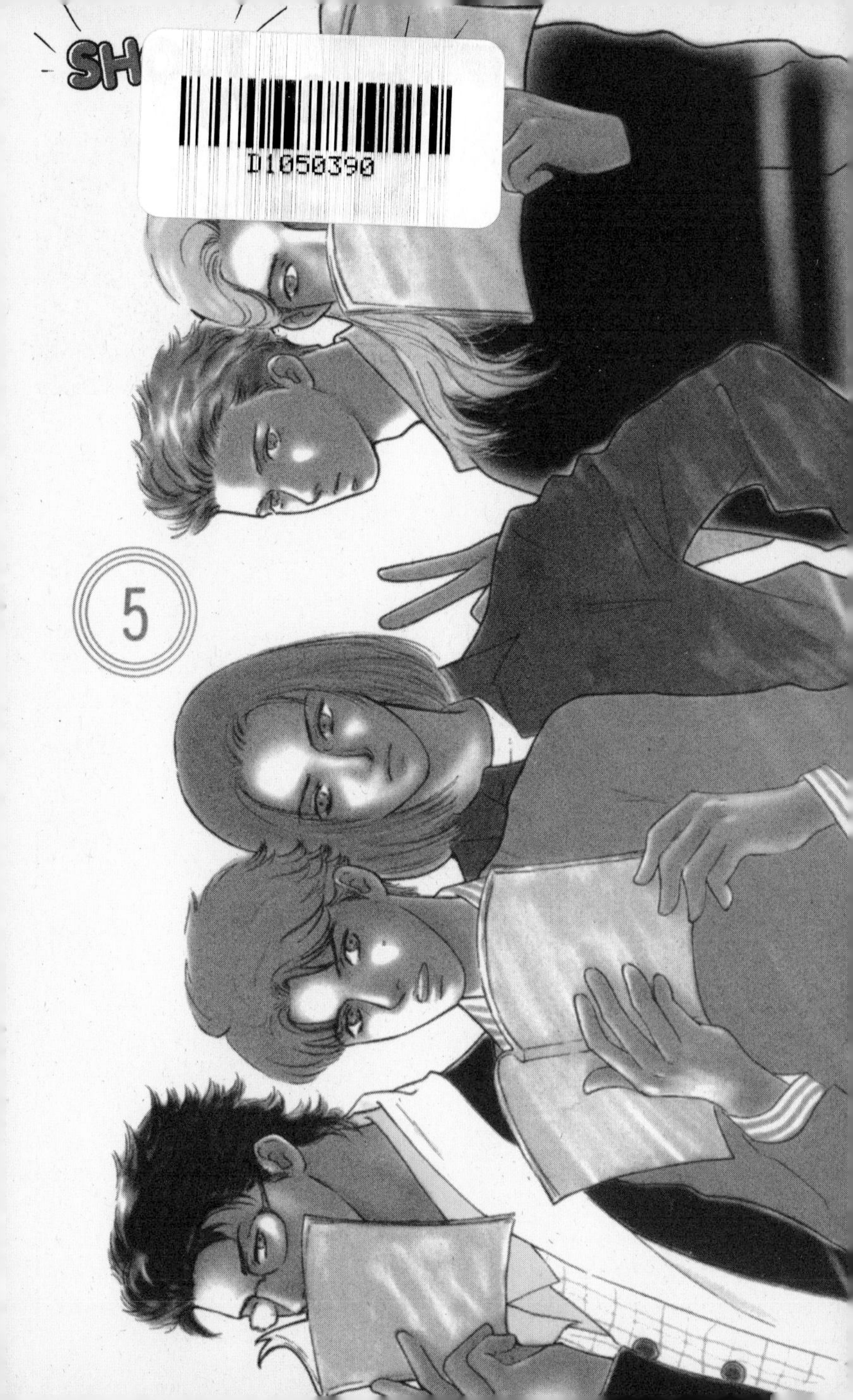
5

CONTENTS

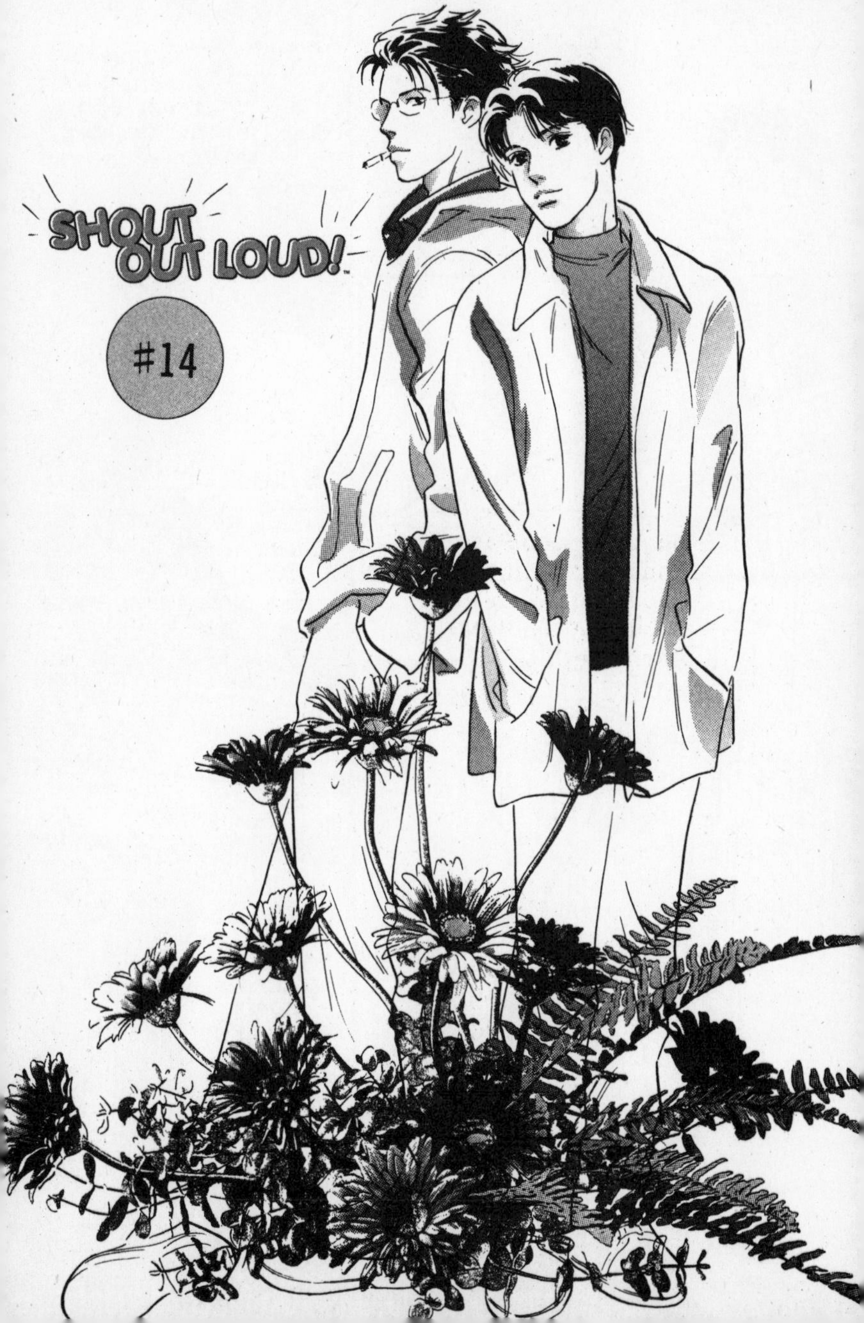
SHOUT OUT LOUD!
#14

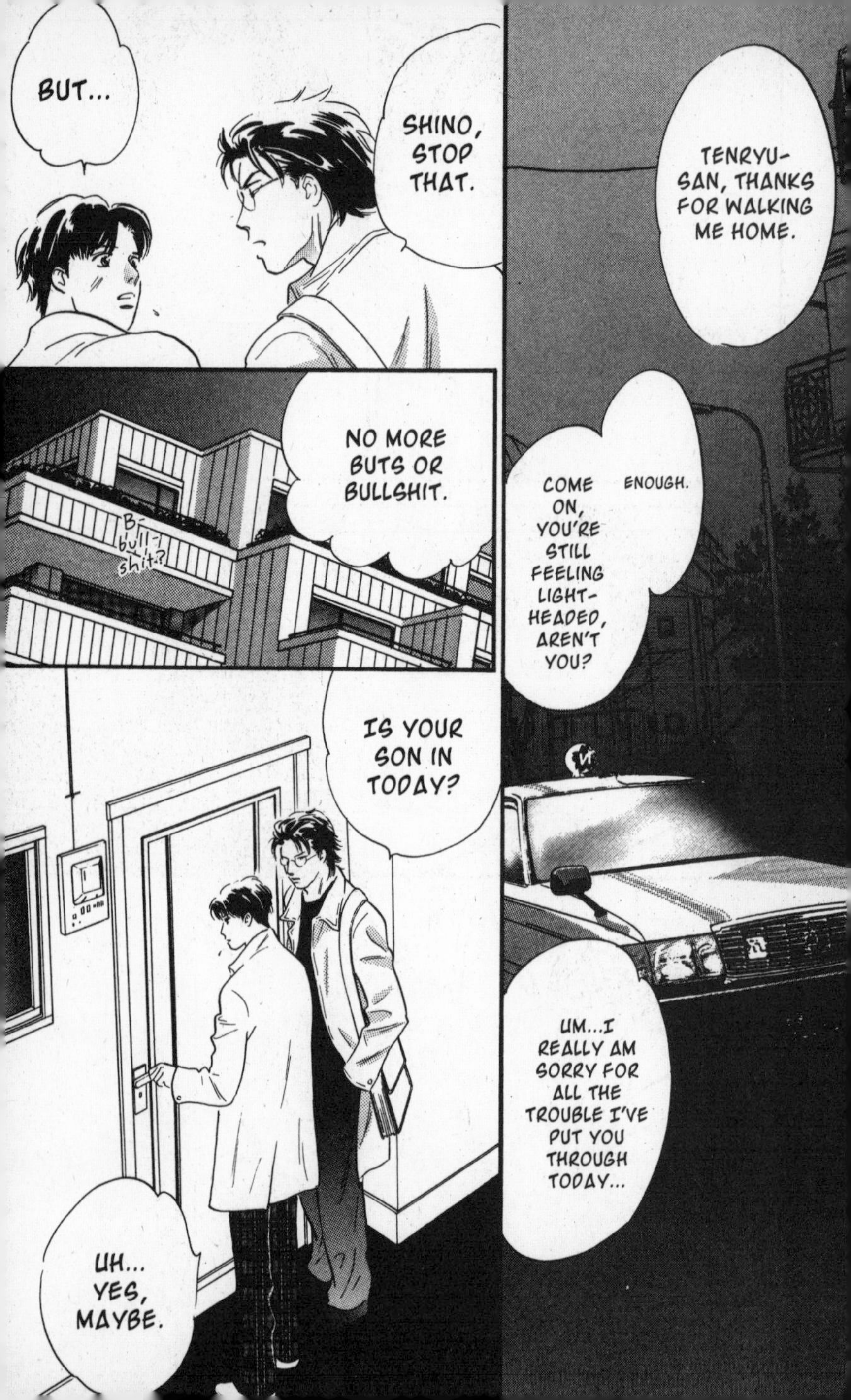
TENRYU-SAN, THANKS FOR WALKING ME HOME.
ENOUGH.
COME ON, YOU'RE STILL FEELING LIGHT-HEADED, AREN'T YOU?
UM...I REALLY AM SORRY FOR ALL THE TROUBLE I'VE PUT YOU THROUGH TODAY...
SHINO, STOP THAT.
BUT...
NO MORE BUTS OR BULLSHIT.
B-bull-shit?
IS YOUR SON IN TODAY?
UH... YES, MAYBE.

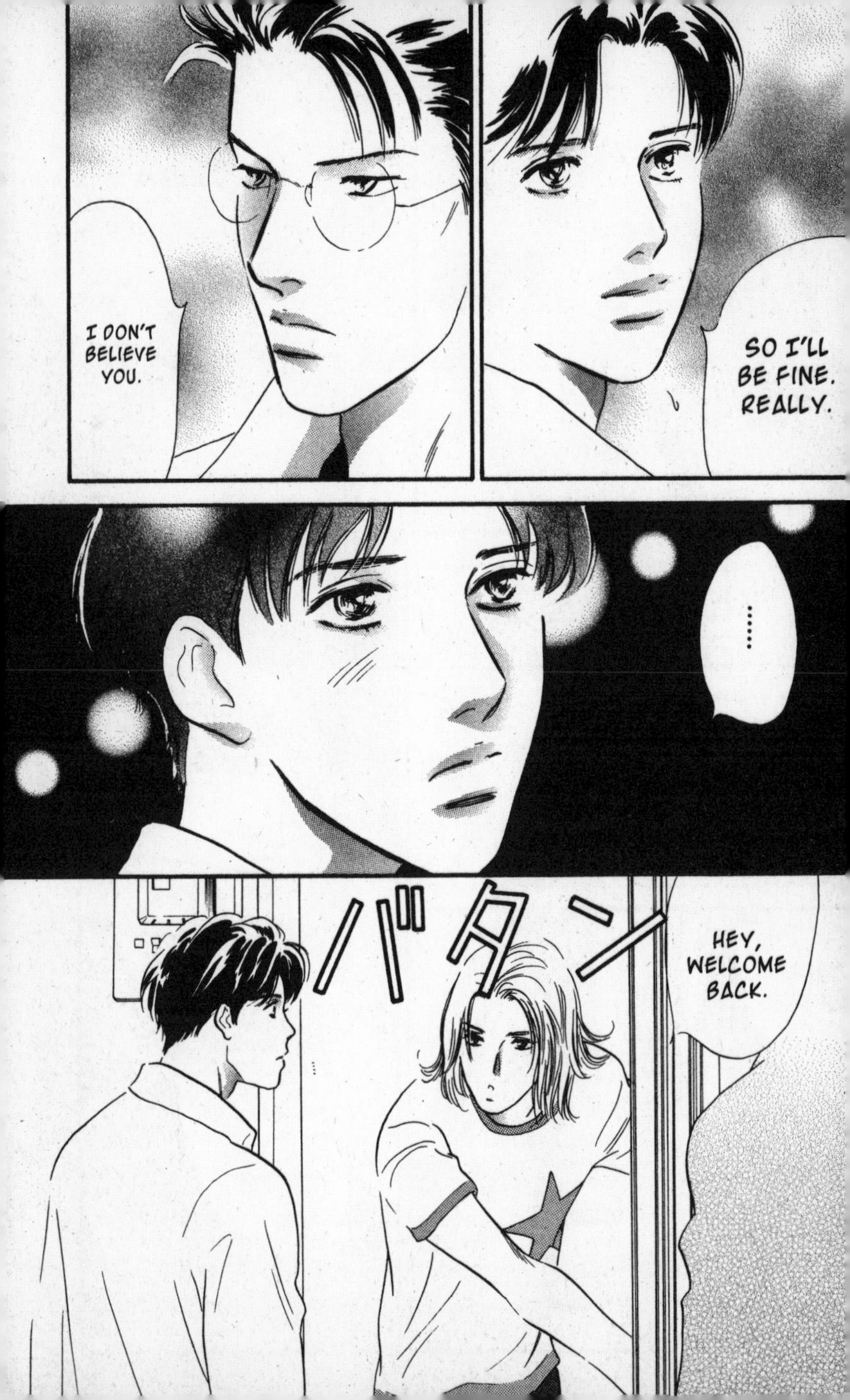
SO I'LL BE FINE. REALLY.
I DON'T BELIEVE YOU.
……
HEY, WELCOME BACK.
バタン
…

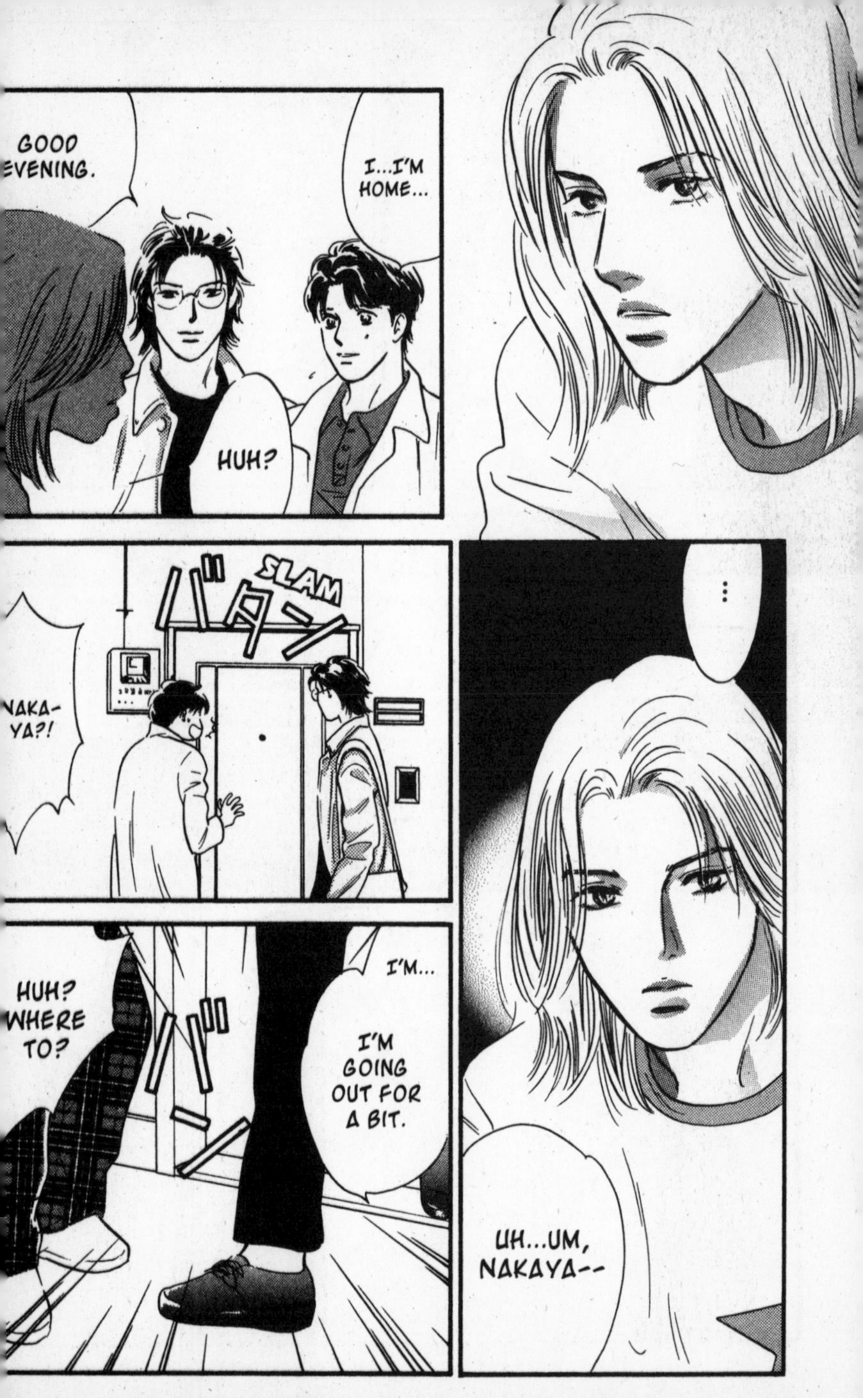
I...I'M HOME...
GOOD EVENING.
HUH?
...
UH...UM, NAKAYA--
SLAM
NAKA-YA?!
I'M...
I'M GOING OUT FOR A BIT.
HUH? WHERE TO?

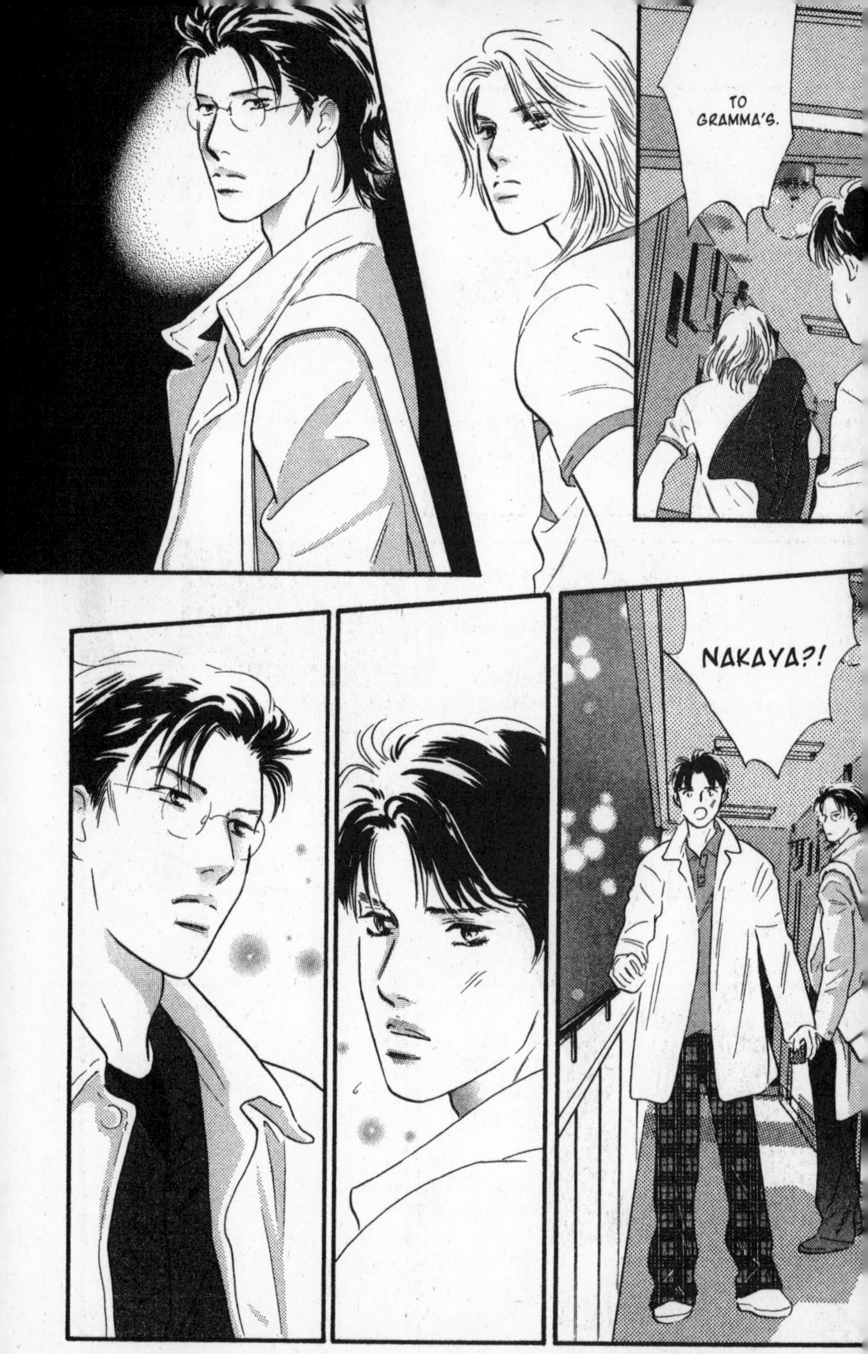
TO GRAMMA'S.
NAKAYA?!

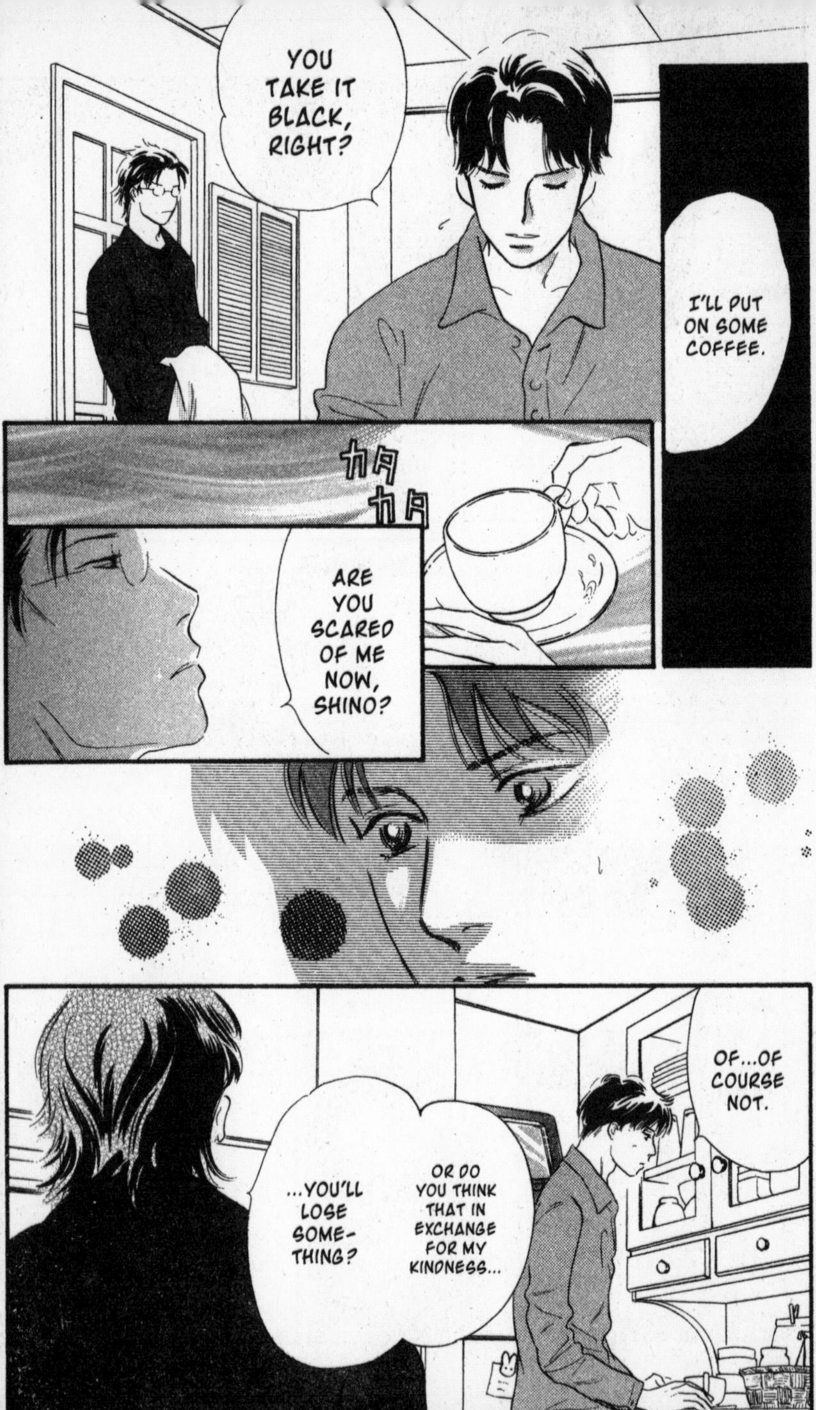

I'LL PUT ON SOME COFFEE.
YOU TAKE IT BLACK, RIGHT?
カタ カタ
ARE YOU SCARED OF ME NOW, SHINO?
OF...OF COURSE NOT.
OR DO YOU THINK THAT IN EXCHANGE FOR MY KINDNESS...
...YOU'LL LOSE SOME-THING?

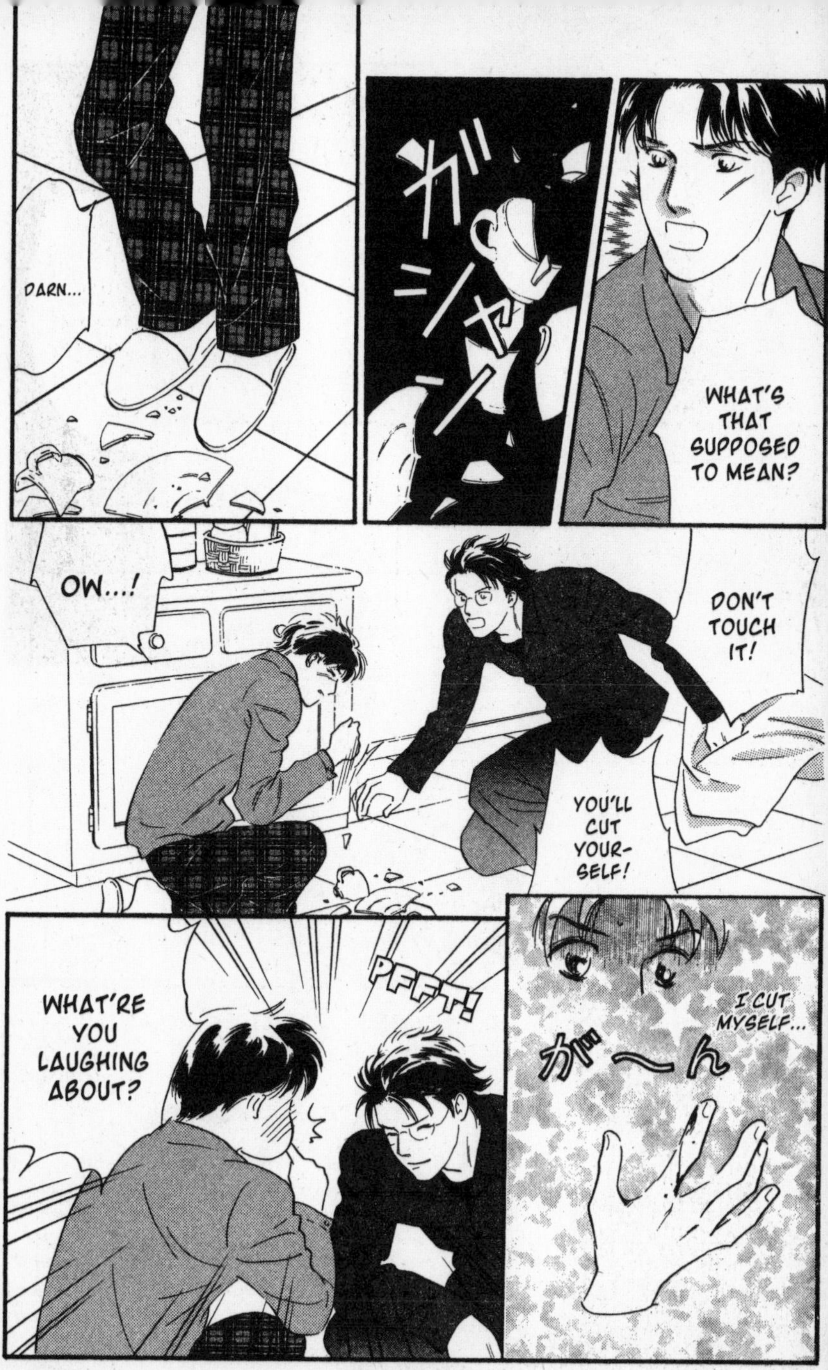
WHAT'S THAT SUPPOSED TO MEAN?
ガシャーン
DARN...
DON'T TOUCH IT!
YOU'LL CUT YOURSELF!
OW...!
I CUT MYSELF...
が～ん
PFFT!
WHAT'RE YOU LAUGHING ABOUT?

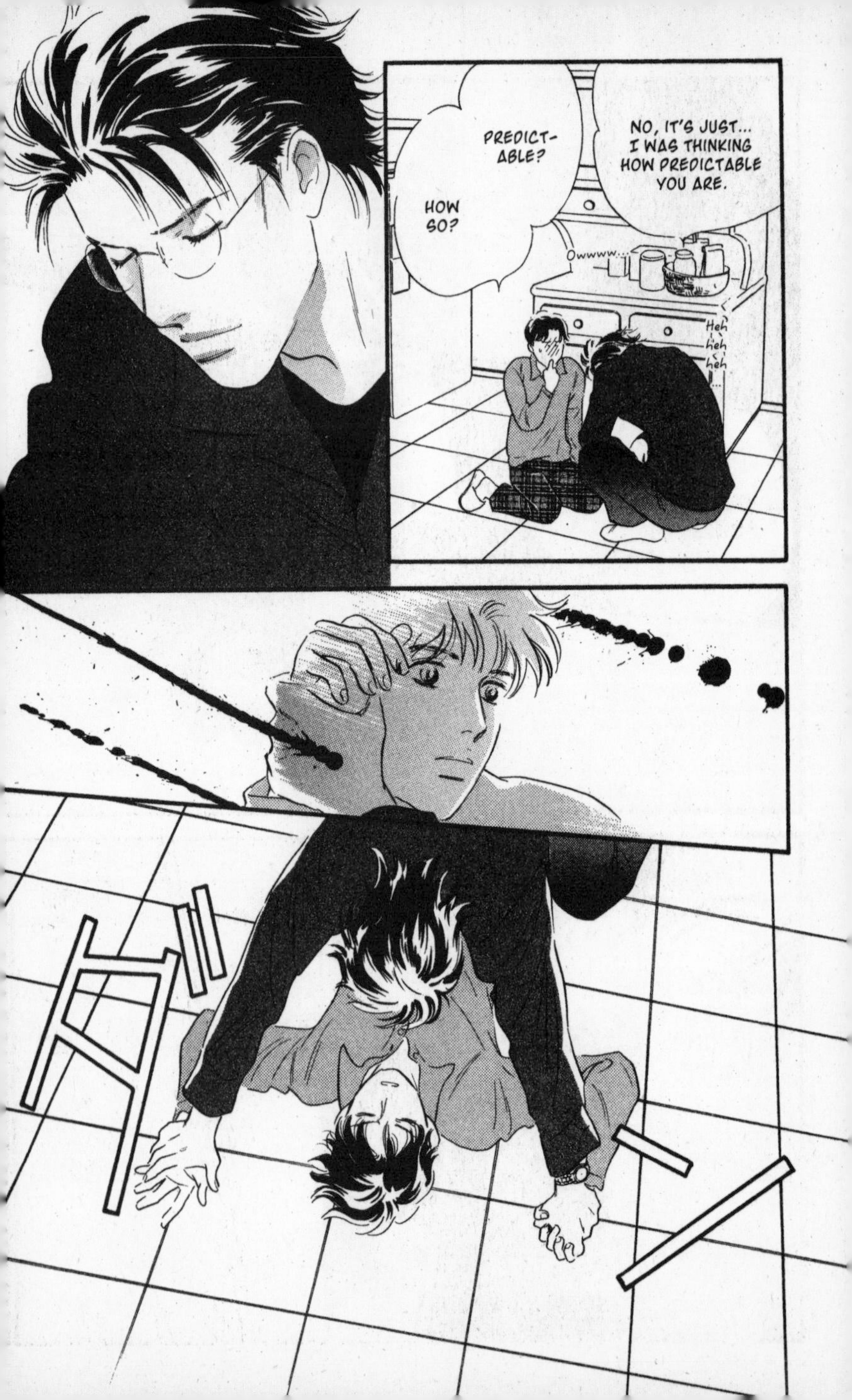
NO, IT'S JUST... I WAS THINKING HOW PREDICTABLE YOU ARE.
PREDICT-ABLE?
HOW SO?
Owwww...
Heh heh heh...

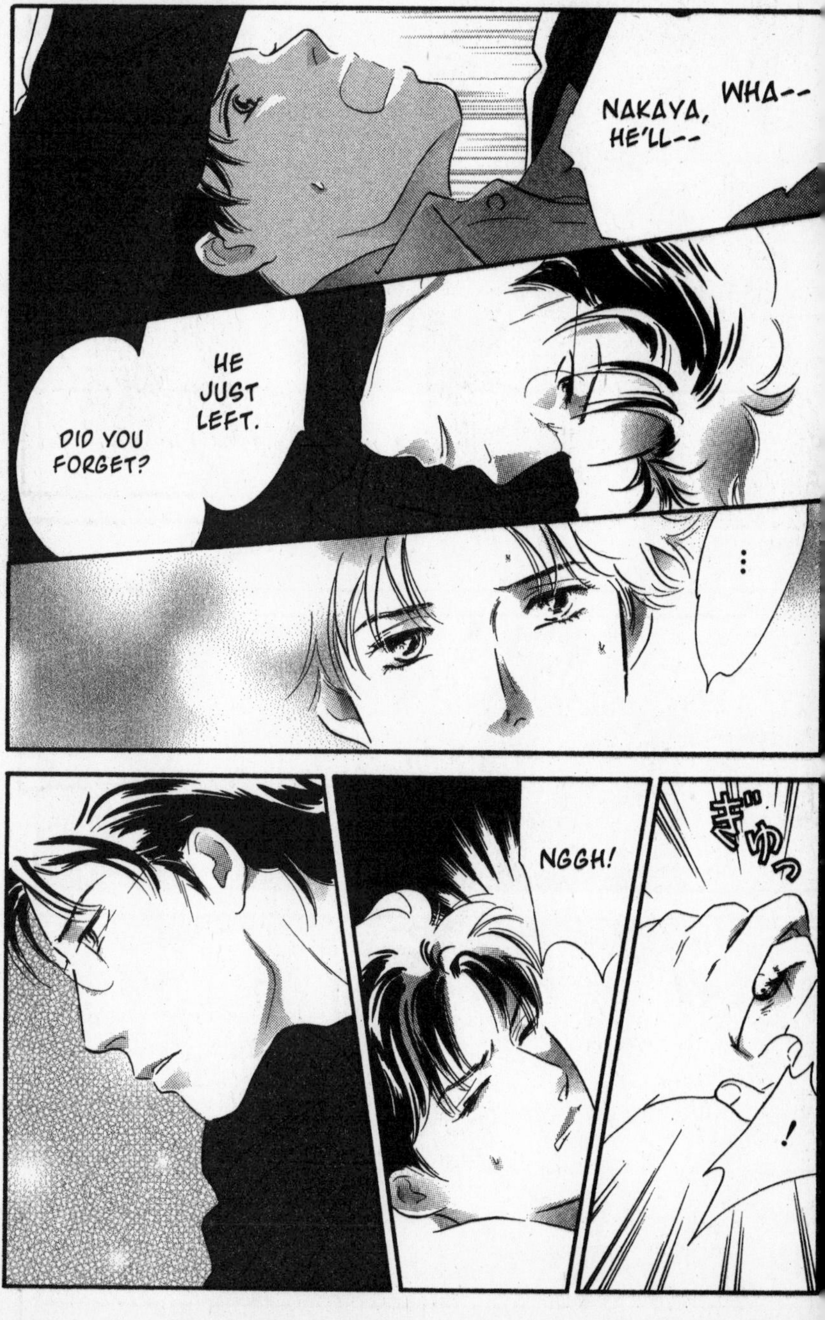
WHA--
NAKAYA, HE'LL--
HE JUST LEFT.
DID YOU FORGET?
...
ぎゅっ
!
NGGH!

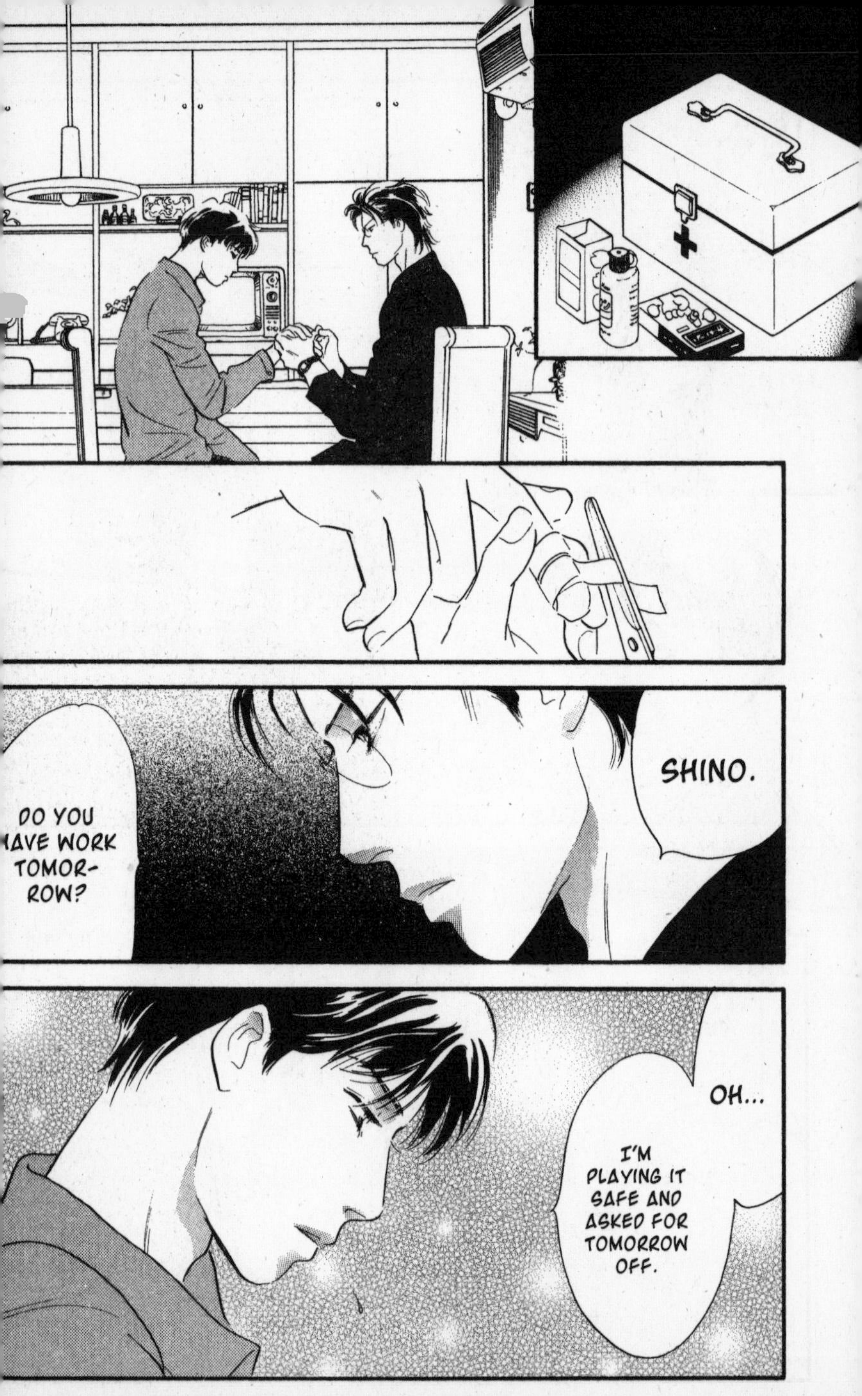
SHINO.
DO YOU HAVE WORK TOMORROW?
OH...
I'M PLAYING IT SAFE AND ASKED FOR TOMORROW OFF.

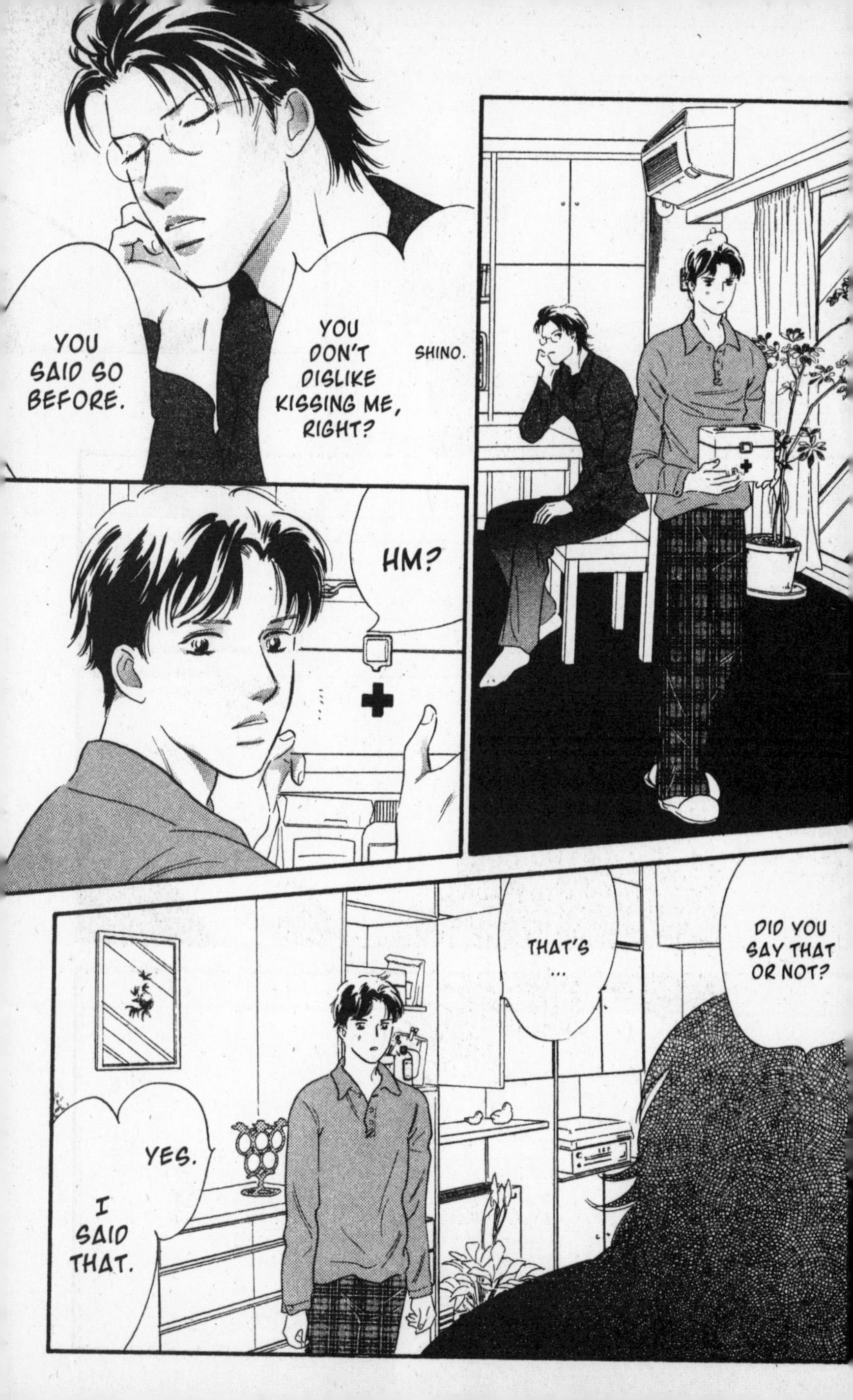
SHINO.
YOU DON'T DISLIKE KISSING ME, RIGHT?
YOU SAID SO BEFORE.
HM?
DID YOU SAY THAT OR NOT?
THAT'S ...
YES.
I SAID THAT.

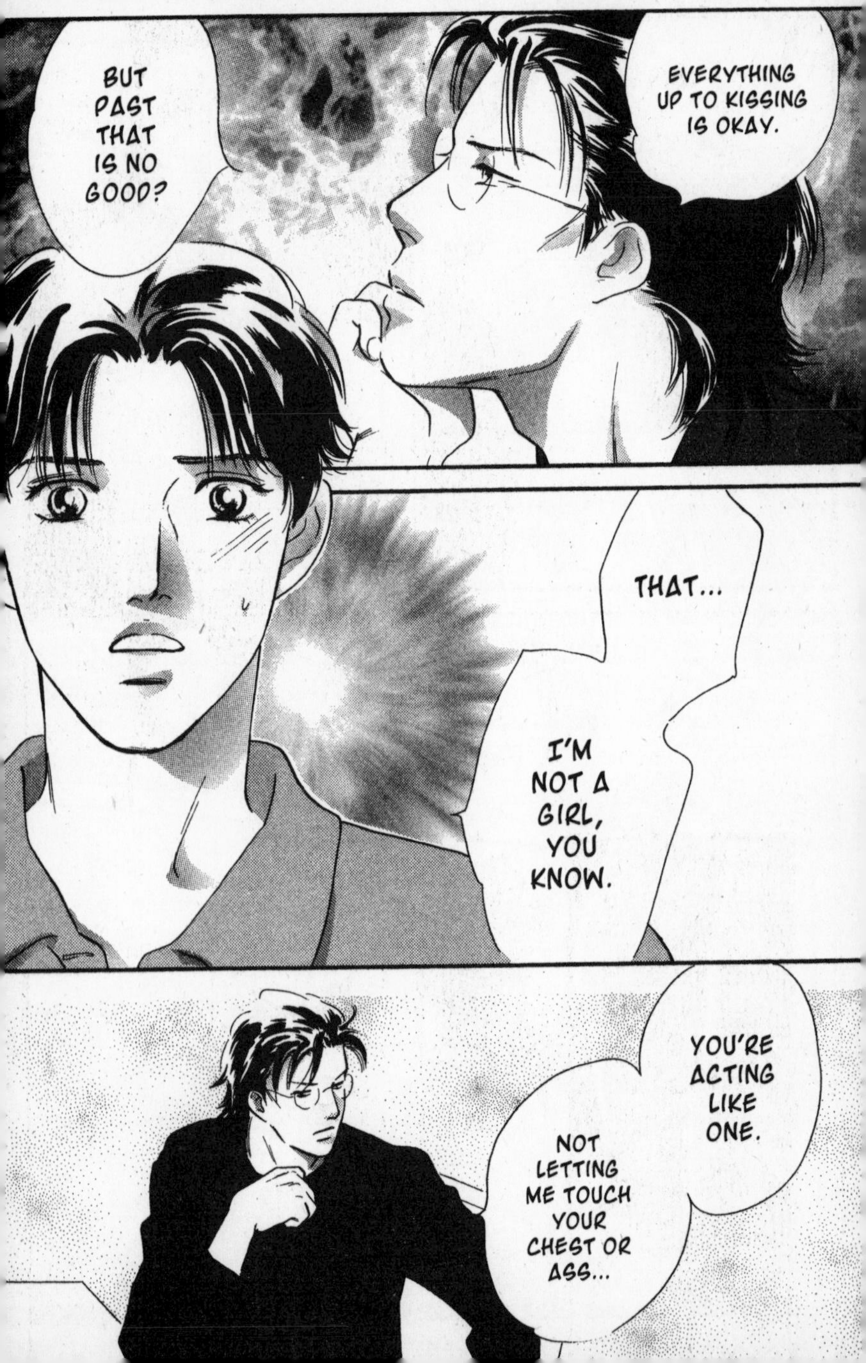
EVERYTHING UP TO KISSING IS OKAY.
BUT PAST THAT IS NO GOOD?
THAT...
I'M NOT A GIRL, YOU KNOW.
YOU'RE ACTING LIKE ONE.
NOT LETTING ME TOUCH YOUR CHEST OR ASS...

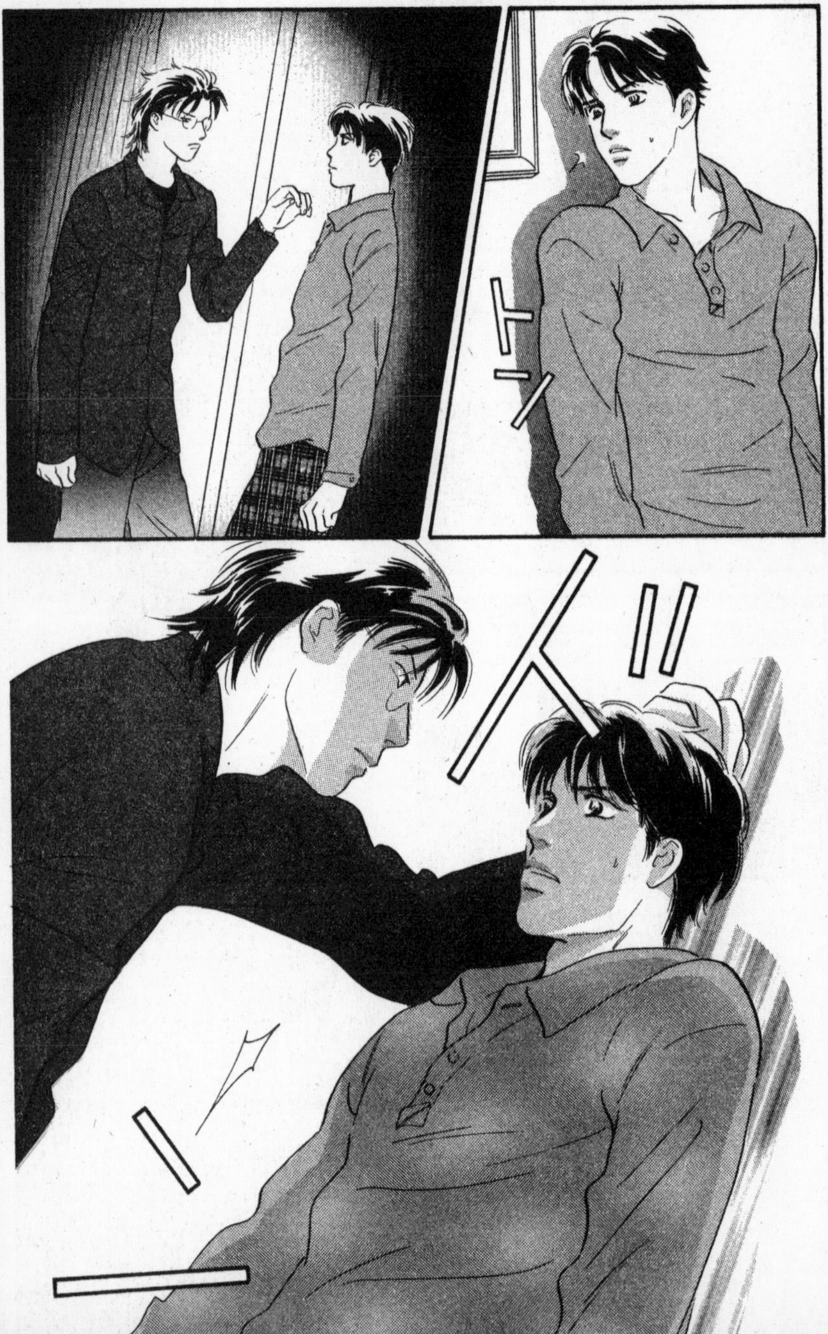

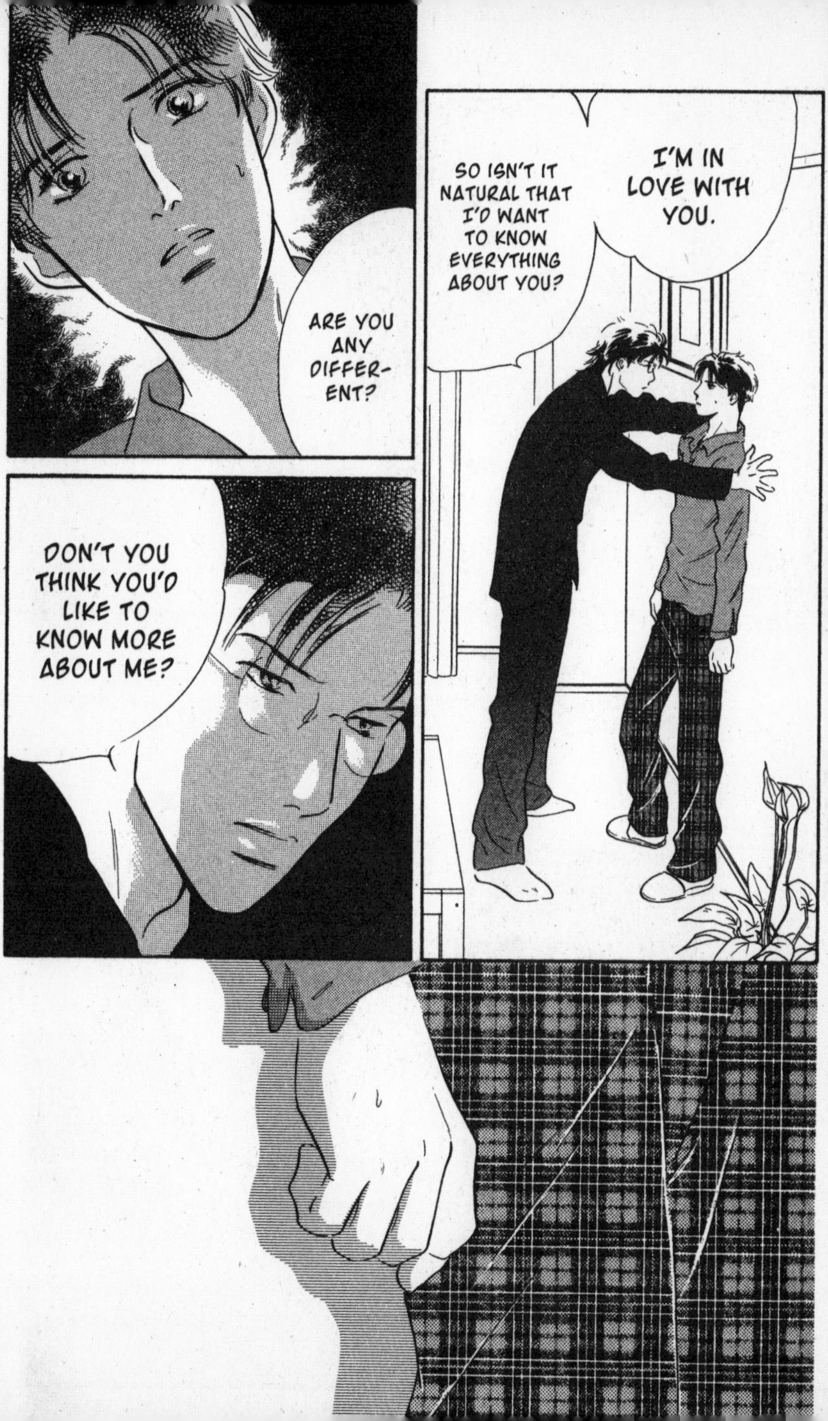
I'M IN LOVE WITH YOU.
SO ISN'T IT NATURAL THAT I'D WANT TO KNOW EVERYTHING ABOUT YOU?
ARE YOU ANY DIFFER-ENT?
DON'T YOU THINK YOU'D LIKE TO KNOW MORE ABOUT ME?

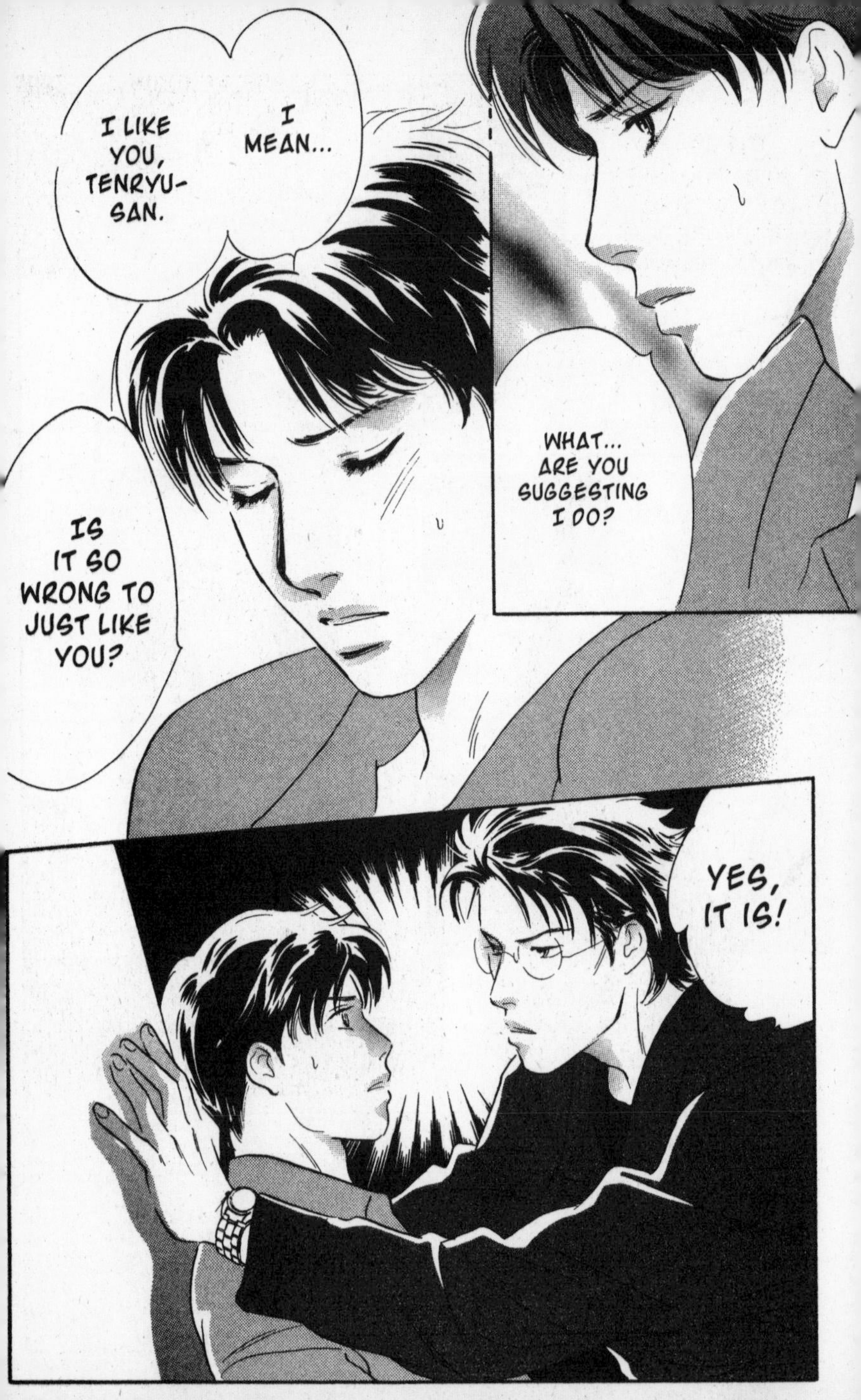
WHAT... ARE YOU SUGGESTING I DO?
I MEAN...
I LIKE YOU, TENRYU-SAN.
IS IT SO WRONG TO JUST LIKE YOU?
YES, IT IS!

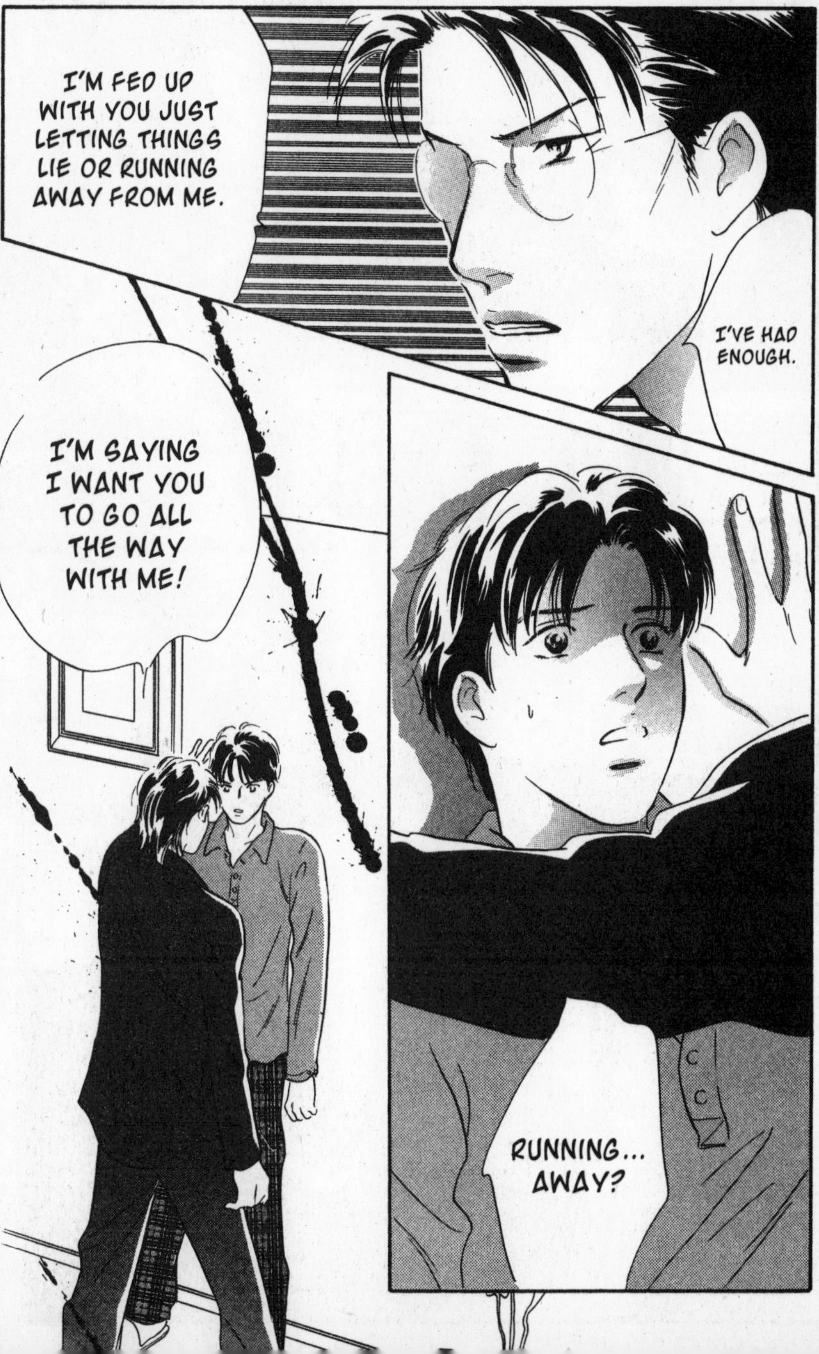
I'VE HAD ENOUGH.
I'M FED UP WITH YOU JUST LETTING THINGS LIE OR RUNNING AWAY FROM ME.
RUNNING... AWAY?
I'M SAYING I WANT YOU TO GO ALL THE WAY WITH ME!

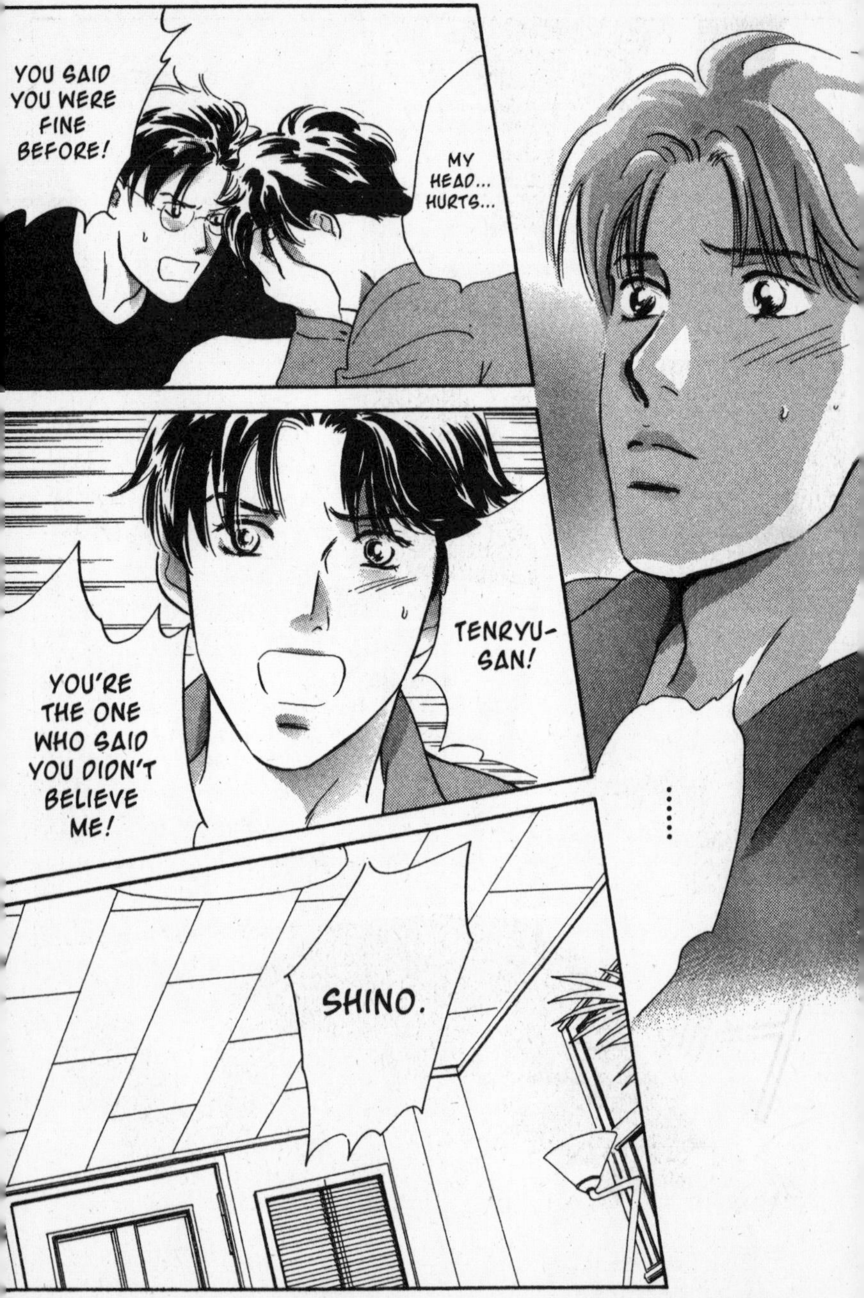

......
MY HEAD... HURTS...
YOU SAID YOU WERE FINE BEFORE!
TENRYU-SAN!
YOU'RE THE ONE WHO SAID YOU DIDN'T BELIEVE ME!
SHINO.

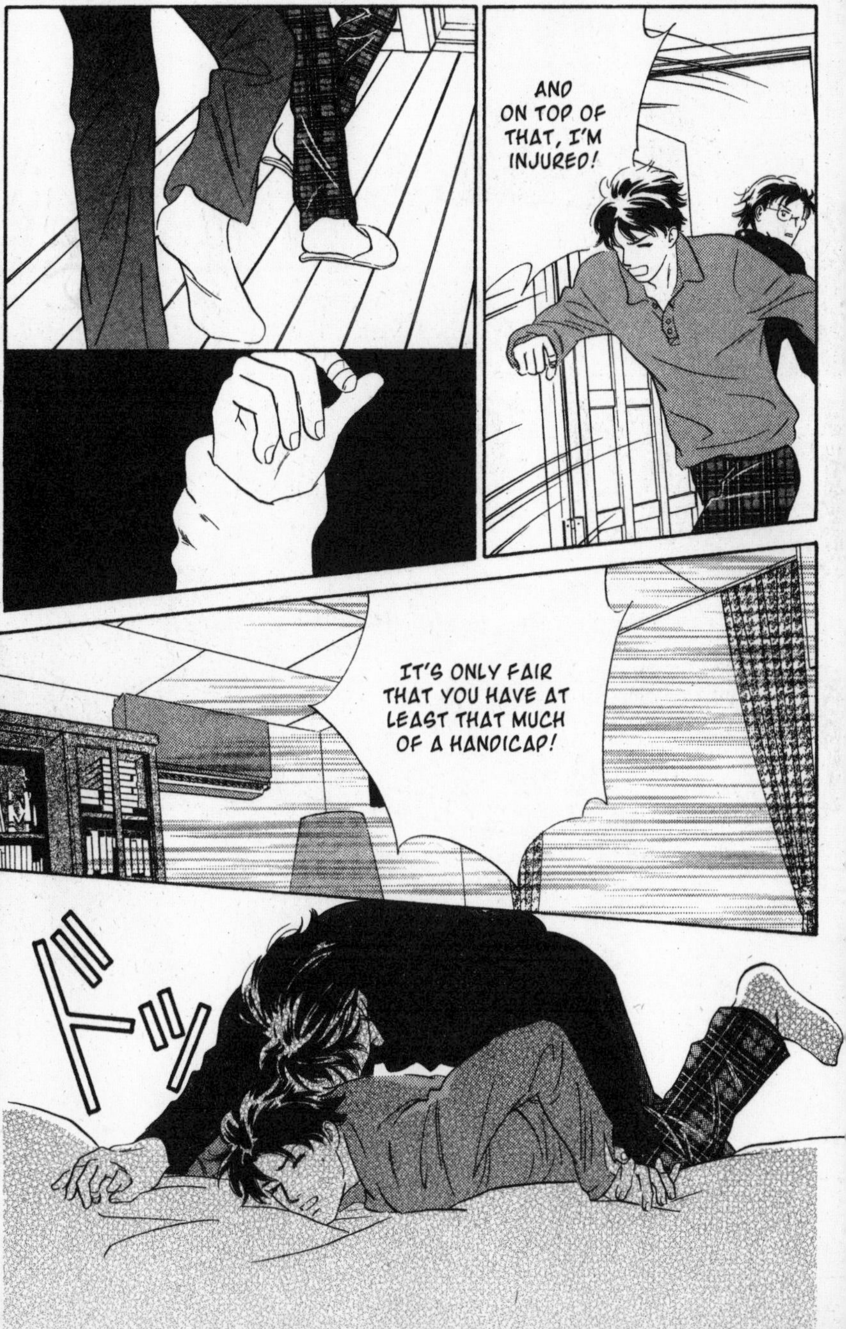
AND ON TOP OF THAT, I'M INJURED!
IT'S ONLY FAIR THAT YOU HAVE AT LEAST THAT MUCH OF A HANDICAP!

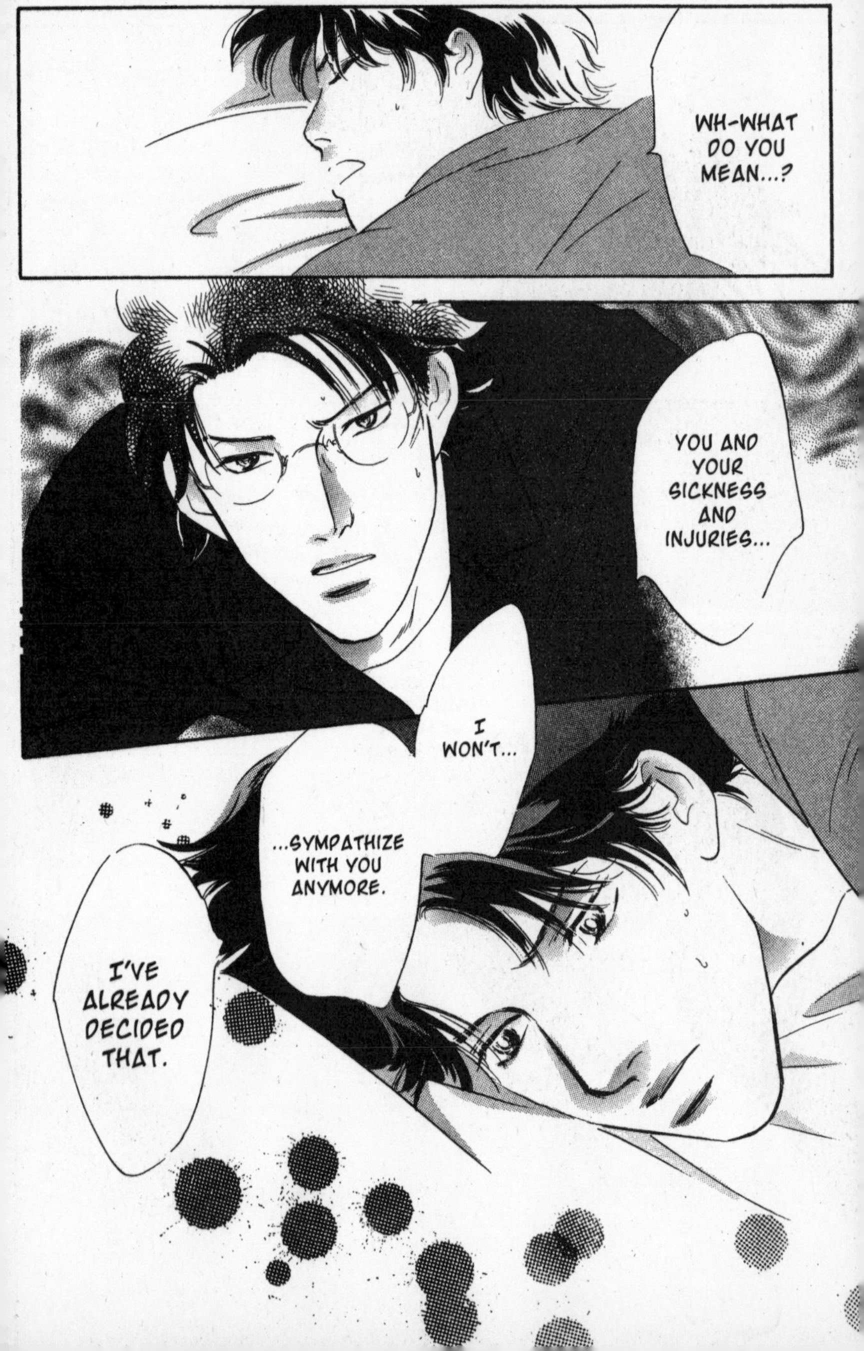
WH-WHAT DO YOU MEAN...?
YOU AND YOUR SICKNESS AND INJURIES...
I WON'T...
...SYMPATHIZE WITH YOU ANYMORE.
I'VE ALREADY DECIDED THAT.

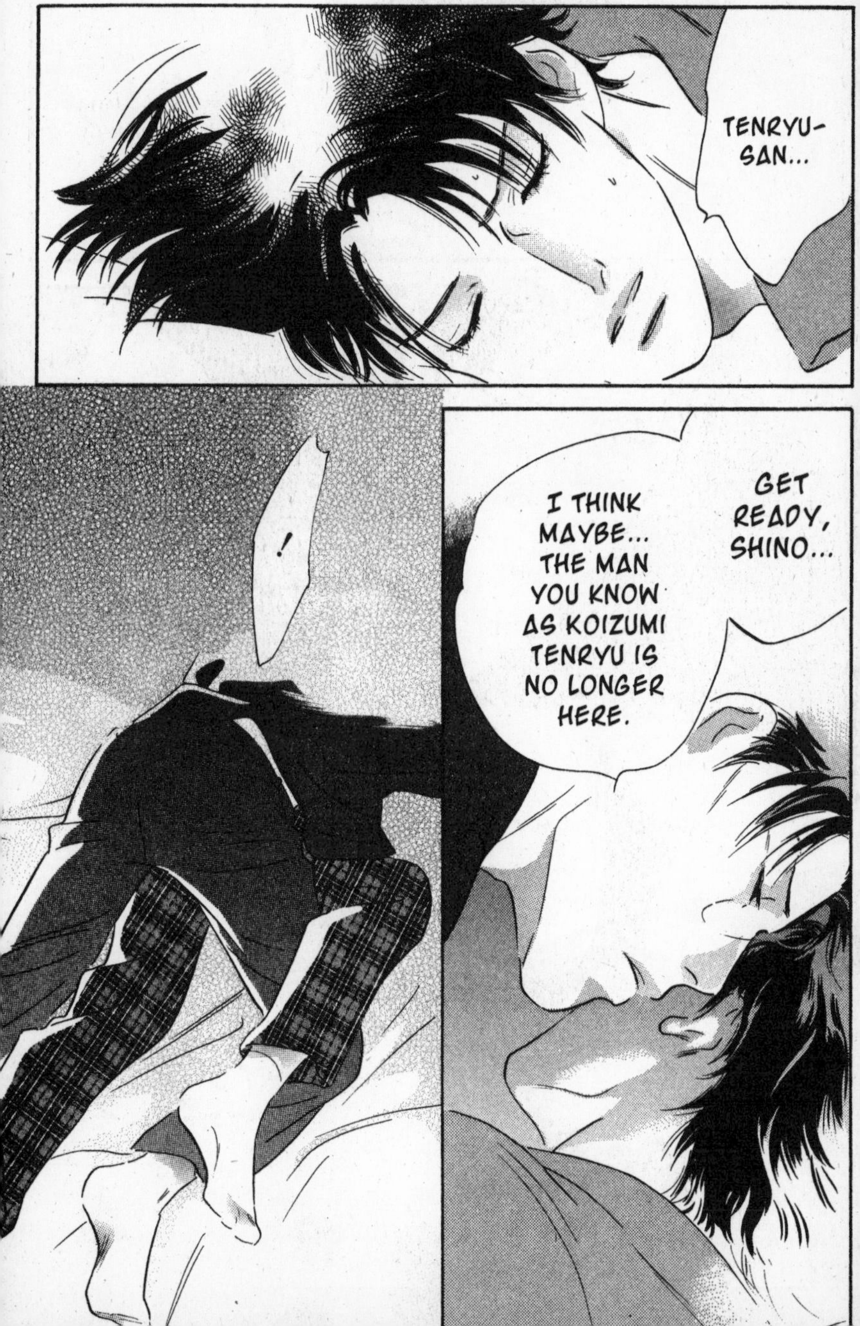
TENRYU-SAN...
GET READY, SHINO...
I THINK MAYBE... THE MAN YOU KNOW AS KOIZUMI TENRYU IS NO LONGER HERE.
!

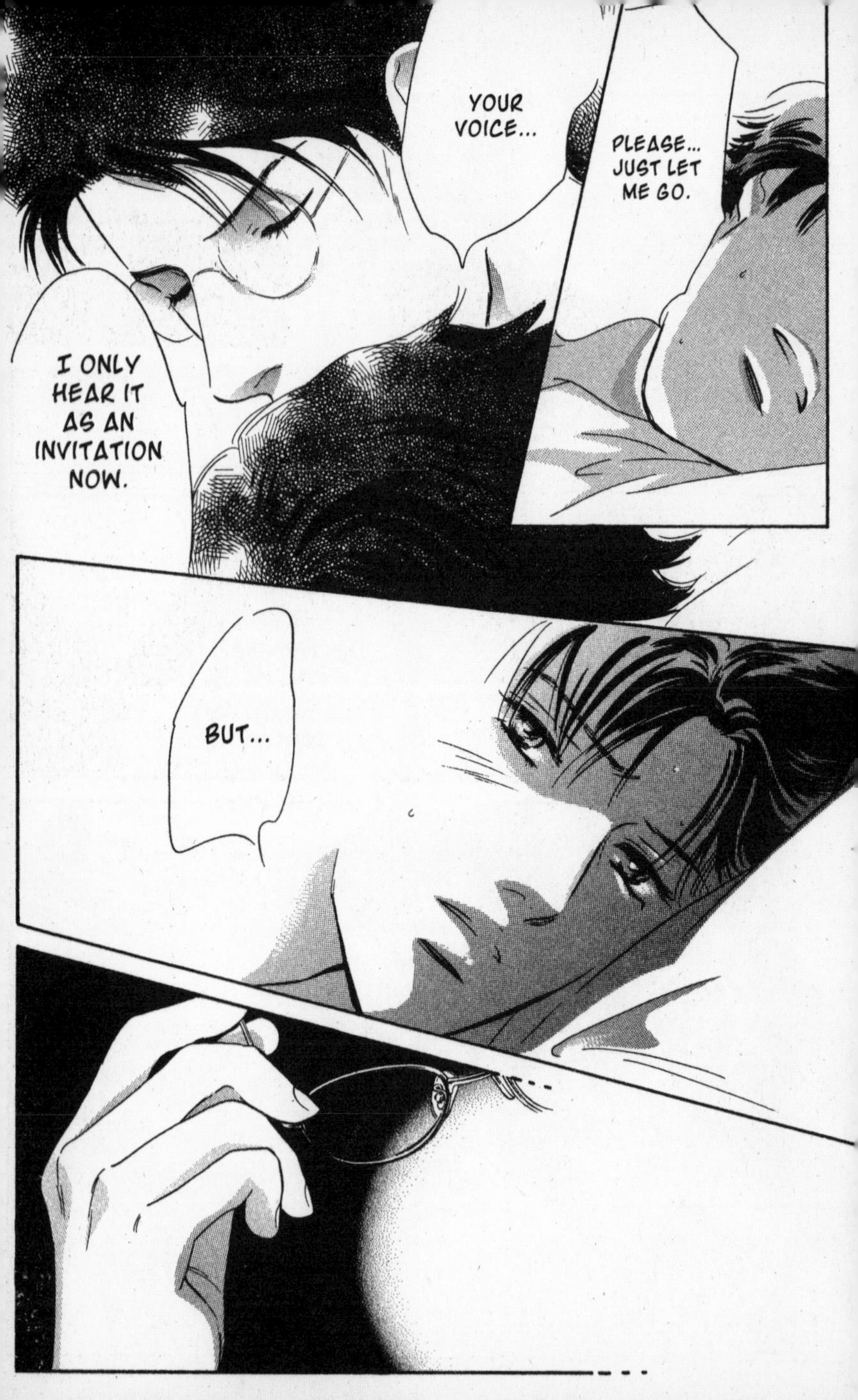
PLEASE... JUST LET ME GO.
YOUR VOICE...
I ONLY HEAR IT AS AN INVITATION NOW.
BUT...

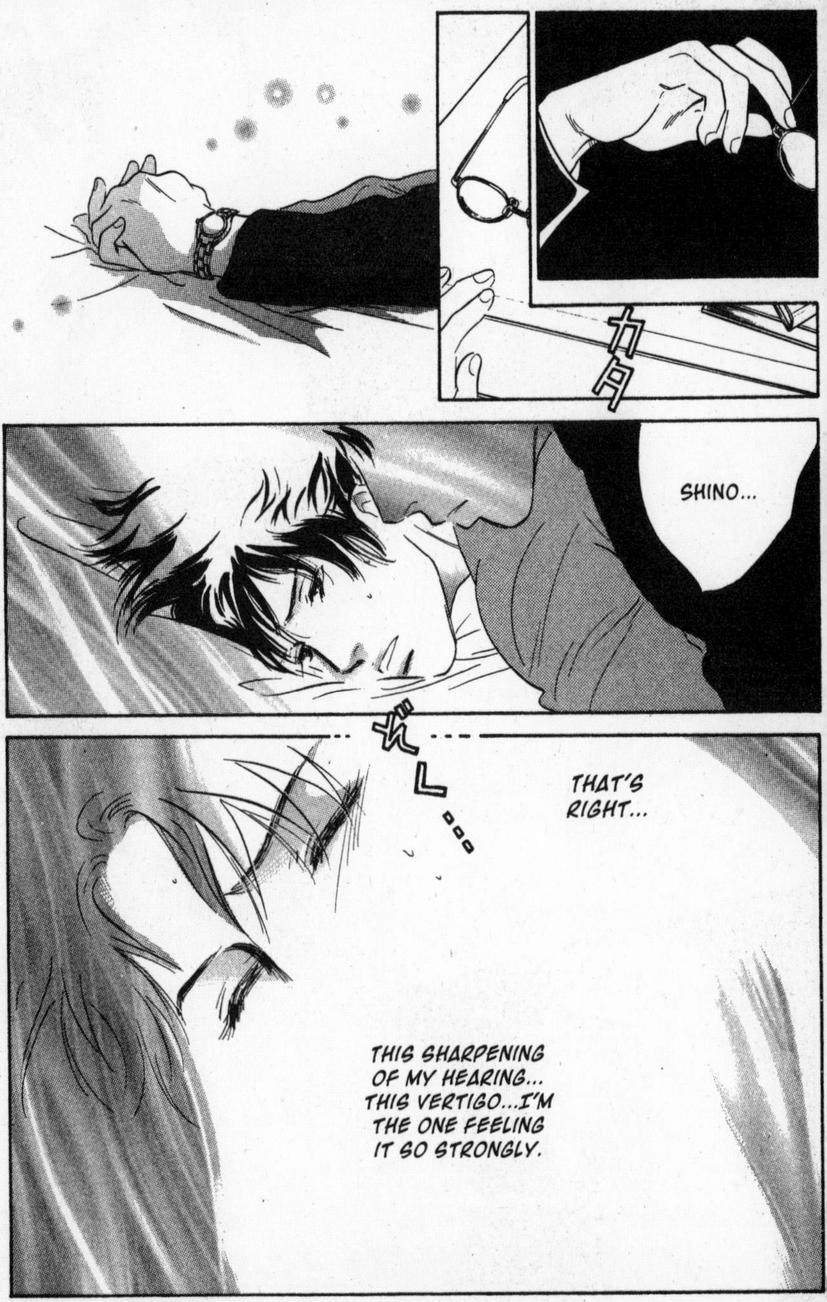
カタ
SHINO...
THAT'S RIGHT...
ぜん...
THIS SHARPENING OF MY HEARING... THIS VERTIGO...I'M THE ONE FEELING IT SO STRONGLY.

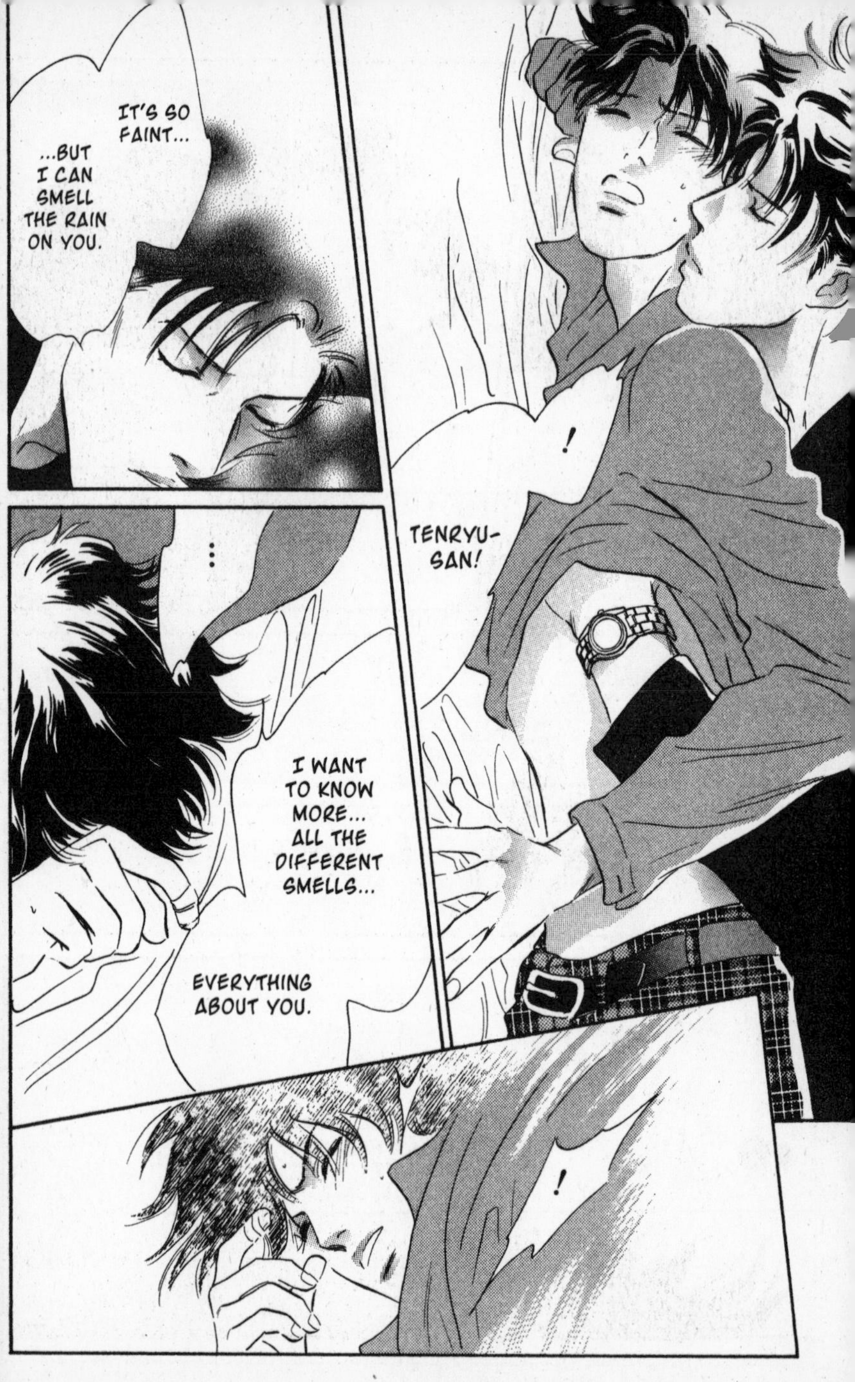
!
TENRYU-SAN!
IT'S SO FAINT...
...BUT I CAN SMELL THE RAIN ON YOU.
...
I WANT TO KNOW MORE... ALL THE DIFFERENT SMELLS...
EVERYTHING ABOUT YOU.
!

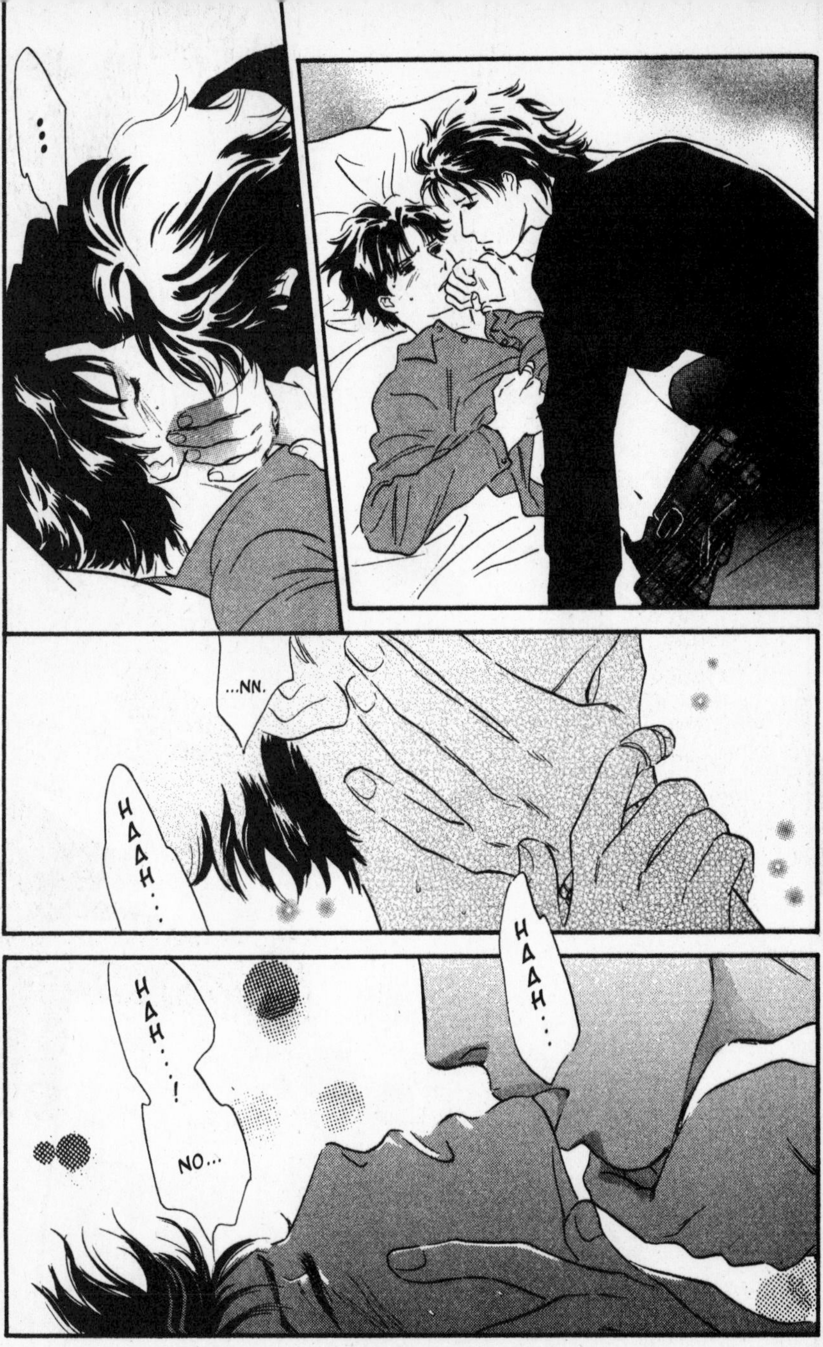
...
...NN.
HAAH...
HAAH...
HAH...!
NO...

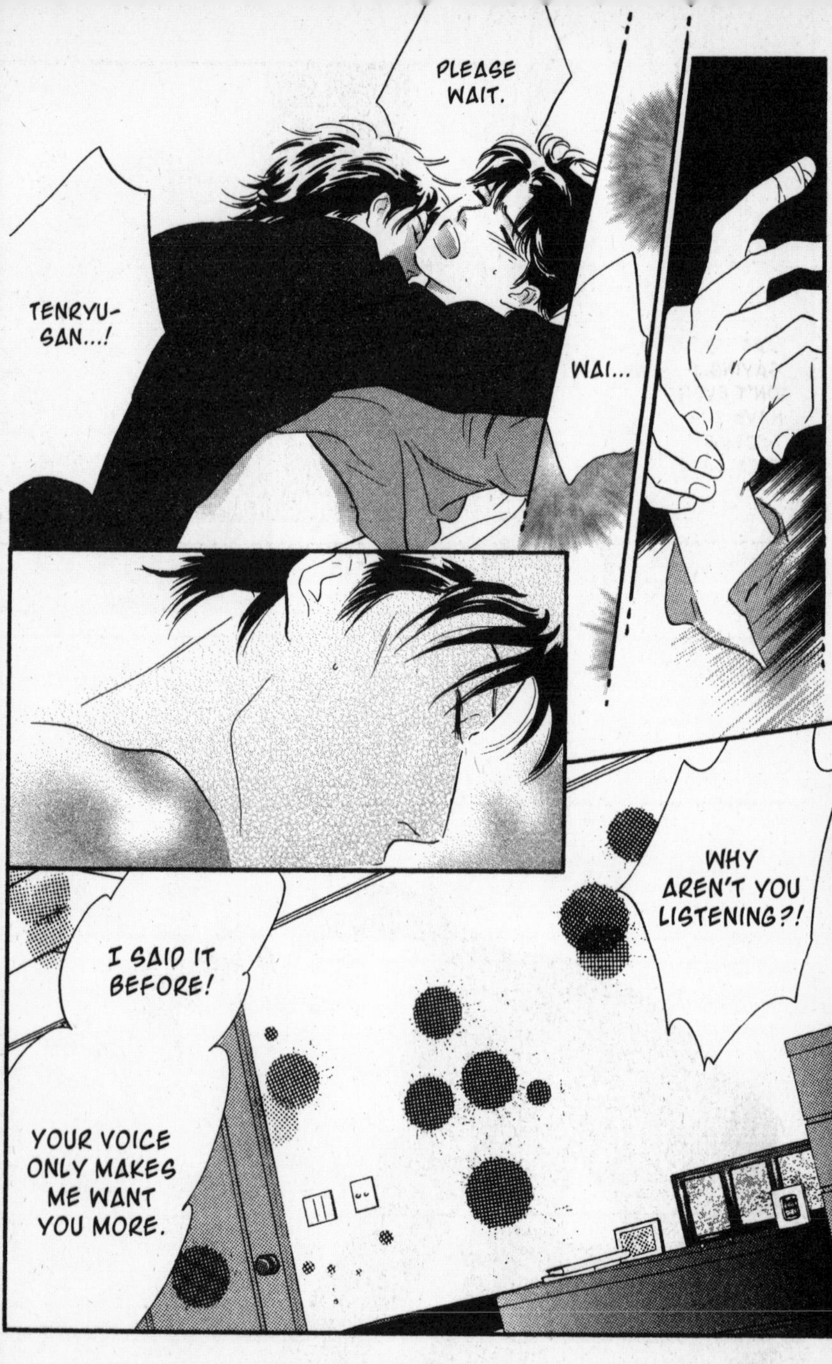
WAI...
PLEASE WAIT.
TENRYU-SAN...!
WHY AREN'T YOU LISTENING?!
I SAID IT BEFORE!
YOUR VOICE ONLY MAKES ME WANT YOU MORE.

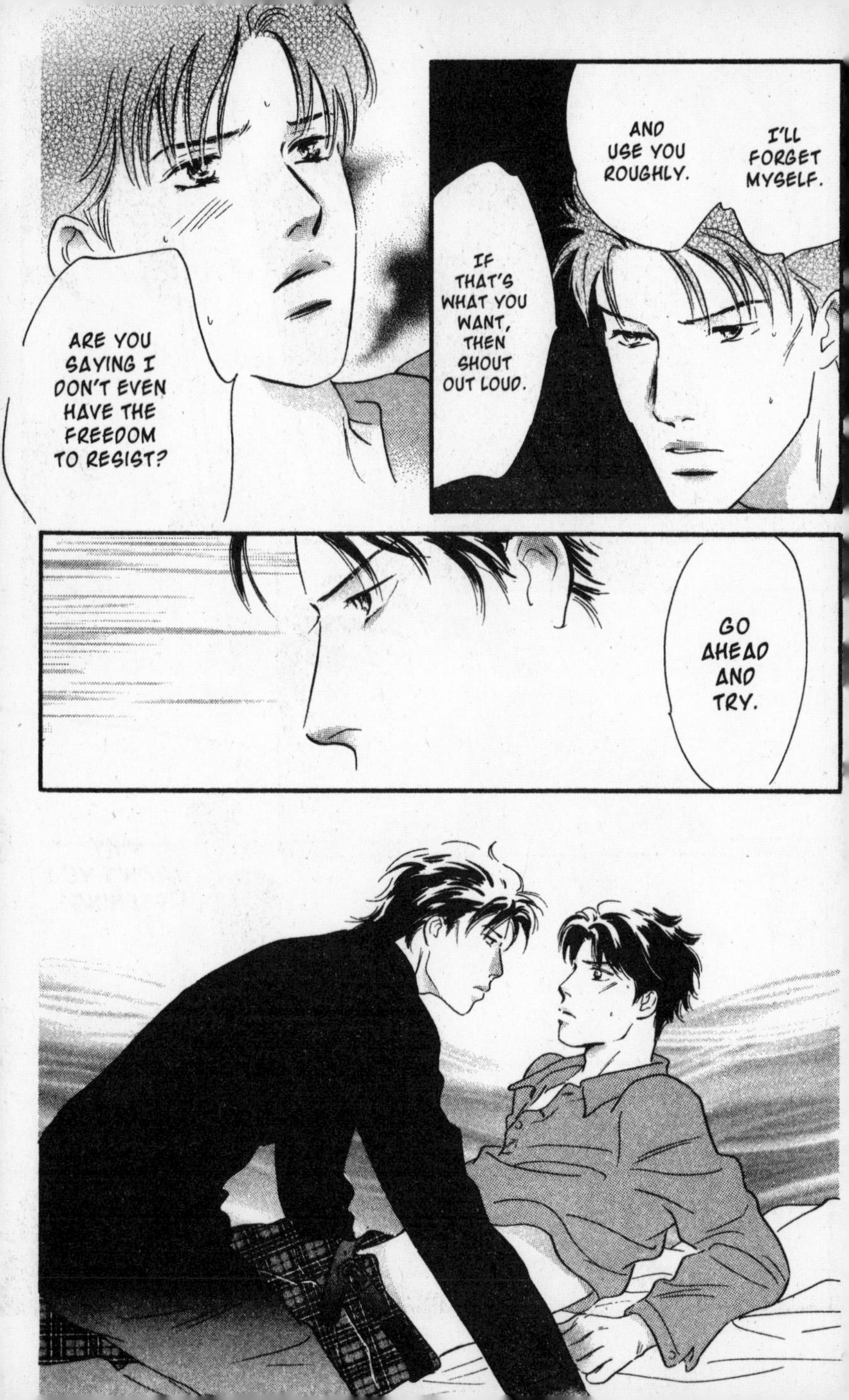
I'LL FORGET MYSELF.
AND USE YOU ROUGHLY.
IF THAT'S WHAT YOU WANT, THEN SHOUT OUT LOUD.
ARE YOU SAYING I DON'T EVEN HAVE THE FREEDOM TO RESIST?
GO AHEAD AND TRY.

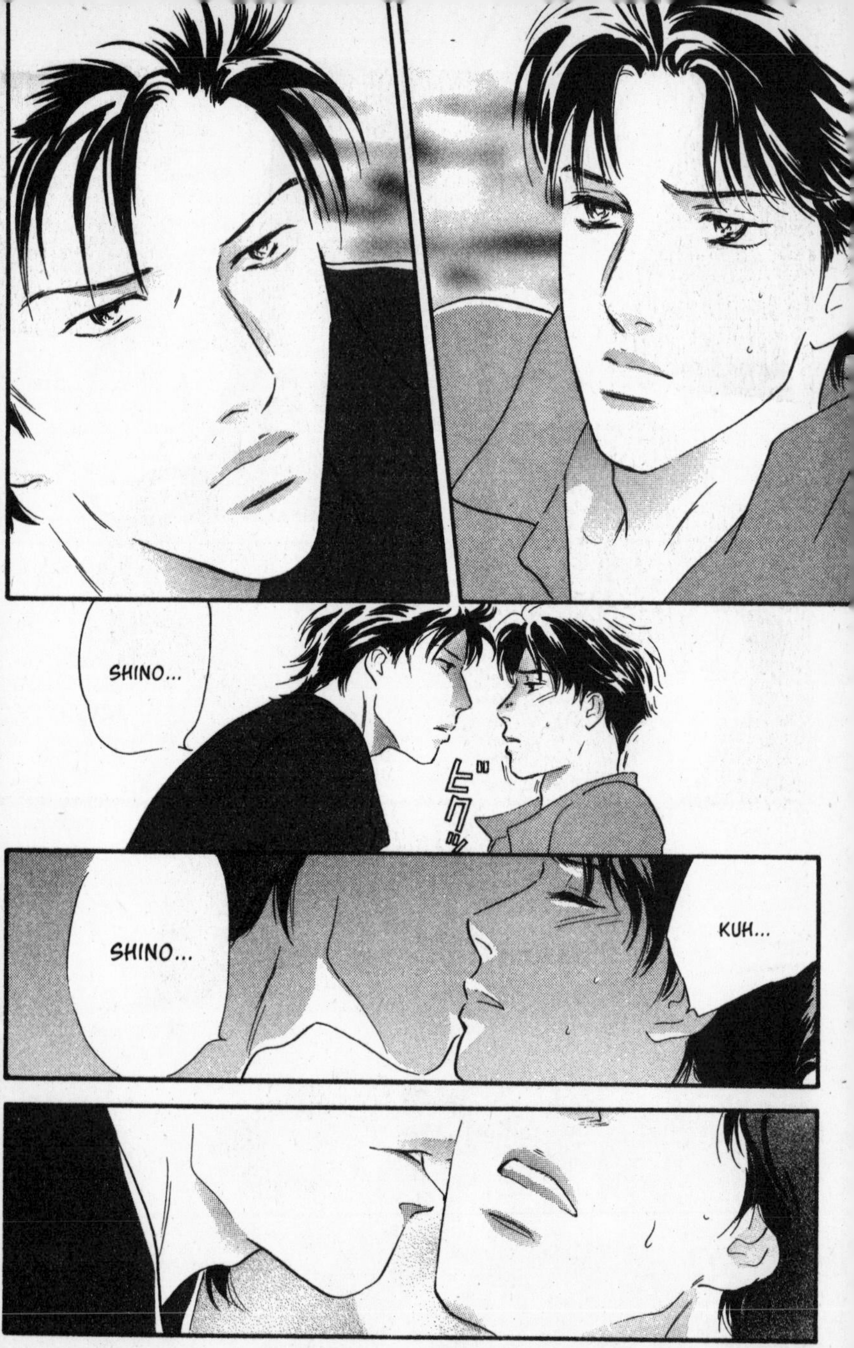
SHINO...
ビクッ
KUH...
SHINO...

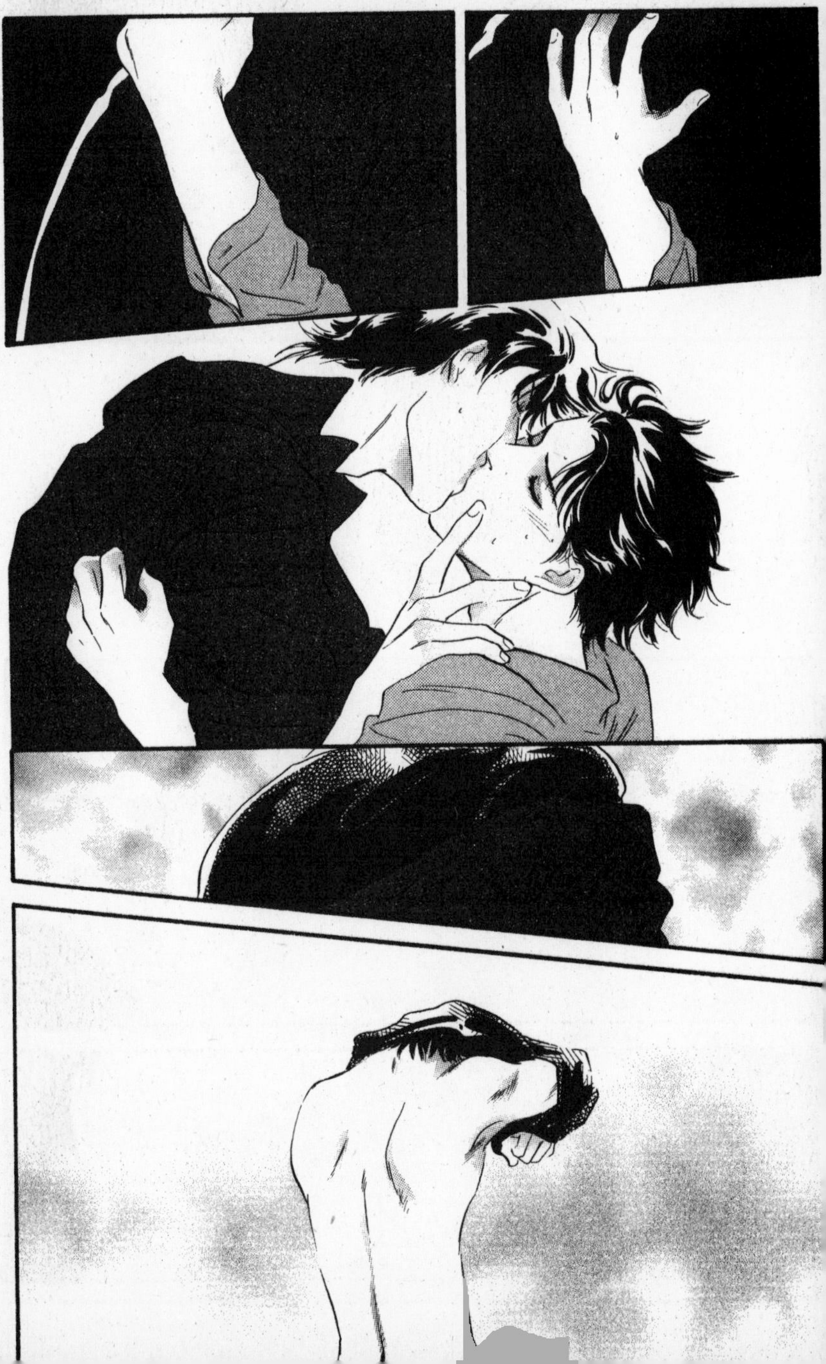

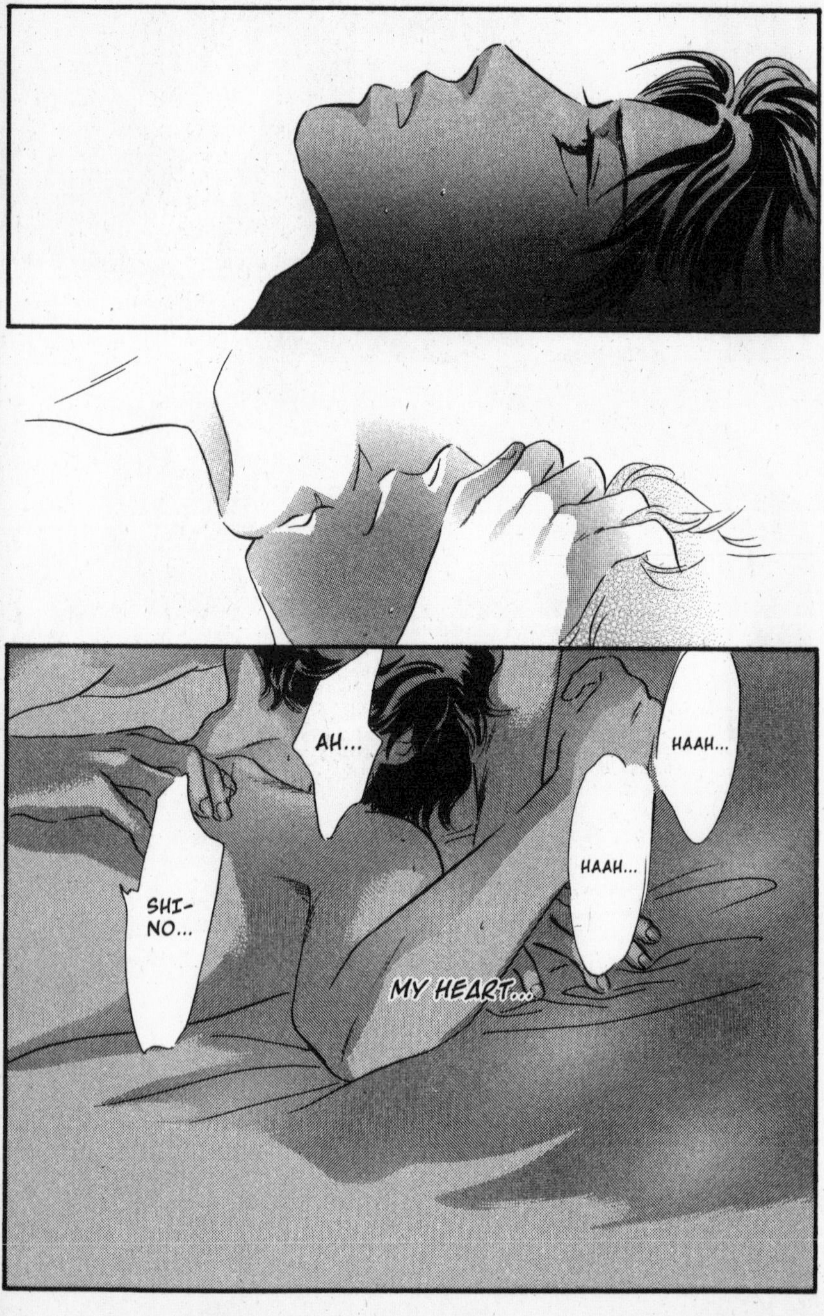
HAAH...
AH...
HAAH...
SHI-NO...
MY HEART...

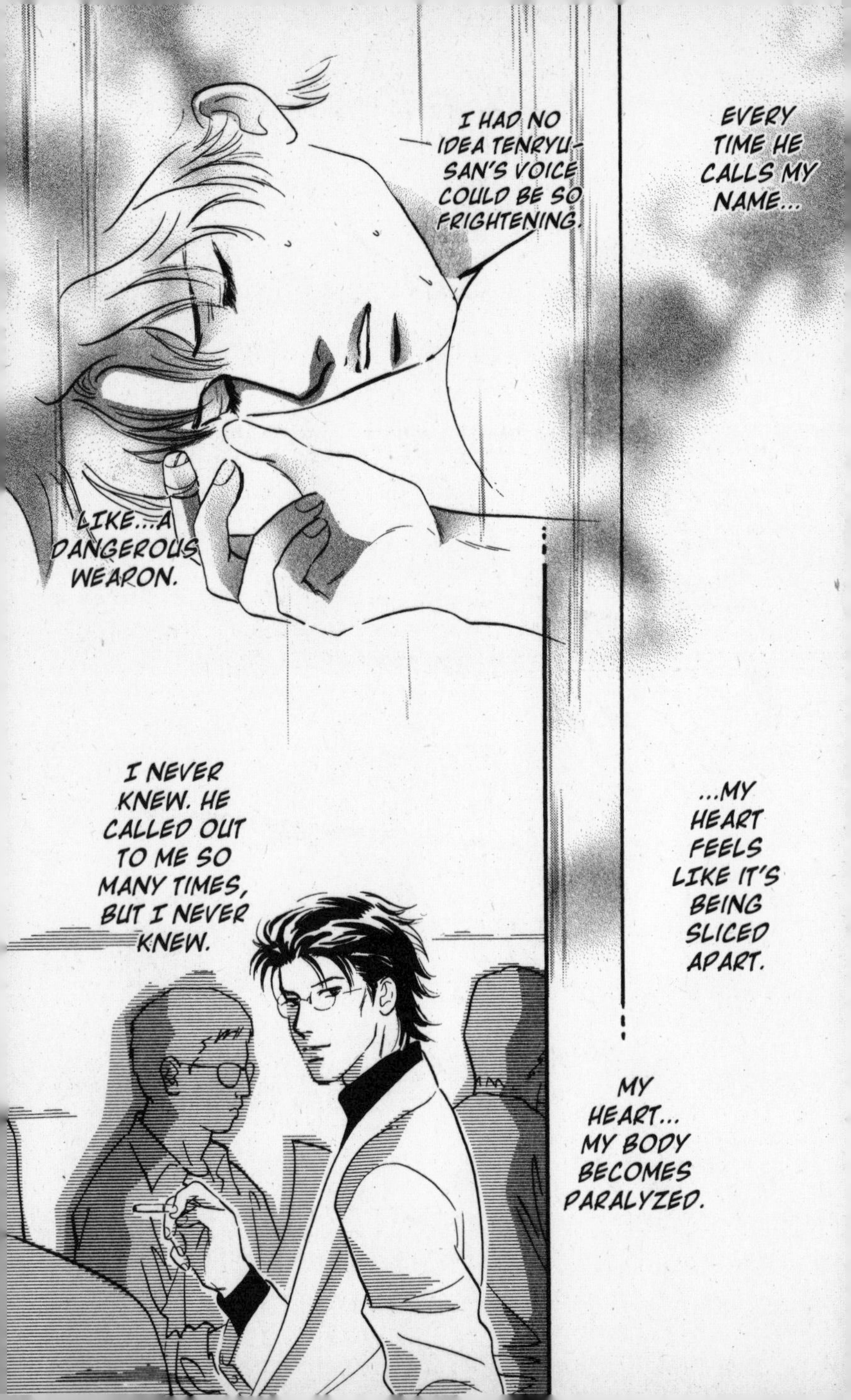
EVERY TIME HE CALLS MY NAME...
...MY HEART FEELS LIKE IT'S BEING SLICED APART.
MY HEART... MY BODY BECOMES PARALYZED.
I HAD NO IDEA TENRYU-SAN'S VOICE COULD BE SO FRIGHTENING.
LIKE...A DANGEROUS WEAPON.
I NEVER KNEW. HE CALLED OUT TO ME SO MANY TIMES, BUT I NEVER KNEW.

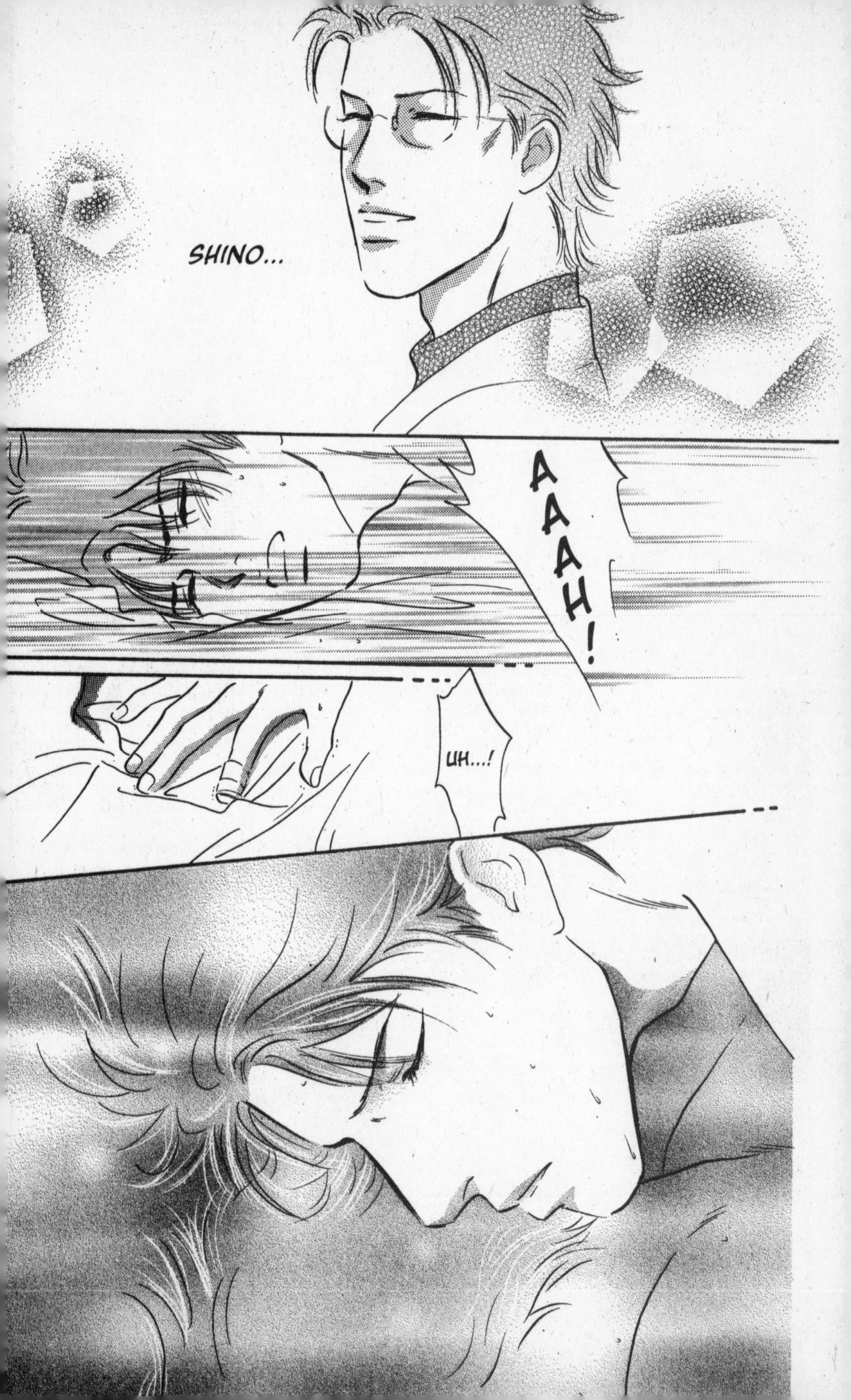
SHINO...
AAAH!
UH...!

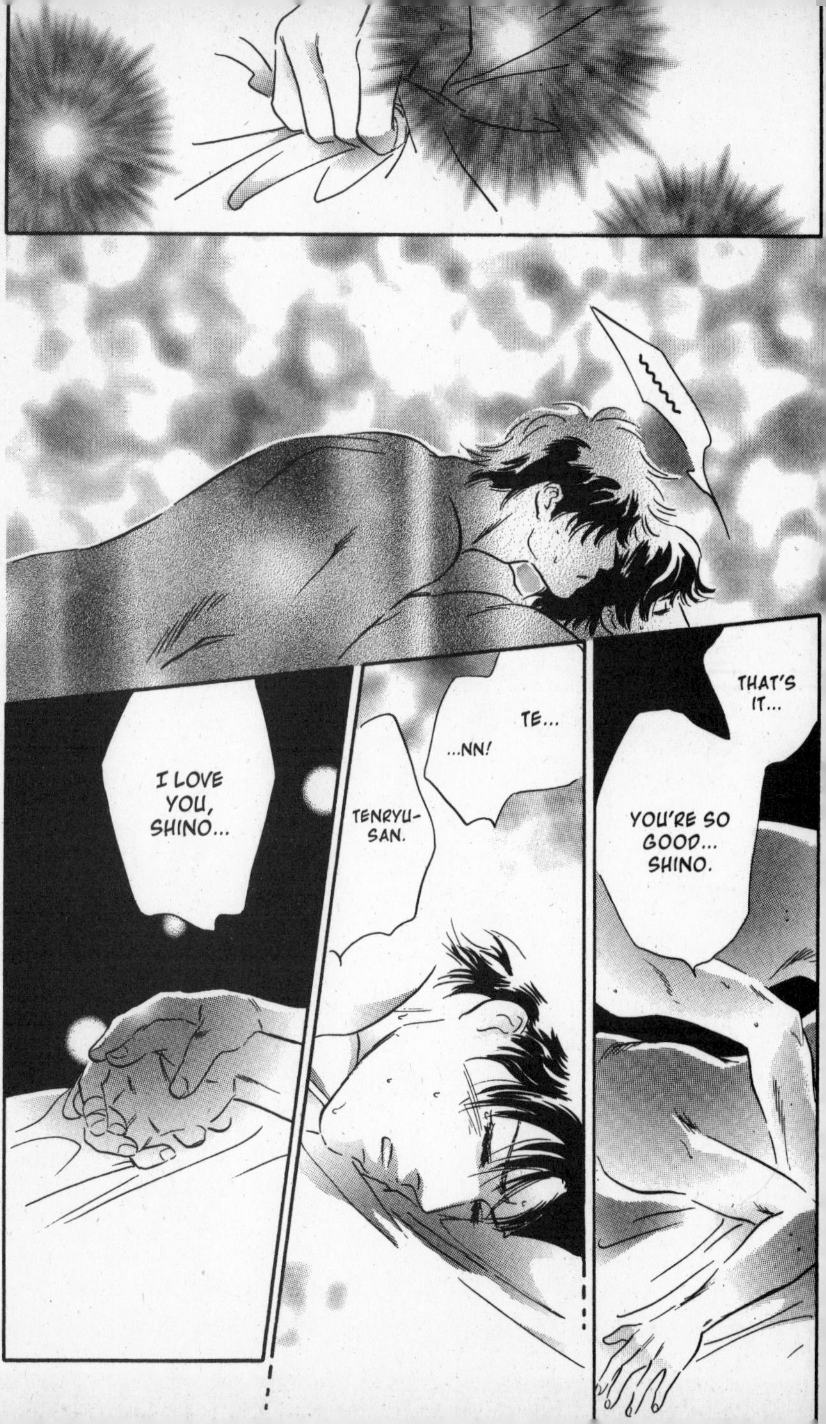
THAT'S IT...
YOU'RE SO GOOD... SHINO.
TE...
...NN!
TENRYU-SAN.
I LOVE YOU, SHINO...

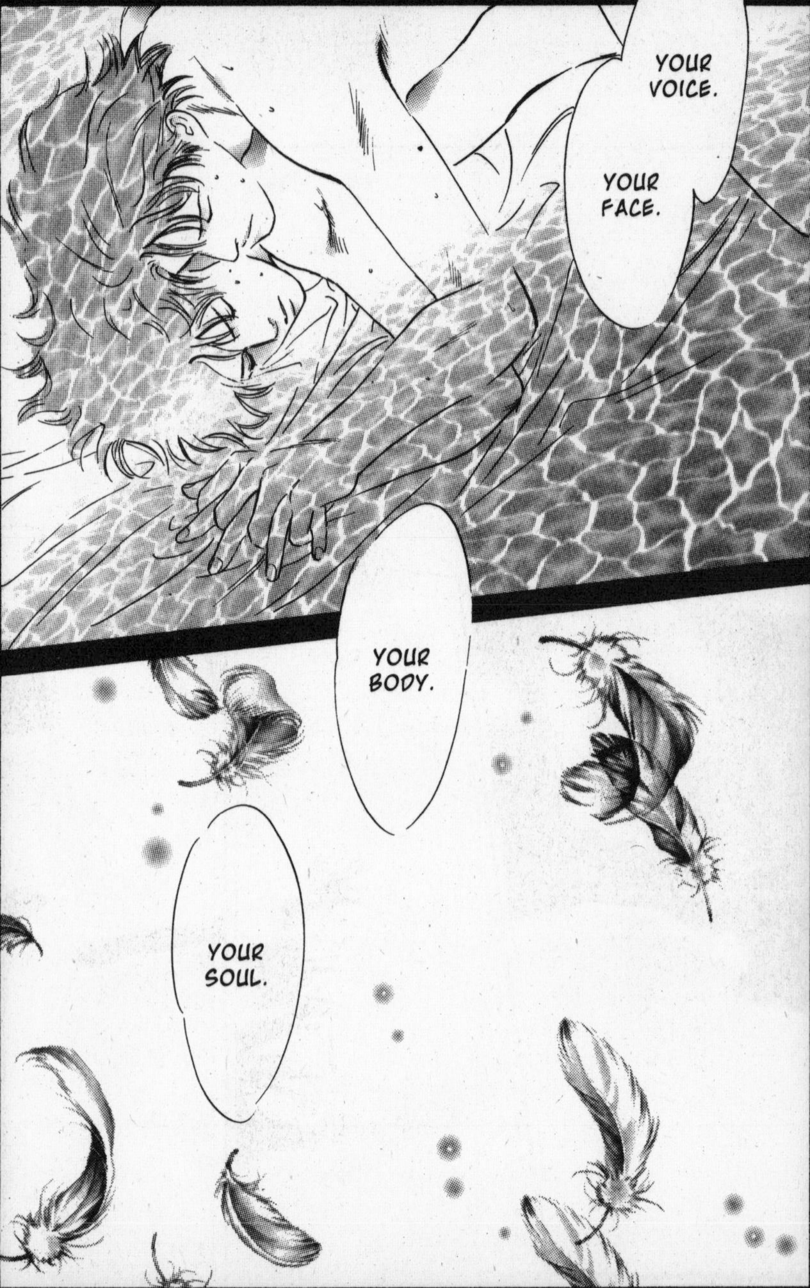
YOUR VOICE.
YOUR FACE.
YOUR BODY.
YOUR SOUL.

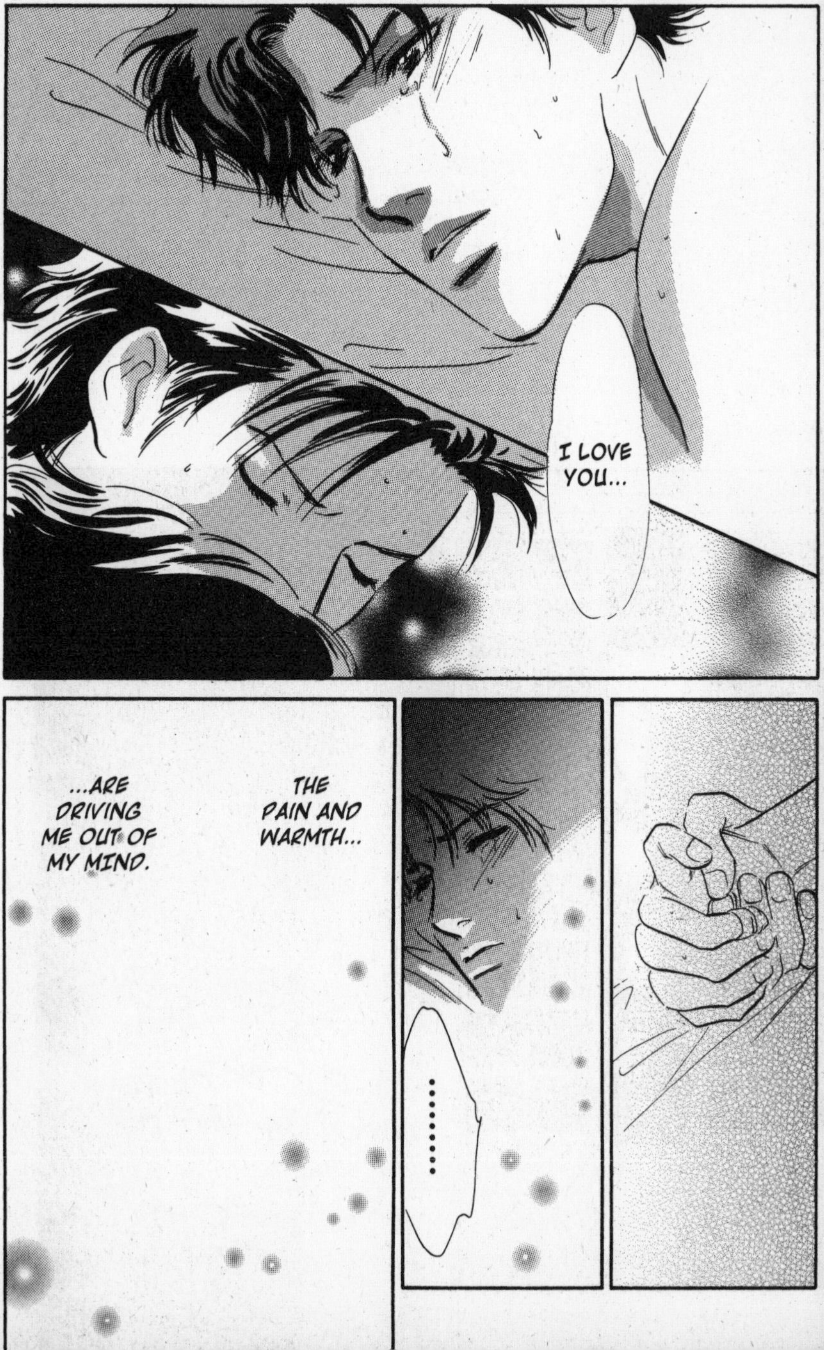
I LOVE YOU...
....
THE PAIN AND WARMTH...
...ARE DRIVING ME OUT OF MY MIND.

I WISH I COULD
JUST LOSE
CONSCIOUSNESS
HERE AND NOW.

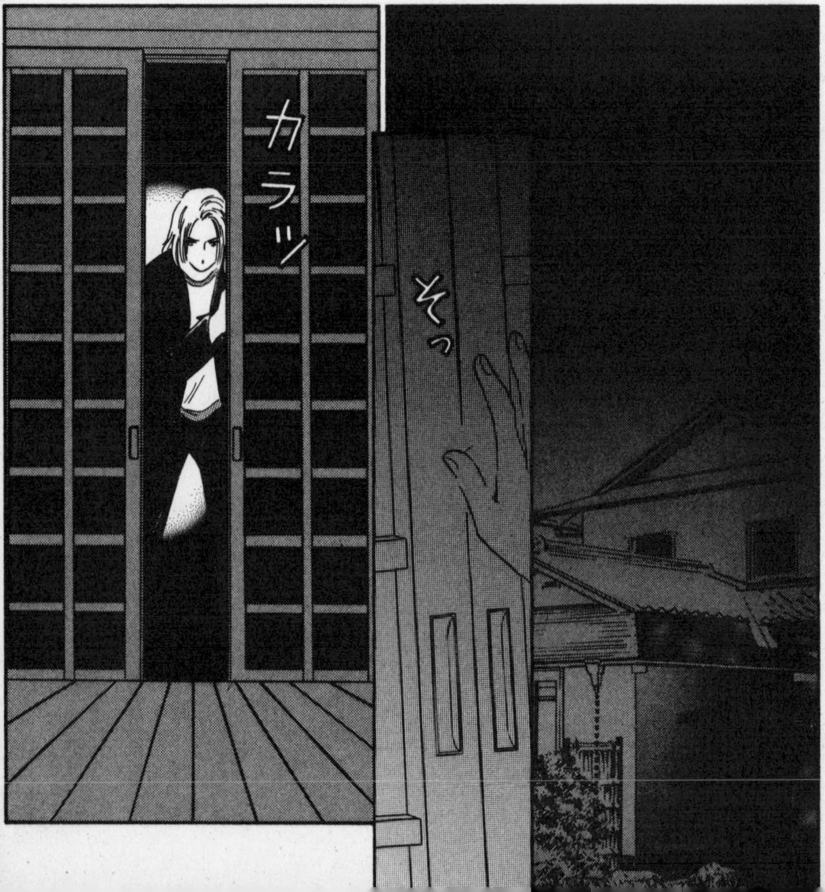
そっ
カラッ

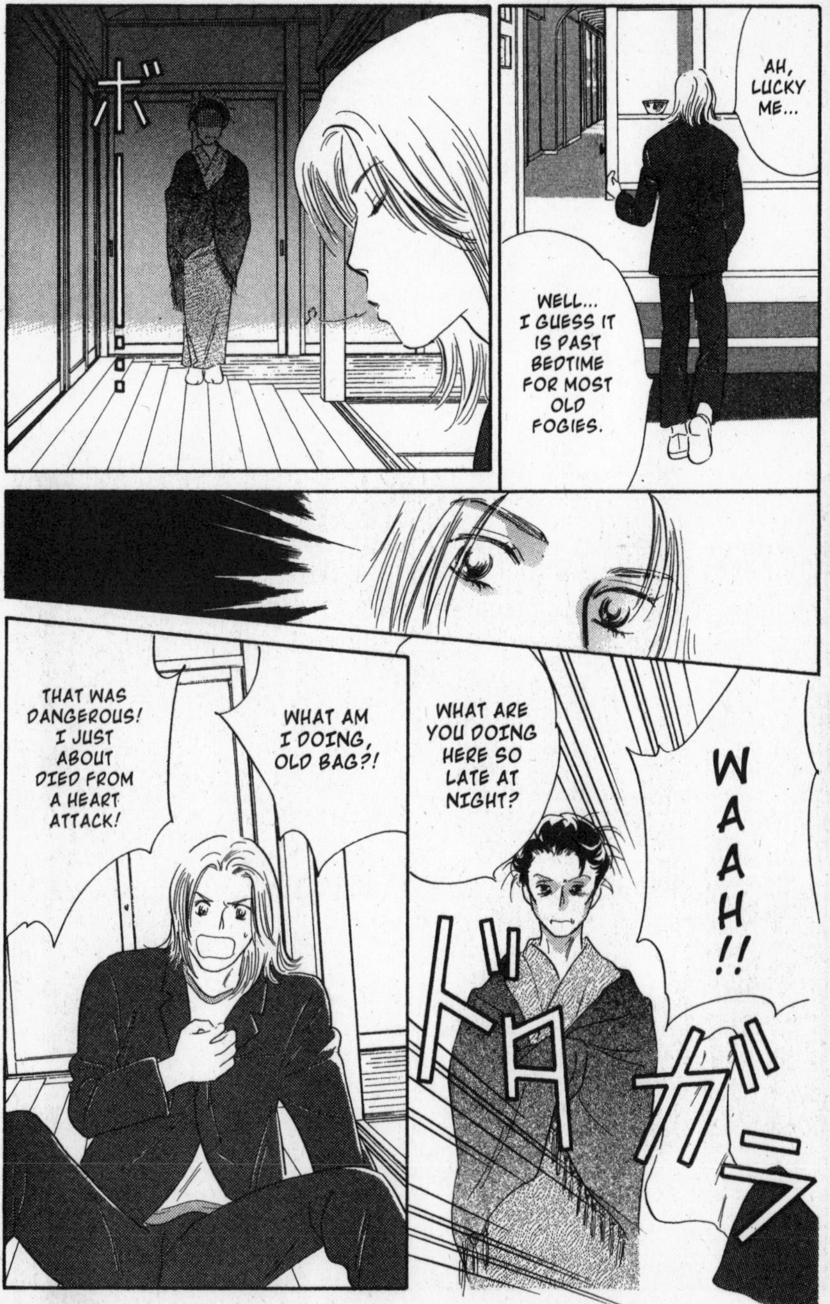
AH, LUCKY ME...
WELL... I GUESS IT IS PAST BEDTIME FOR MOST OLD FOGIES.
WAAAH!!
WHAT ARE YOU DOING HERE SO LATE AT NIGHT?
WHAT AM I DOING, OLD BAG?!
THAT WAS DANGEROUS! I JUST ABOUT DIED FROM A HEART ATTACK!

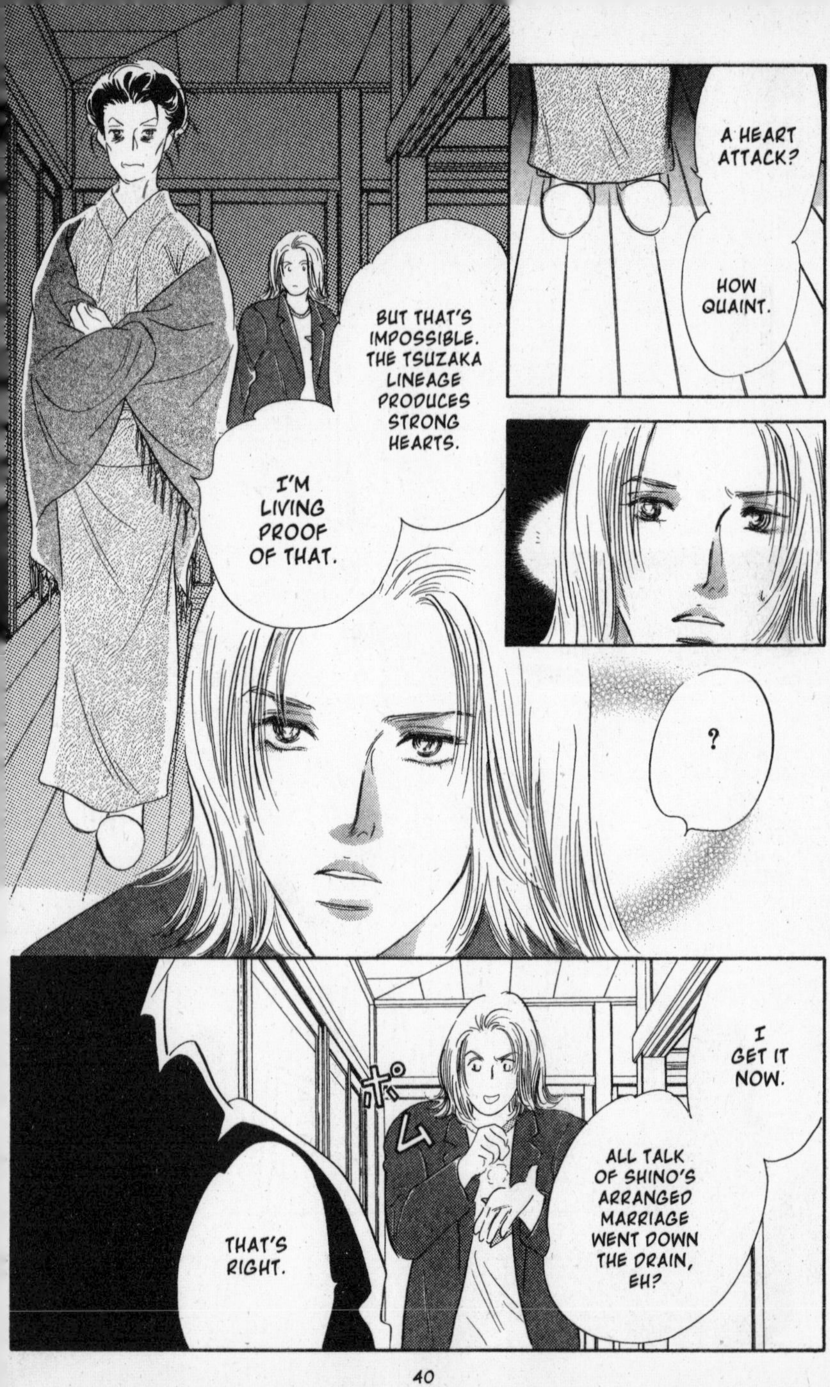

A HEART ATTACK?
HOW QUAINT.
BUT THAT'S IMPOSSIBLE. THE TSUZAKA LINEAGE PRODUCES STRONG HEARTS.
I'M LIVING PROOF OF THAT.
?
I GET IT NOW.
ALL TALK OF SHINO'S ARRANGED MARRIAGE WENT DOWN THE DRAIN, EH?
ポン
THAT'S RIGHT.

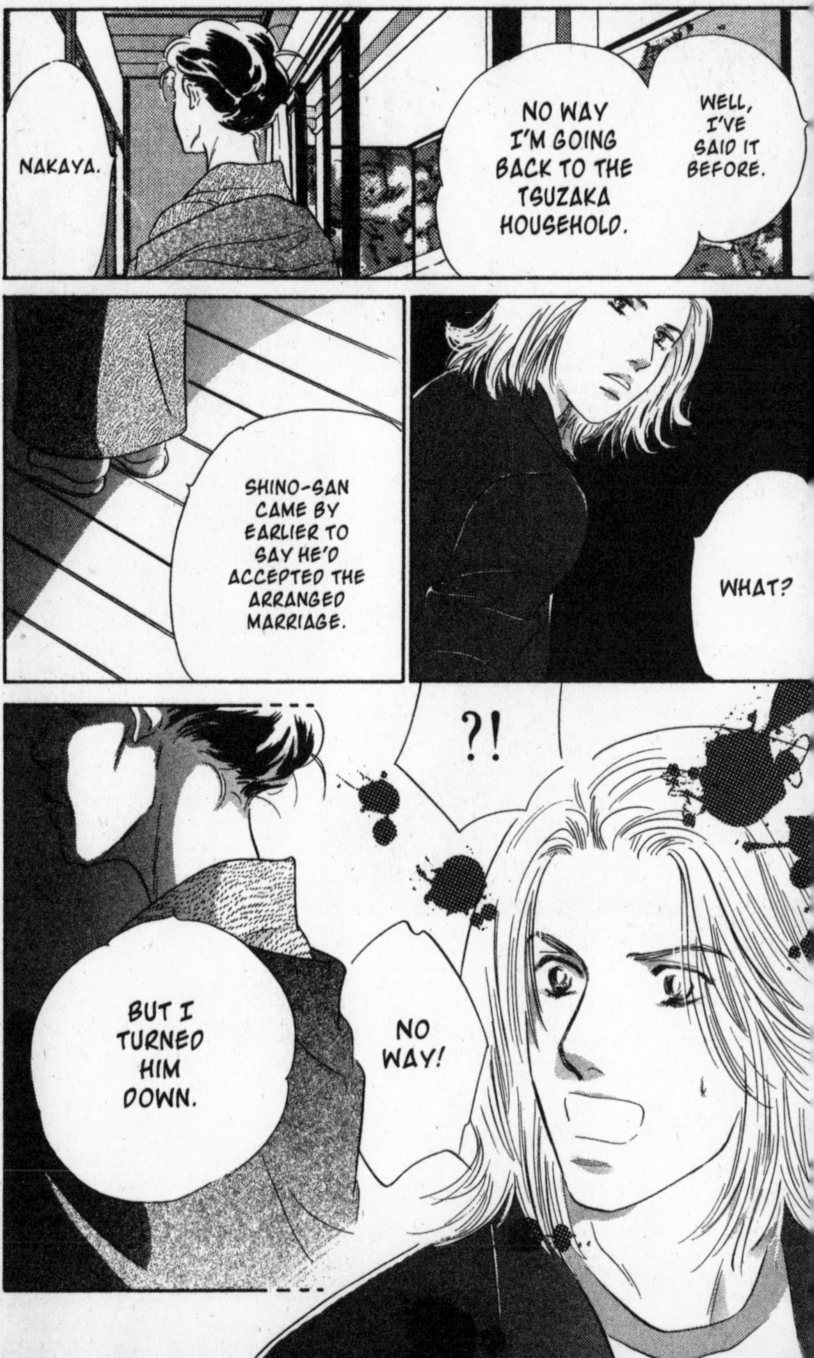
WELL, I'VE SAID IT BEFORE.
NO WAY I'M GOING BACK TO THE TSUZAKA HOUSEHOLD.
NAKAYA.
WHAT?
SHINO-SAN CAME BY EARLIER TO SAY HE'D ACCEPTED THE ARRANGED MARRIAGE.
?!
NO WAY!
BUT I TURNED HIM DOWN.

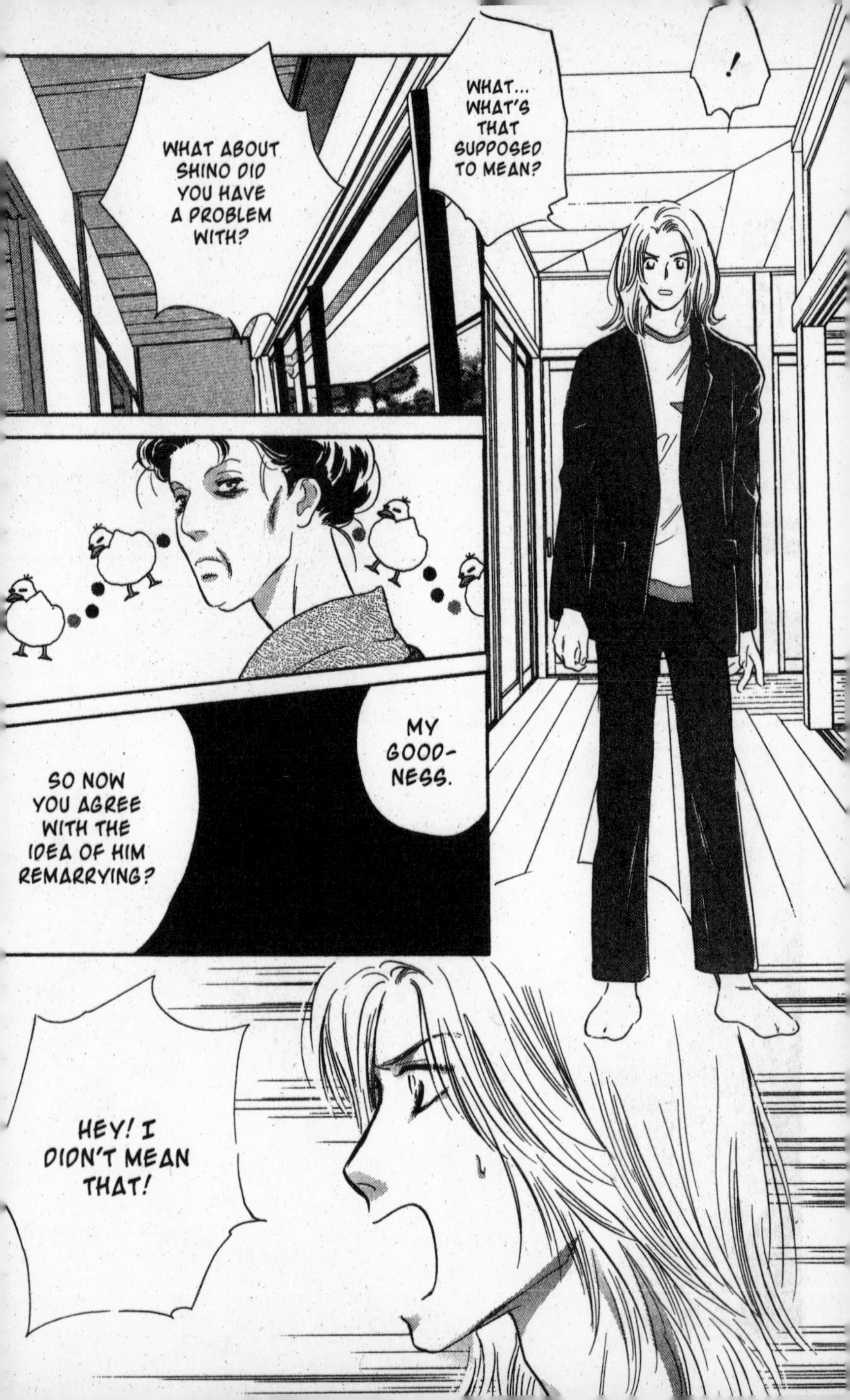
!
WHAT... WHAT'S THAT SUPPOSED TO MEAN?
WHAT ABOUT SHINO DID YOU HAVE A PROBLEM WITH?
MY GOODNESS.
SO NOW YOU AGREE WITH THE IDEA OF HIM REMARRYING?
HEY! I DIDN'T MEAN THAT!

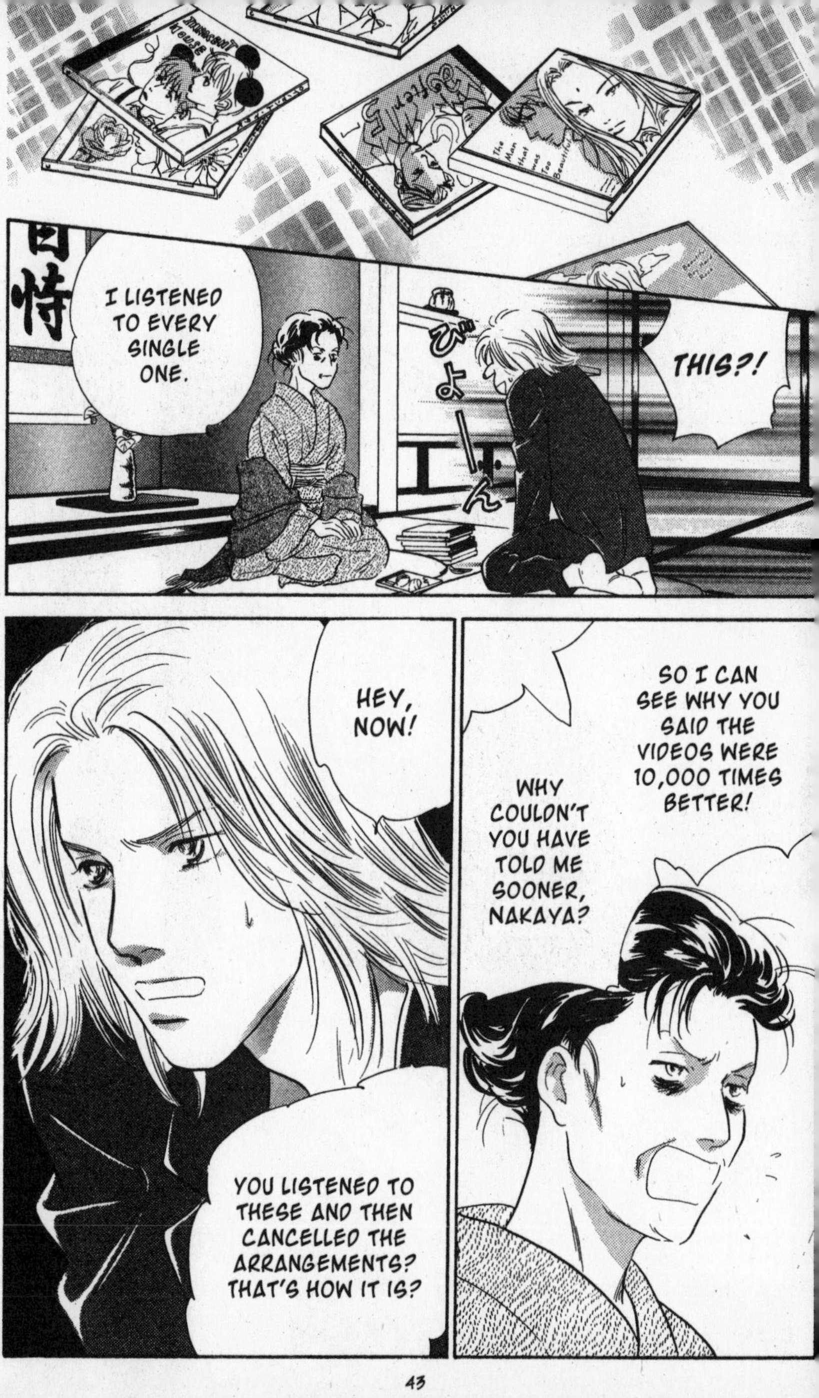

The Man that was Too Beautiful
THIS?!
びょーーん
I LISTENED TO EVERY SINGLE ONE.
SO I CAN SEE WHY YOU SAID THE VIDEOS WERE 10,000 TIMES BETTER!
WHY COULDN'T YOU HAVE TOLD ME SOONER, NAKAYA?
HEY, NOW!
YOU LISTENED TO THESE AND THEN CANCELLED THE ARRANGEMENTS? THAT'S HOW IT IS?

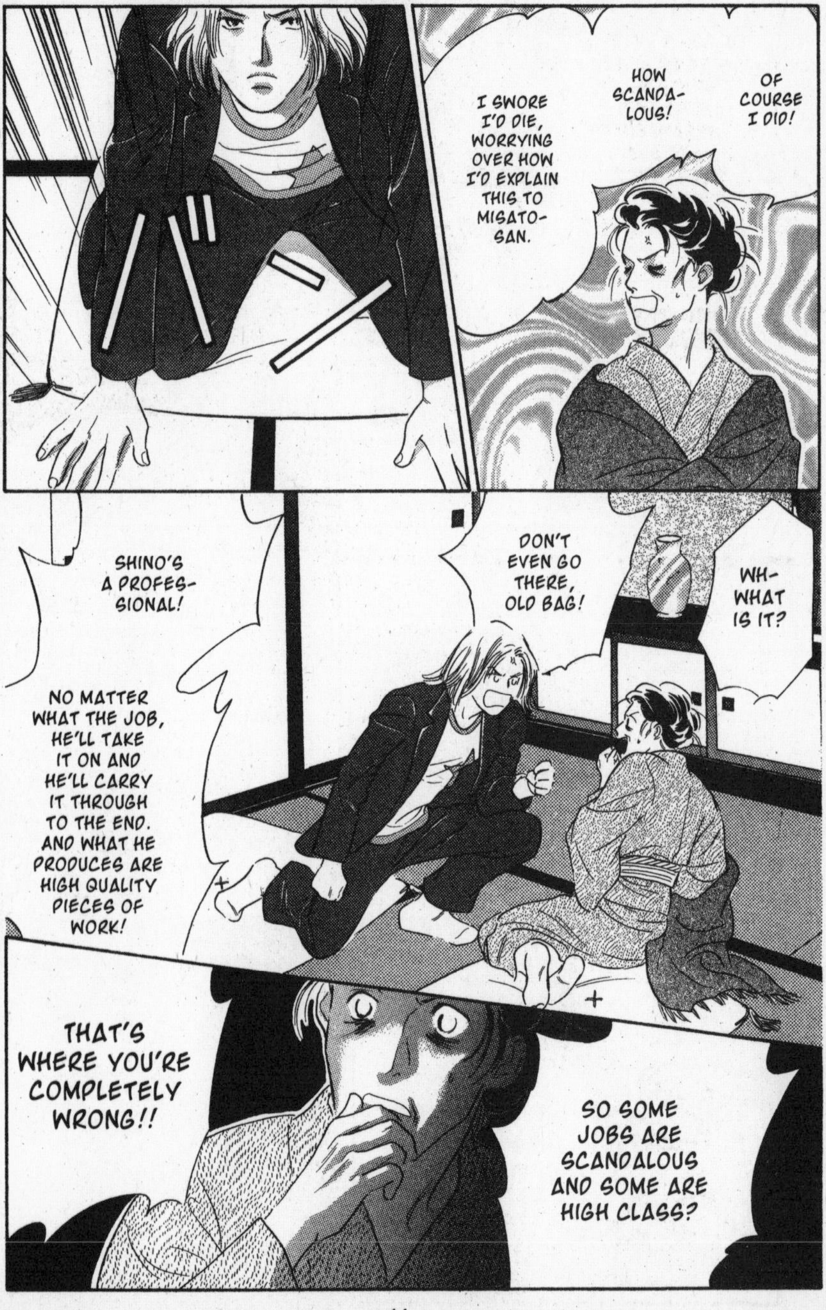
OF COURSE I DID!
HOW SCANDALOUS!
I SWORE I'D DIE, WORRYING OVER HOW I'D EXPLAIN THIS TO MISATO-SAN.
WH-WHAT IS IT?
DON'T EVEN GO THERE, OLD BAG!
SHINO'S A PROFESSIONAL!
NO MATTER WHAT THE JOB, HE'LL TAKE IT ON AND HE'LL CARRY IT THROUGH TO THE END. AND WHAT HE PRODUCES ARE HIGH QUALITY PIECES OF WORK!
SO SOME JOBS ARE SCANDALOUS AND SOME ARE HIGH CLASS?
THAT'S WHERE YOU'RE COMPLETELY WRONG!!

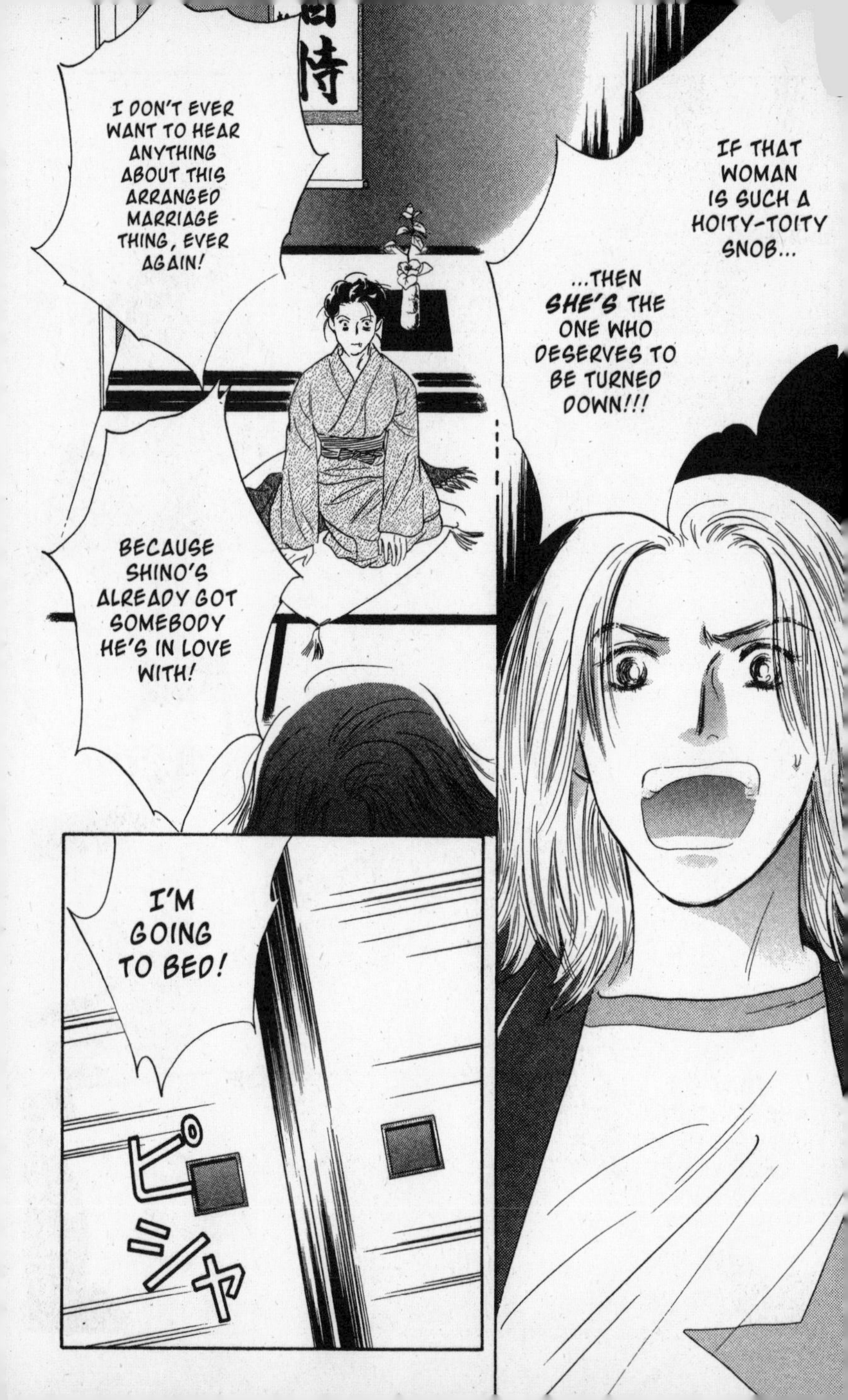
IF THAT WOMAN IS SUCH A HOITY-TOITY SNOB...
...THEN ***SHE'S*** THE ONE WHO DESERVES TO BE TURNED DOWN!!!
I DON'T EVER WANT TO HEAR ANYTHING ABOUT THIS ARRANGED MARRIAGE THING, EVER AGAIN!
BECAUSE SHINO'S ALREADY GOT SOMEBODY HE'S IN LOVE WITH!
I'M GOING TO BED!
ピシャ

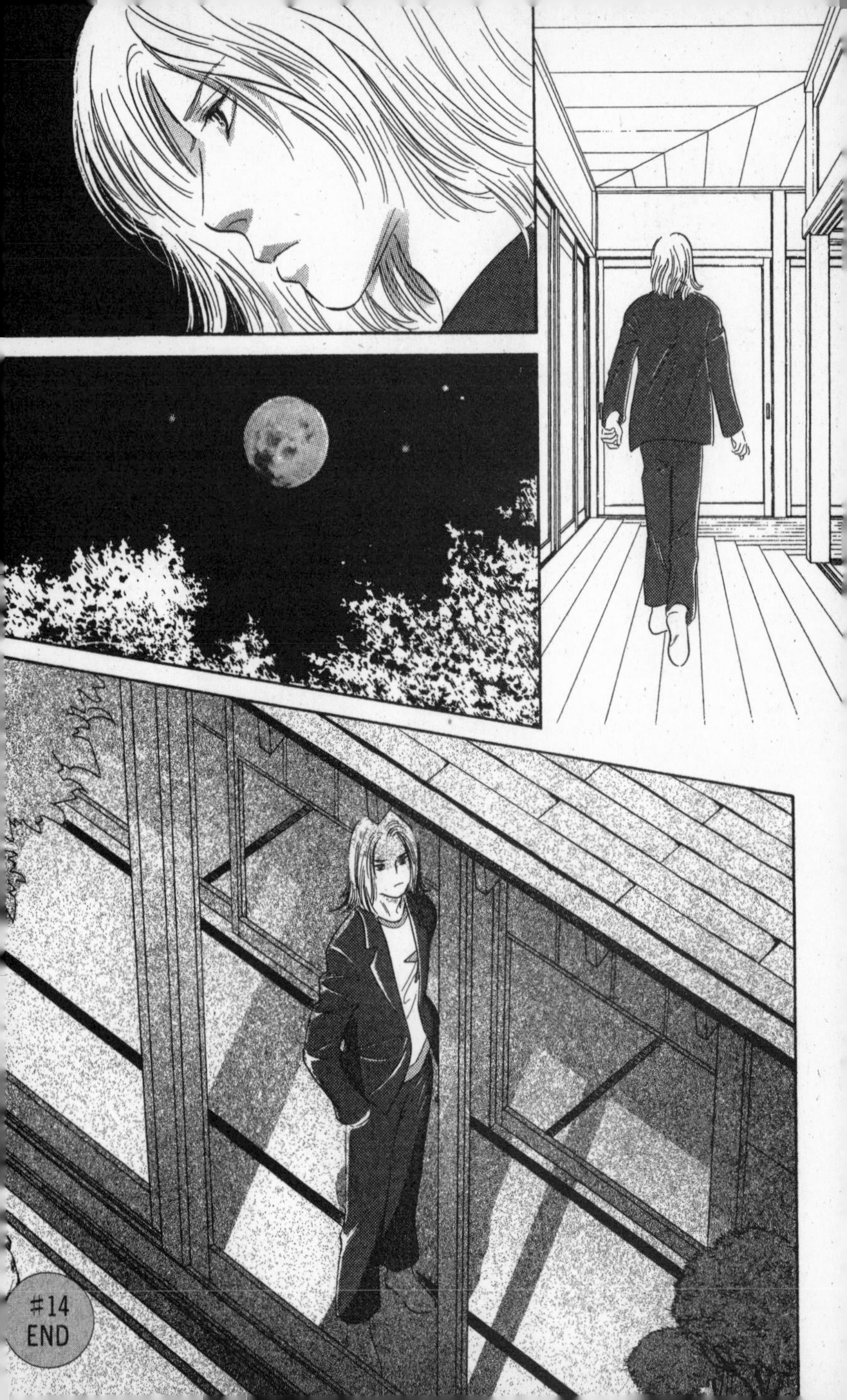
#14
END

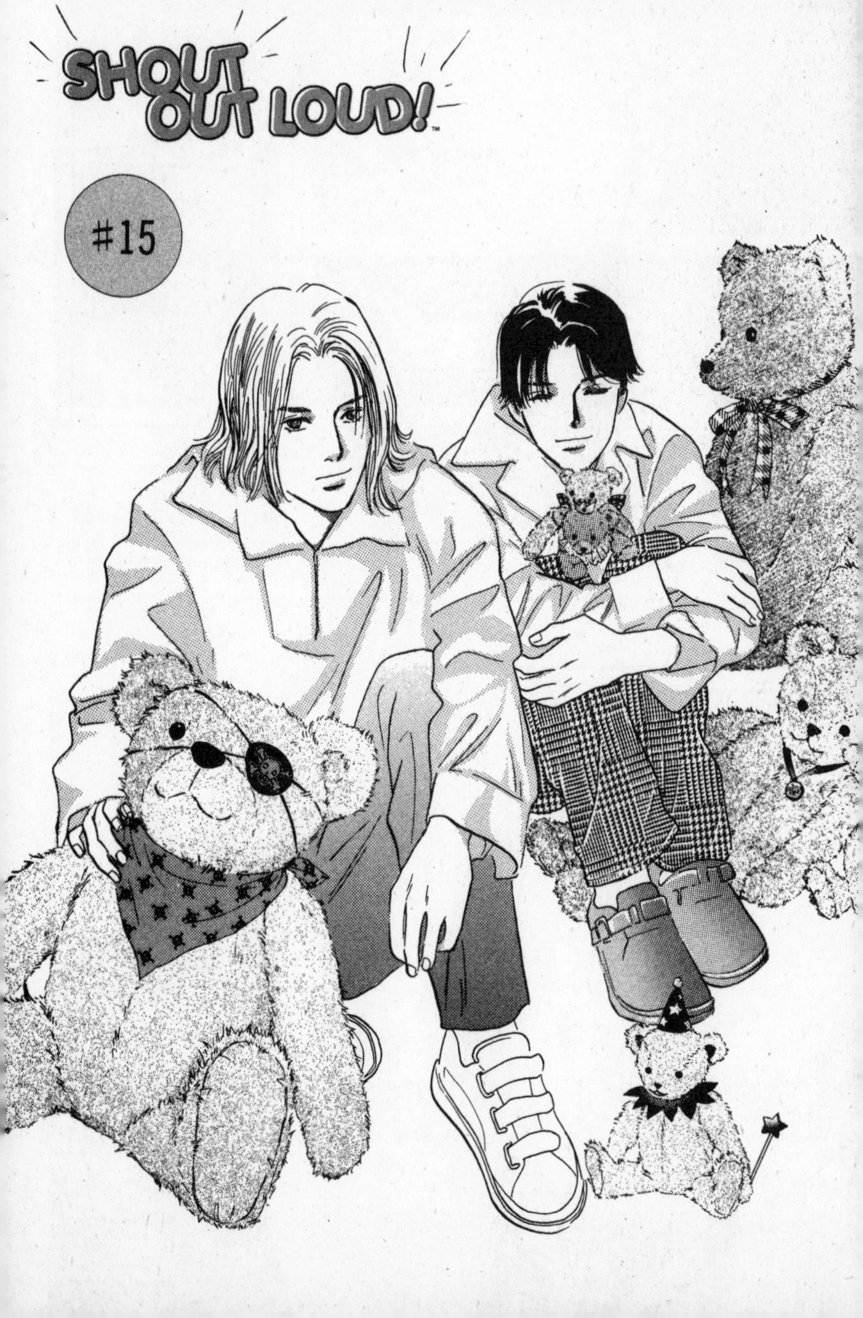
SHOUT OUT LOUD!™
#15

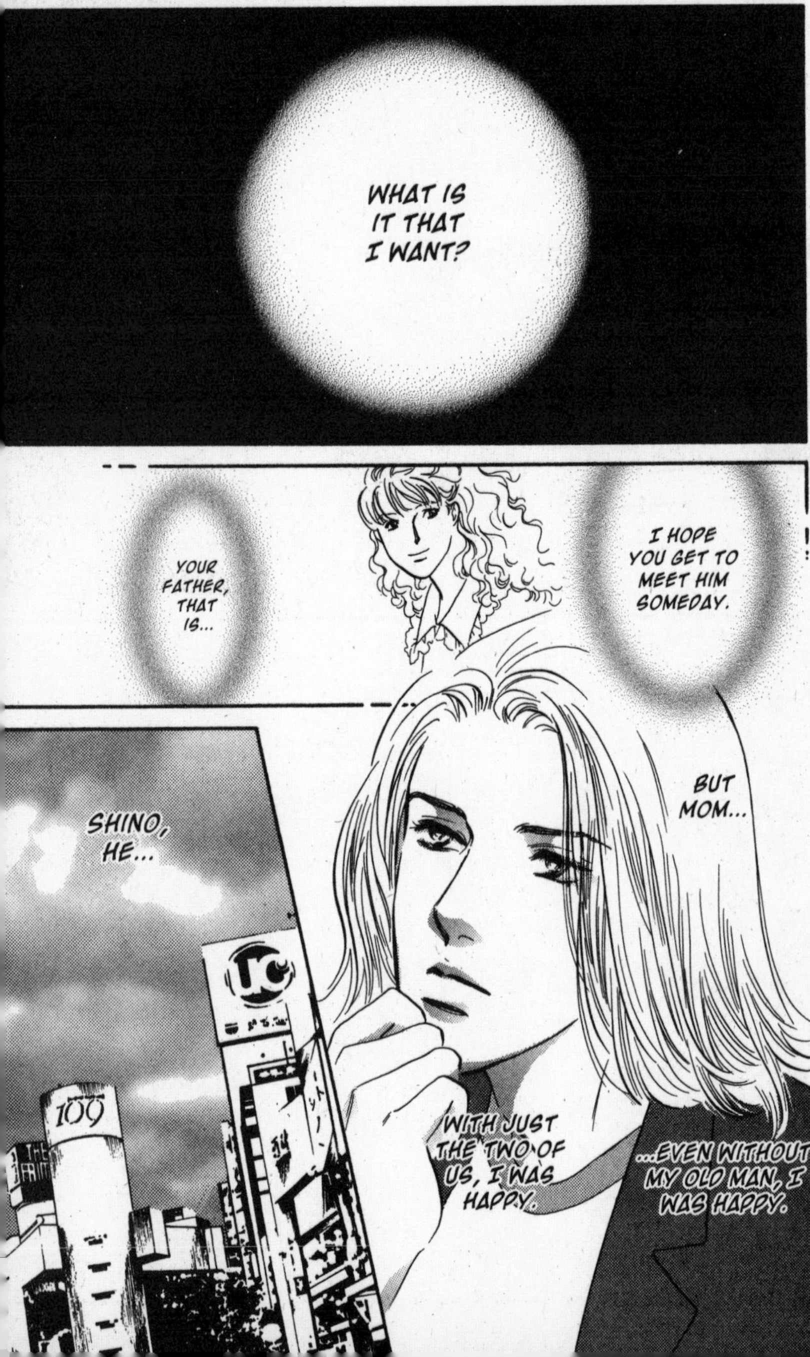
WHAT IS IT THAT I WANT?
I HOPE YOU GET TO MEET HIM SOMEDAY.
YOUR FATHER, THAT IS...
BUT MOM...
SHINO, HE...
...EVEN WITHOUT MY OLD MAN, I WAS HAPPY.
WITH JUST THE TWO OF US, I WAS HAPPY.

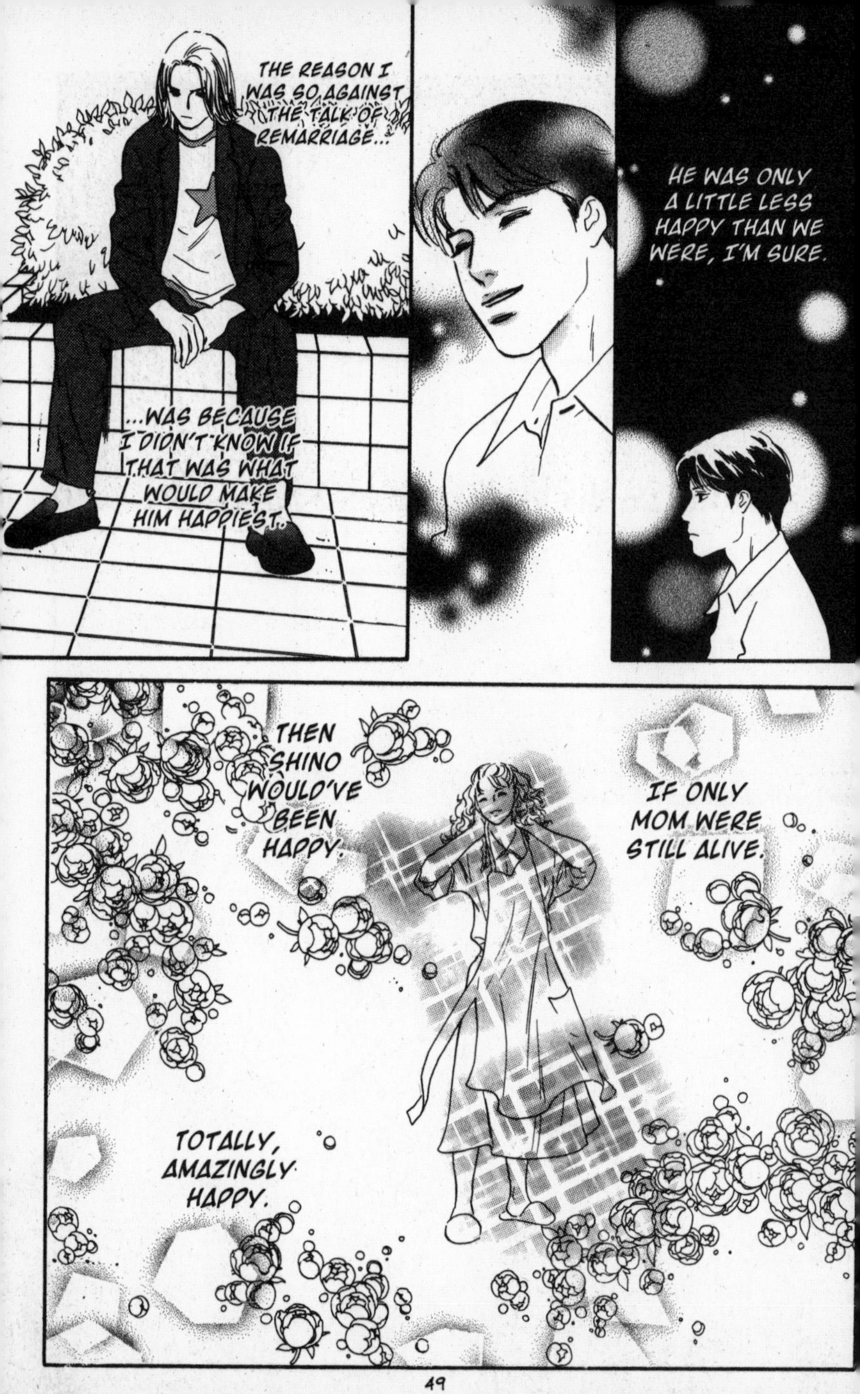
HE WAS ONLY A LITTLE LESS HAPPY THAN WE WERE, I'M SURE.
THE REASON I WAS SO AGAINST THE TALK OF REMARRIAGE...
...WAS BECAUSE I DIDN'T KNOW IF THAT WAS WHAT WOULD MAKE HIM HAPPIEST.
IF ONLY MOM WERE STILL ALIVE.
THEN SHINO WOULD'VE BEEN HAPPY.
TOTALLY, AMAZINGLY HAPPY.

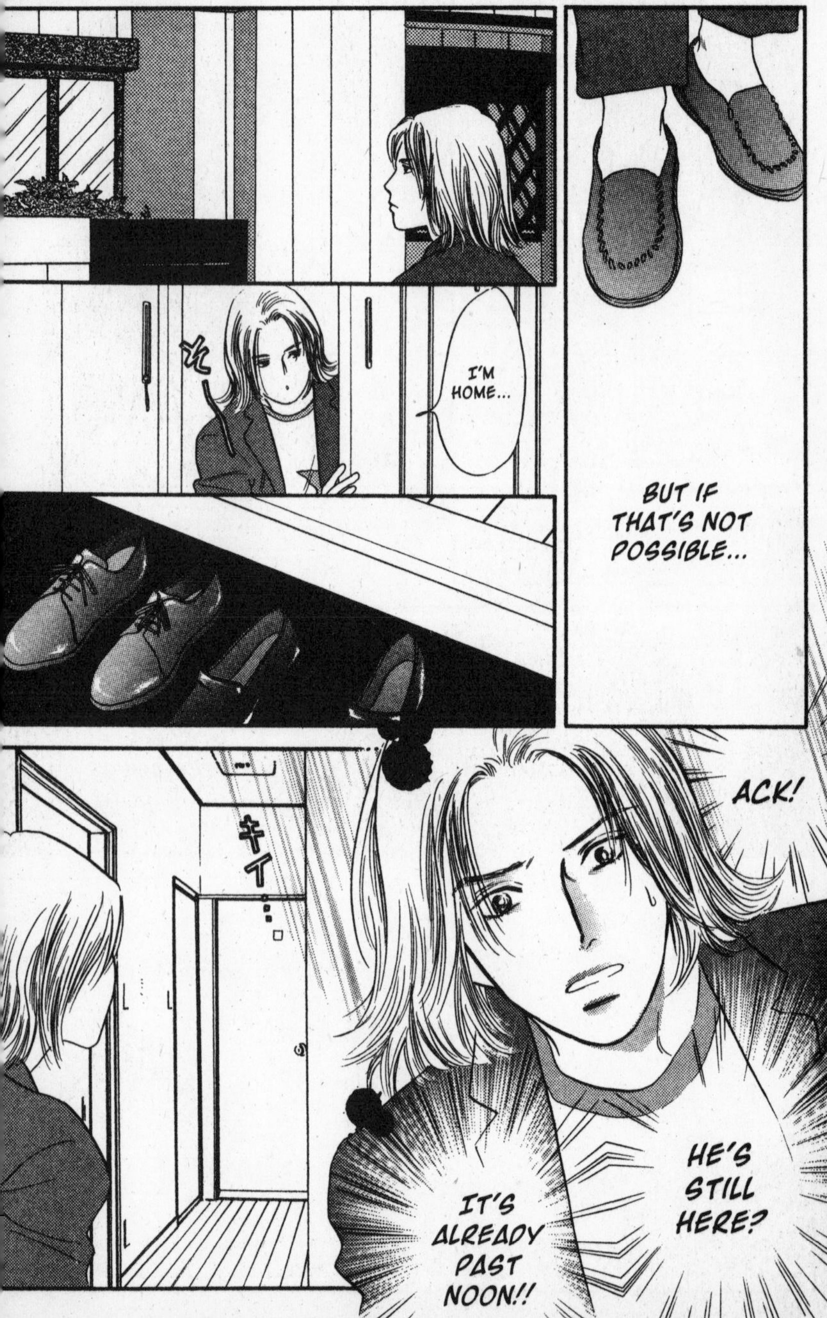
BUT IF THAT'S NOT POSSIBLE...
I'M HOME...
ACK!
HE'S STILL HERE?
IT'S ALREADY PAST NOON!!
キイ

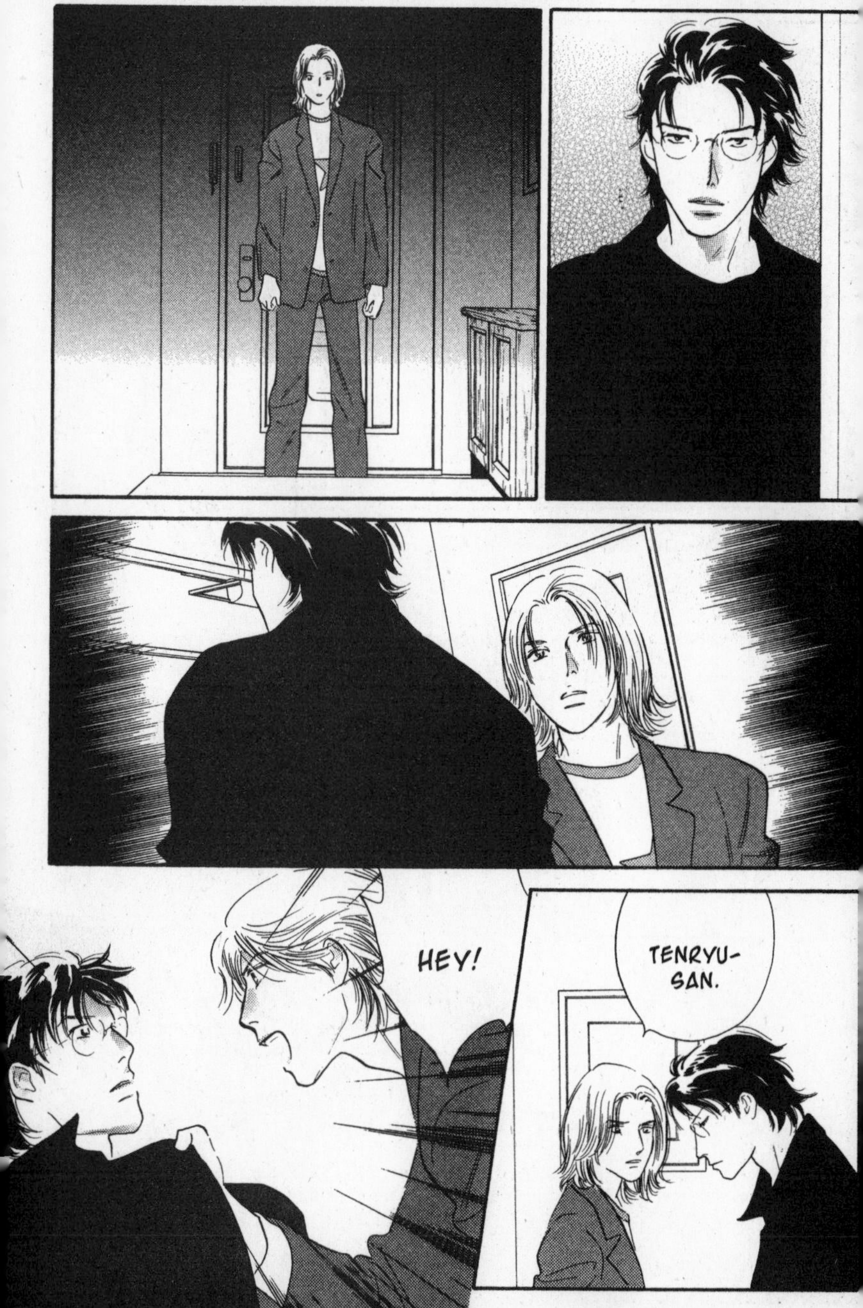
TENRYU-SAN.
HEY!

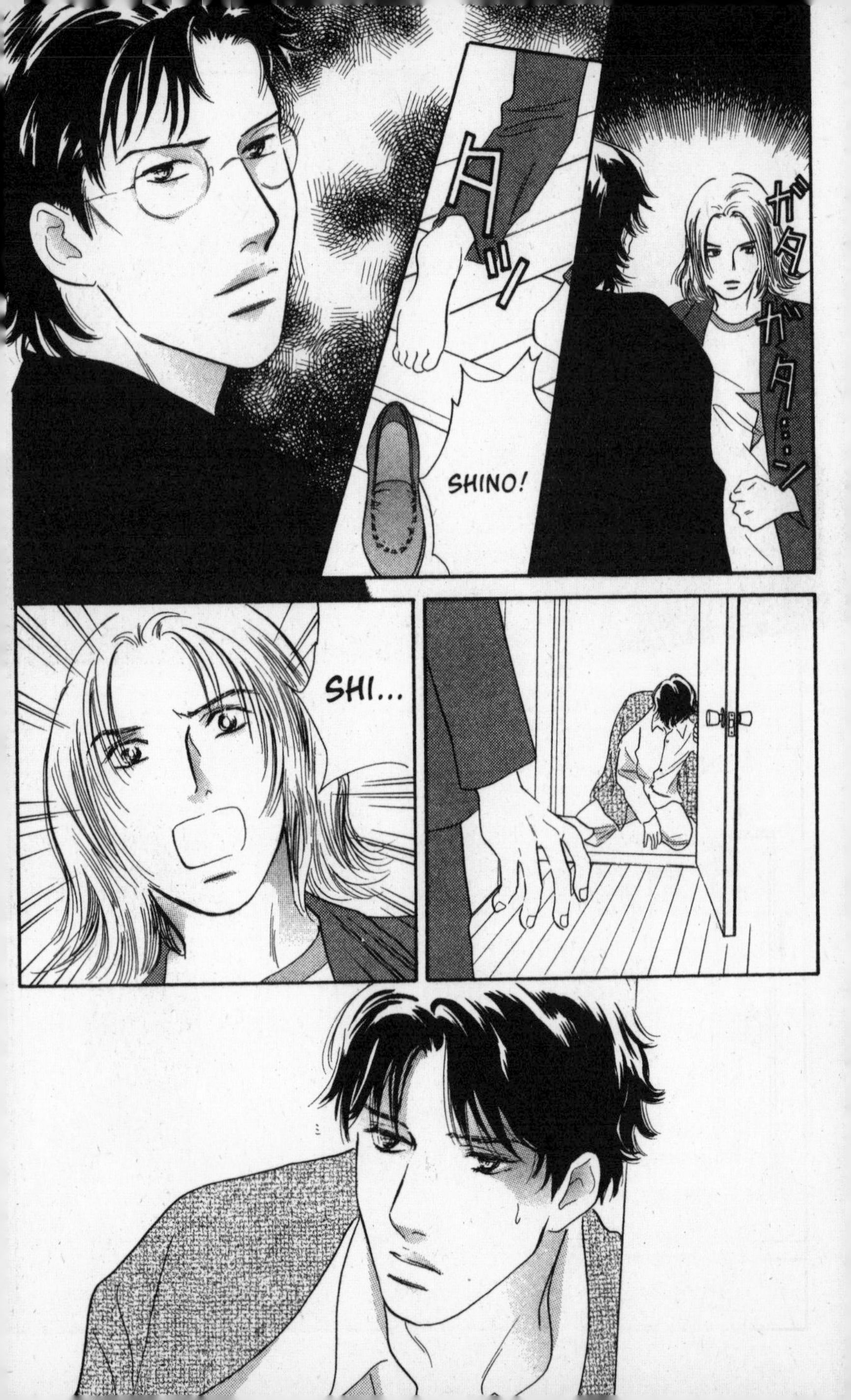
ガタガタ…
SHINO!
SHI...

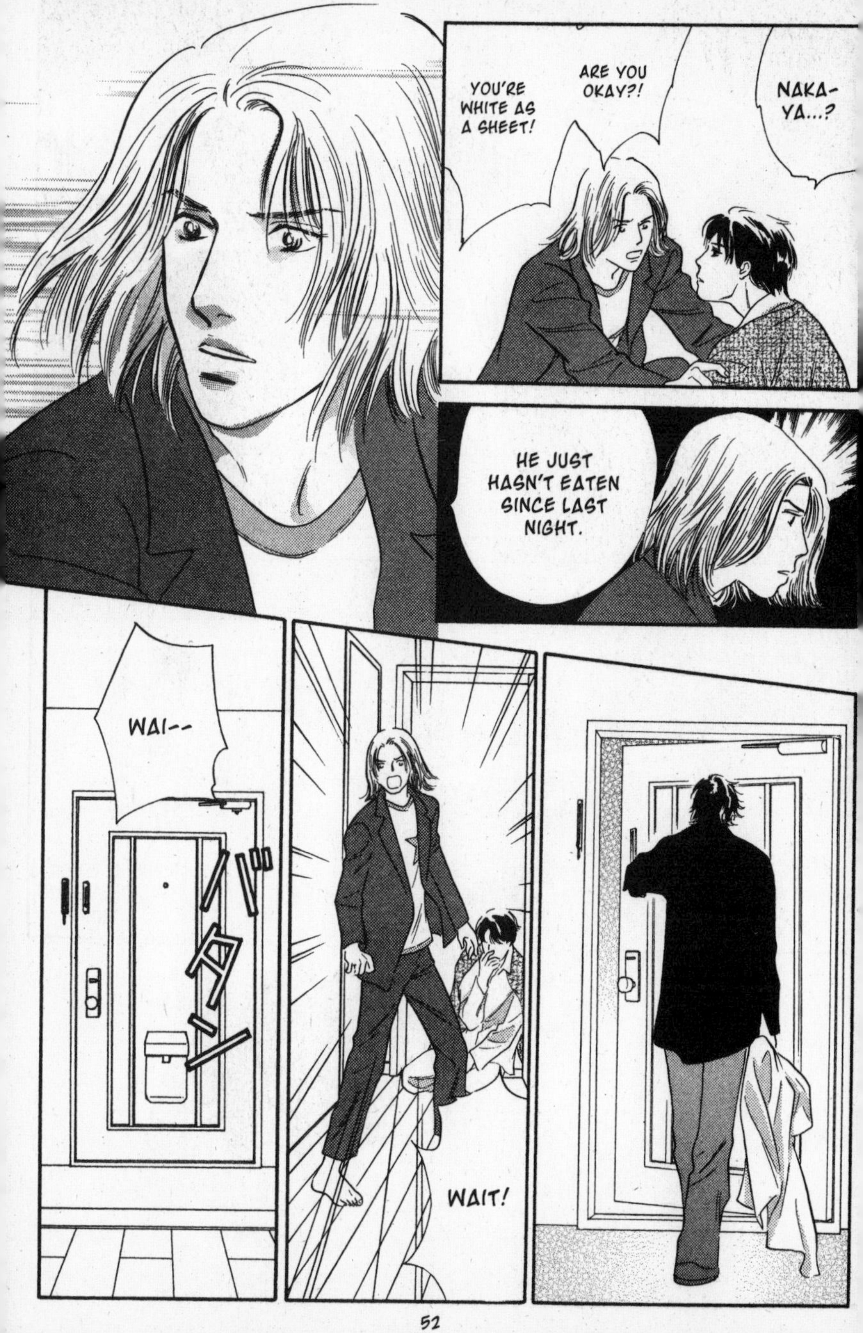
NAKA-YA...?
ARE YOU OKAY?!
YOU'RE WHITE AS A SHEET!
HE JUST HASN'T EATEN SINCE LAST NIGHT.
WAIT!
WAI--
バタン

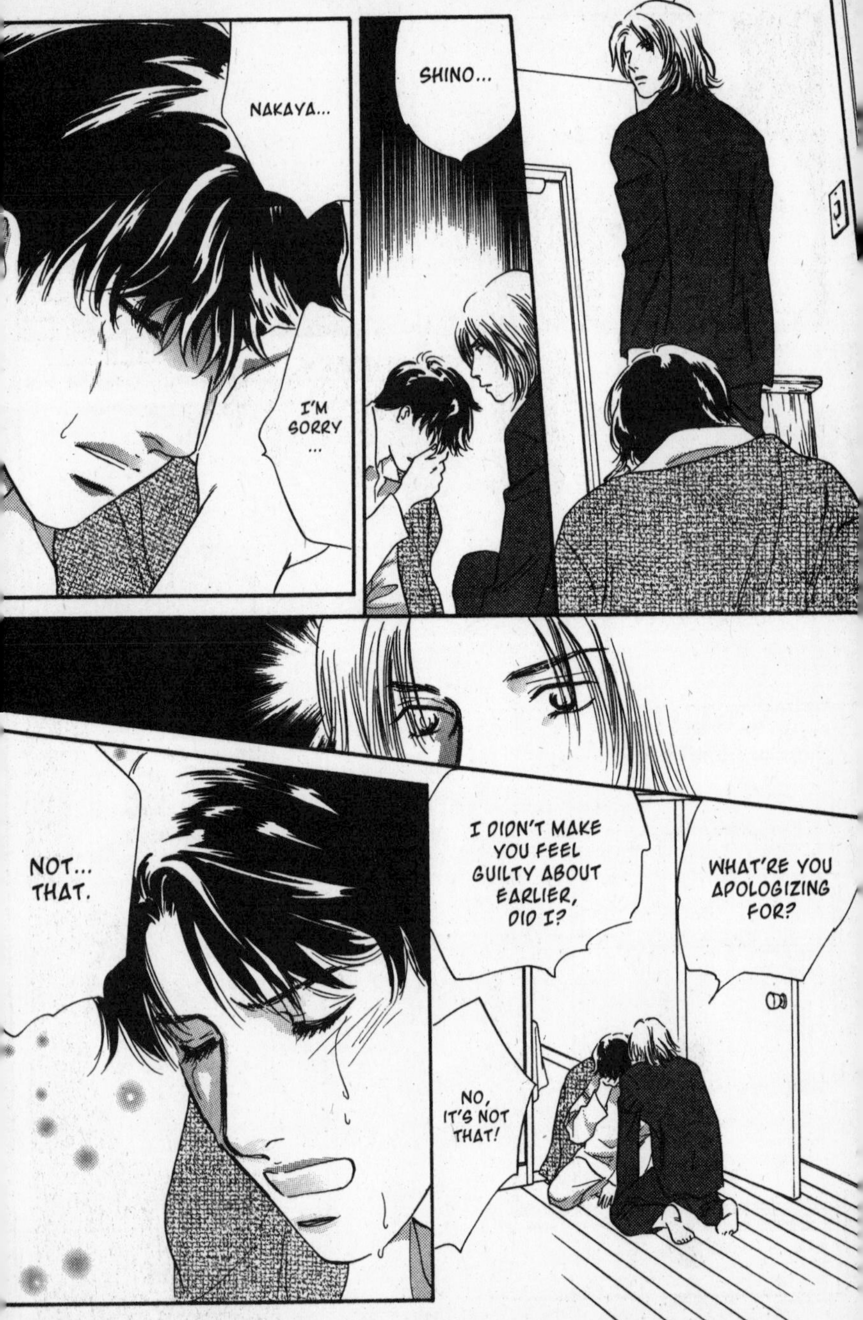
SHINO...
NAKAYA...
I'M SORRY ...
WHAT'RE YOU APOLOGIZING FOR?
I DIDN'T MAKE YOU FEEL GUILTY ABOUT EARLIER, DID I?
NO, IT'S NOT THAT!
NOT... THAT.

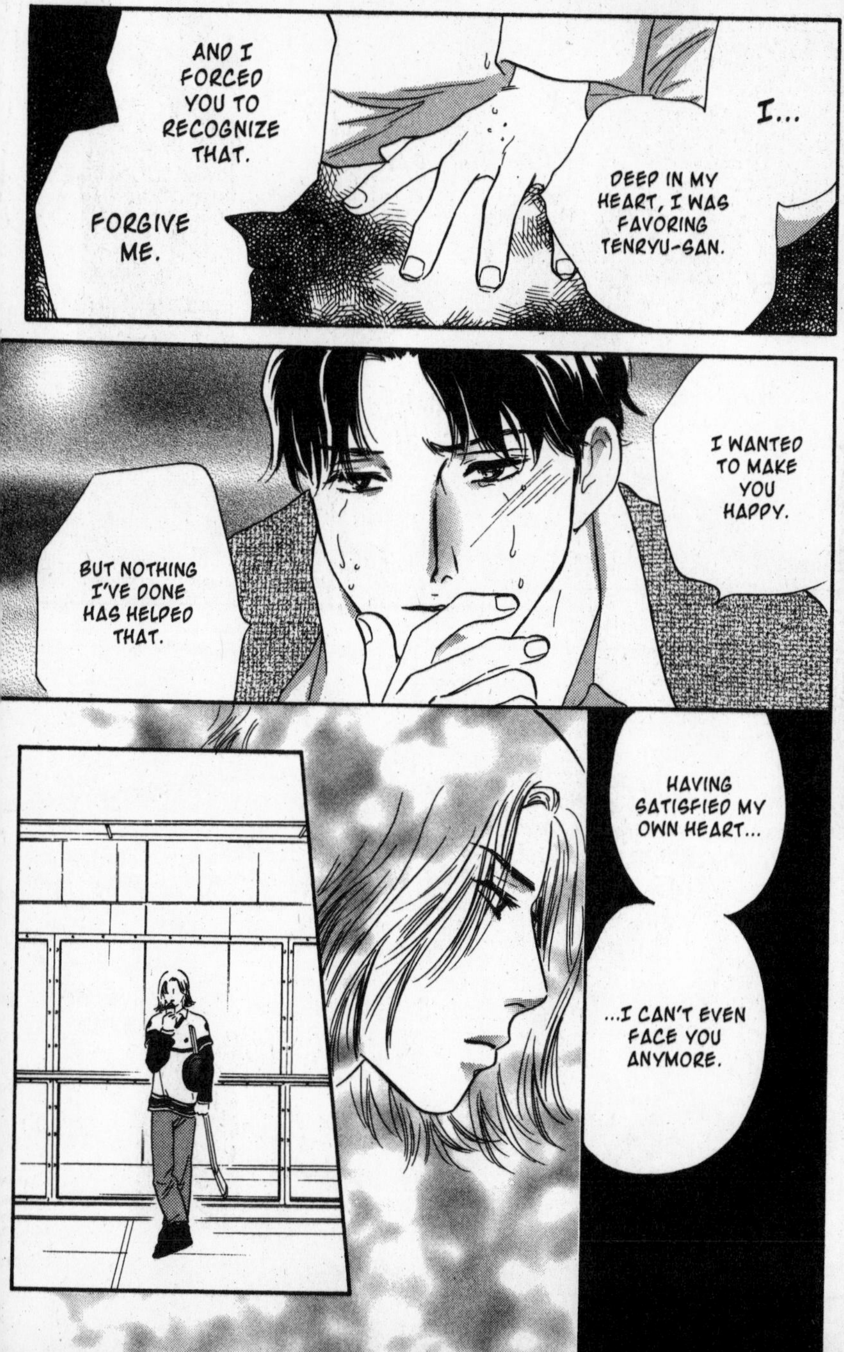
I...
DEEP IN MY HEART, I WAS FAVORING TENRYU-SAN.
AND I FORCED YOU TO RECOGNIZE THAT.
FORGIVE ME.
I WANTED TO MAKE YOU HAPPY.
BUT NOTHING I'VE DONE HAS HELPED THAT.
HAVING SATISFIED MY OWN HEART...
...I CAN'T EVEN FACE YOU ANYMORE.

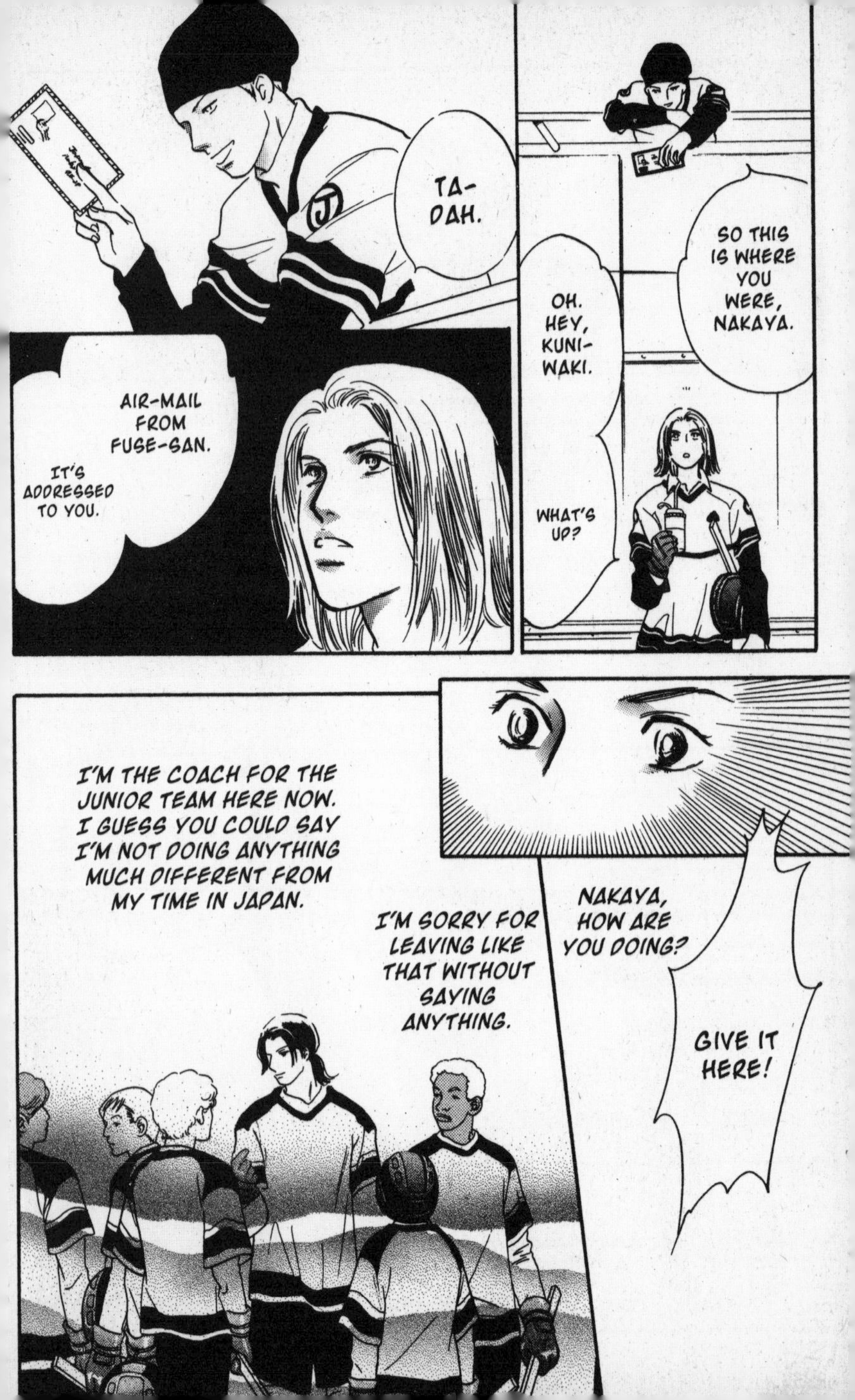

SO THIS IS WHERE YOU WERE, NAKAYA.
...
OH. HEY, KUNI-WAKI.
WHAT'S UP?
TA-DAH.
AIR-MAIL FROM FUSE-SAN.
IT'S ADDRESSED TO YOU.
NAKAYA, HOW ARE YOU DOING?
GIVE IT HERE!
I'M SORRY FOR LEAVING LIKE THAT WITHOUT SAYING ANYTHING.
I'M THE COACH FOR THE JUNIOR TEAM HERE NOW. I GUESS YOU COULD SAY I'M NOT DOING ANYTHING MUCH DIFFERENT FROM MY TIME IN JAPAN.

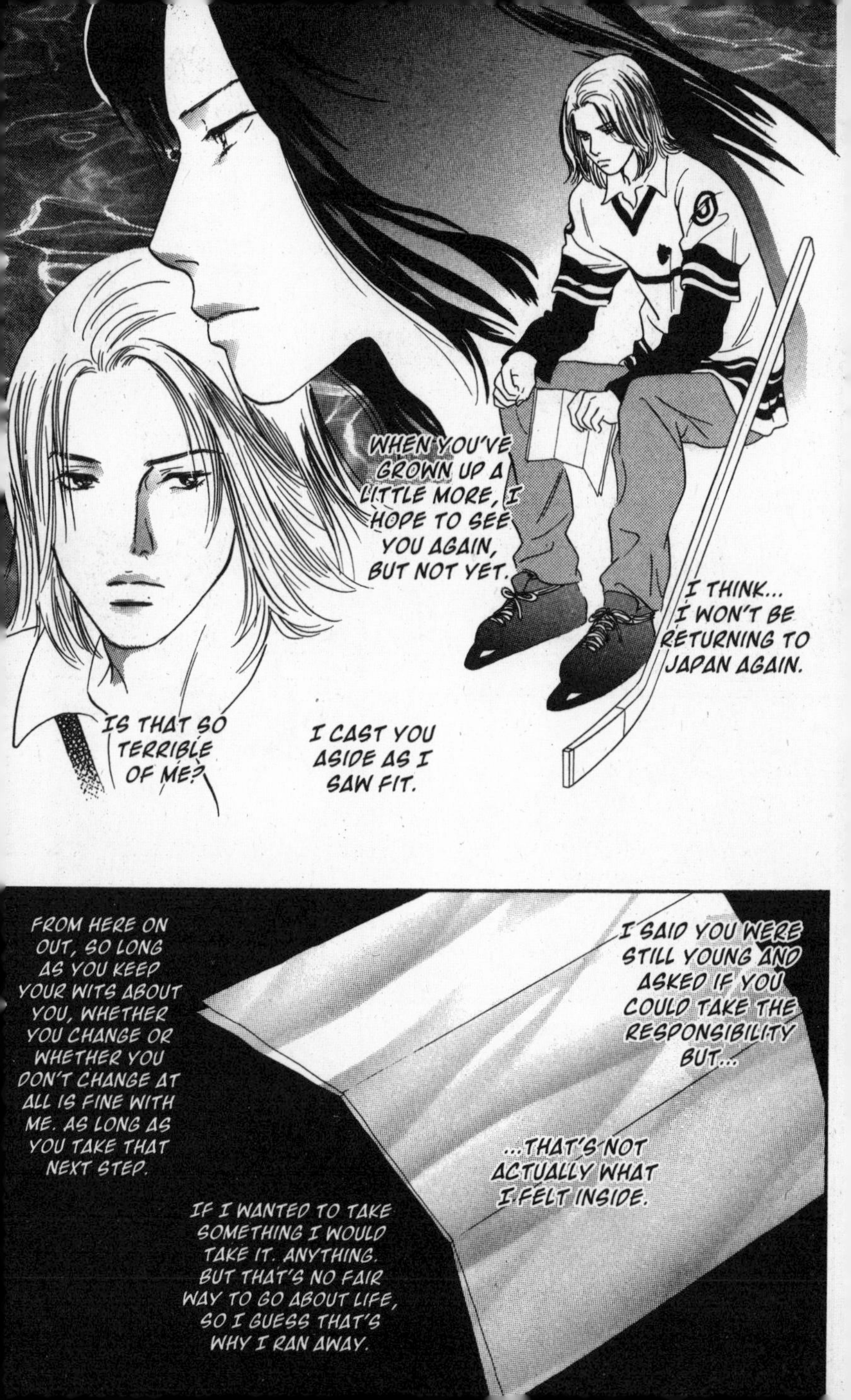
I THINK... I WON'T BE RETURNING TO JAPAN AGAIN.
WHEN YOU'VE GROWN UP A LITTLE MORE, I HOPE TO SEE YOU AGAIN, BUT NOT YET.
I CAST YOU ASIDE AS I SAW FIT.
IS THAT SO TERRIBLE OF ME?
I SAID YOU WERE STILL YOUNG AND ASKED IF YOU COULD TAKE THE RESPONSIBILITY BUT...
...THAT'S NOT ACTUALLY WHAT I FELT INSIDE.
FROM HERE ON OUT, SO LONG AS YOU KEEP YOUR WITS ABOUT YOU, WHETHER YOU CHANGE OR WHETHER YOU DON'T CHANGE AT ALL IS FINE WITH ME. AS LONG AS YOU TAKE THAT NEXT STEP.
IF I WANTED TO TAKE SOMETHING I WOULD TAKE IT. ANYTHING. BUT THAT'S NO FAIR WAY TO GO ABOUT LIFE, SO I GUESS THAT'S WHY I RAN AWAY.

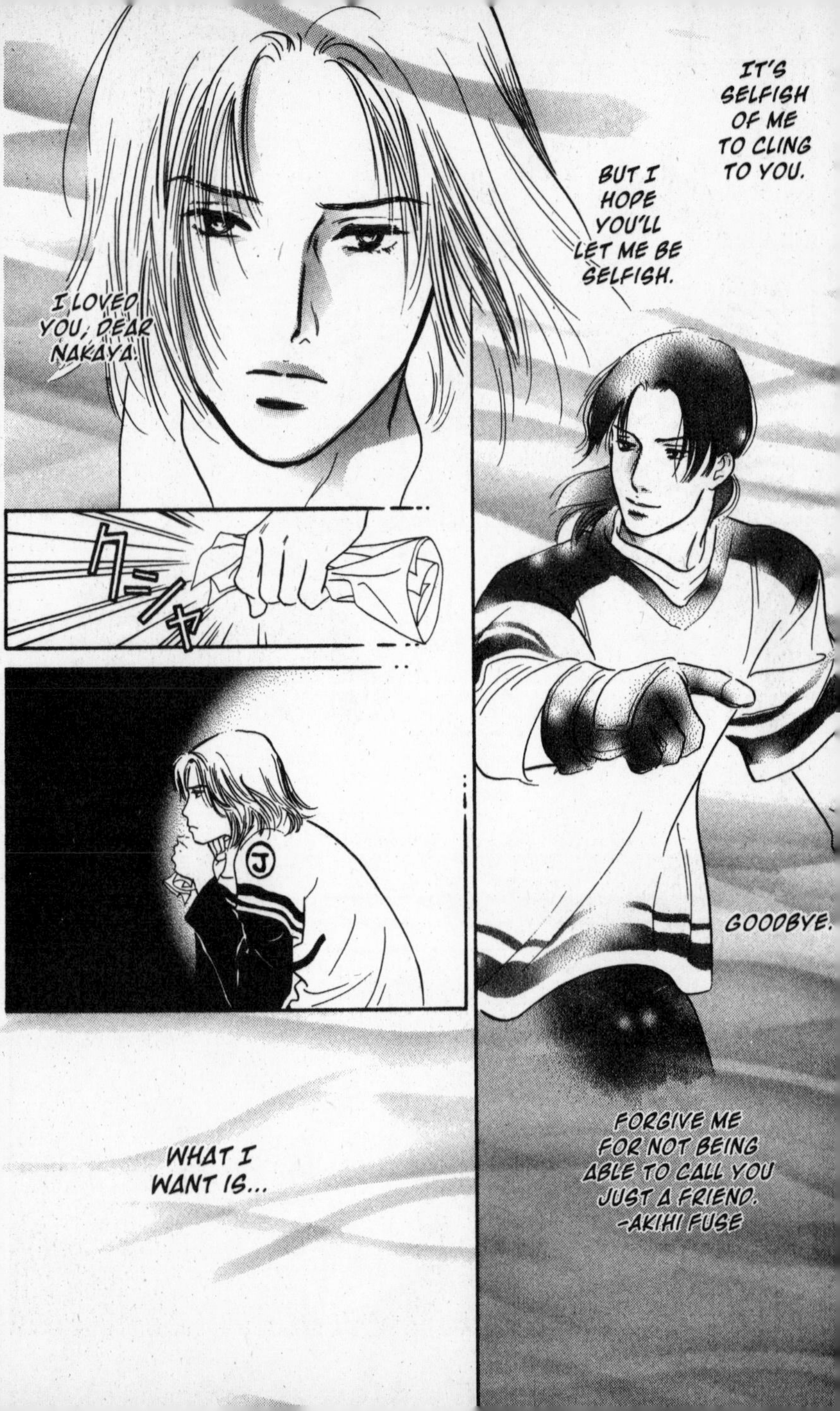
IT'S SELFISH OF ME TO CLING TO YOU.
BUT I HOPE YOU'LL LET ME BE SELFISH.
GOODBYE.
FORGIVE ME FOR NOT BEING ABLE TO CALL YOU JUST A FRIEND.
-AKIHI FUSE
I LOVED YOU, DEAR NAKAYA.
グシャ
WHAT I WANT IS...

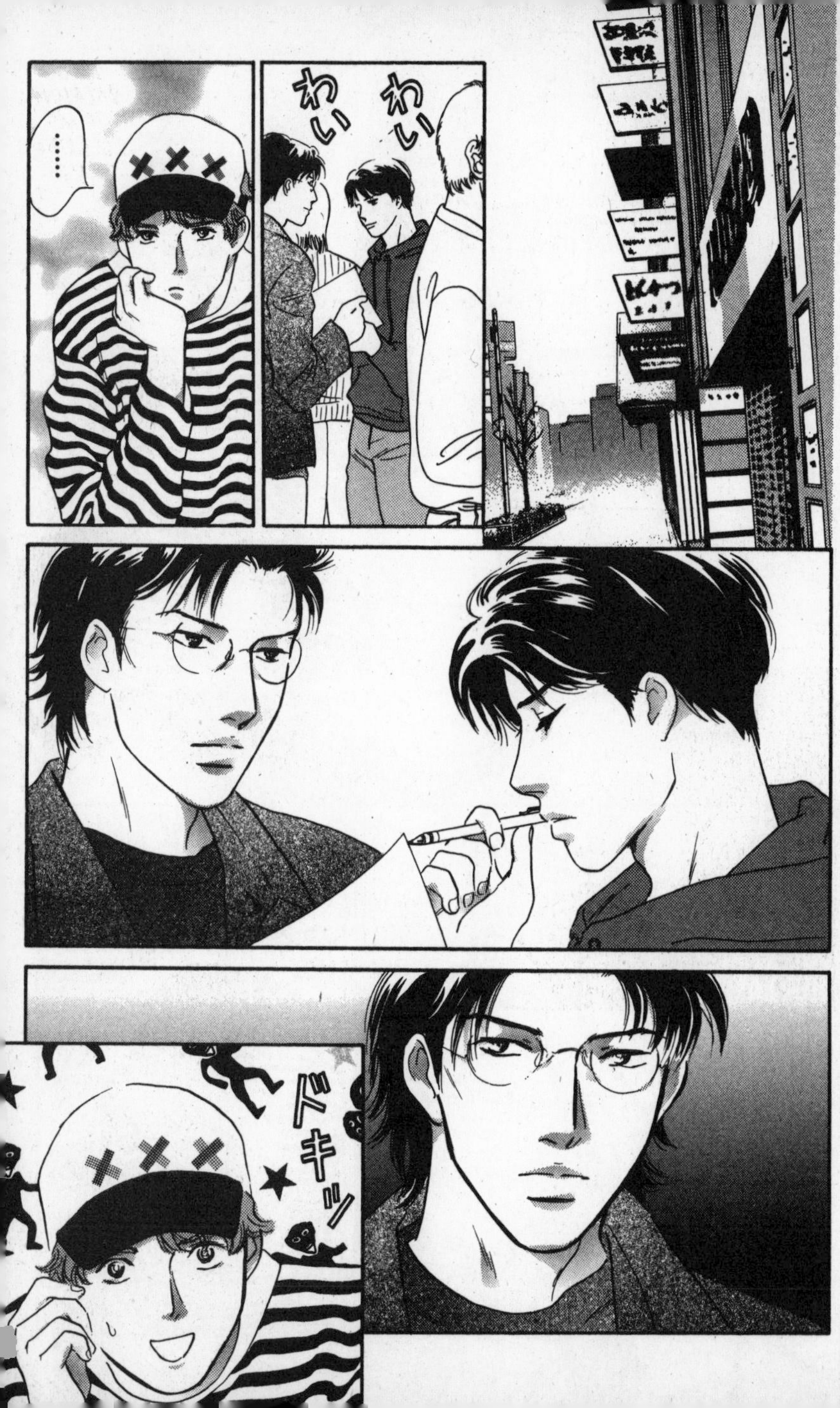
わい わい
……
ドキッ

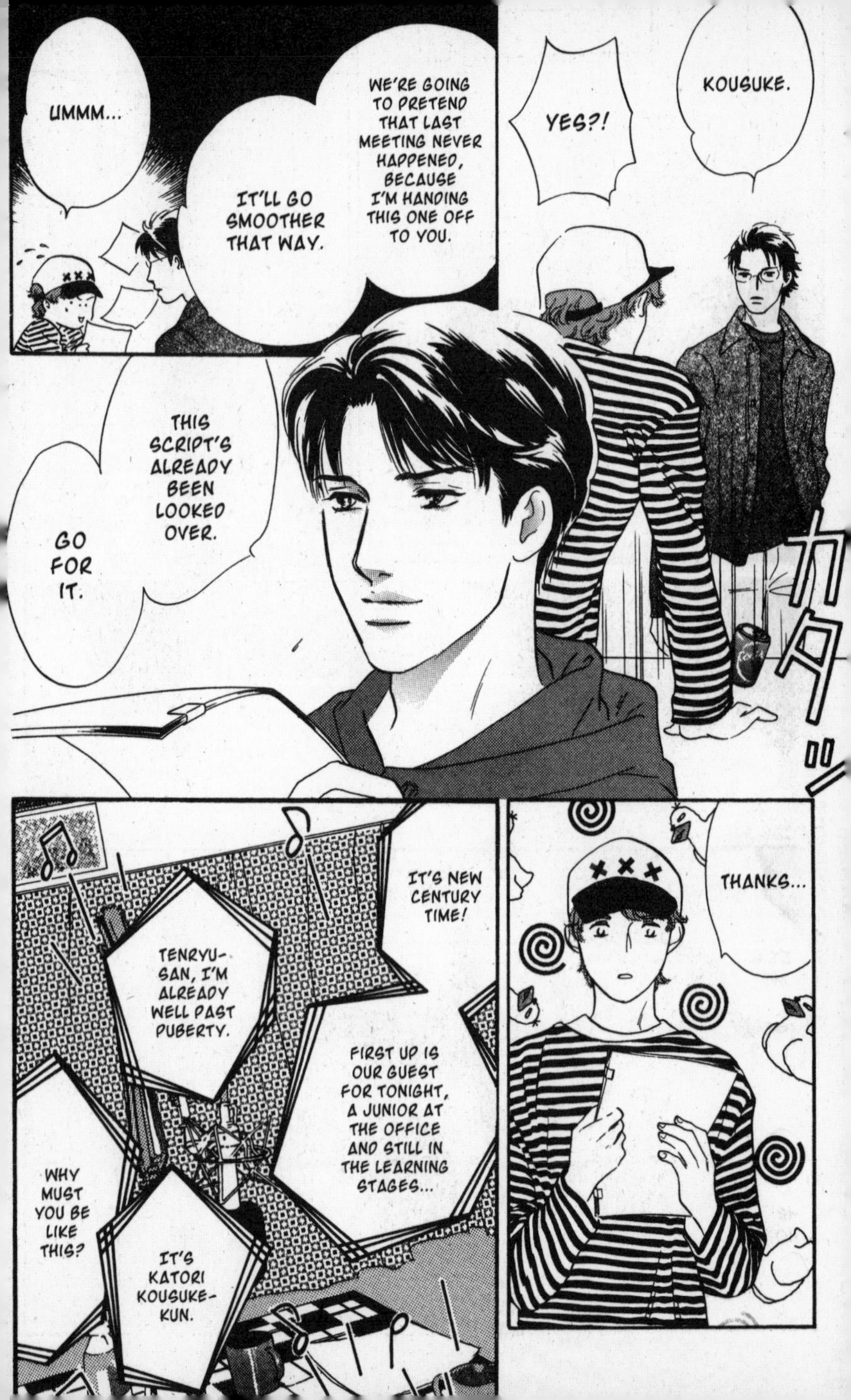
KOUSUKE.
YES?!
WE'RE GOING TO PRETEND THAT LAST MEETING NEVER HAPPENED, BECAUSE I'M HANDING THIS ONE OFF TO YOU.
IT'LL GO SMOOTHER THAT WAY.
UMMM...
カタッ
THIS SCRIPT'S ALREADY BEEN LOOKED OVER.
GO FOR IT.
THANKS...
IT'S NEW CENTURY TIME!
FIRST UP IS OUR GUEST FOR TONIGHT, A JUNIOR AT THE OFFICE AND STILL IN THE LEARNING STAGES...
IT'S KATORI KOUSUKE-KUN.
TENRYU-SAN, I'M ALREADY WELL PAST PUBERTY.
WHY MUST YOU BE LIKE THIS?

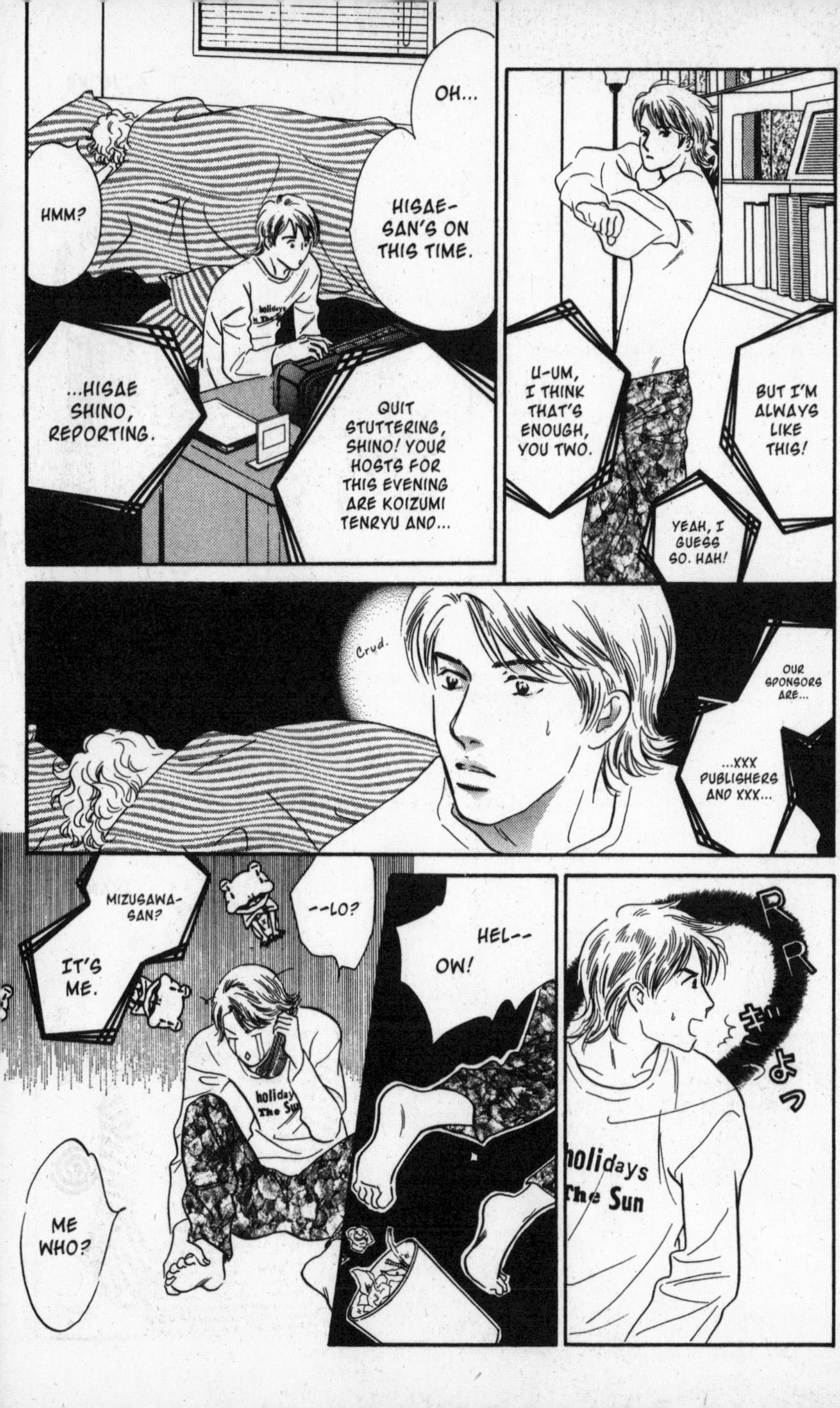
BUT I'M ALWAYS LIKE THIS!
U-UM, I THINK THAT'S ENOUGH, YOU TWO.
YEAH, I GUESS SO. HAH!
OH...
HISAE-SAN'S ON THIS TIME.
HMM?
...HISAE SHINO, REPORTING.
QUIT STUTTERING, SHINO! YOUR HOSTS FOR THIS EVENING ARE KOIZUMI TENRYU AND...
OUR SPONSORS ARE...
...XXX PUBLISHERS AND XXX...
Crud.
RR
ぎょっ
HEL--
OW!
--LO?
MIZUSAWA-SAN?
IT'S ME.
ME WHO?

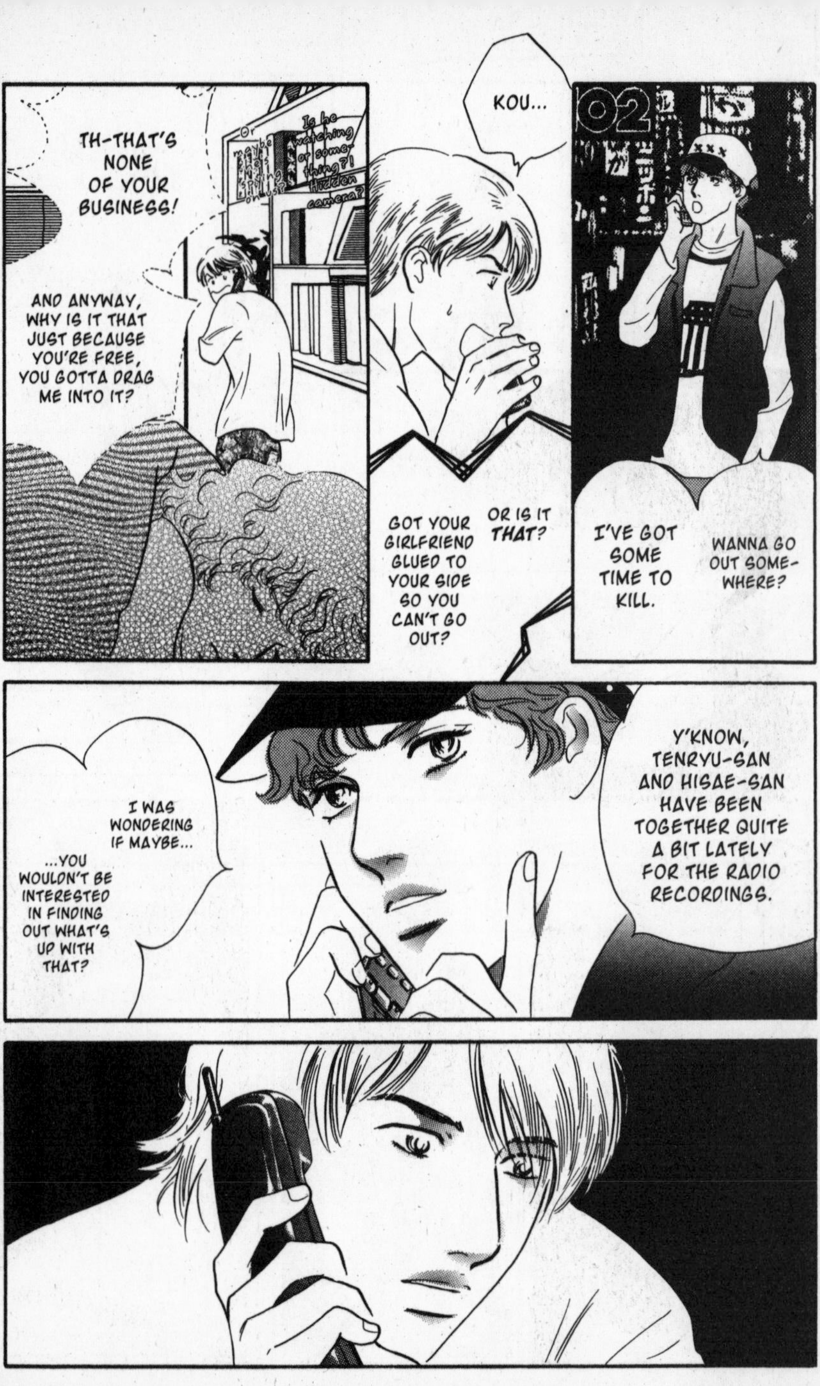
WANNA GO OUT SOME-WHERE?
I'VE GOT SOME TIME TO KILL.
KOU...
OR IS IT *THAT*?
GOT YOUR GIRLFRIEND GLUED TO YOUR SIDE SO YOU CAN'T GO OUT?
Is he watching or some-thing?! Hidden camera?
Or maybe he's spying on us?
TH-THAT'S NONE OF YOUR BUSINESS!
AND ANYWAY, WHY IS IT THAT JUST BECAUSE YOU'RE FREE, YOU GOTTA DRAG ME INTO IT?
Y'KNOW, TENRYU-SAN AND HISAE-SAN HAVE BEEN TOGETHER QUITE A BIT LATELY FOR THE RADIO RECORDINGS.
I WAS WONDERING IF MAYBE...
...YOU WOULDN'T BE INTERESTED IN FINDING OUT WHAT'S UP WITH THAT?

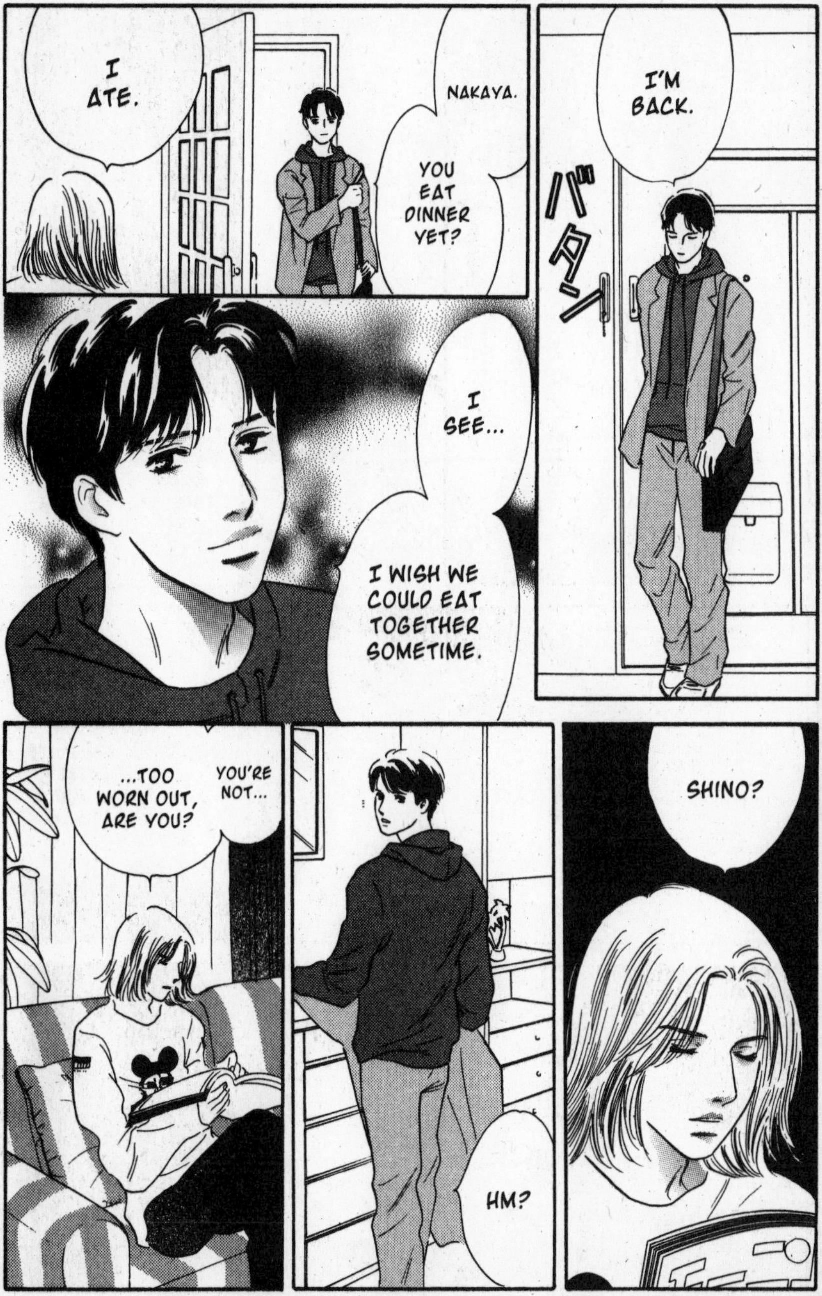
I'M BACK.
バタン
NAKAYA.
YOU EAT DINNER YET?
I ATE.
I SEE...
I WISH WE COULD EAT TOGETHER SOMETIME.
SHINO?
HM?
YOU'RE NOT...
...TOO WORN OUT, ARE YOU?

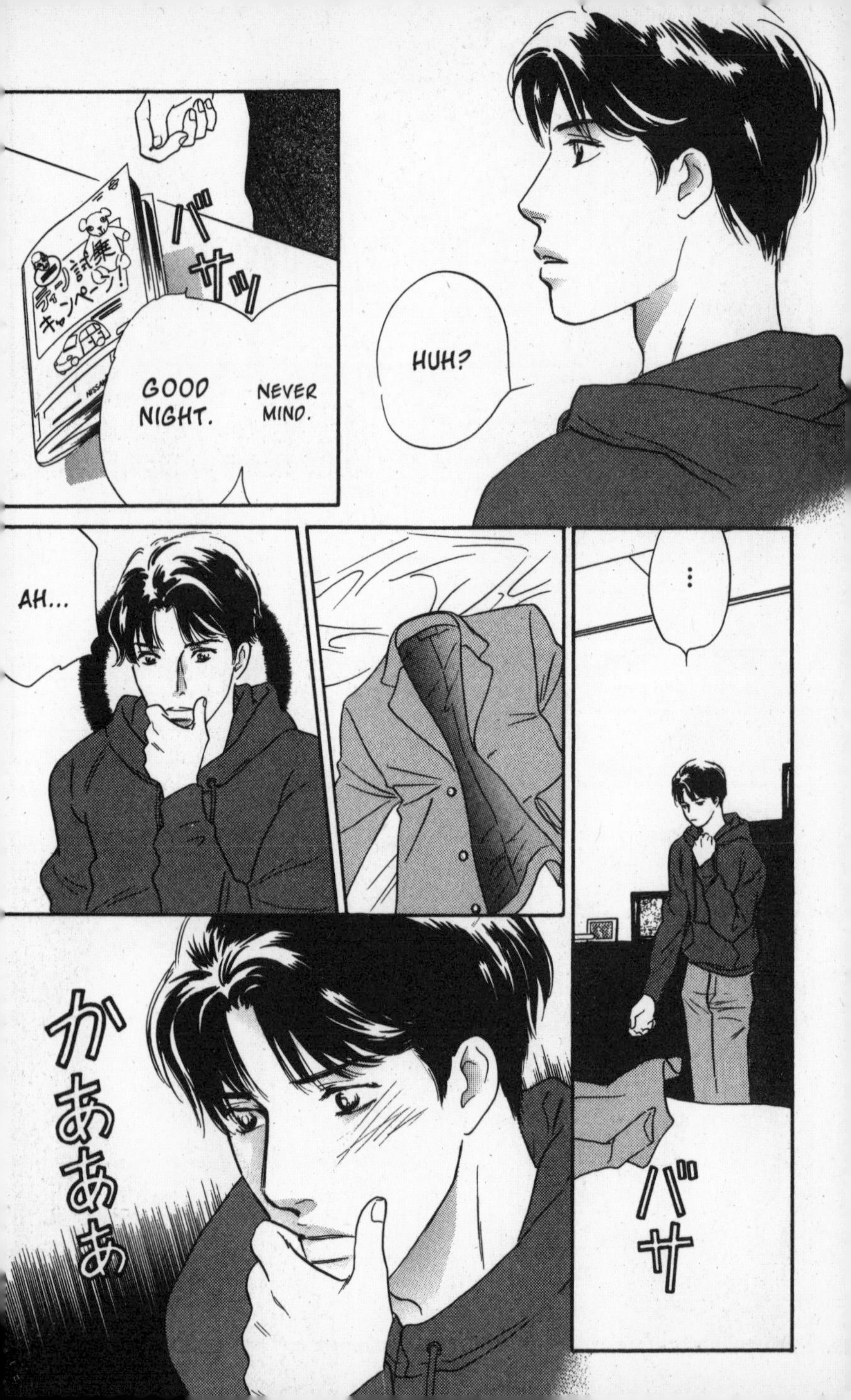
HUH?
バサッ
NEVER MIND.
GOOD NIGHT.
...
バサ
AH...
かあああ

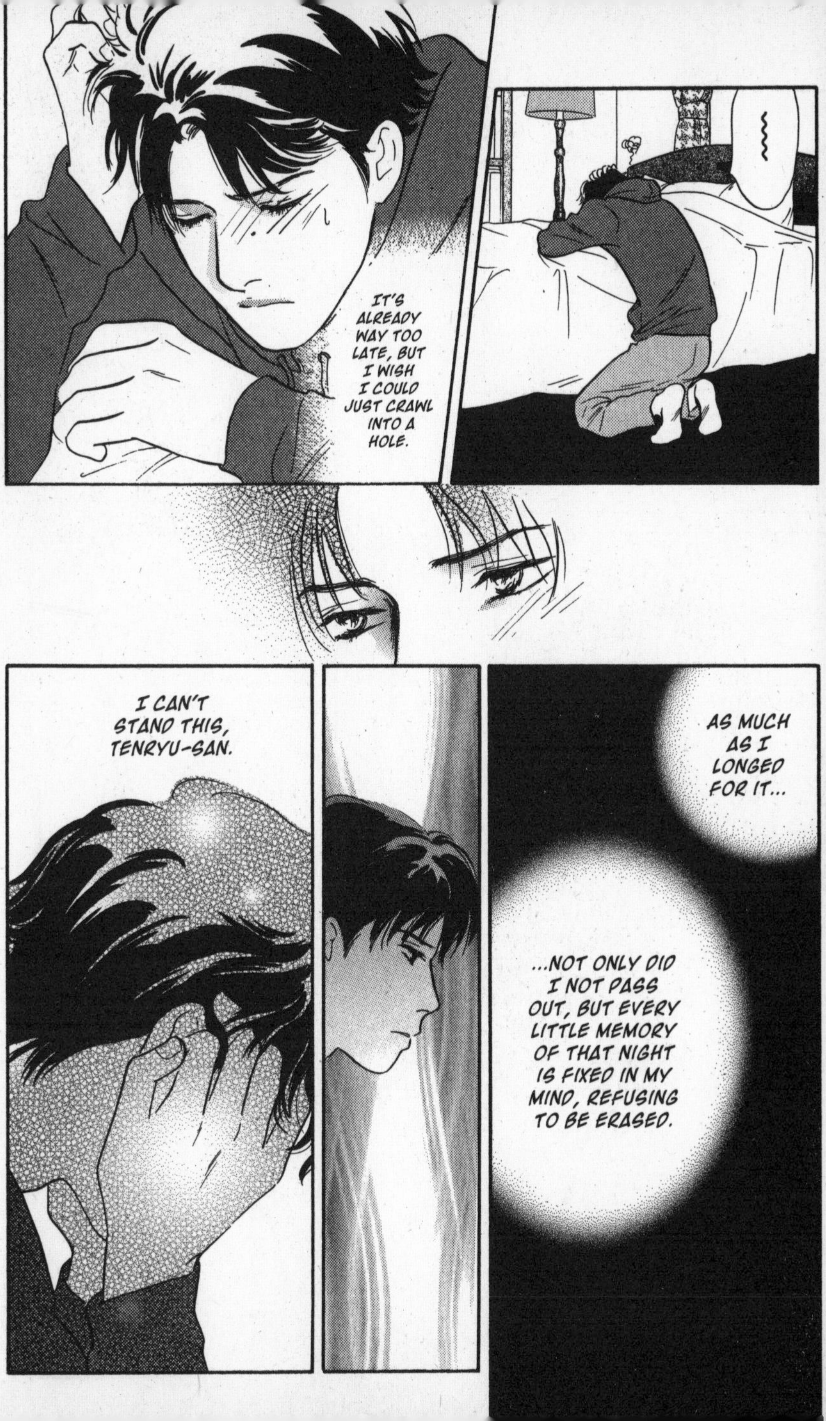
...
IT'S ALREADY WAY TOO LATE, BUT I WISH I COULD JUST CRAWL INTO A HOLE.
AS MUCH AS I LONGED FOR IT...
...NOT ONLY DID I NOT PASS OUT, BUT EVERY LITTLE MEMORY OF THAT NIGHT IS FIXED IN MY MIND, REFUSING TO BE ERASED.
I CAN'T STAND THIS, TENRYU-SAN.

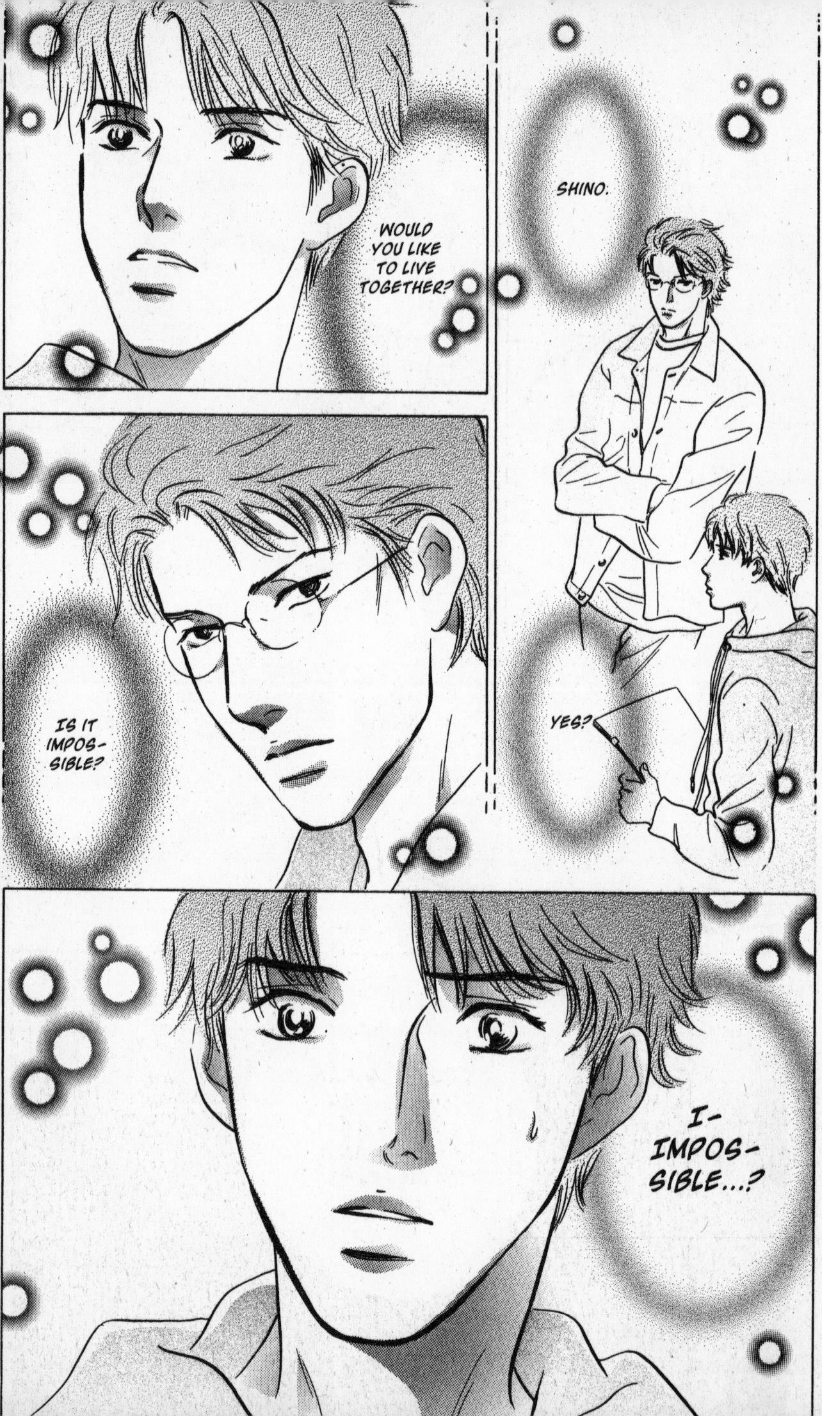
SHINO.
YES?
WOULD YOU LIKE TO LIVE TOGETHER?
IS IT IMPOS-SIBLE?
I-IMPOS-SIBLE...?

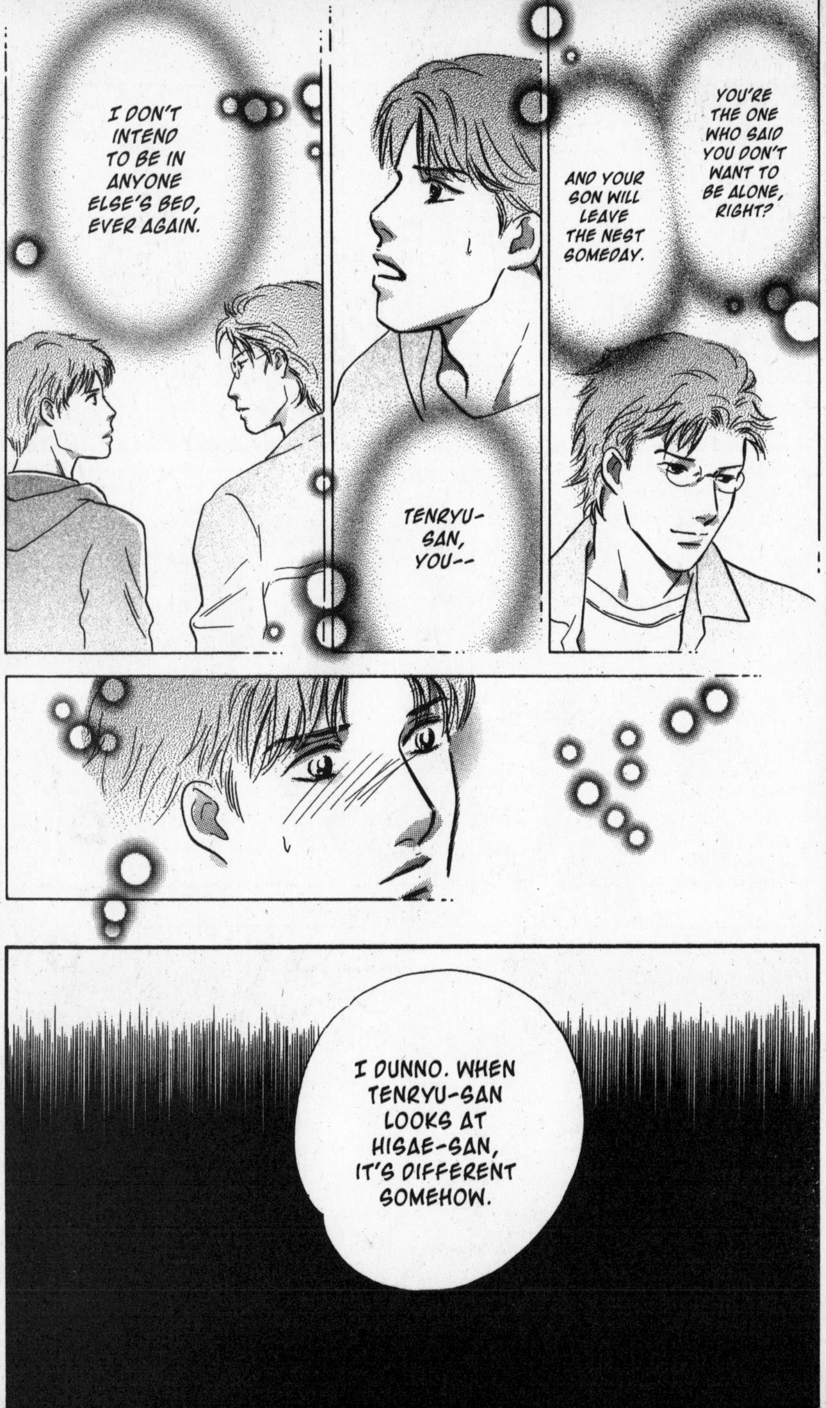
YOU'RE THE ONE WHO SAID YOU DON'T WANT TO BE ALONE, RIGHT?
AND YOUR SON WILL LEAVE THE NEST SOMEDAY.
TENRYU-SAN, YOU--
I DON'T INTEND TO BE IN ANYONE ELSE'S BED, EVER AGAIN.
I DUNNO. WHEN TENRYU-SAN LOOKS AT HISAE-SAN, IT'S DIFFERENT SOMEHOW.

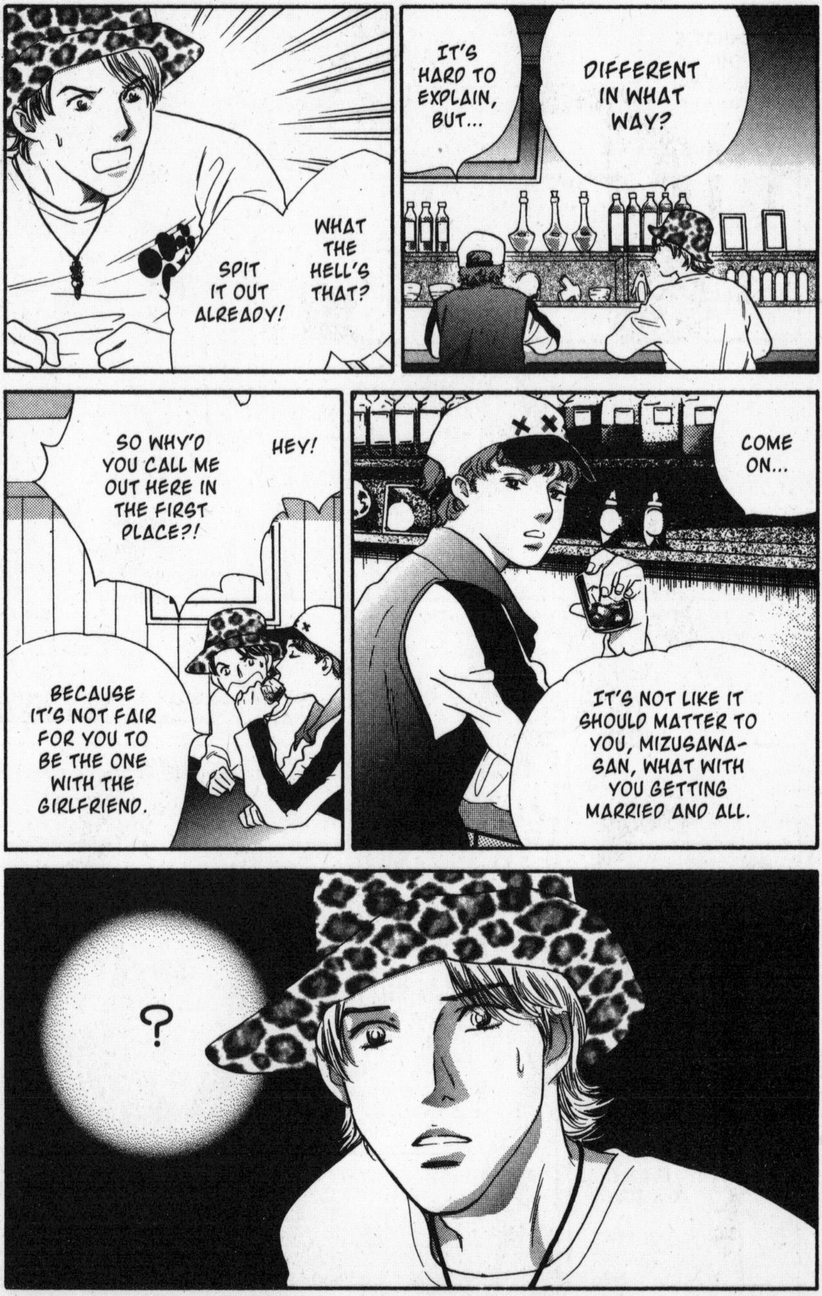
DIFFERENT IN WHAT WAY?
IT'S HARD TO EXPLAIN, BUT...
WHAT THE HELL'S THAT?
SPIT IT OUT ALREADY!
COME ON...
IT'S NOT LIKE IT SHOULD MATTER TO YOU, MIZUSAWA-SAN, WHAT WITH YOU GETTING MARRIED AND ALL.
HEY!
SO WHY'D YOU CALL ME OUT HERE IN THE FIRST PLACE?!
BECAUSE IT'S NOT FAIR FOR YOU TO BE THE ONE WITH THE GIRLFRIEND.
?

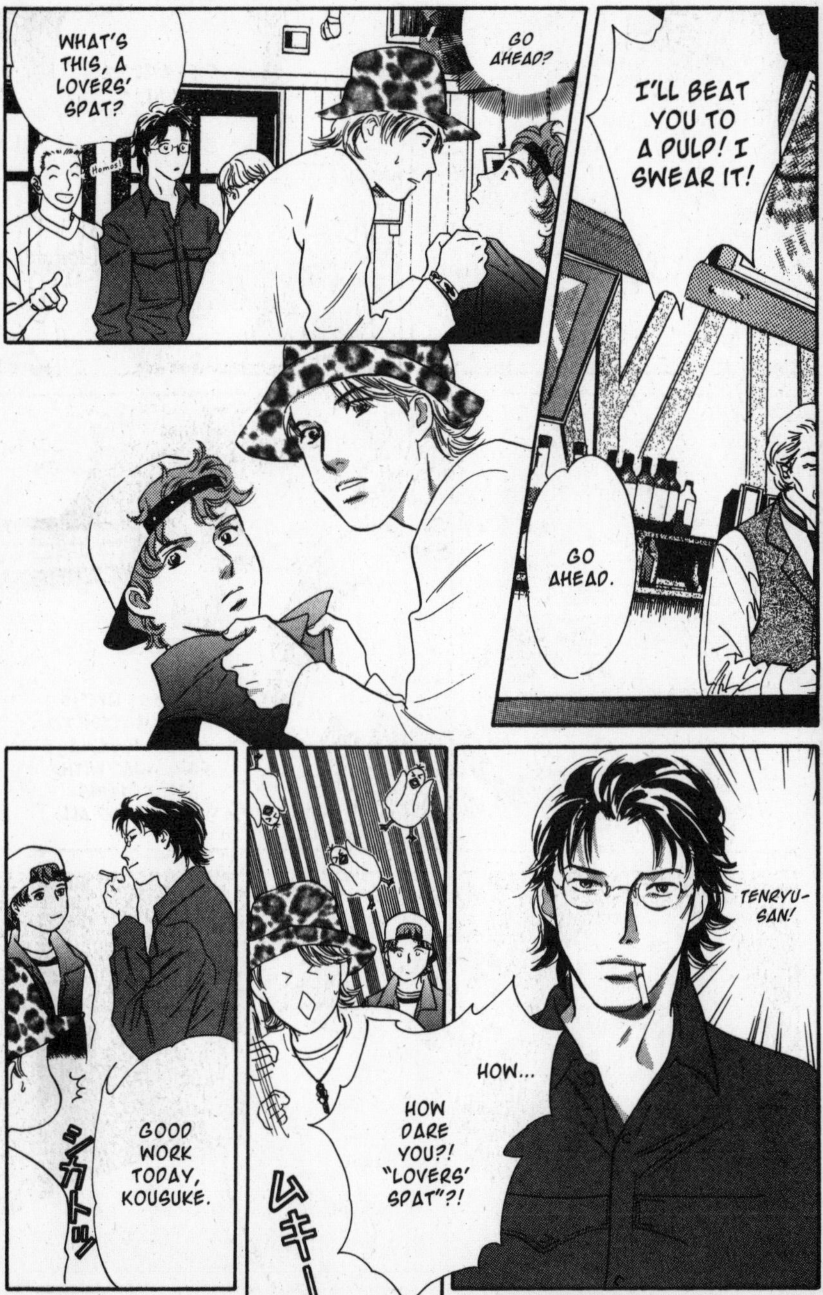
I'LL BEAT YOU TO A PULP! I SWEAR IT!
GO AHEAD.
GO AHEAD?
WHAT'S THIS, A LOVERS' SPAT?
Homos!
TENRYU-SAN!
HOW...
HOW DARE YOU?! "LOVERS' SPAT"?!
ムキー
GOOD WORK TODAY, KOUSUKE.
シカトッ

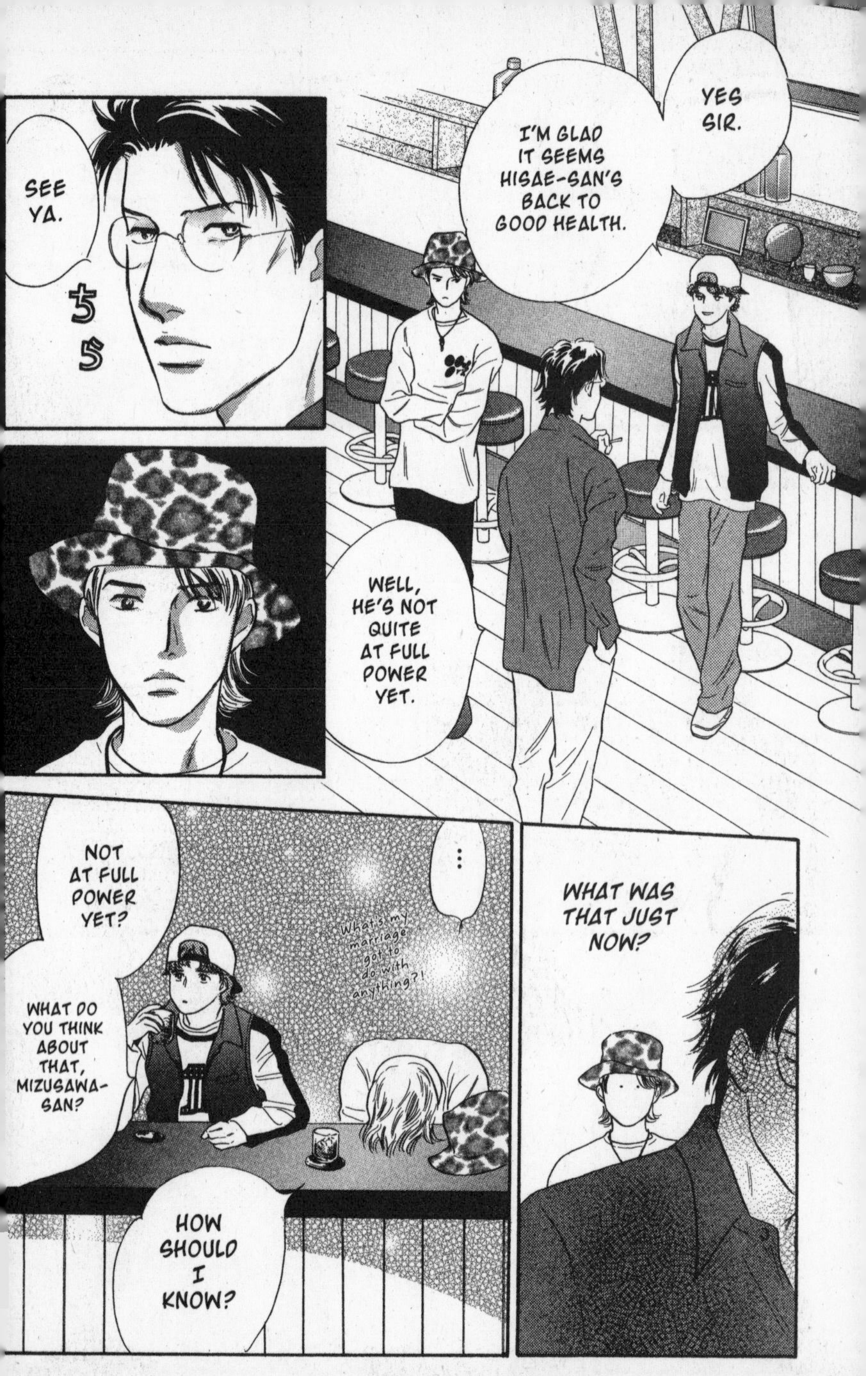
YES SIR.
I'M GLAD IT SEEMS HISAE-SAN'S BACK TO GOOD HEALTH.
WELL, HE'S NOT QUITE AT FULL POWER YET.
SEE YA.
ちら
WHAT WAS THAT JUST NOW?
...
NOT AT FULL POWER YET?
What's my marriage got to do with anything?!
WHAT DO YOU THINK ABOUT THAT, MIZUSAWA-SAN?
HOW SHOULD I KNOW?

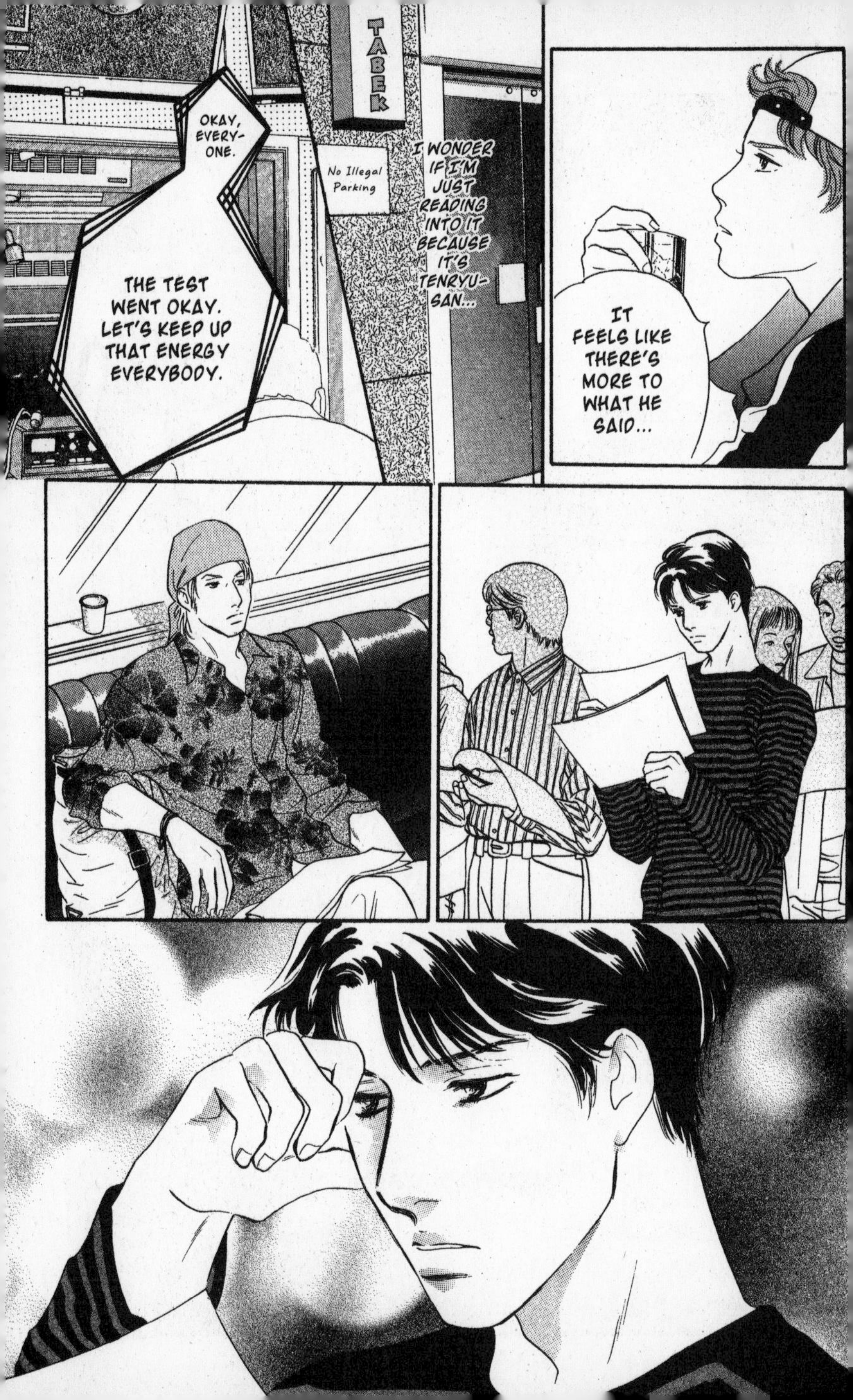

IT FEELS LIKE THERE'S MORE TO WHAT HE SAID...
I WONDER IF I'M JUST READING INTO IT BECAUSE IT'S TENRYU-SAN...
TABEK
No Illegal Parking
OKAY, EVERY-ONE.
THE TEST WENT OKAY. LET'S KEEP UP THAT ENERGY EVERYBODY.

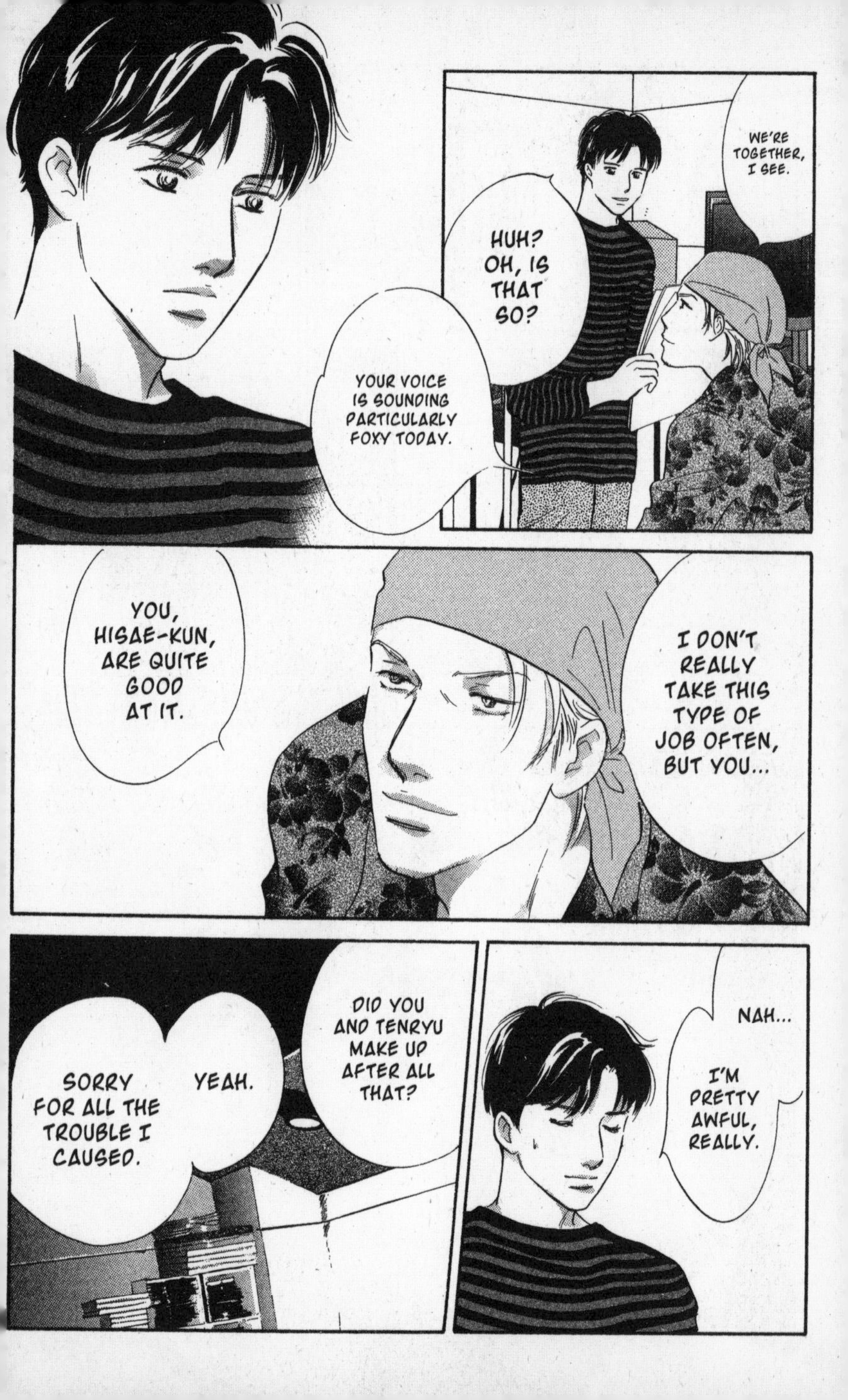
WE'RE TOGETHER, I SEE.
HUH? OH, IS THAT SO?
YOUR VOICE IS SOUNDING PARTICULARLY FOXY TODAY.
I DON'T REALLY TAKE THIS TYPE OF JOB OFTEN, BUT YOU...
YOU, HISAE-KUN, ARE QUITE GOOD AT IT.
NAH...
I'M PRETTY AWFUL, REALLY.
DID YOU AND TENRYU MAKE UP AFTER ALL THAT?
YEAH.
SORRY FOR ALL THE TROUBLE I CAUSED.

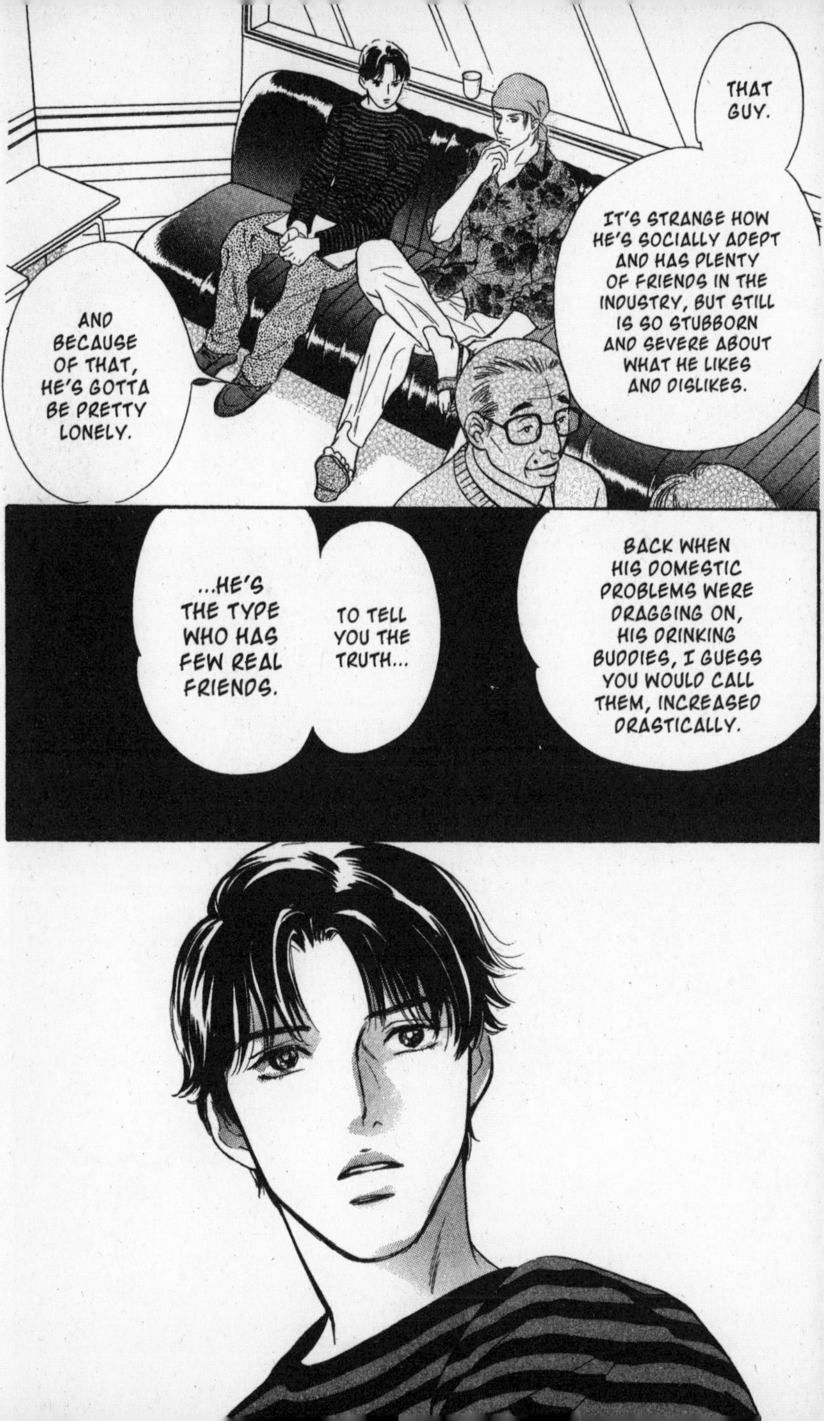
THAT GUY.
IT'S STRANGE HOW HE'S SOCIALLY ADEPT AND HAS PLENTY OF FRIENDS IN THE INDUSTRY, BUT STILL IS SO STUBBORN AND SEVERE ABOUT WHAT HE LIKES AND DISLIKES.
AND BECAUSE OF THAT, HE'S GOTTA BE PRETTY LONELY.
BACK WHEN HIS DOMESTIC PROBLEMS WERE DRAGGING ON, HIS DRINKING BUDDIES, I GUESS YOU WOULD CALL THEM, INCREASED DRASTICALLY.
TO TELL YOU THE TRUTH...
...HE'S THE TYPE WHO HAS FEW REAL FRIENDS.

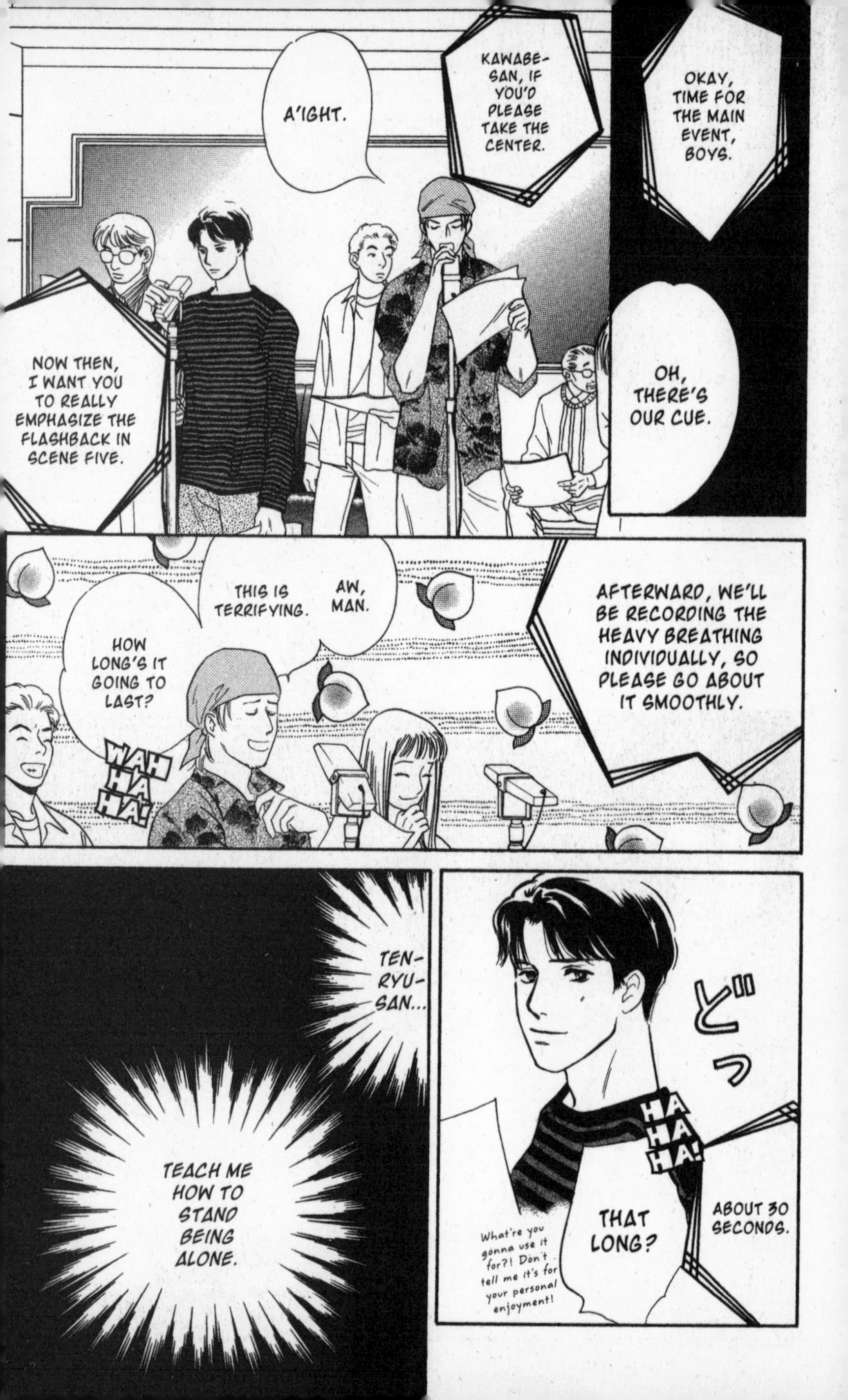
OKAY, TIME FOR THE MAIN EVENT, BOYS.
OH, THERE'S OUR CUE.
KAWABE-SAN, IF YOU'D PLEASE TAKE THE CENTER.
A'IGHT.
NOW THEN, I WANT YOU TO REALLY EMPHASIZE THE FLASHBACK IN SCENE FIVE.
AFTERWARD, WE'LL BE RECORDING THE HEAVY BREATHING INDIVIDUALLY, SO PLEASE GO ABOUT IT SMOOTHLY.
AW, MAN.
THIS IS TERRIFYING.
HOW LONG'S IT GOING TO LAST?
WAH HA HA HA!
ABOUT 30 SECONDS.
どっ
HA HA HA HA!
THAT LONG?
What're you gonna use it for?! Don't tell me it's for your personal enjoyment!
TEN-RYU-SAN...
TEACH ME HOW TO STAND BEING ALONE.

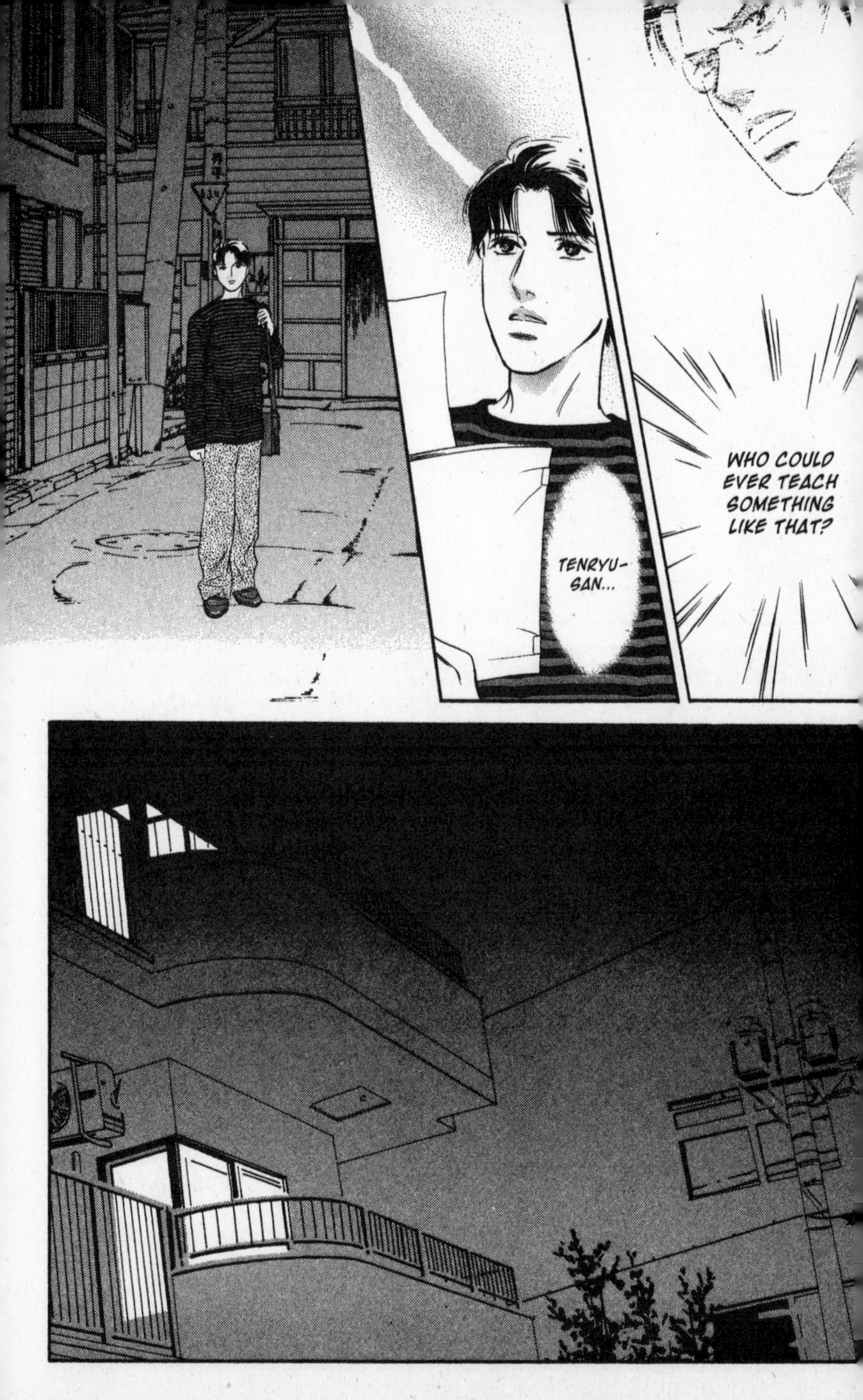
WHO COULD EVER TEACH SOMETHING LIKE THAT?
TENRYU-SAN...

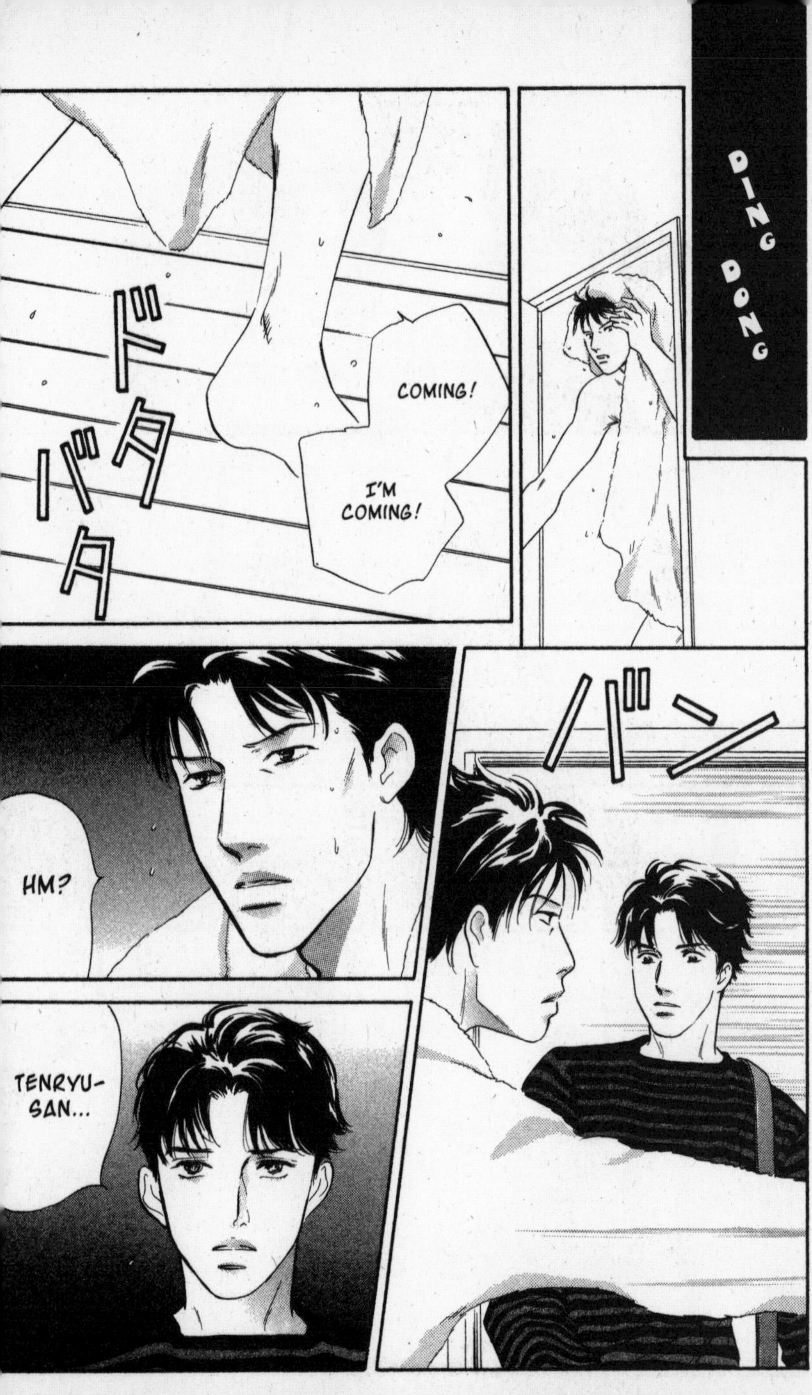
DING DONG
COMING!
I'M COMING!
ドタバタ
バーン
HM?
TENRYU-SAN...

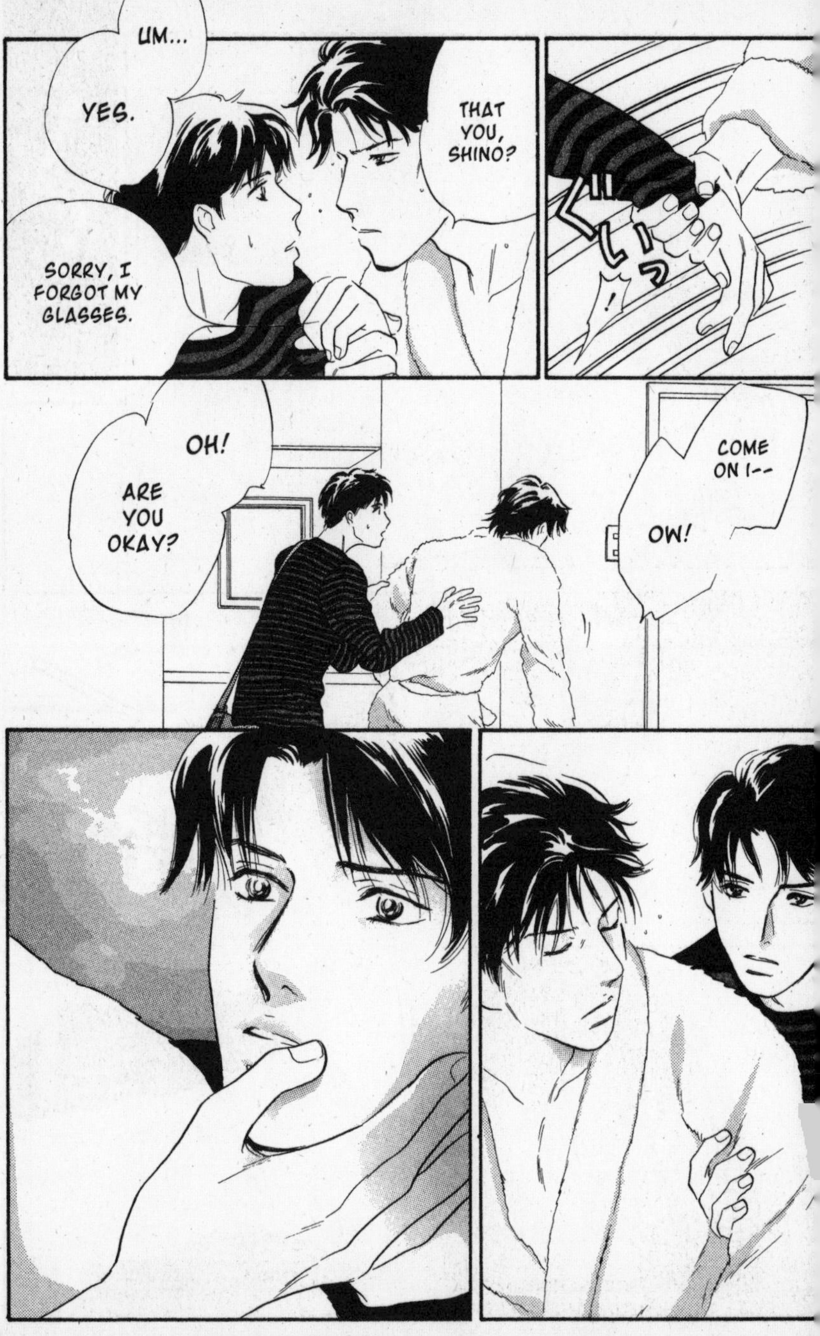
THAT YOU, SHINO?
UM... YES.
SORRY, I FORGOT MY GLASSES.
COME ON I-- OW!
OH! ARE YOU OKAY?

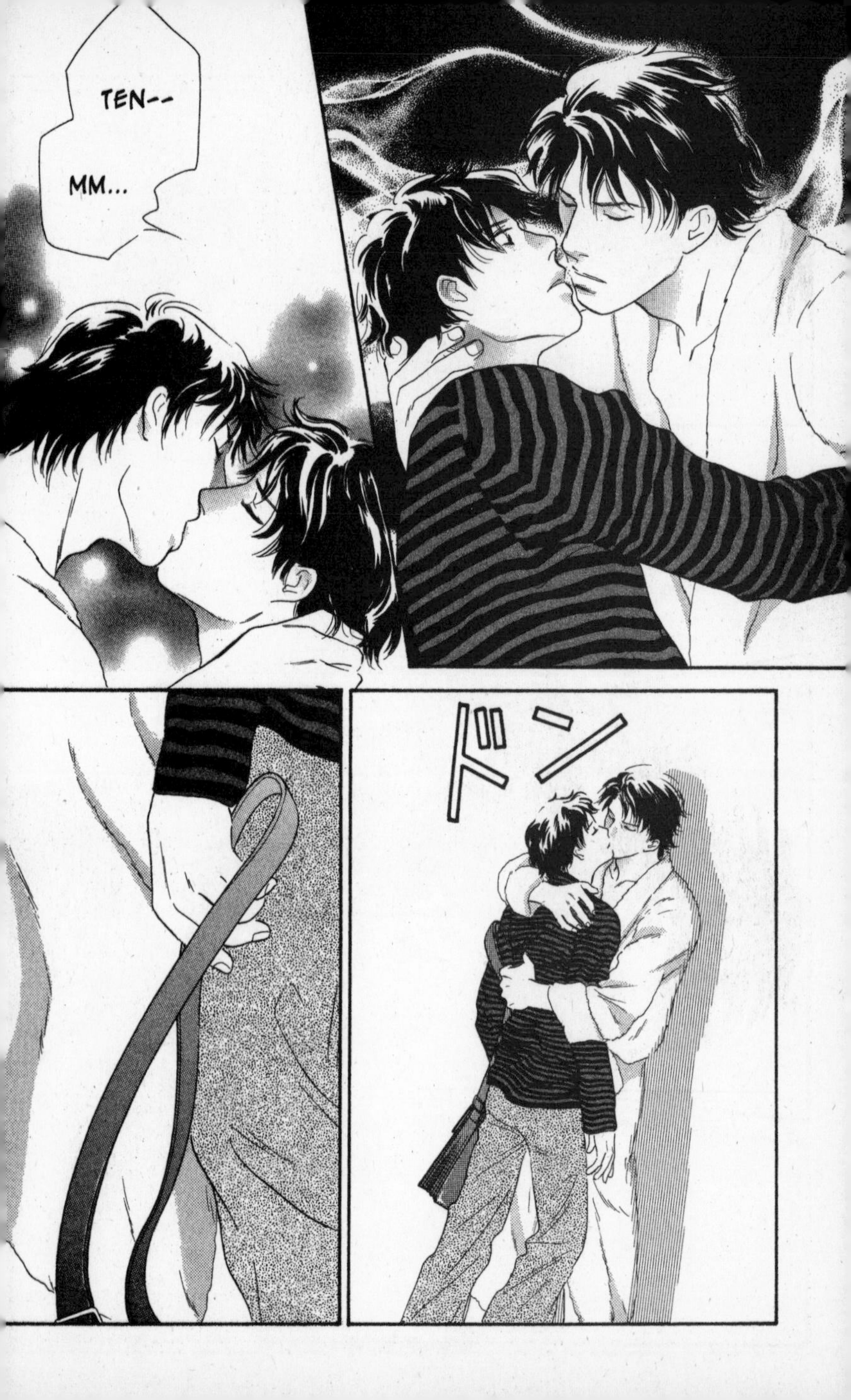
TEN--
MM...
ドン

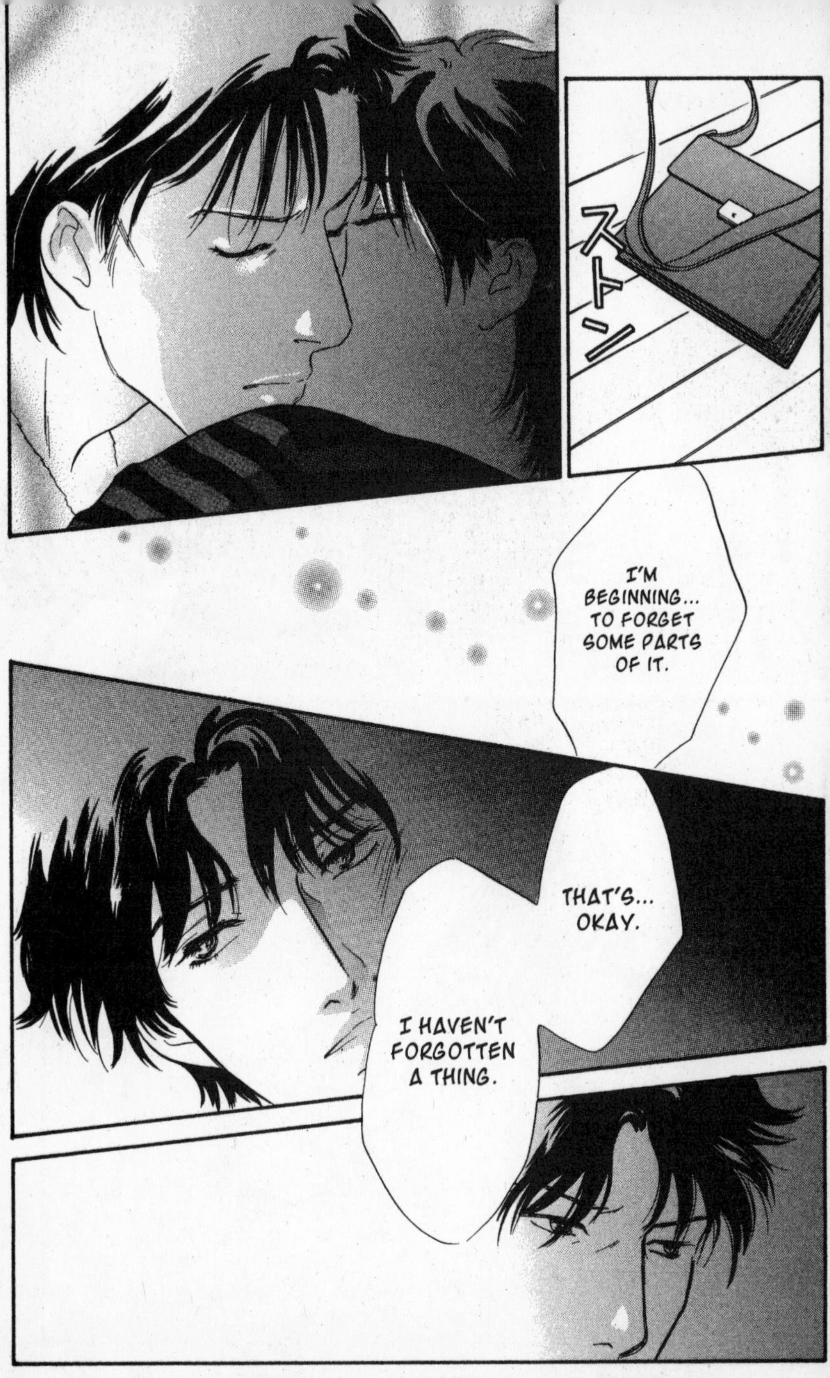
ストン
I'M BEGINNING... TO FORGET SOME PARTS OF IT.
THAT'S... OKAY.
I HAVEN'T FORGOTTEN A THING.

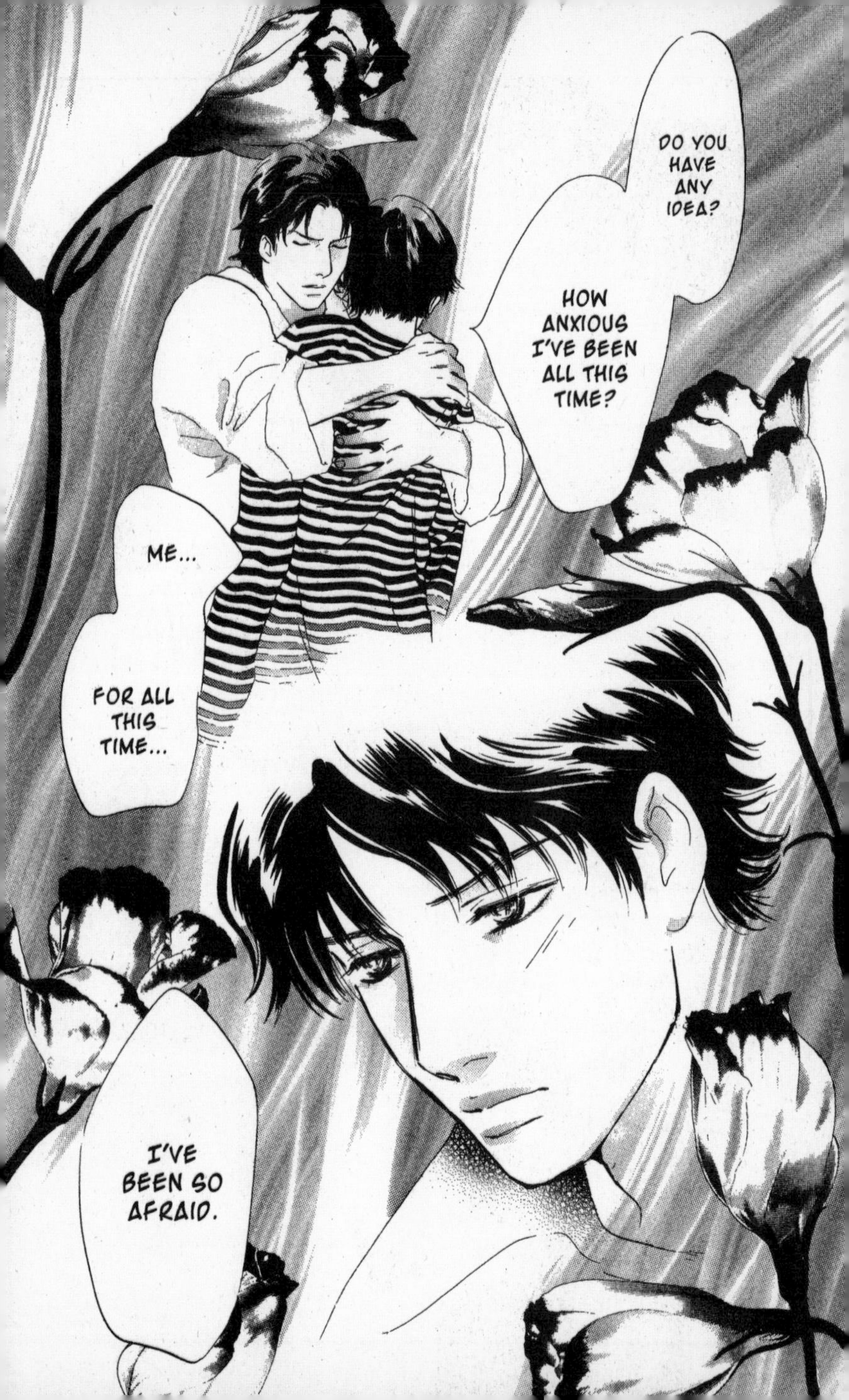
DO YOU HAVE ANY IDEA?
HOW ANXIOUS I'VE BEEN ALL THIS TIME?
ME...
FOR ALL THIS TIME...
I'VE BEEN SO AFRAID.

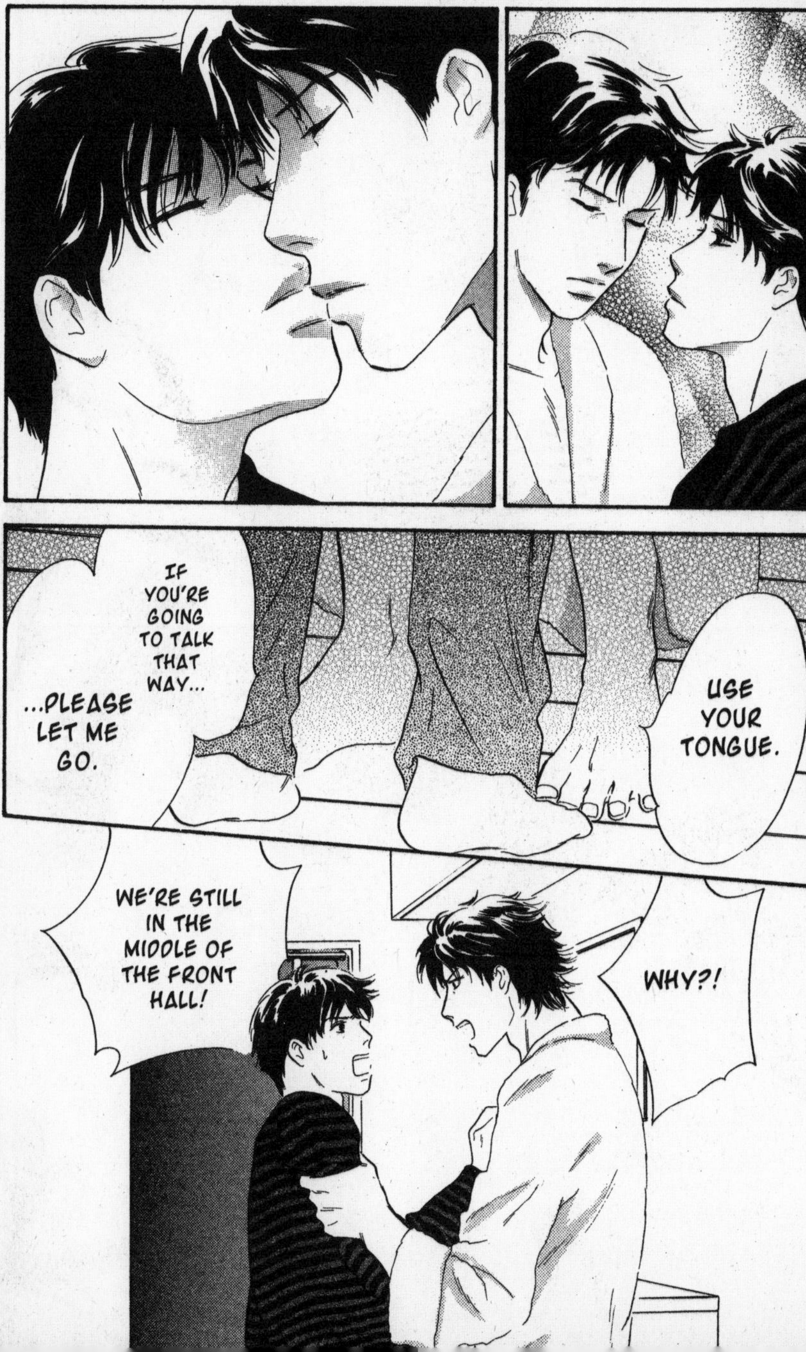
USE YOUR TONGUE.
IF YOU'RE GOING TO TALK THAT WAY...
...PLEASE LET ME GO.
WHY?!
WE'RE STILL IN THE MIDDLE OF THE FRONT HALL!

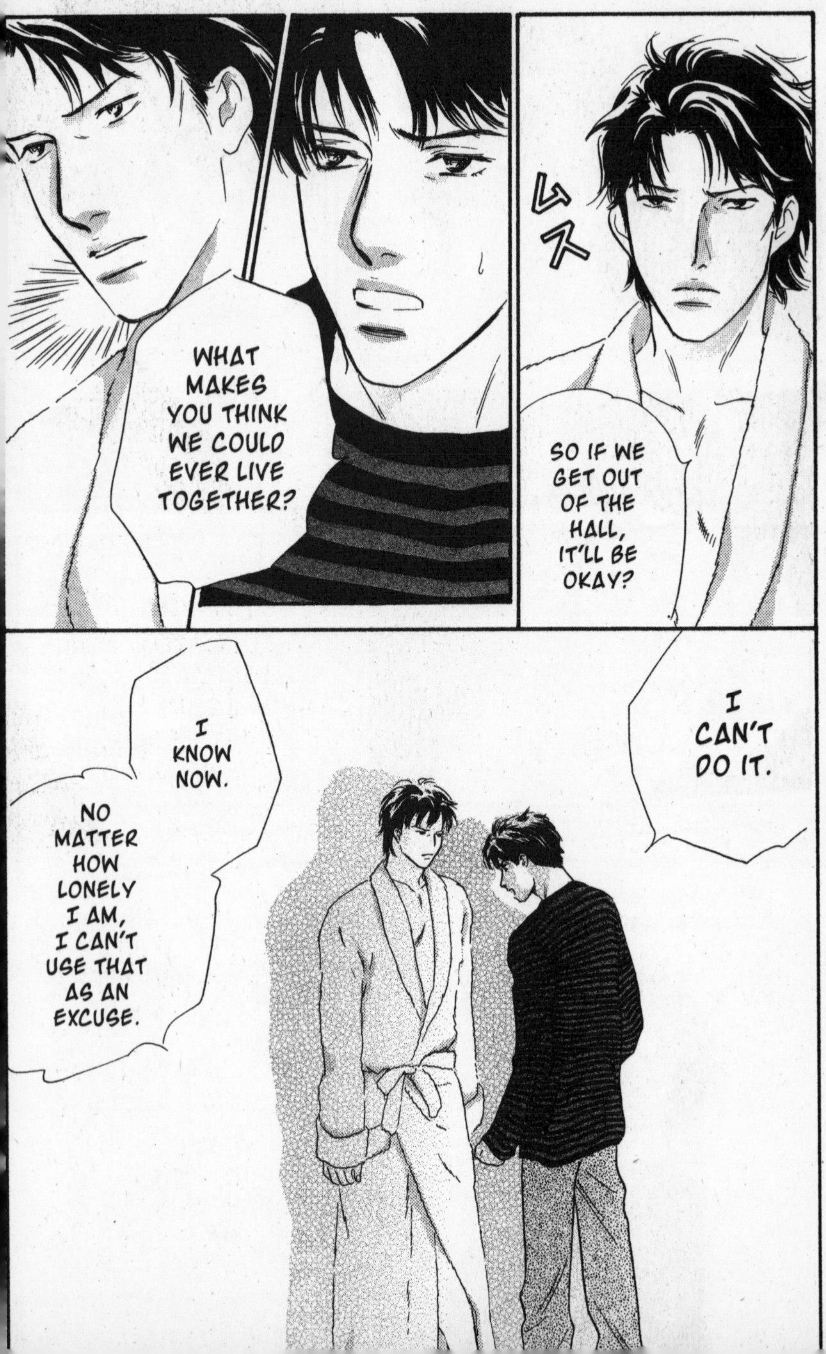
ムス
SO IF WE GET OUT OF THE HALL, IT'LL BE OKAY?
WHAT MAKES YOU THINK WE COULD EVER LIVE TOGETHER?
I CAN'T DO IT.
I KNOW NOW.
NO MATTER HOW LONELY I AM, I CAN'T USE THAT AS AN EXCUSE.

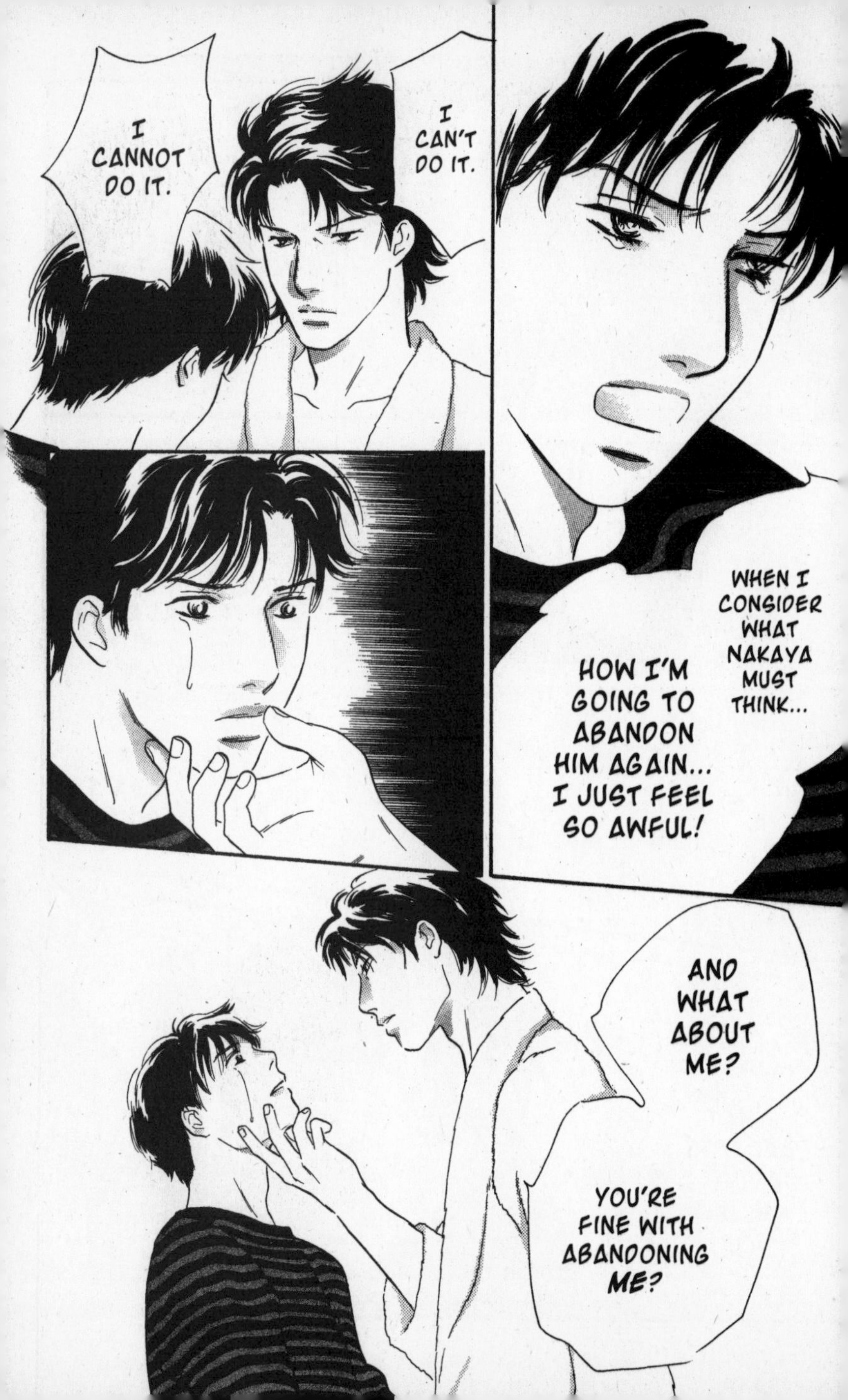
WHEN I CONSIDER WHAT NAKAYA MUST THINK...
HOW I'M GOING TO ABANDON HIM AGAIN... I JUST FEEL SO AWFUL!
I CAN'T DO IT.
I CANNOT DO IT.
AND WHAT ABOUT ME?
YOU'RE FINE WITH ABANDONING *ME*?

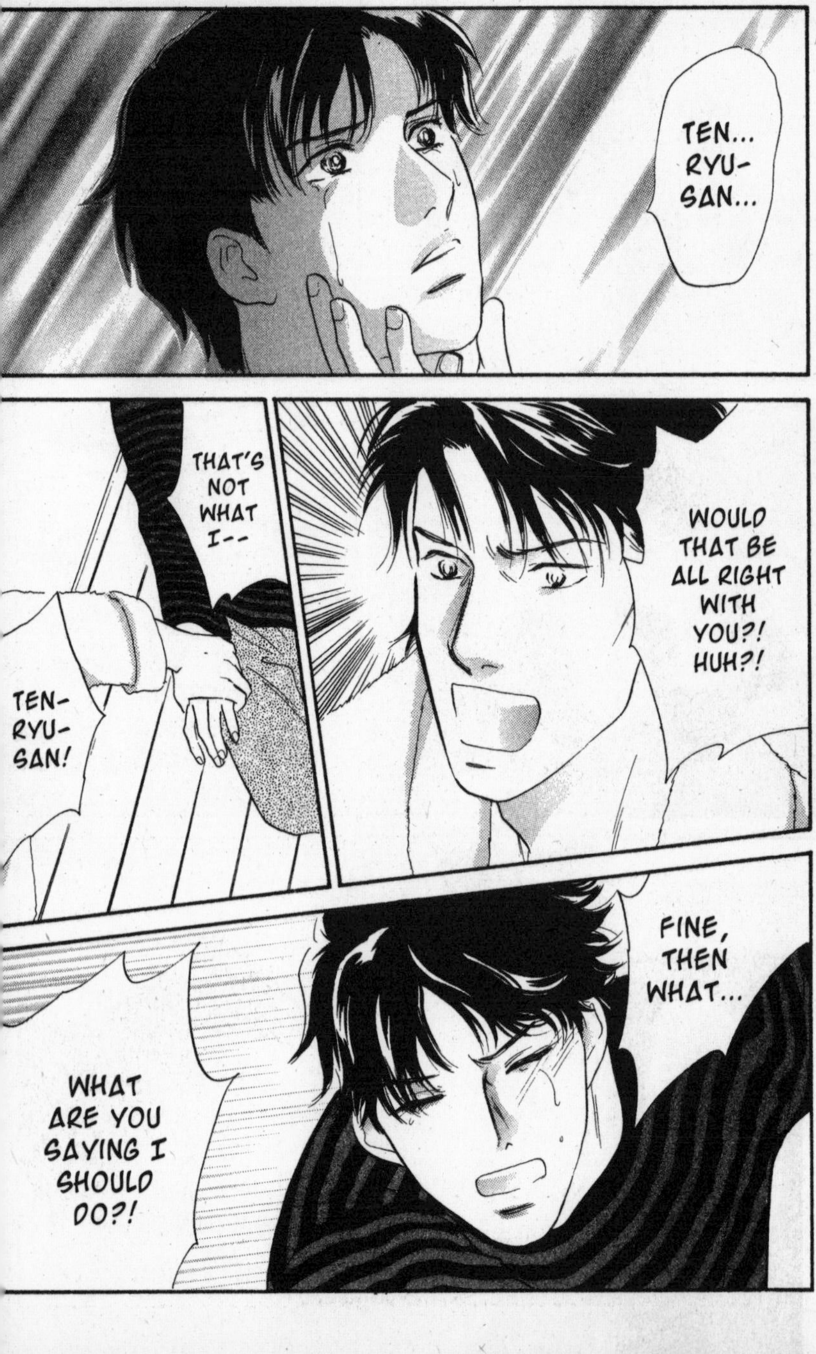
TEN... RYU-SAN...
WOULD THAT BE ALL RIGHT WITH YOU?! HUH?!
THAT'S NOT WHAT I--
TEN-RYU-SAN!
FINE, THEN WHAT...
WHAT ARE YOU SAYING I SHOULD DO?!

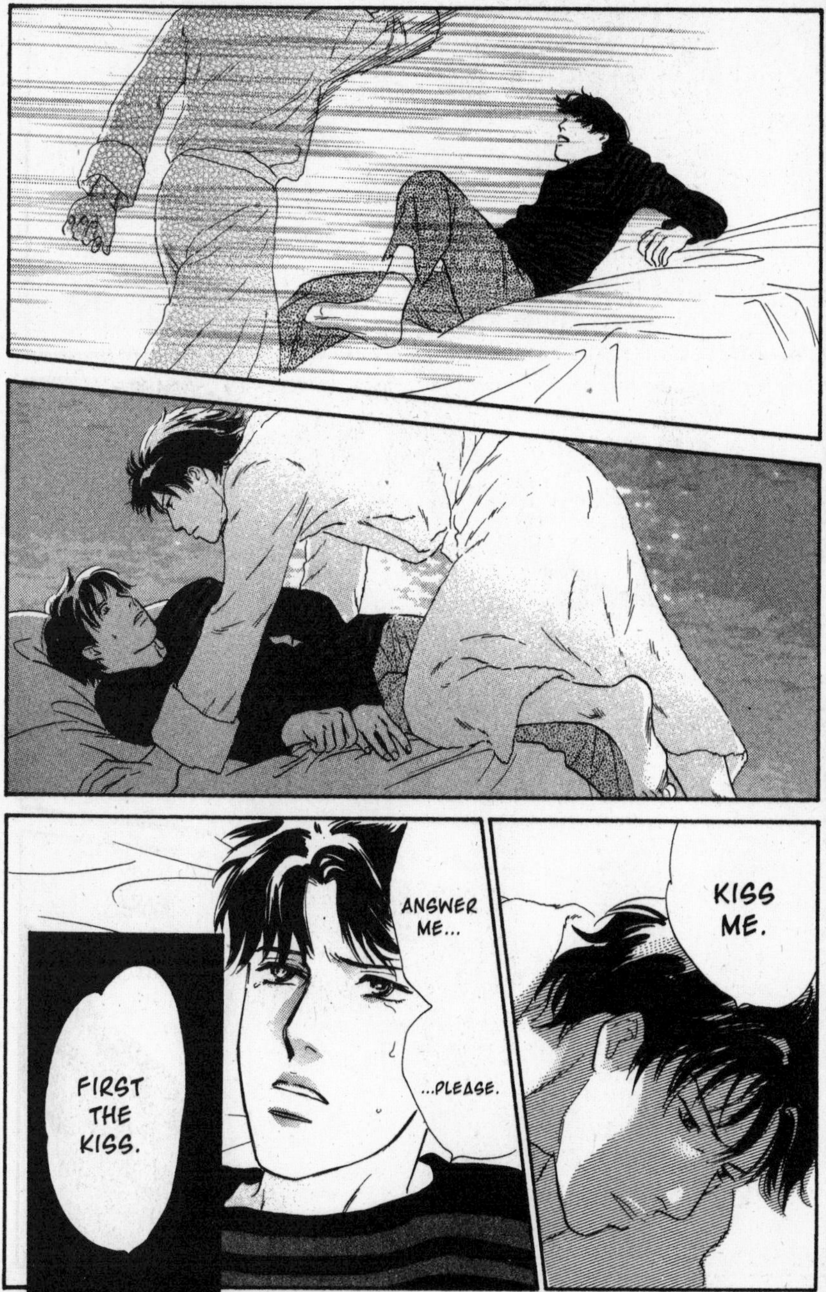
KISS ME.
ANSWER ME...
...PLEASE.
FIRST THE KISS.

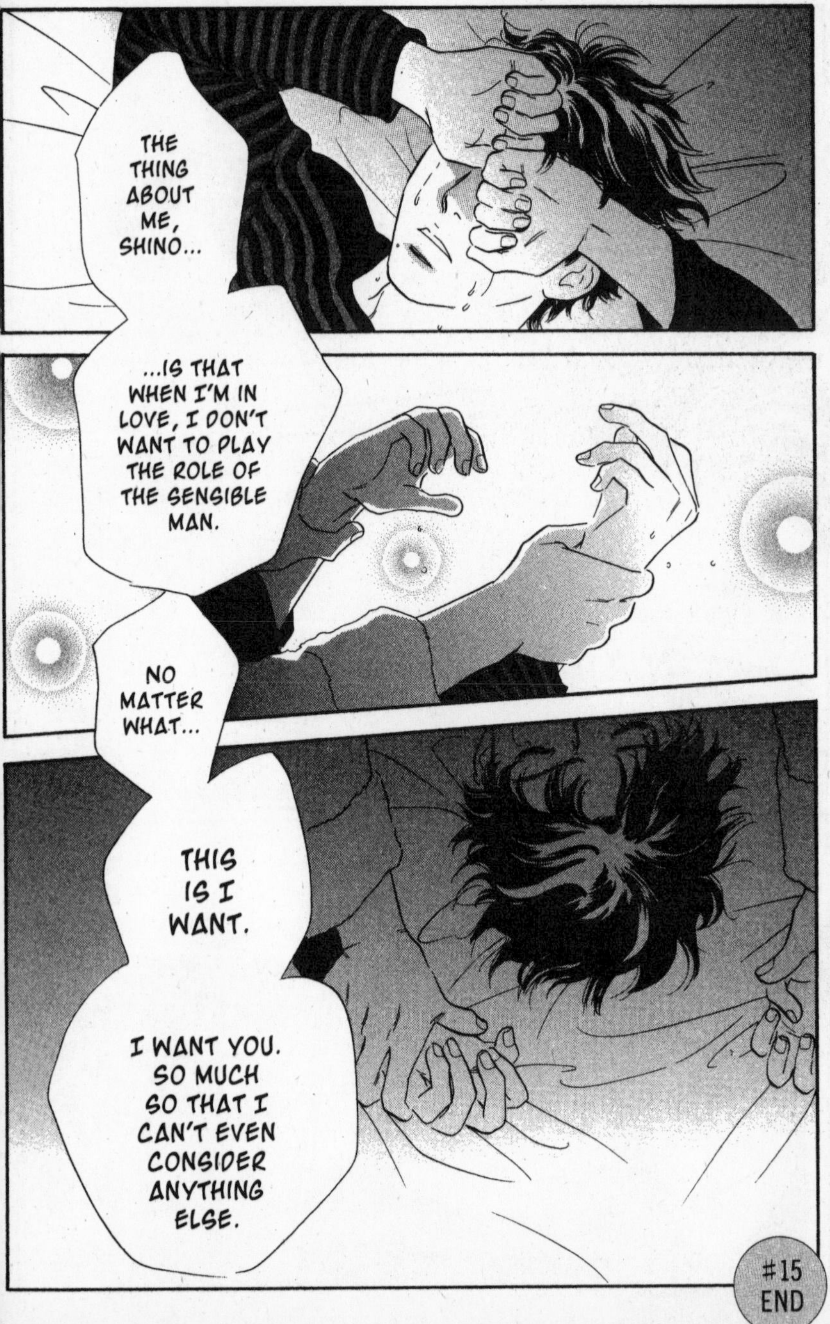
THE THING ABOUT ME, SHINO...
...IS THAT WHEN I'M IN LOVE, I DON'T WANT TO PLAY THE ROLE OF THE SENSIBLE MAN.
NO MATTER WHAT...
THIS IS I WANT.
I WANT YOU. SO MUCH SO THAT I CAN'T EVEN CONSIDER ANYTHING ELSE.
#15 END

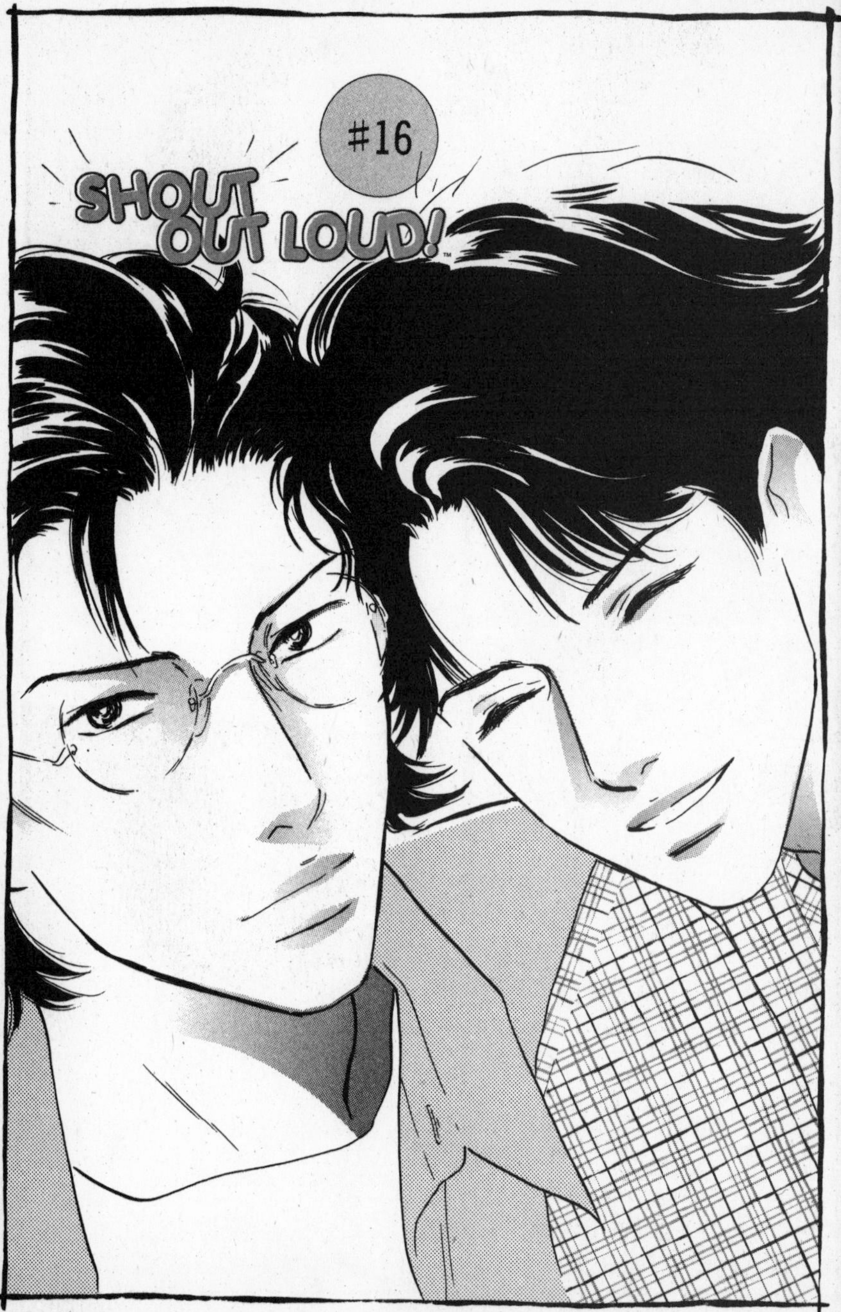
#16
SHOUT OUT LOUD!™

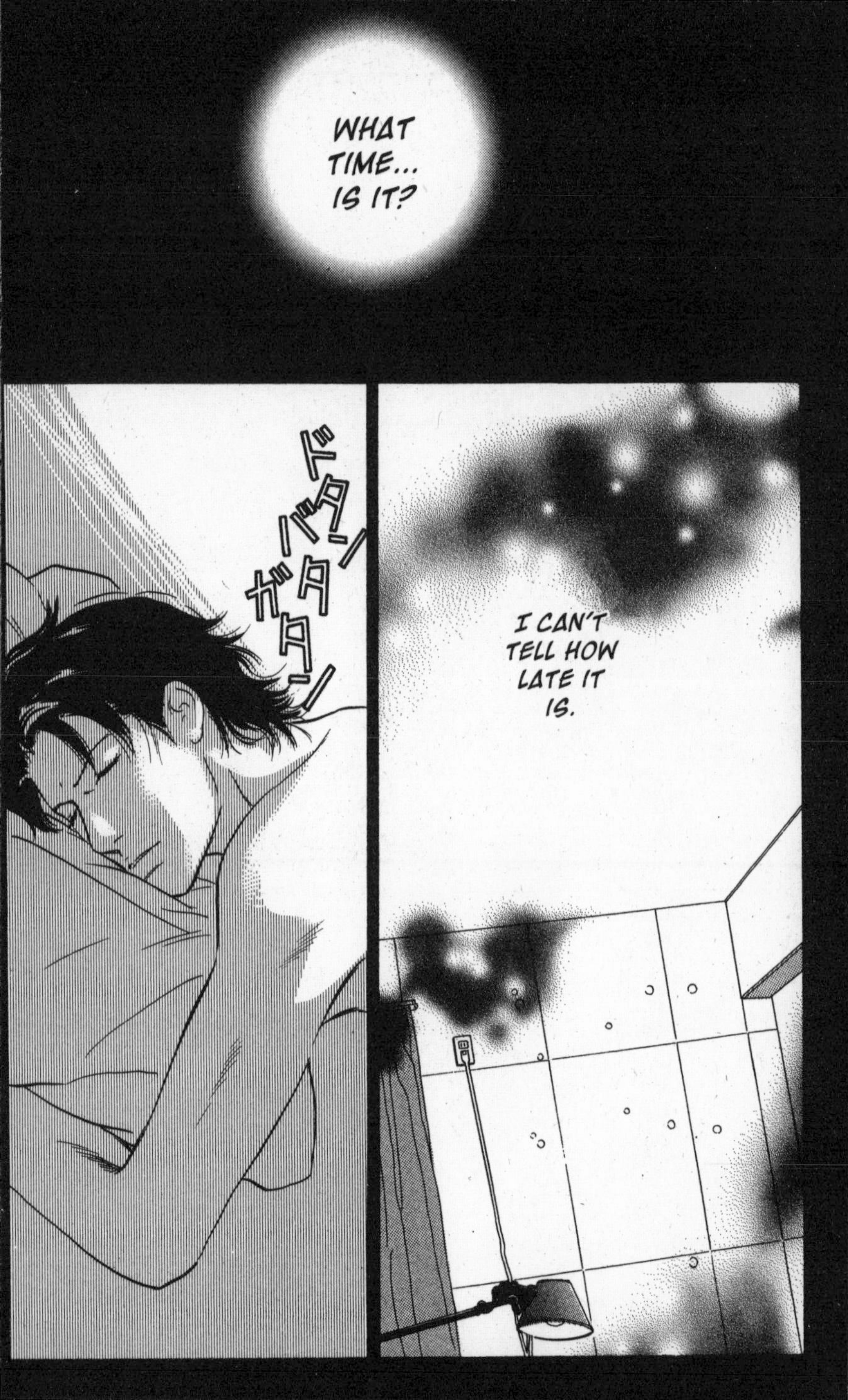
WHAT TIME... IS IT?
I CAN'T TELL HOW LATE IT IS.
ドターン
バタ
ガターン

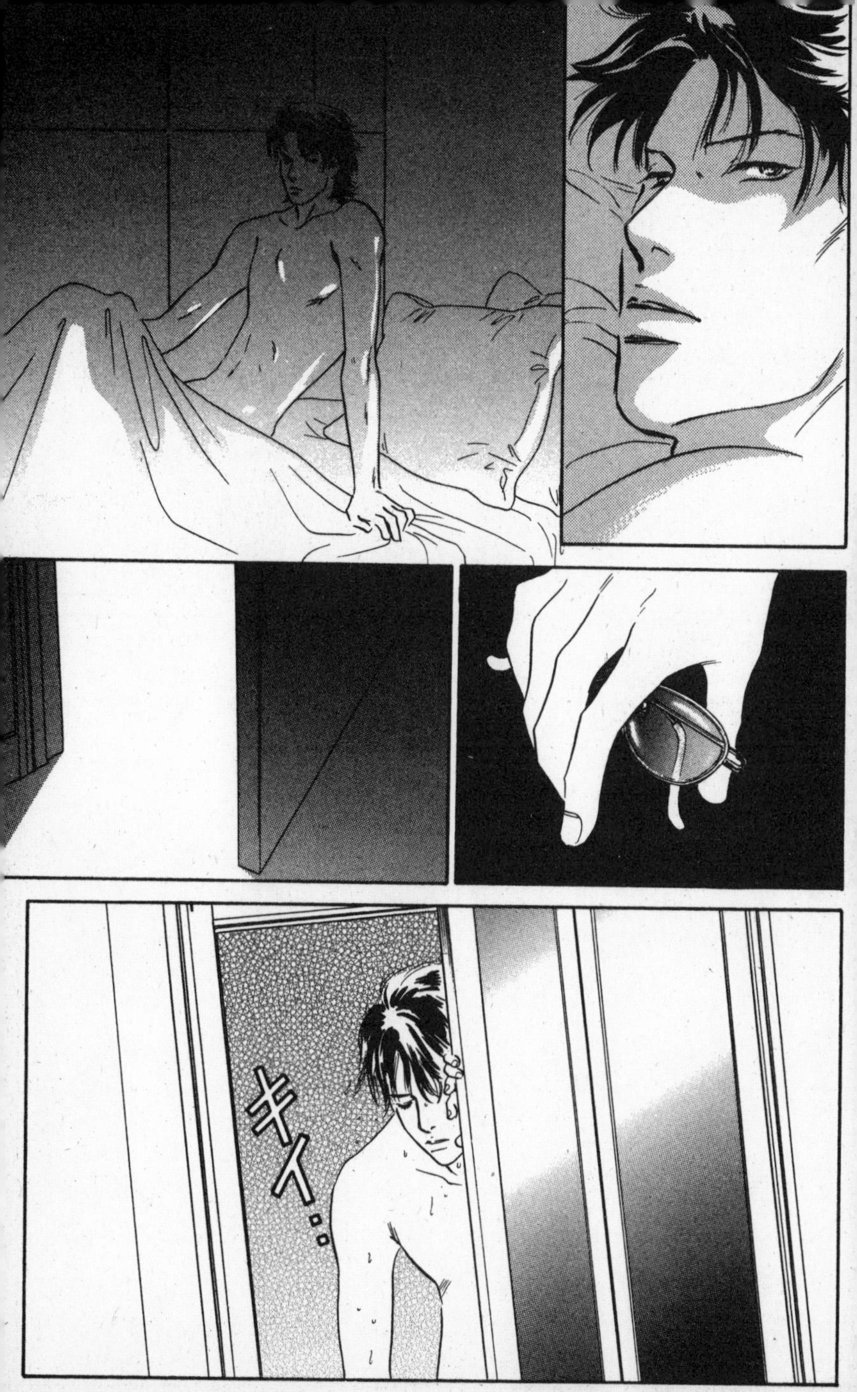
キィ…

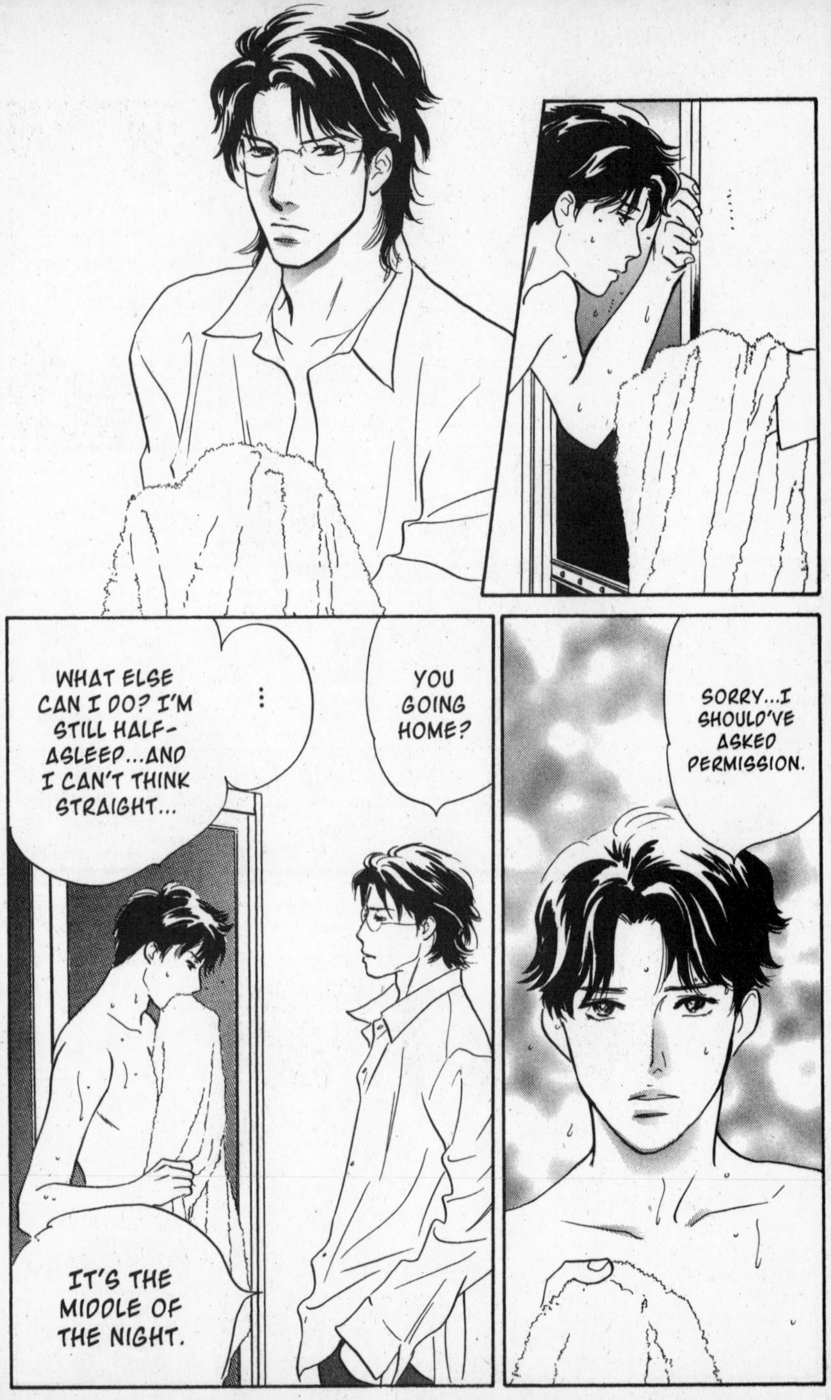
.....
SORRY...I SHOULD'VE ASKED PERMISSION.
YOU GOING HOME?
...
WHAT ELSE CAN I DO? I'M STILL HALF-ASLEEP...AND I CAN'T THINK STRAIGHT...
IT'S THE MIDDLE OF THE NIGHT.

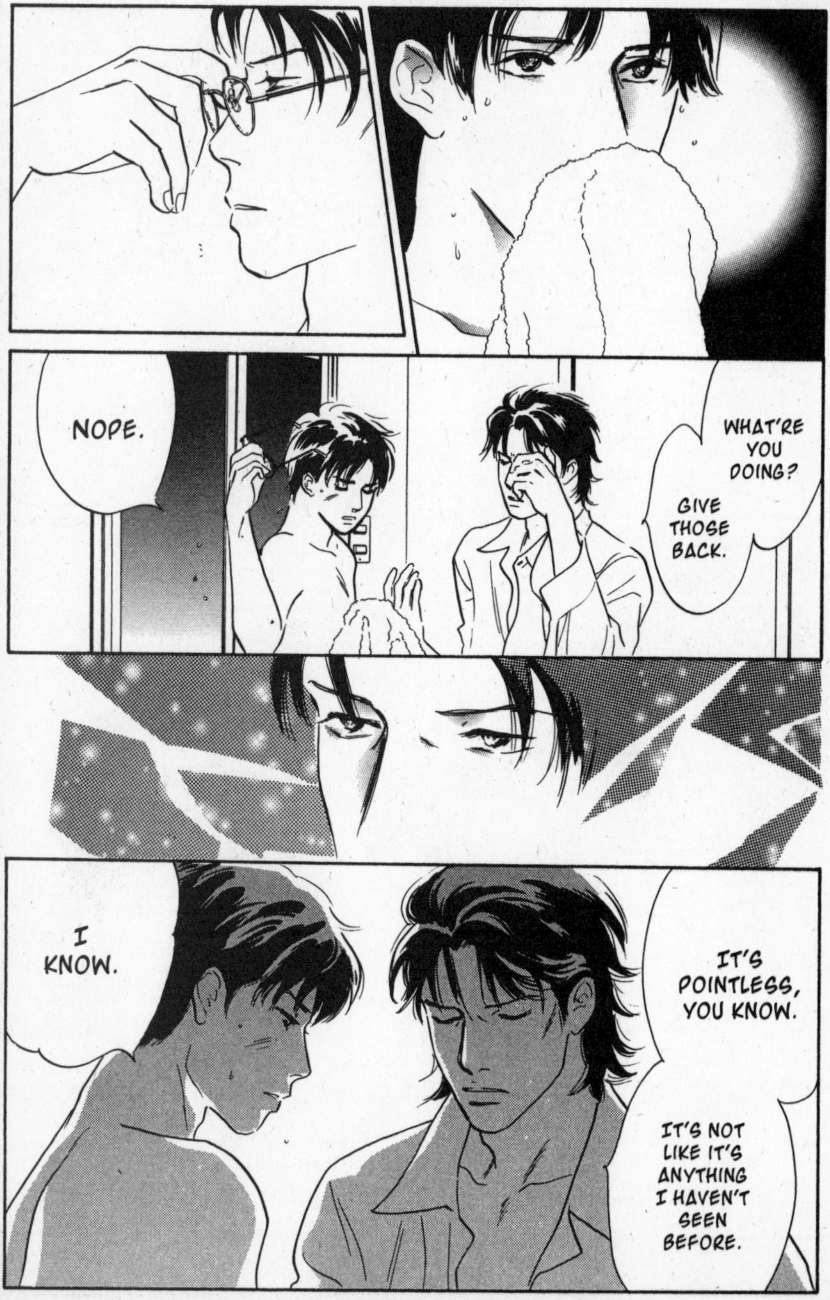
WHAT'RE YOU DOING?
GIVE THOSE BACK.
NOPE.
IT'S POINTLESS, YOU KNOW.
IT'S NOT LIKE IT'S ANYTHING I HAVEN'T SEEN BEFORE.
I KNOW.

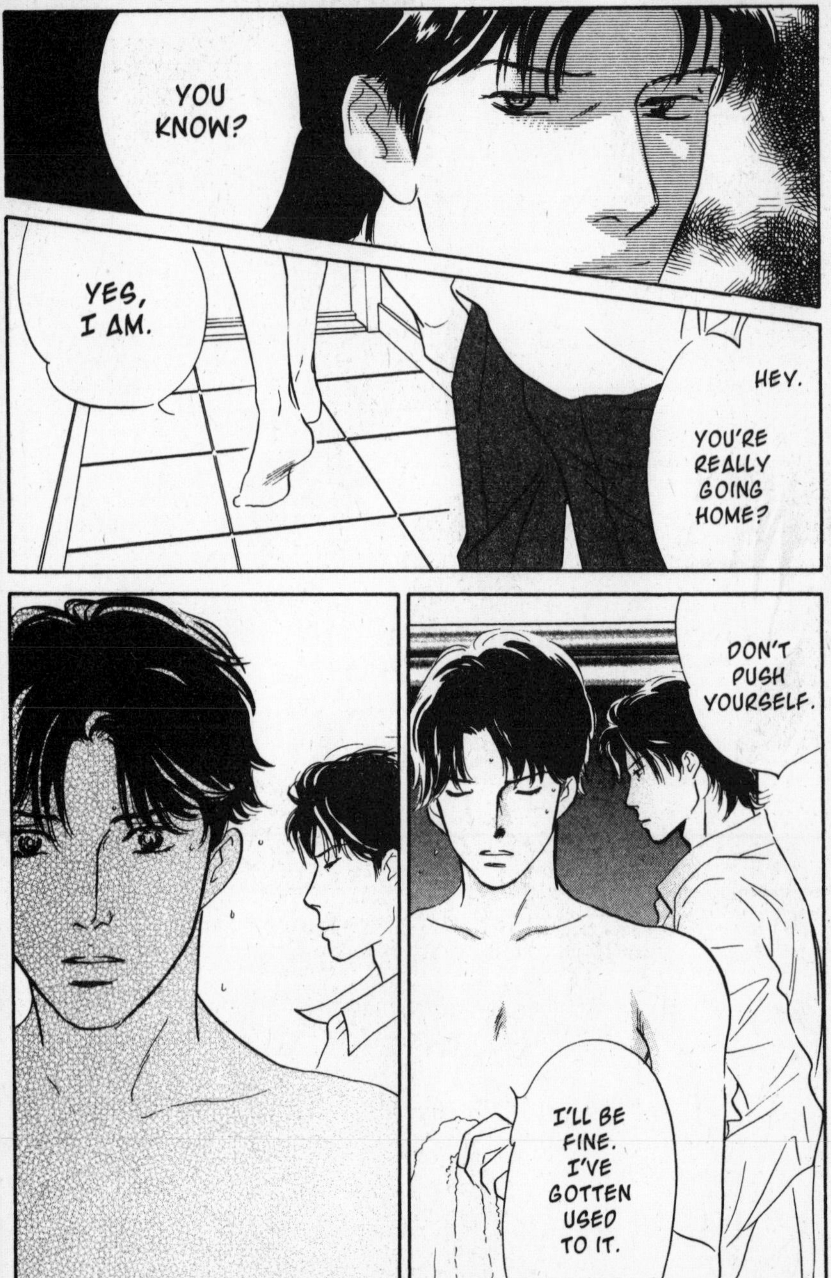
YOU KNOW?
HEY.
YOU'RE REALLY GOING HOME?
YES, I AM.
DON'T PUSH YOURSELF.
I'LL BE FINE. I'VE GOTTEN USED TO IT.

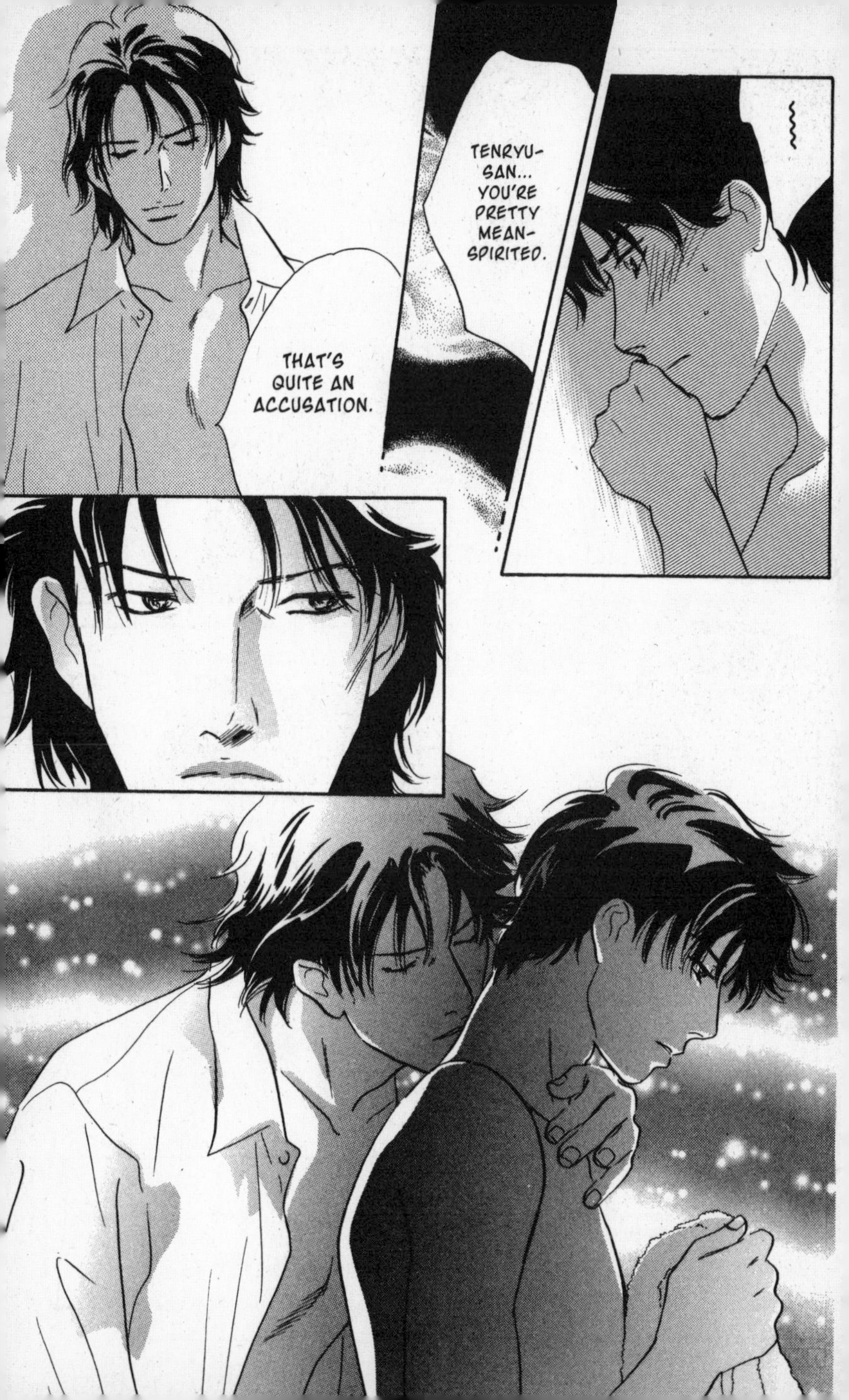
~
TENRYU-SAN... YOU'RE PRETTY MEAN-SPIRITED.
THAT'S QUITE AN ACCUSATION.

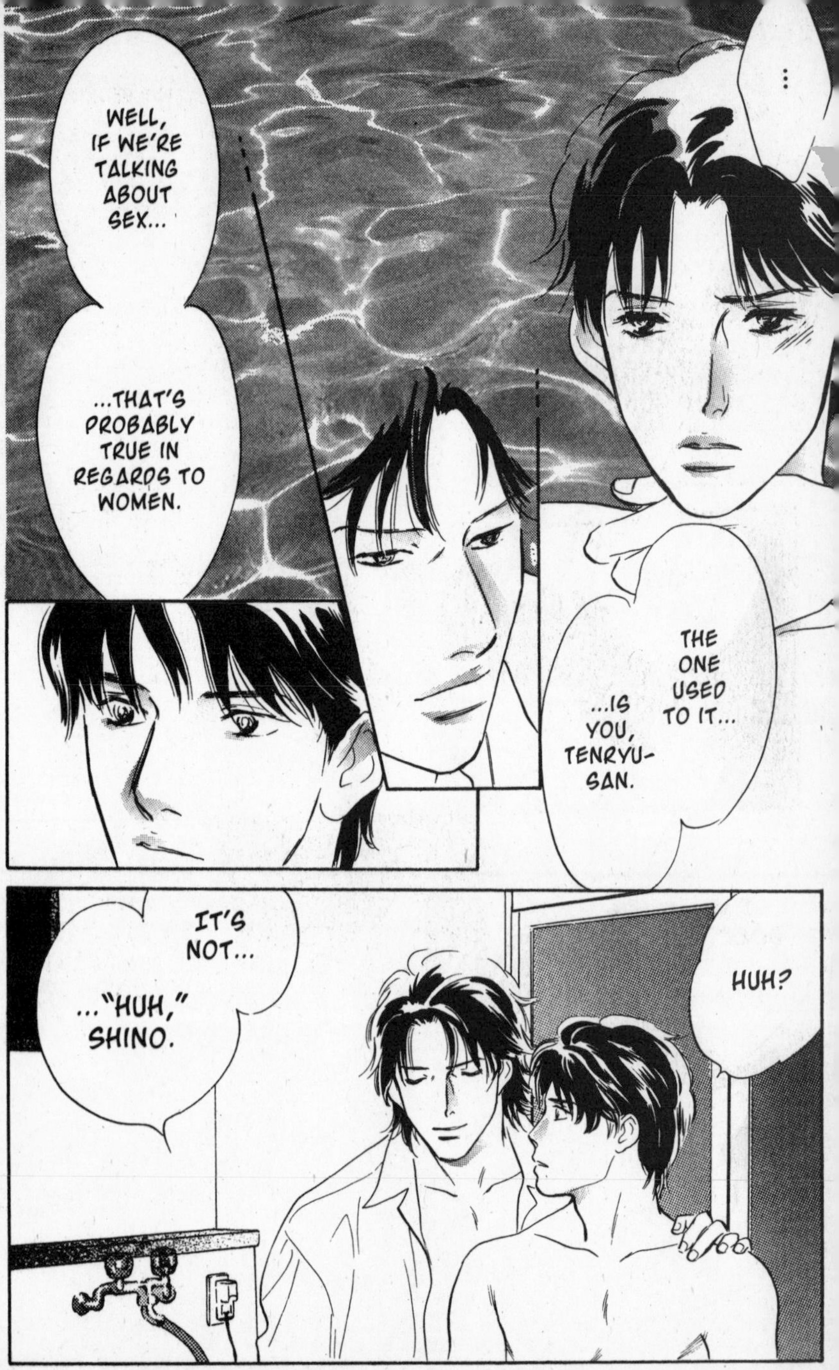
...
WELL, IF WE'RE TALKING ABOUT SEX...
...THAT'S PROBABLY TRUE IN REGARDS TO WOMEN.
THE ONE USED TO IT...
...IS YOU, TENRYU-SAN.
HUH?
IT'S NOT...
..."HUH," SHINO.

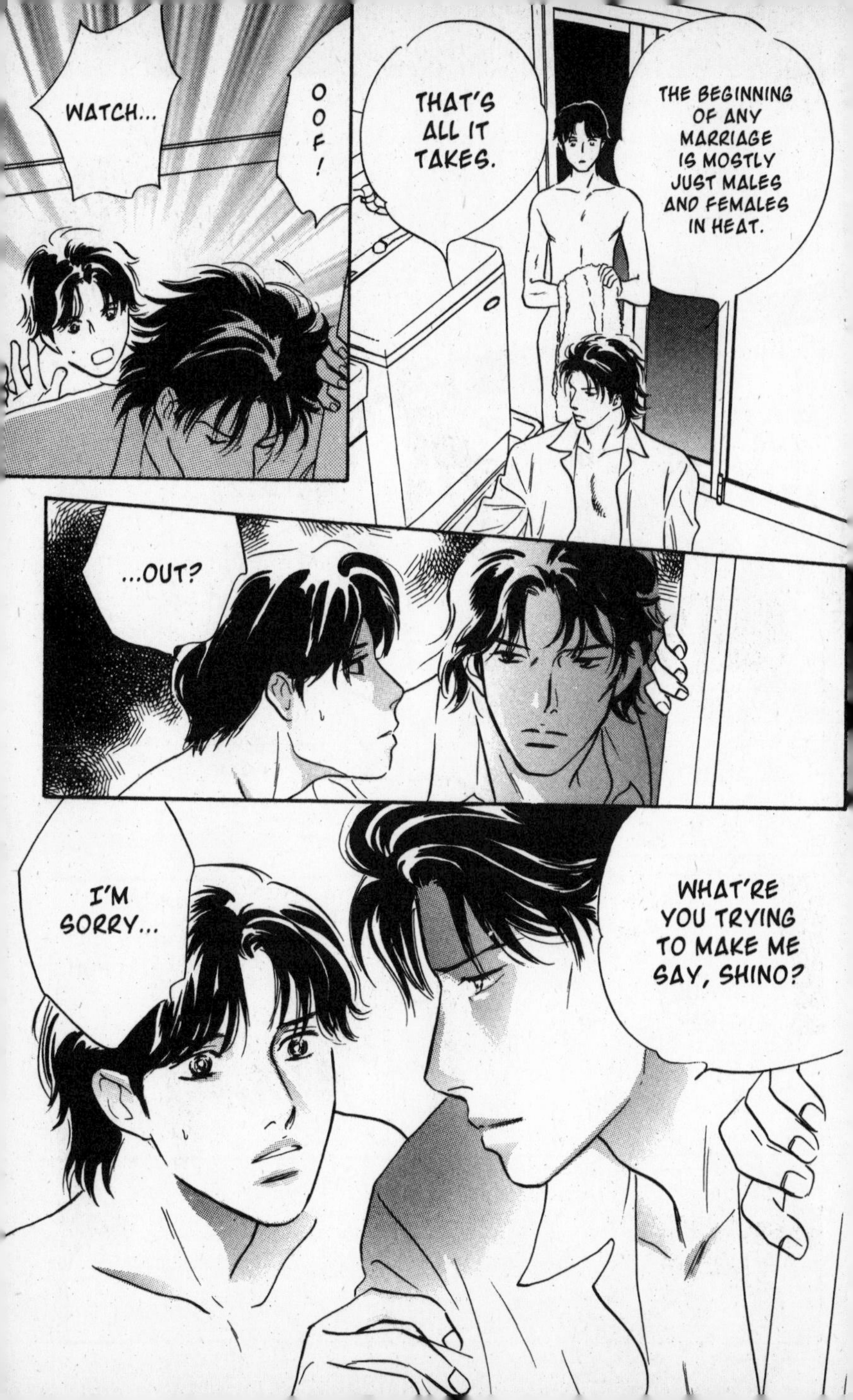
THE BEGINNING OF ANY MARRIAGE IS MOSTLY JUST MALES AND FEMALES IN HEAT.
THAT'S ALL IT TAKES.
OOF!
WATCH...
...OUT?
WHAT'RE YOU TRYING TO MAKE ME SAY, SHINO?
I'M SORRY...

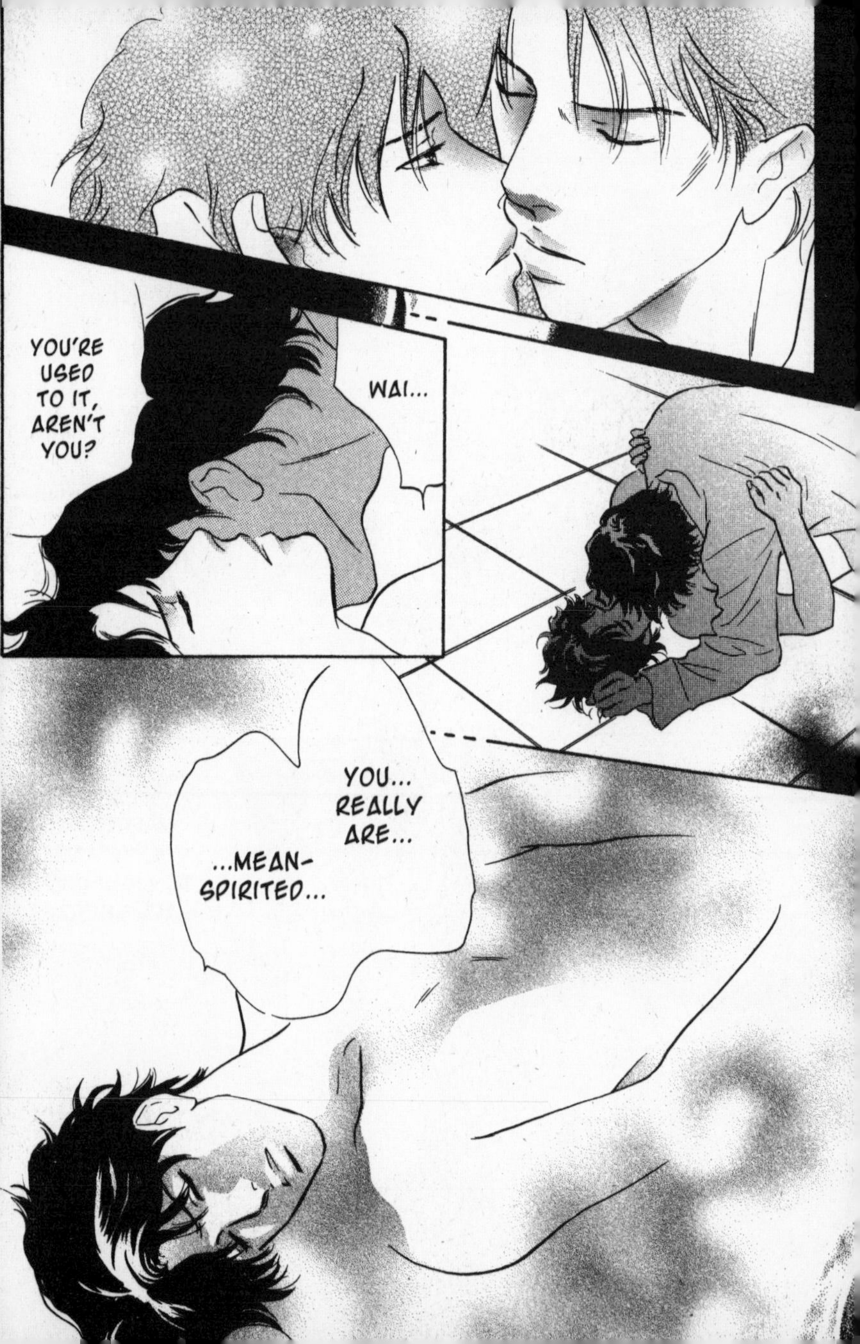
WAI...
YOU'RE USED TO IT, AREN'T YOU?
YOU... REALLY ARE... ...MEAN-SPIRITED...

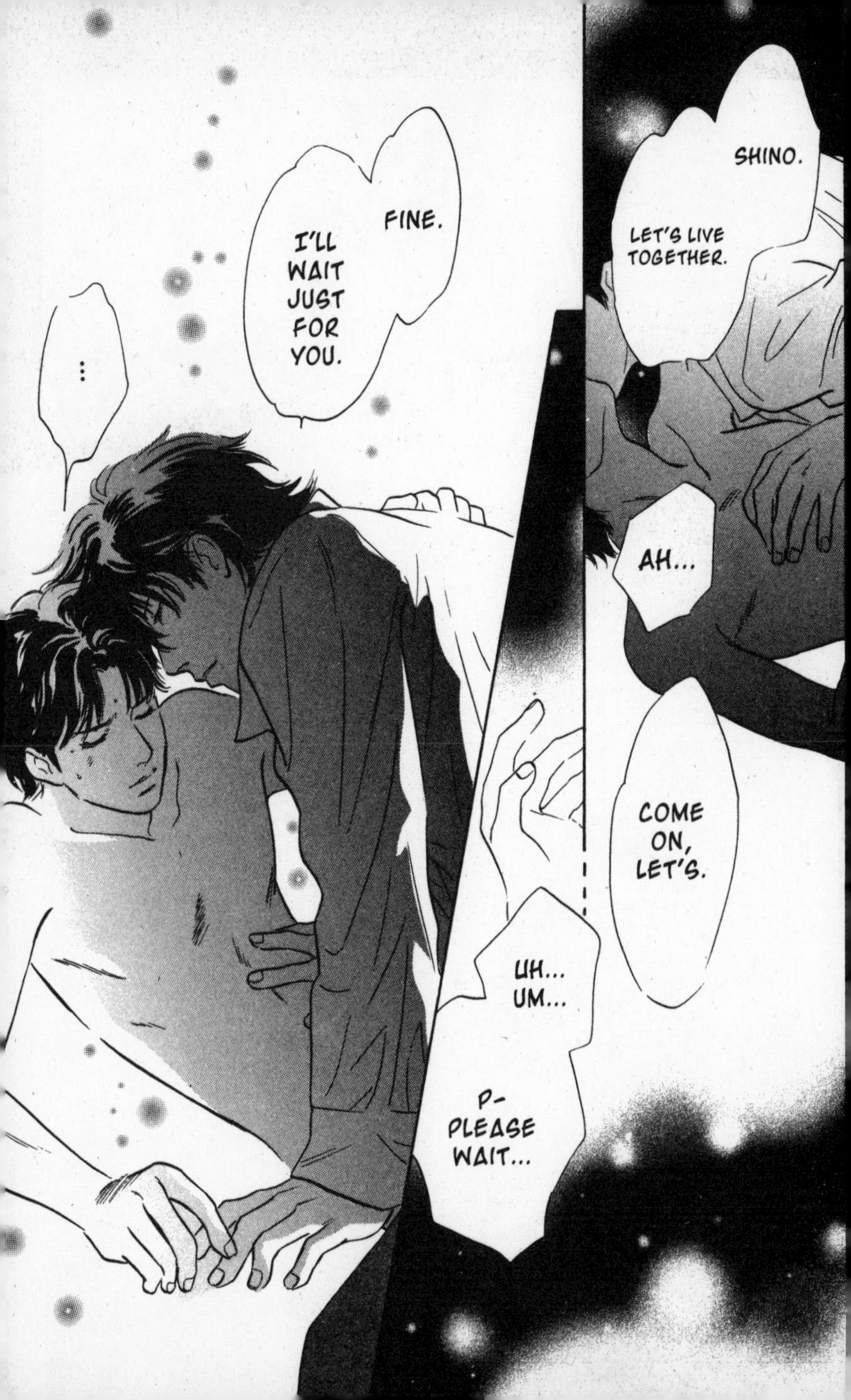
SHINO.
LET'S LIVE TOGETHER.
AH...
COME ON, LET'S.
UH... UM...
P-PLEASE WAIT...
FINE.
I'LL WAIT JUST FOR YOU.
...

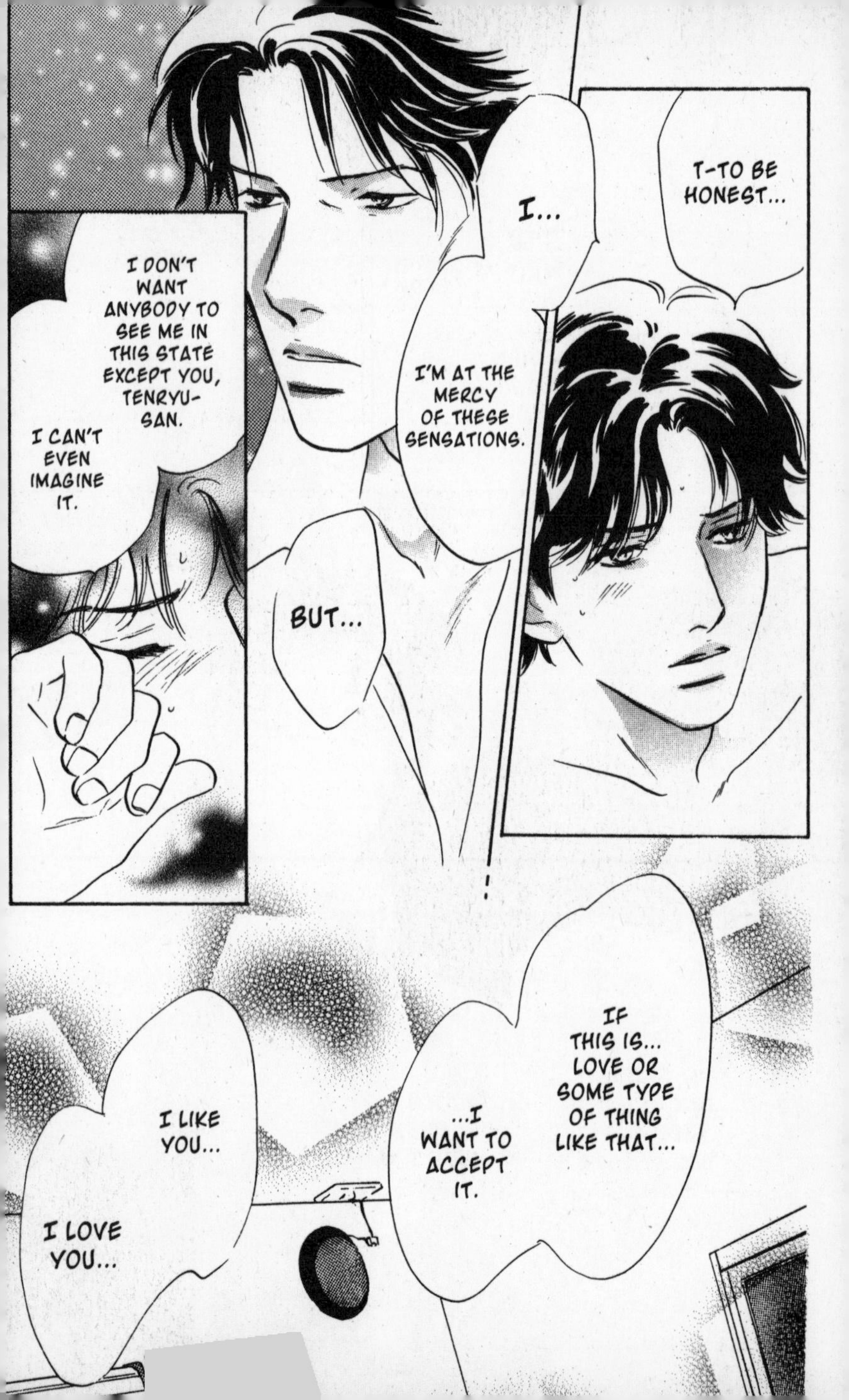
T-TO BE HONEST...
I...
I'M AT THE MERCY OF THESE SENSATIONS.
BUT...
I DON'T WANT ANYBODY TO SEE ME IN THIS STATE EXCEPT YOU, TENRYU-SAN.
I CAN'T EVEN IMAGINE IT.
IF THIS IS... LOVE OR SOME TYPE OF THING LIKE THAT...
...I WANT TO ACCEPT IT.
I LIKE YOU...
I LOVE YOU...

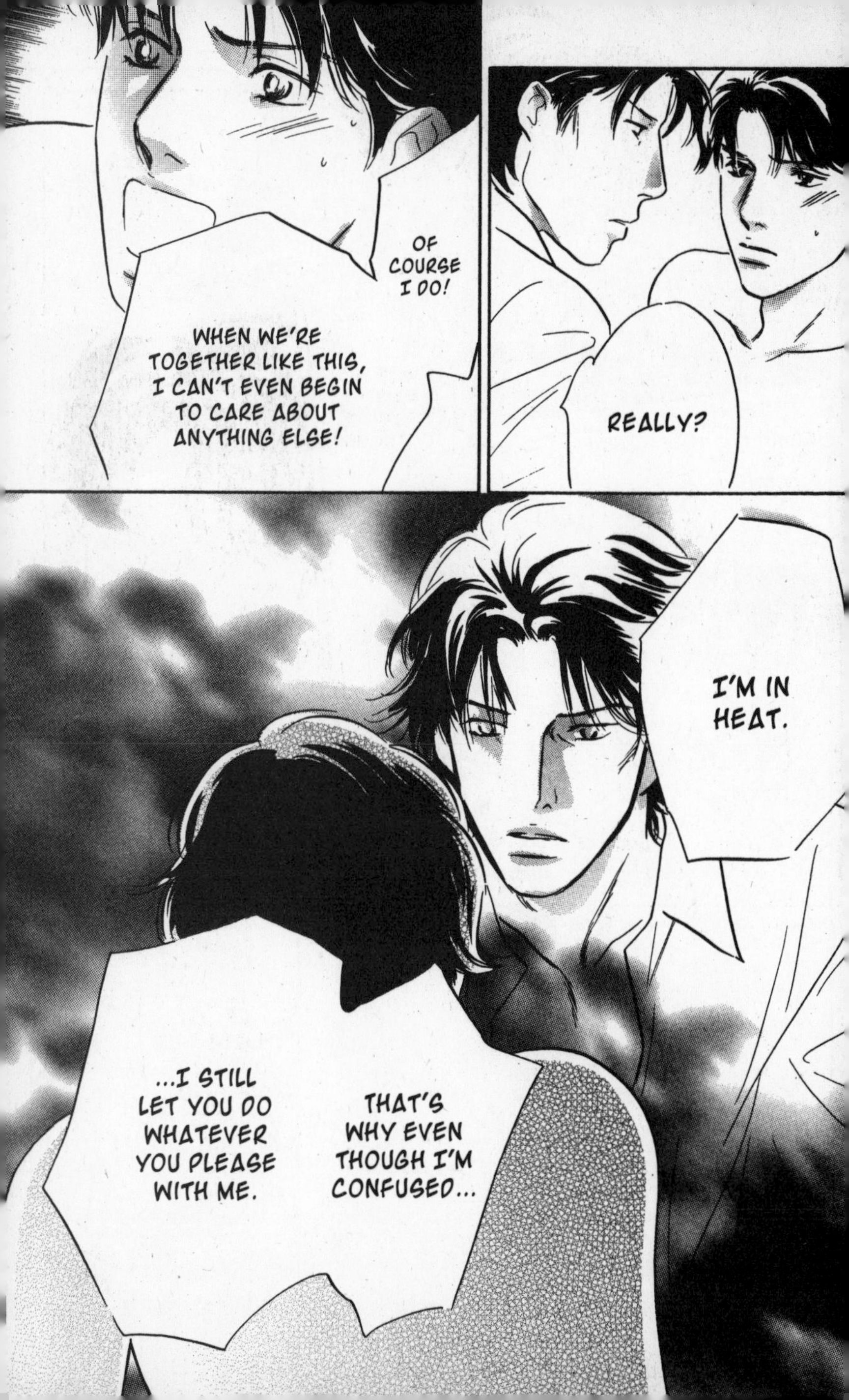
REALLY?
OF COURSE I DO!
WHEN WE'RE TOGETHER LIKE THIS, I CAN'T EVEN BEGIN TO CARE ABOUT ANYTHING ELSE!
I'M IN HEAT.
THAT'S WHY EVEN THOUGH I'M CONFUSED...
...I STILL LET YOU DO WHATEVER YOU PLEASE WITH ME.

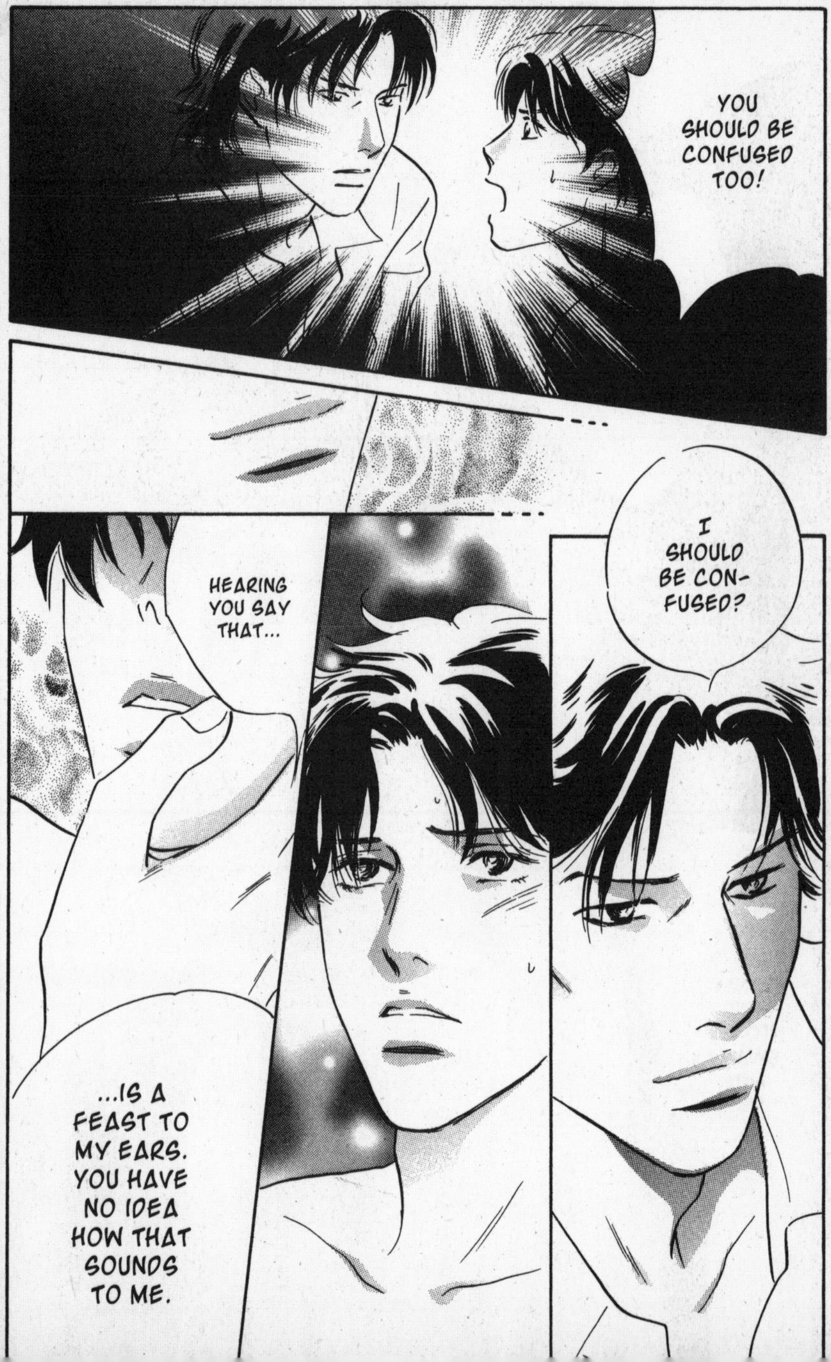
YOU SHOULD BE CONFUSED TOO!
I SHOULD BE CON-FUSED?
HEARING YOU SAY THAT...
...IS A FEAST TO MY EARS. YOU HAVE NO IDEA HOW THAT SOUNDS TO ME.

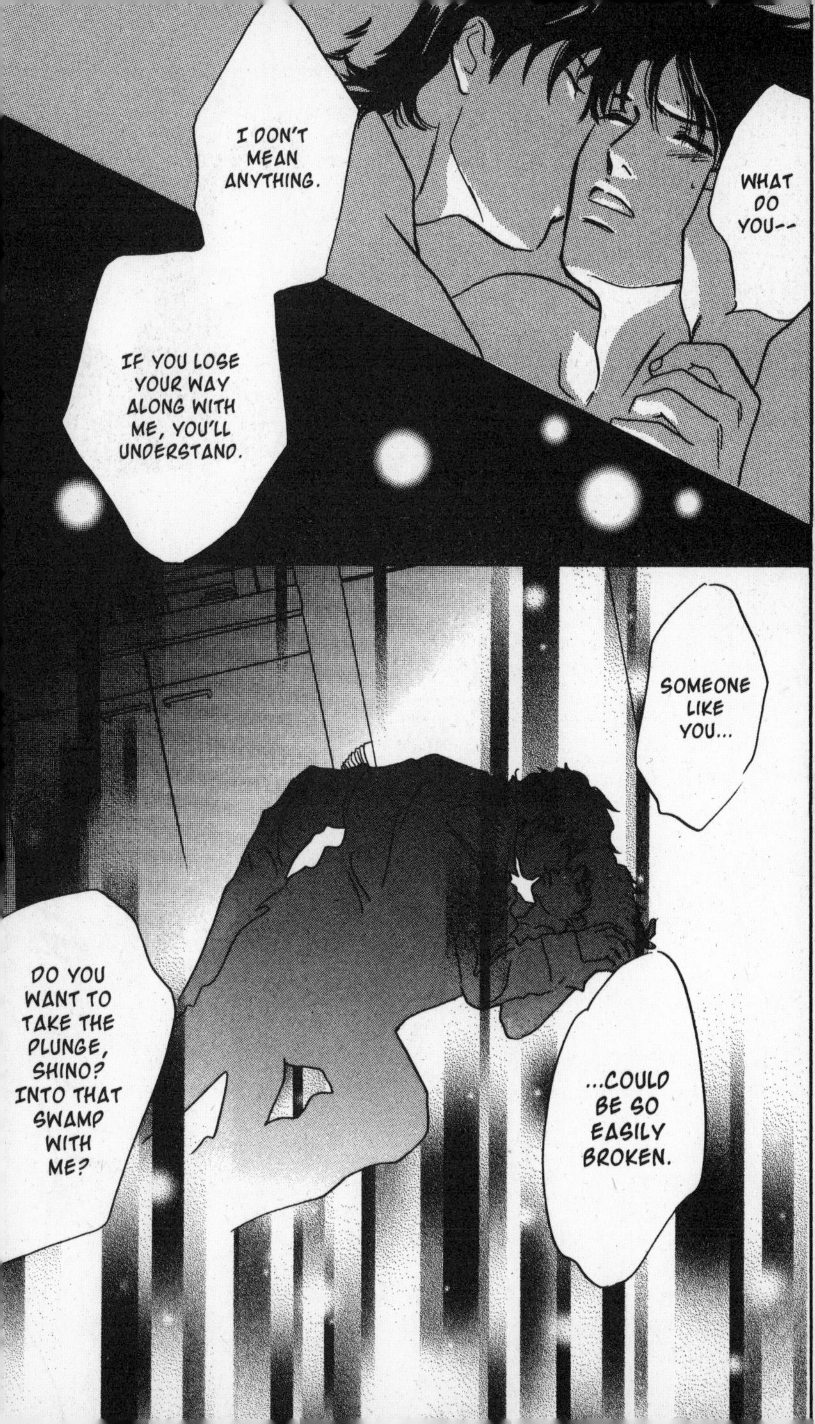
WHAT DO YOU--
I DON'T MEAN ANYTHING.
IF YOU LOSE YOUR WAY ALONG WITH ME, YOU'LL UNDERSTAND.
SOMEONE LIKE YOU...
...COULD BE SO EASILY BROKEN.
DO YOU WANT TO TAKE THE PLUNGE, SHINO? INTO THAT SWAMP WITH ME?

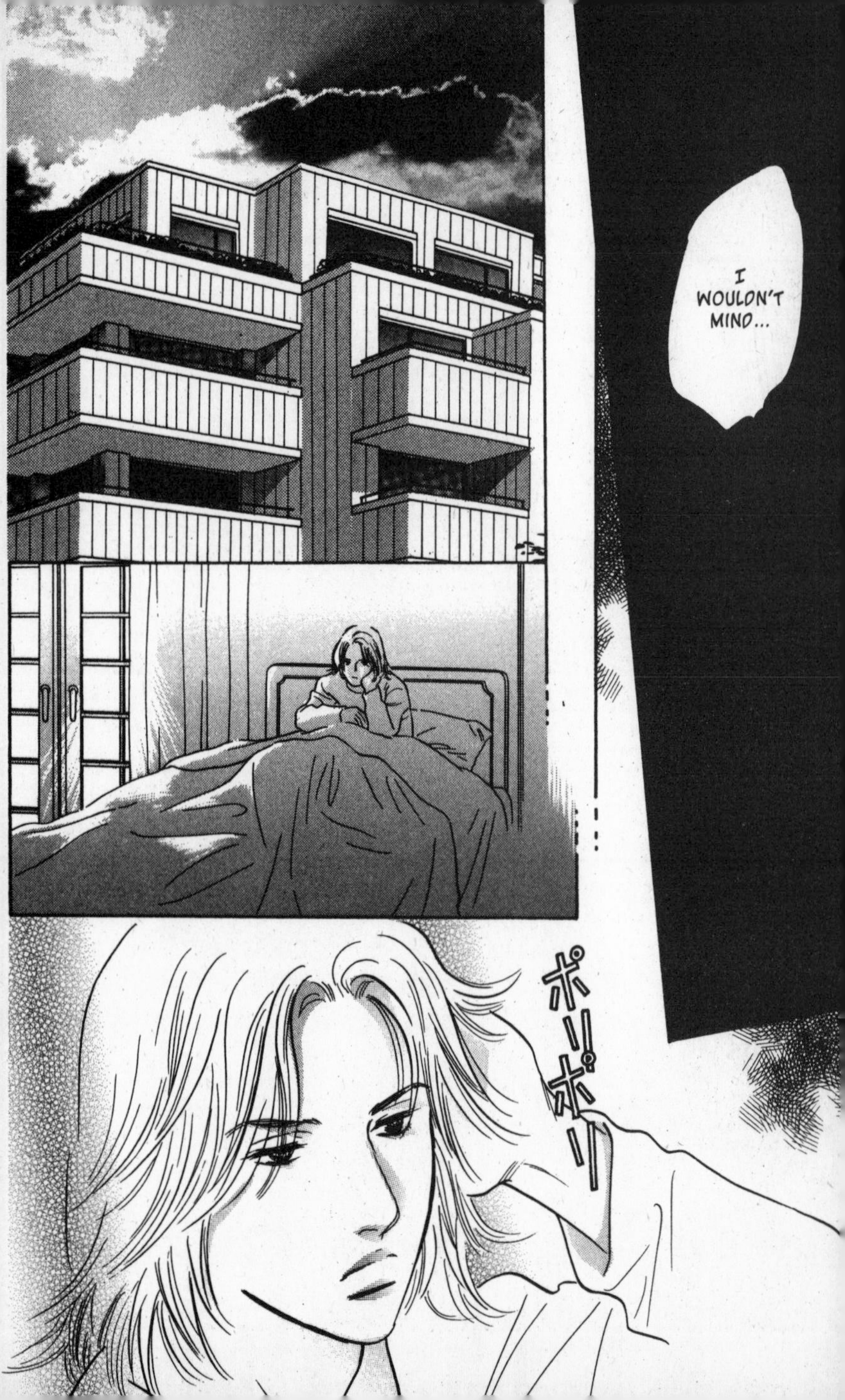
I WOULDN'T MIND...
ポリポリ

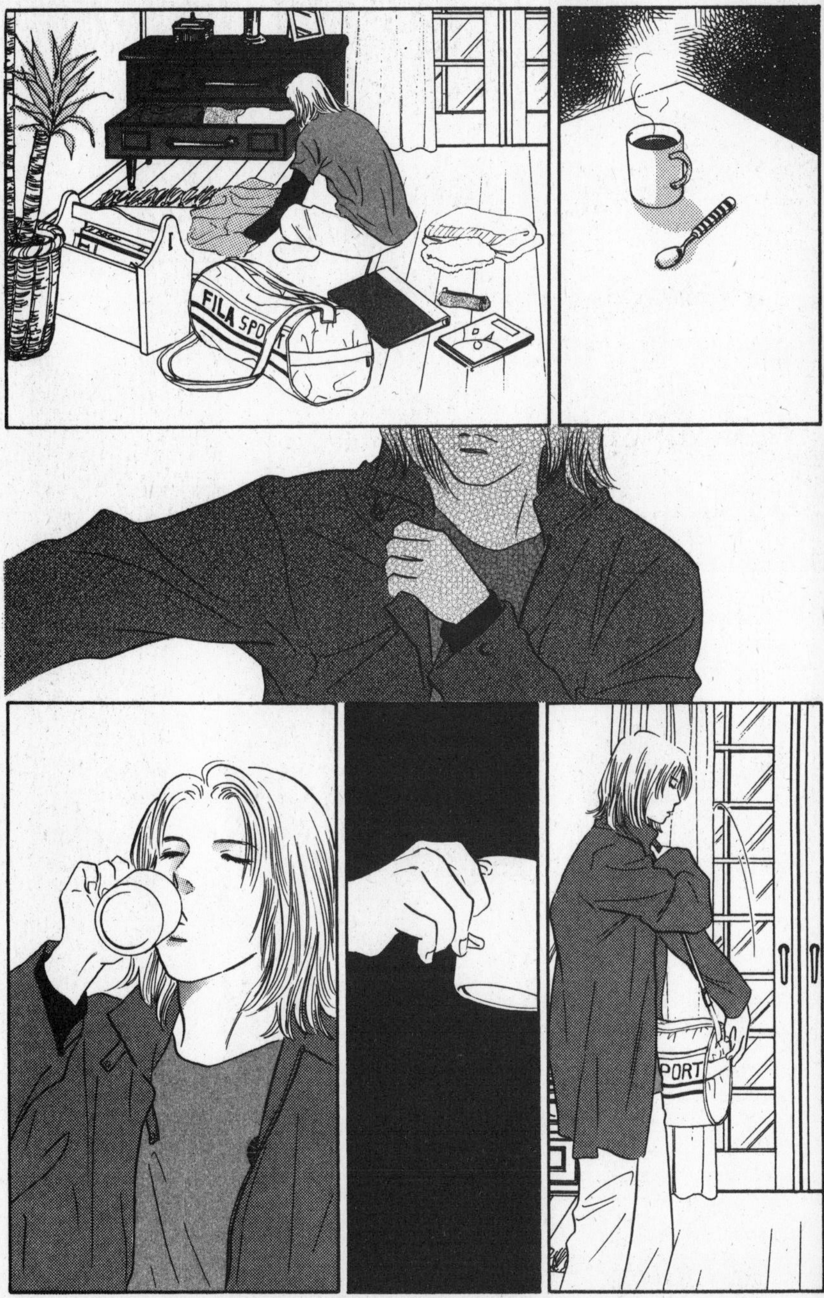
FILA
SPORT

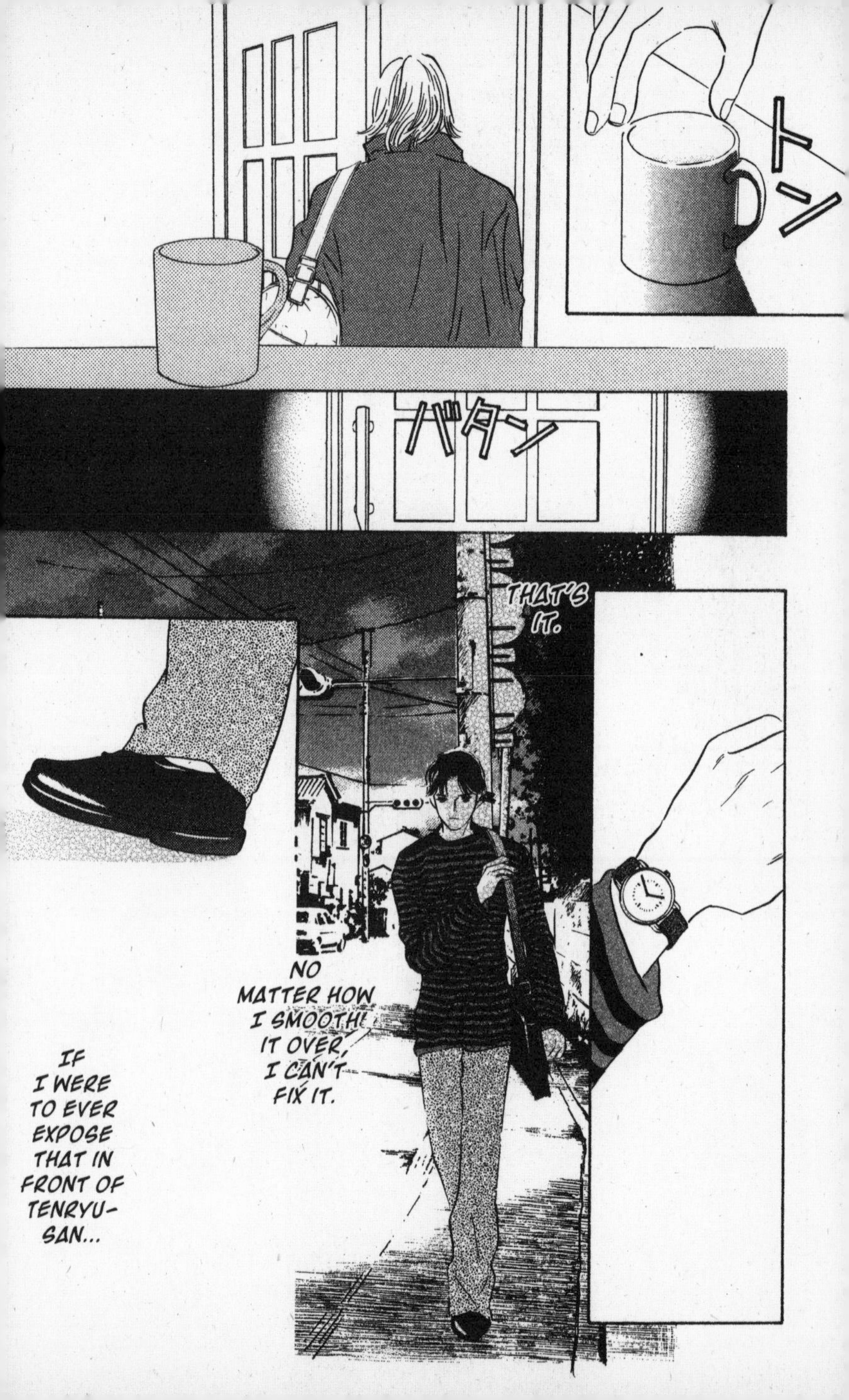
トーン
バタン
THAT'S IT.
NO MATTER HOW I SMOOTH IT OVER, I CAN'T FIX IT.
IF I WERE TO EVER EXPOSE THAT IN FRONT OF TENRYU-SAN...

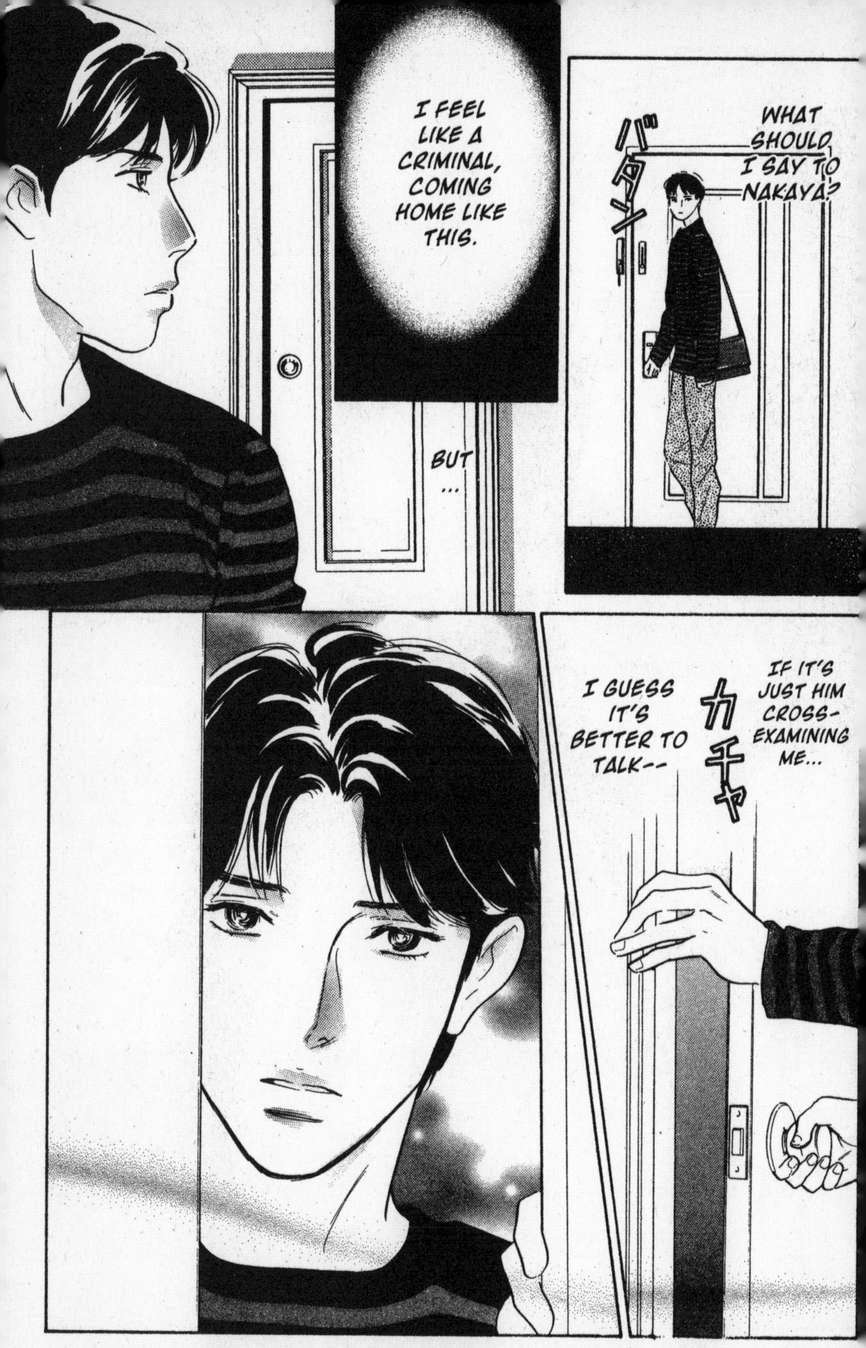
WHAT SHOULD I SAY TO NAKAYA?
バタン
I FEEL LIKE A CRIMINAL, COMING HOME LIKE THIS.
BUT ...
IF IT'S JUST HIM CROSS-EXAMINING ME...
カチャ
I GUESS IT'S BETTER TO TALK--

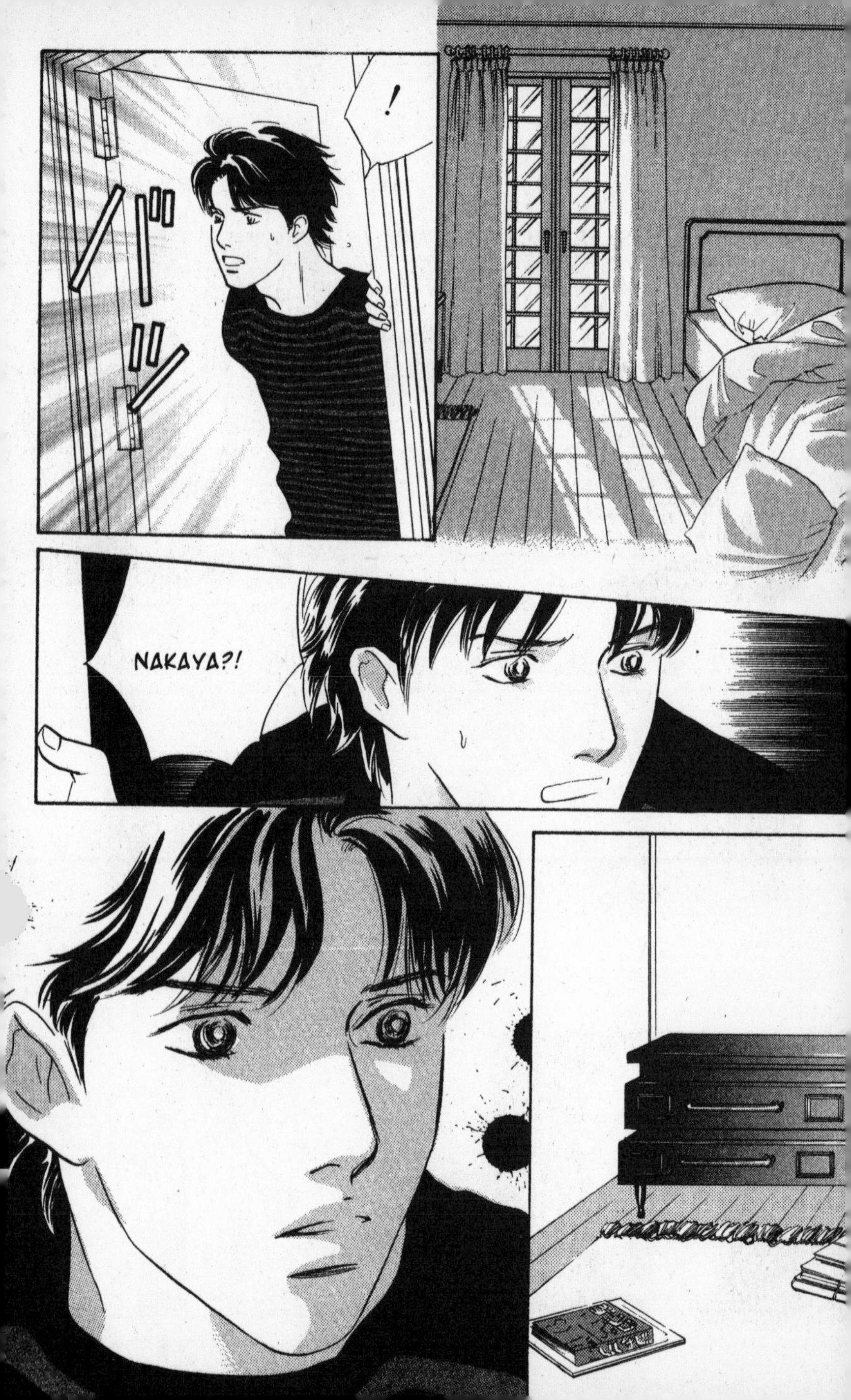
!
NAKAYA?!

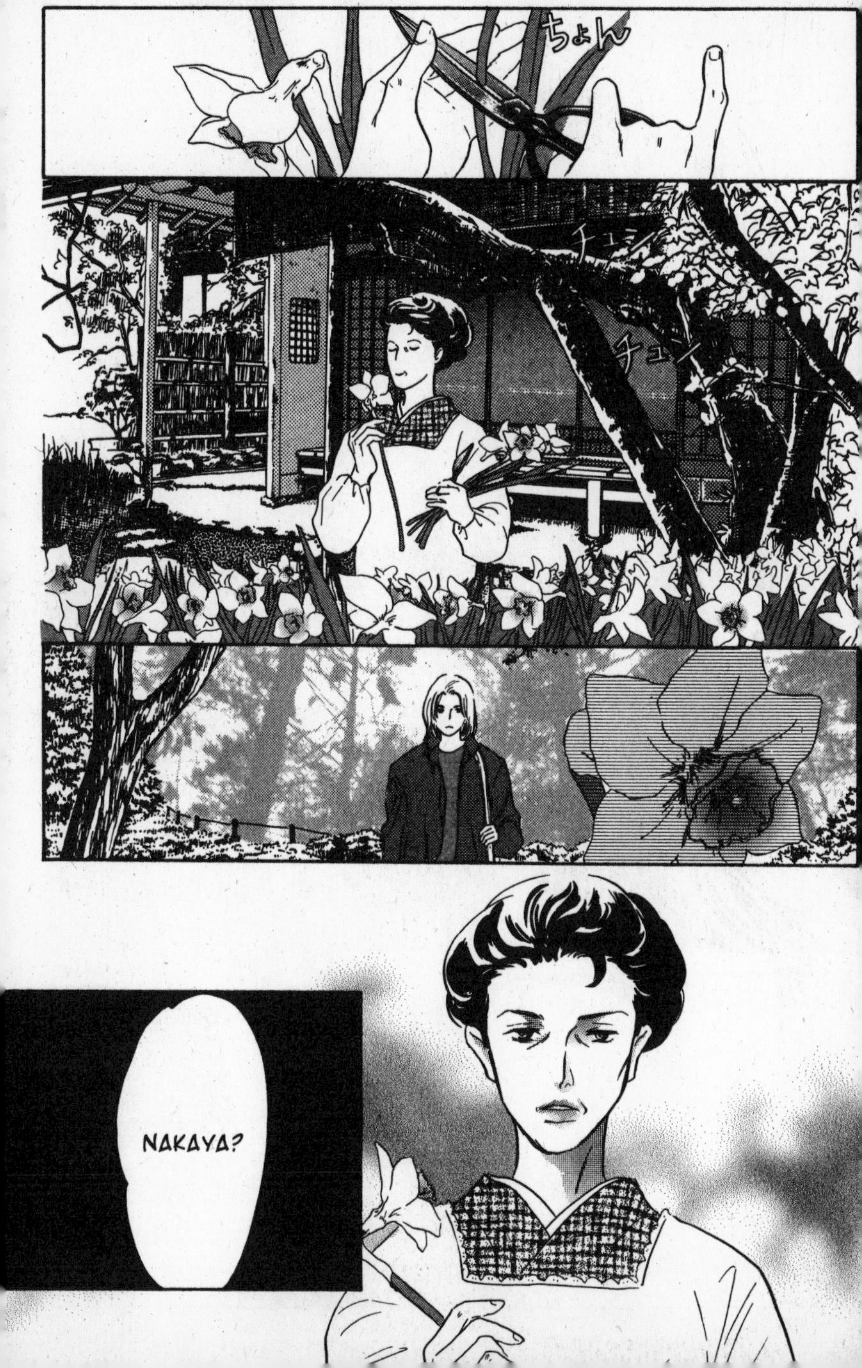
ちょん
チュン
チュン
NAKAYA?

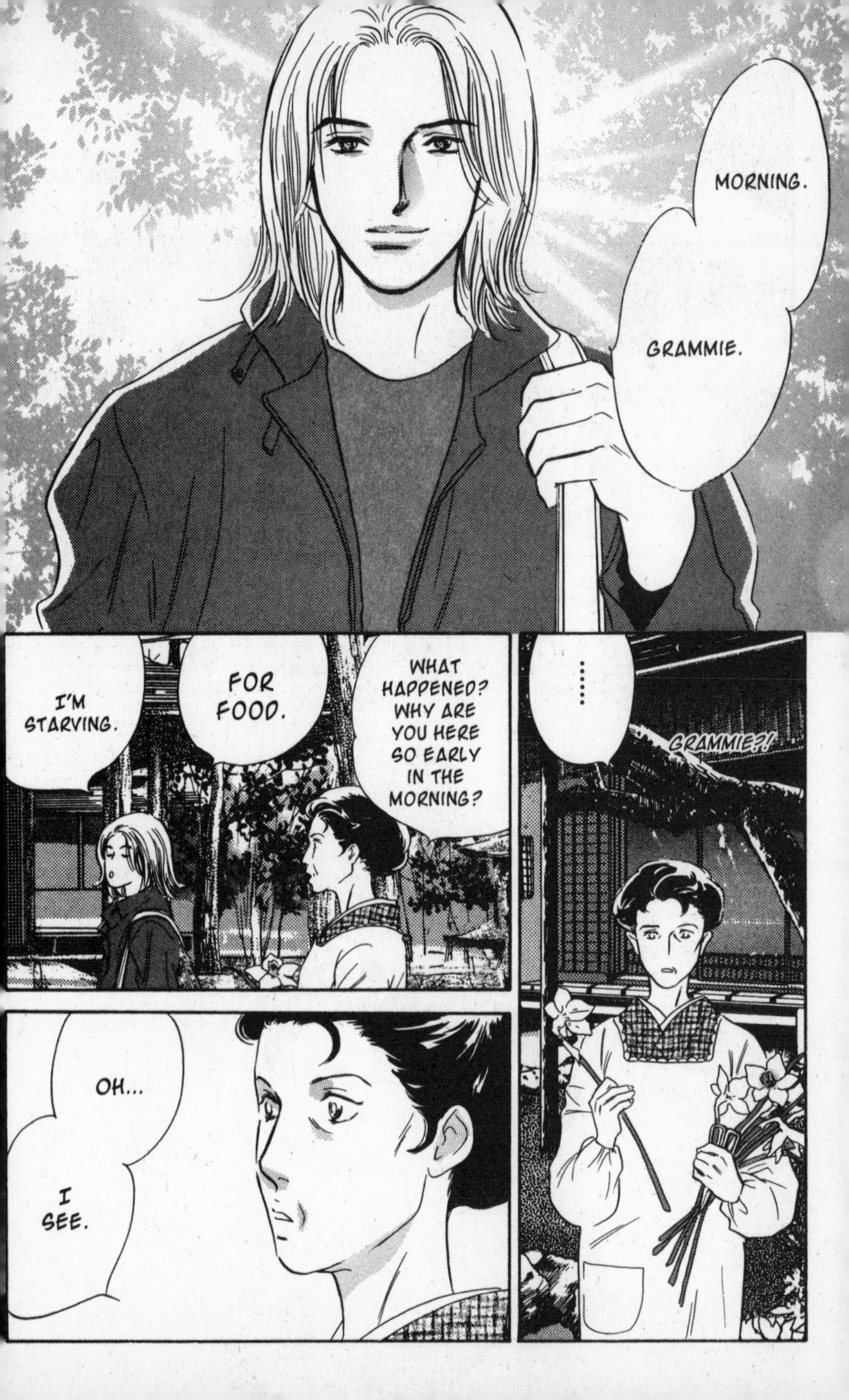
MORNING.
GRAMMIE.
......
GRAMMIE?!
WHAT HAPPENED? WHY ARE YOU HERE SO EARLY IN THE MORNING?
FOR FOOD.
I'M STARVING.
OH... I SEE.

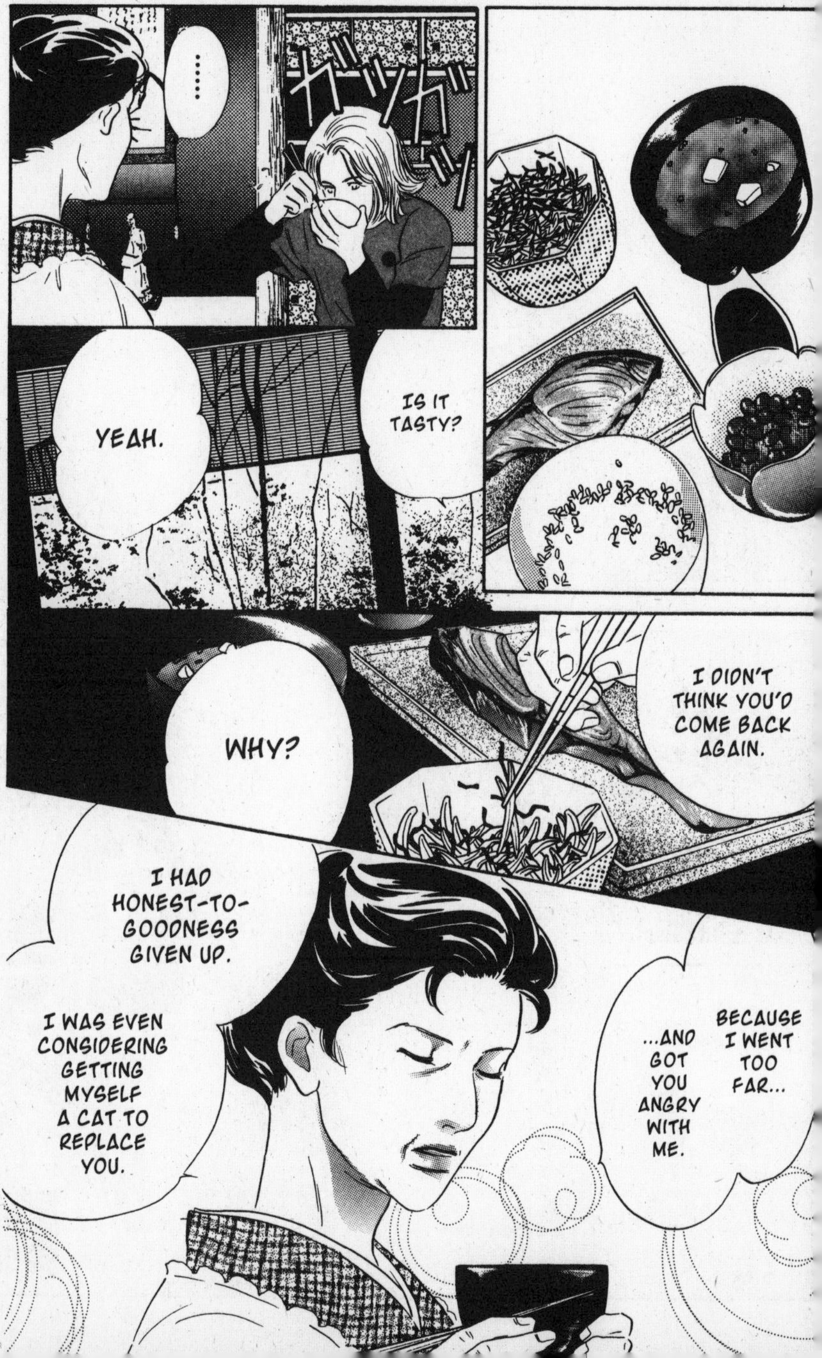
......
IS IT TASTY?
YEAH.
I DIDN'T THINK YOU'D COME BACK AGAIN.
WHY?
BECAUSE I WENT TOO FAR...
...AND GOT YOU ANGRY WITH ME.
I HAD HONEST-TO-GOODNESS GIVEN UP.
I WAS EVEN CONSIDERING GETTING MYSELF A CAT TO REPLACE YOU.

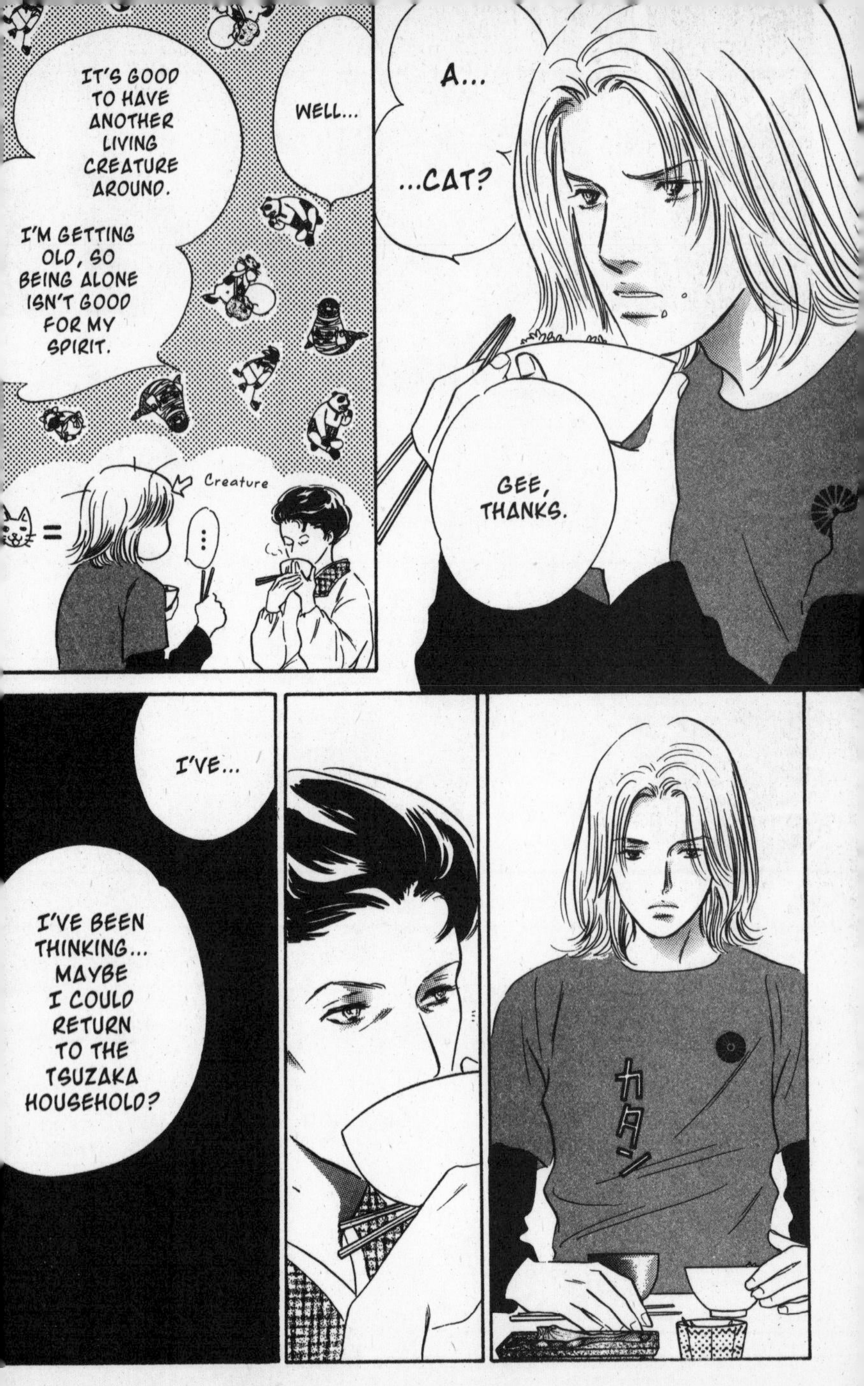
A...
...CAT?
GEE, THANKS.
WELL...
IT'S GOOD TO HAVE ANOTHER LIVING CREATURE AROUND.
I'M GETTING OLD, SO BEING ALONE ISN'T GOOD FOR MY SPIRIT.
Creature
...
=
カタン
I'VE...
I'VE BEEN THINKING... MAYBE I COULD RETURN TO THE TSUZAKA HOUSEHOLD?

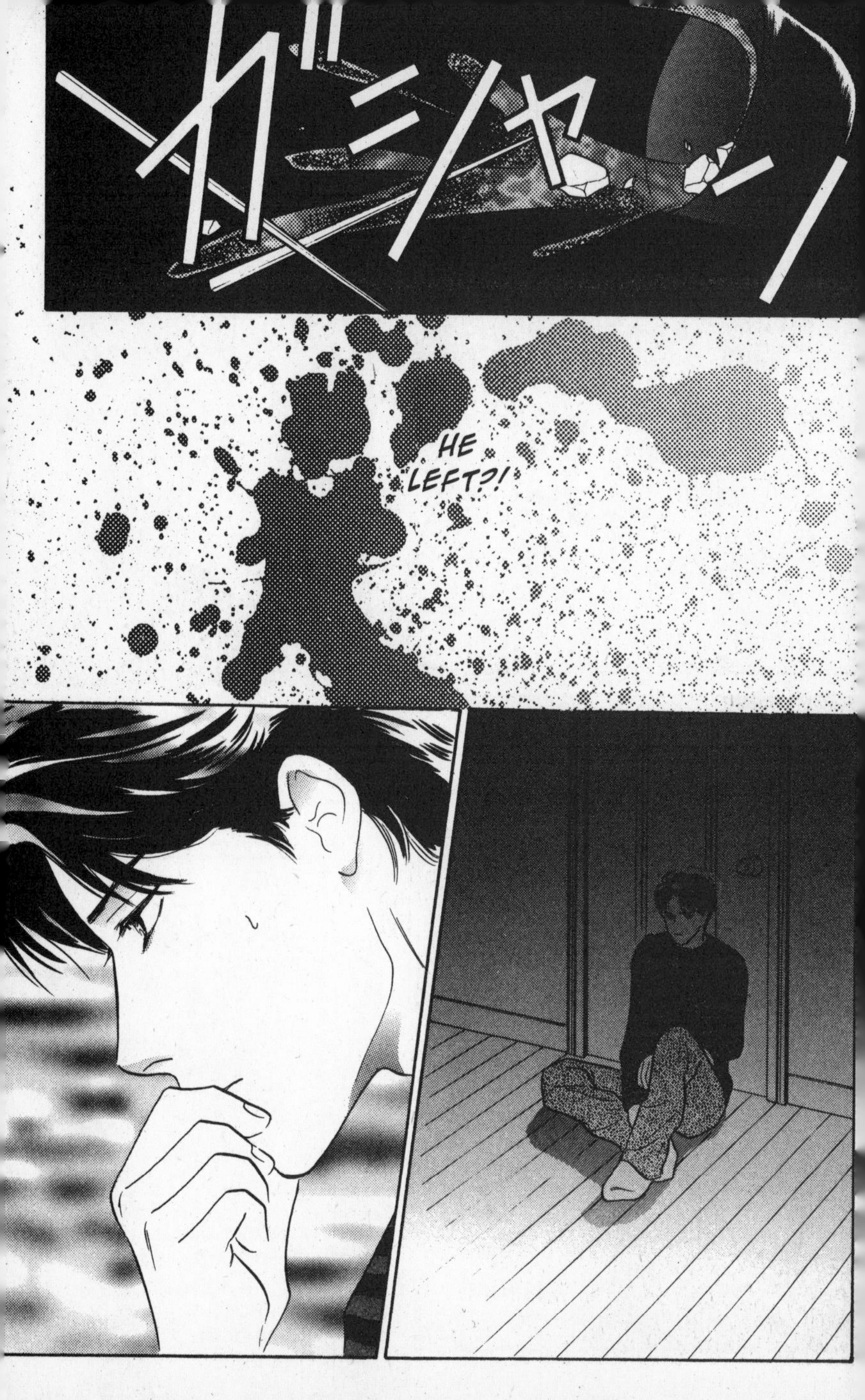
HE LEFT?!

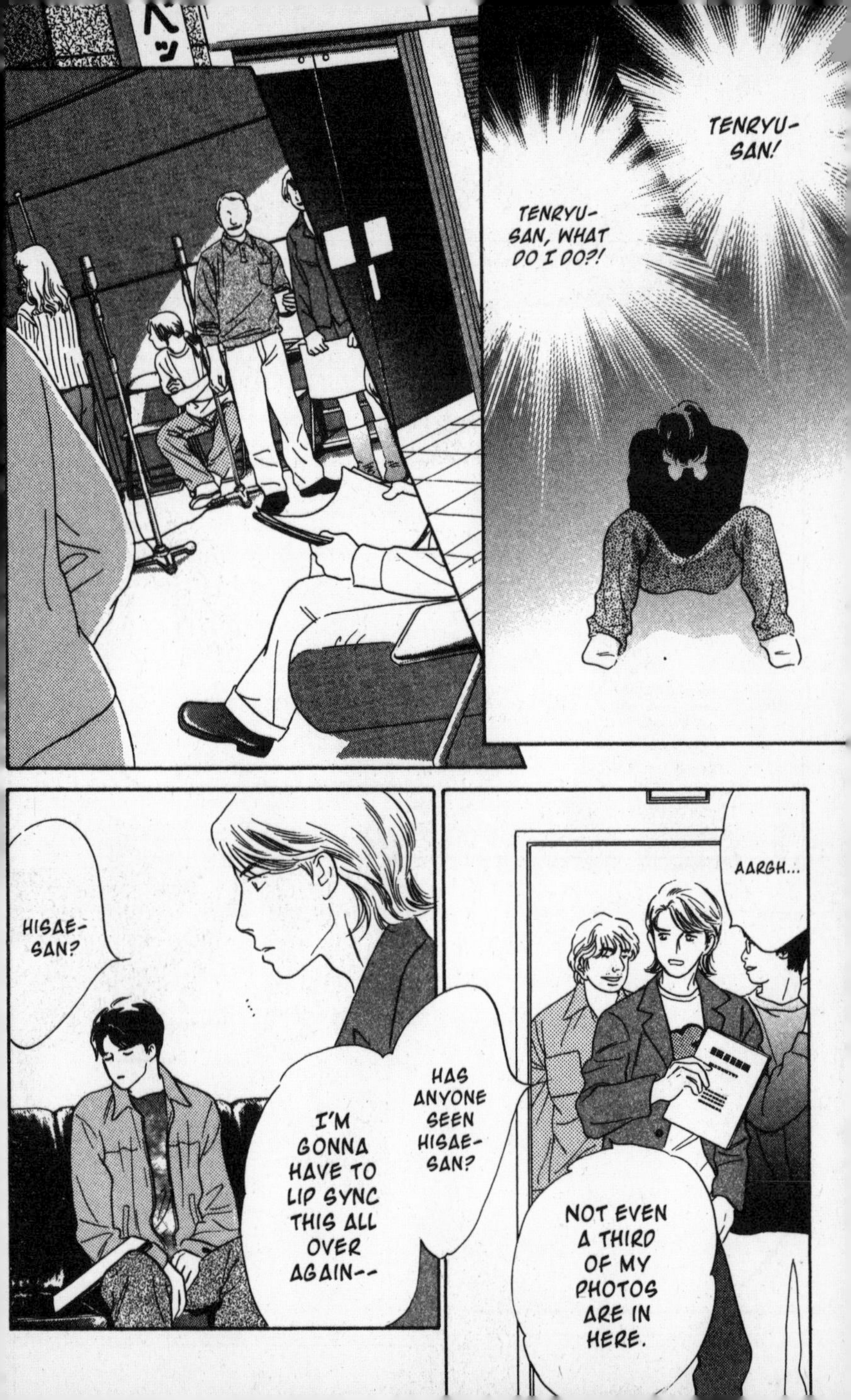
TENRYU-SAN!
TENRYU-SAN, WHAT DO I DO?!
AARGH...
HAS ANYONE SEEN HISAE-SAN?
NOT EVEN A THIRD OF MY PHOTOS ARE IN HERE.
I'M GONNA HAVE TO LIP SYNC THIS ALL OVER AGAIN--
HISAE-SAN?
...

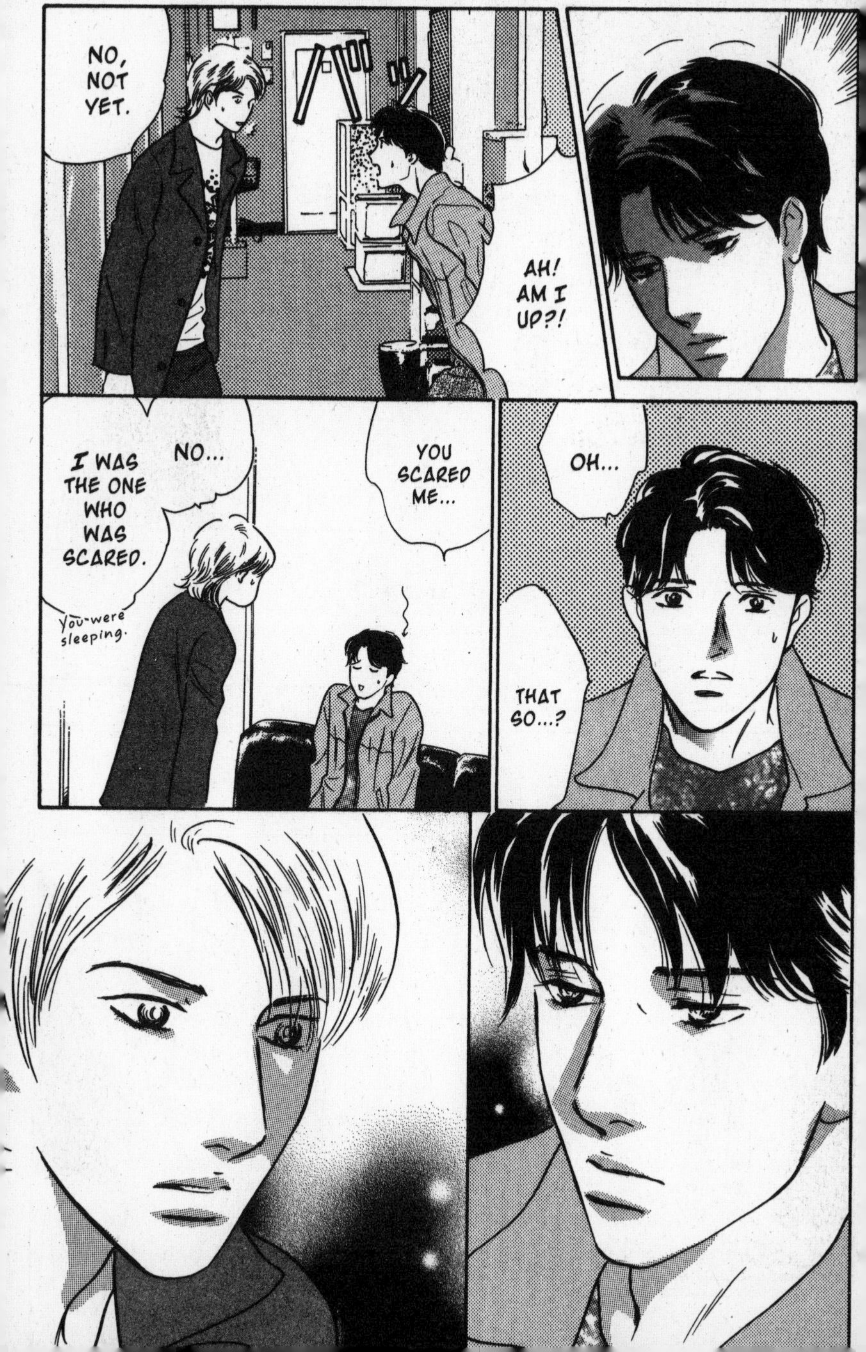
AH! AM I UP?!
NO, NOT YET.
OH...
THAT SO...?
YOU SCARED ME...
NO...
I WAS THE ONE WHO WAS SCARED.
You were sleeping.

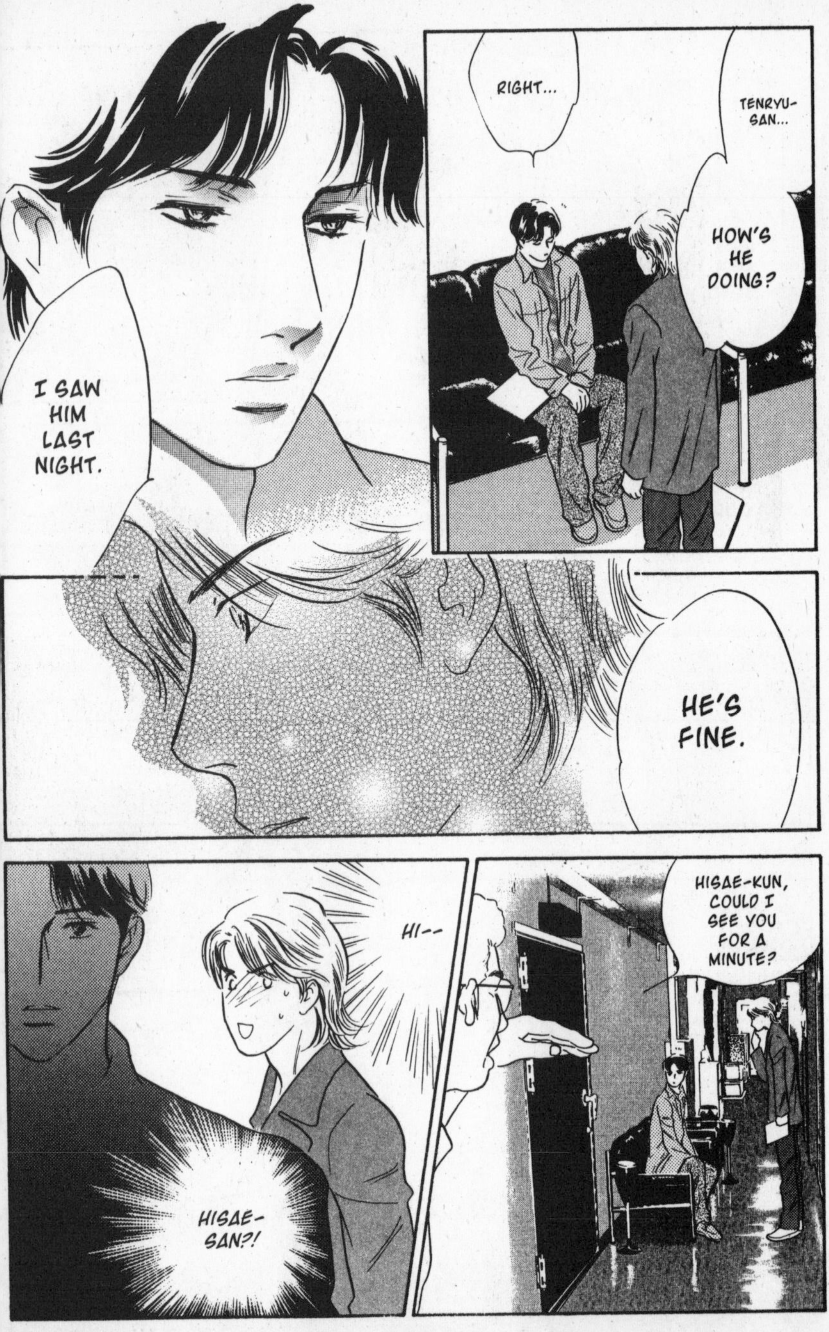
RIGHT...
TENRYU-SAN...
HOW'S HE DOING?
I SAW HIM LAST NIGHT.
HE'S FINE.
HISAE-KUN, COULD I SEE YOU FOR A MINUTE?
HI--
HISAE-SAN?!

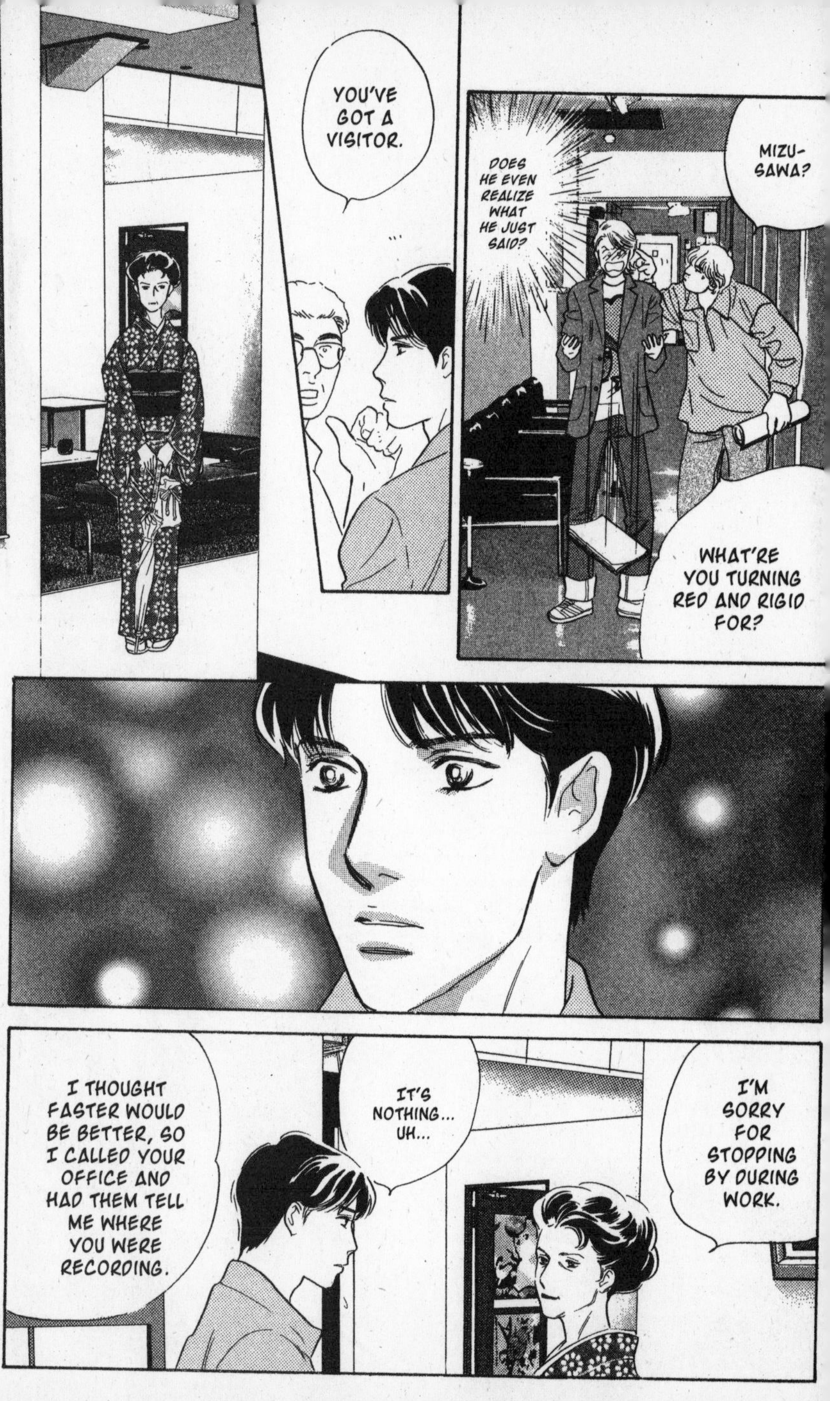
MIZU-SAWA?
DOES HE EVEN REALIZE WHAT HE JUST SAID?
WHAT'RE YOU TURNING RED AND RIGID FOR?
YOU'VE GOT A VISITOR.
...
I'M SORRY FOR STOPPING BY DURING WORK.
IT'S NOTHING... UH...
I THOUGHT FASTER WOULD BE BETTER, SO I CALLED YOUR OFFICE AND HAD THEM TELL ME WHERE YOU WERE RECORDING.

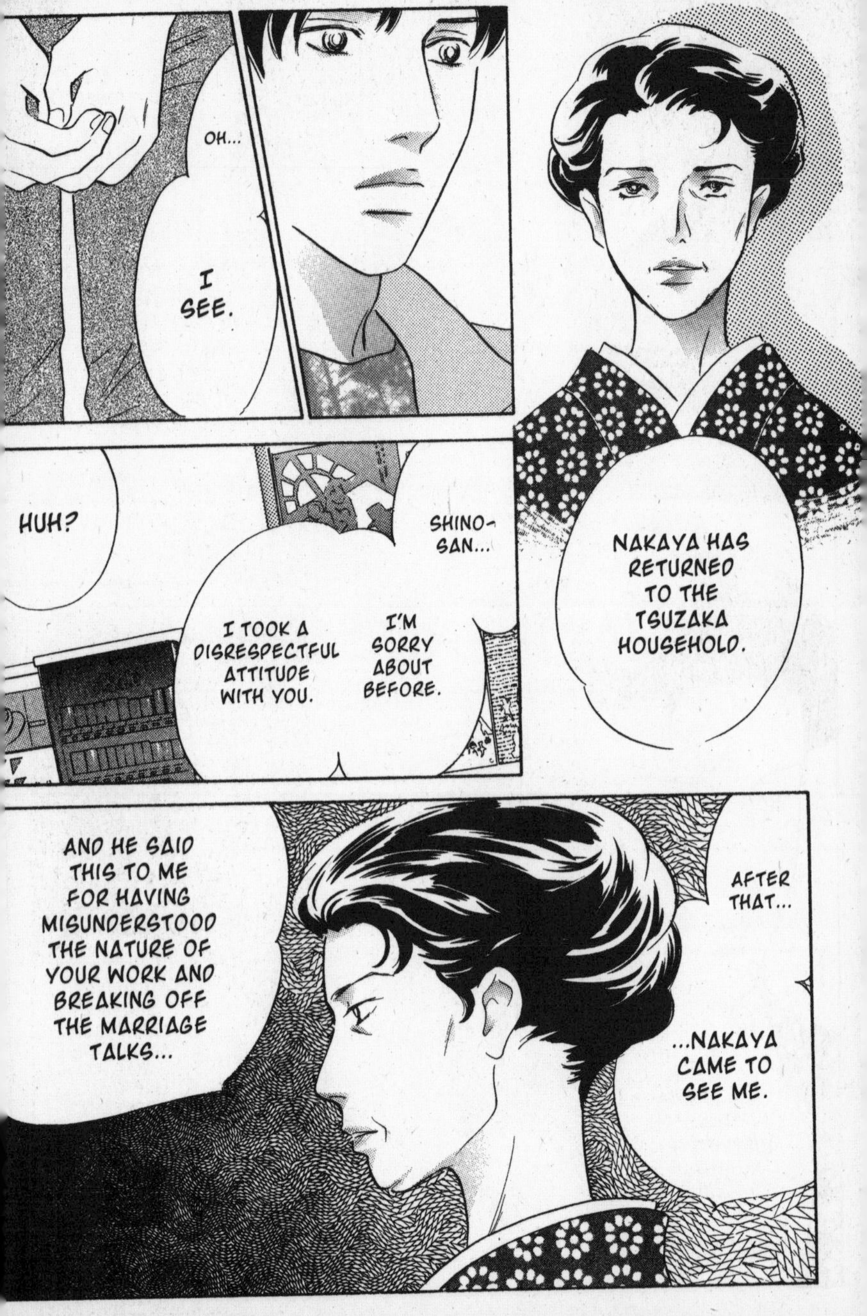
NAKAYA HAS RETURNED TO THE TSUZAKA HOUSEHOLD.
OH...
I SEE.
SHINO-SAN...
I'M SORRY ABOUT BEFORE.
I TOOK A DISRESPECTFUL ATTITUDE WITH YOU.
HUH?
AFTER THAT...
...NAKAYA CAME TO SEE ME.
AND HE SAID THIS TO ME FOR HAVING MISUNDERSTOOD THE NATURE OF YOUR WORK AND BREAKING OFF THE MARRIAGE TALKS...

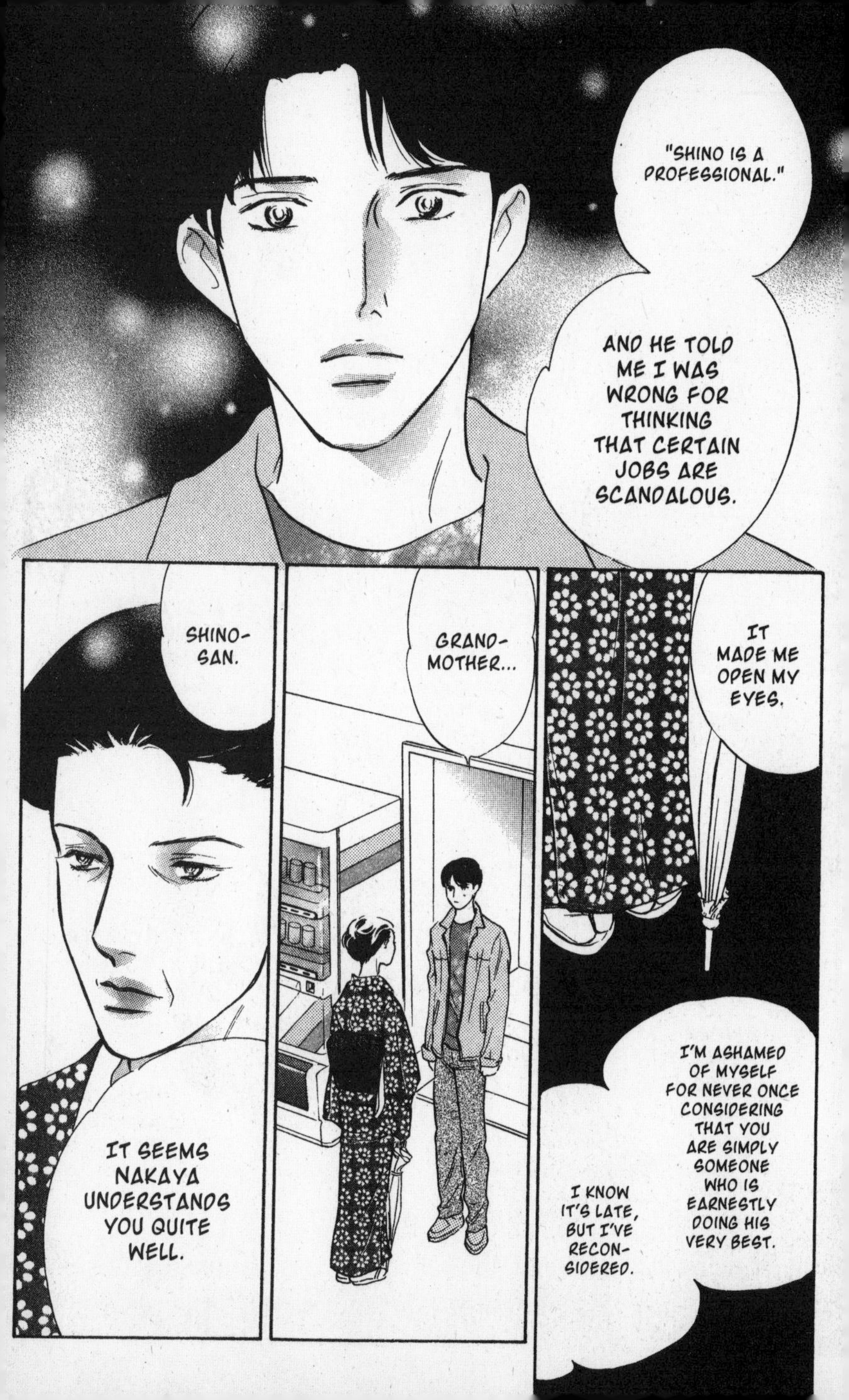
"SHINO IS A PROFESSIONAL."
AND HE TOLD ME I WAS WRONG FOR THINKING THAT CERTAIN JOBS ARE SCANDALOUS.
IT MADE ME OPEN MY EYES.
I'M ASHAMED OF MYSELF FOR NEVER ONCE CONSIDERING THAT YOU ARE SIMPLY SOMEONE WHO IS EARNESTLY DOING HIS VERY BEST.
I KNOW IT'S LATE, BUT I'VE RECON-SIDERED.
GRAND-MOTHER...
SHINO-SAN.
IT SEEMS NAKAYA UNDERSTANDS YOU QUITE WELL.

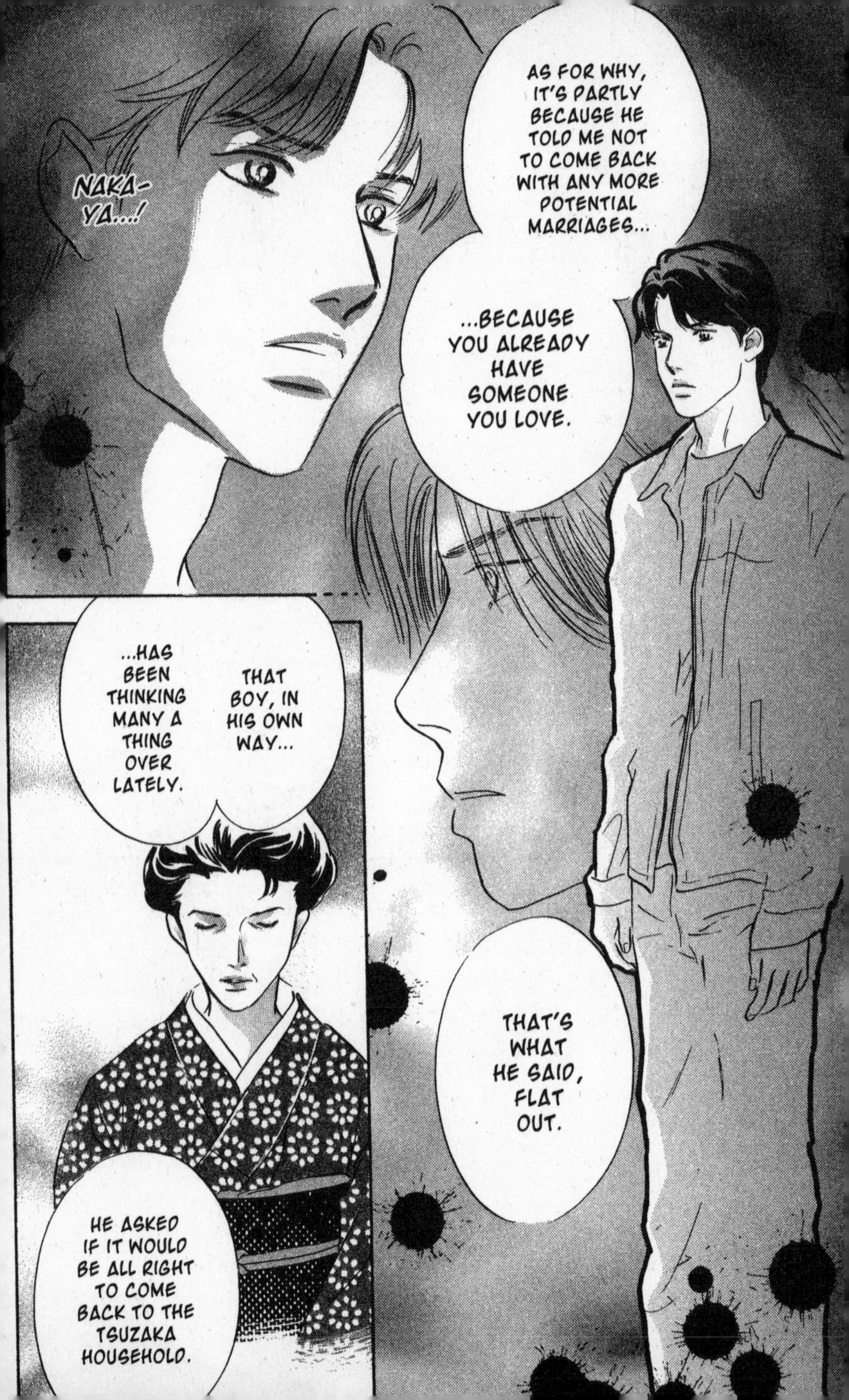
AS FOR WHY, IT'S PARTLY BECAUSE HE TOLD ME NOT TO COME BACK WITH ANY MORE POTENTIAL MARRIAGES...
...BECAUSE YOU ALREADY HAVE SOMEONE YOU LOVE.
NAKA-YA...!
THAT'S WHAT HE SAID, FLAT OUT.
THAT BOY, IN HIS OWN WAY...
...HAS BEEN THINKING MANY A THING OVER LATELY.
HE ASKED IF IT WOULD BE ALL RIGHT TO COME BACK TO THE TSUZAKA HOUSEHOLD.

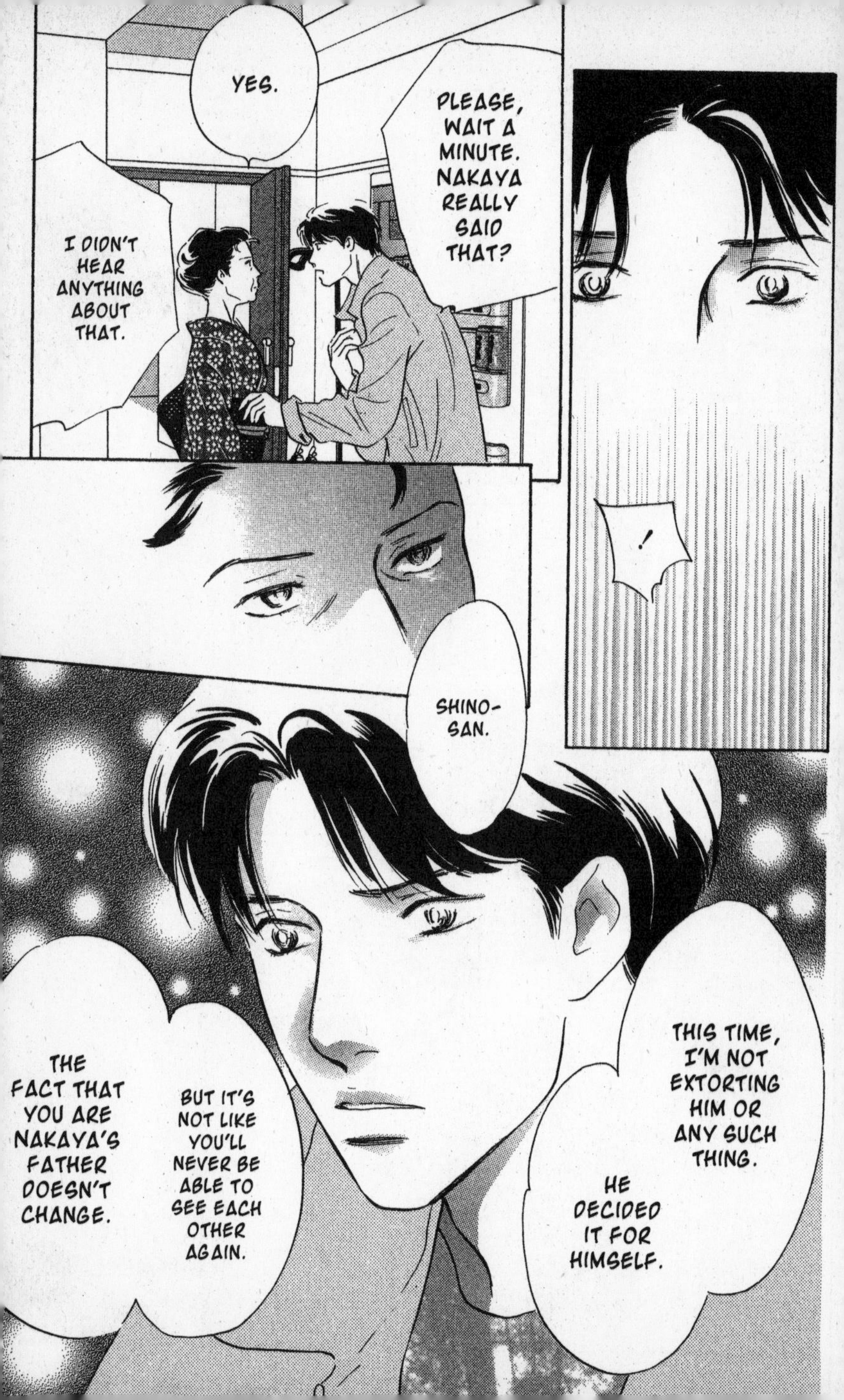
PLEASE, WAIT A MINUTE. NAKAYA REALLY SAID THAT?
YES.
I DIDN'T HEAR ANYTHING ABOUT THAT.
!
SHINO-SAN.
THIS TIME, I'M NOT EXTORTING HIM OR ANY SUCH THING.
HE DECIDED IT FOR HIMSELF.
BUT IT'S NOT LIKE YOU'LL NEVER BE ABLE TO SEE EACH OTHER AGAIN.
THE FACT THAT YOU ARE NAKAYA'S FATHER DOESN'T CHANGE.

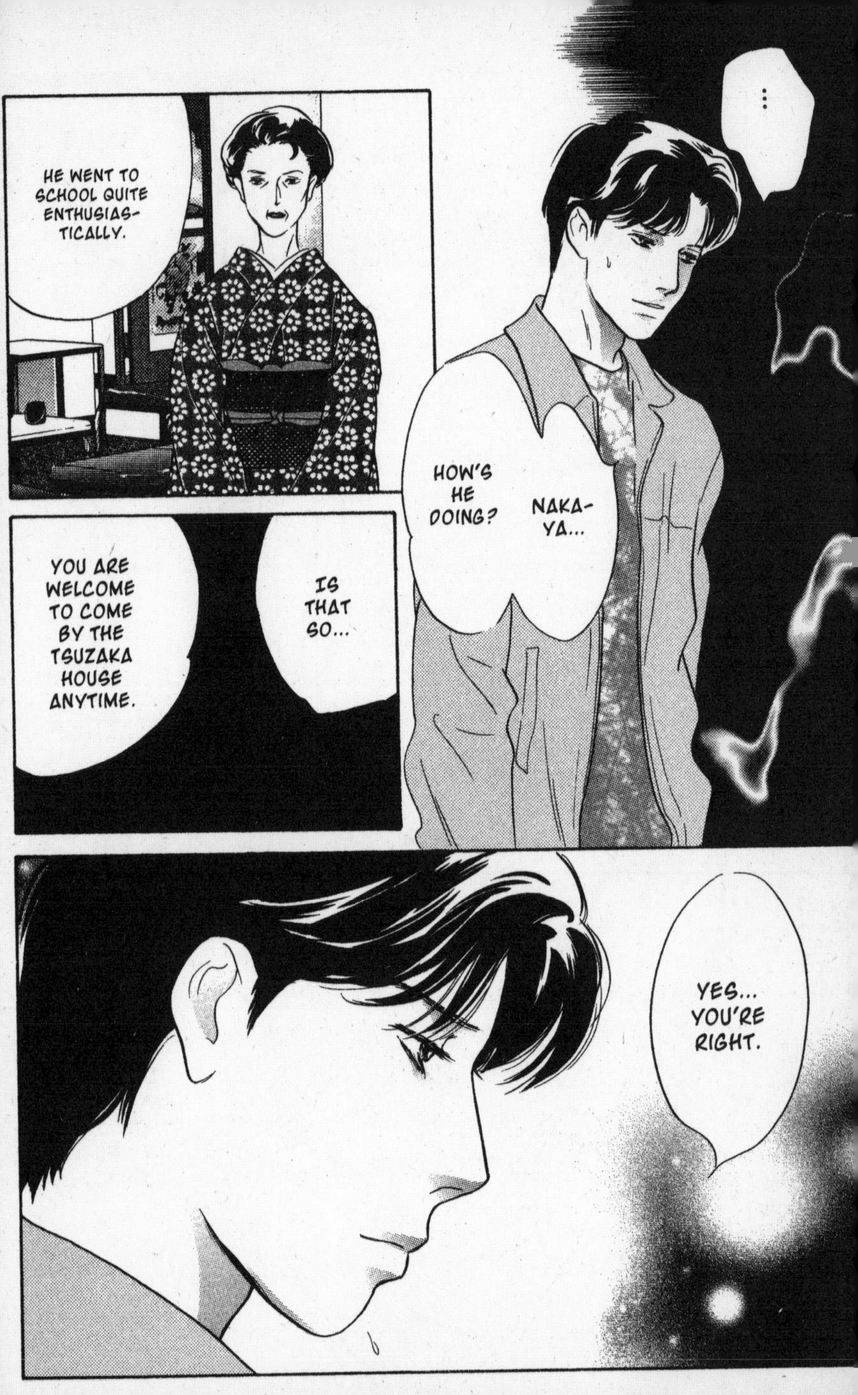
...
NAKA-YA...
HOW'S HE DOING?
HE WENT TO SCHOOL QUITE ENTHUSIASTICALLY.
IS THAT SO...
YOU ARE WELCOME TO COME BY THE TSUZAKA HOUSE ANYTIME.
YES... YOU'RE RIGHT.

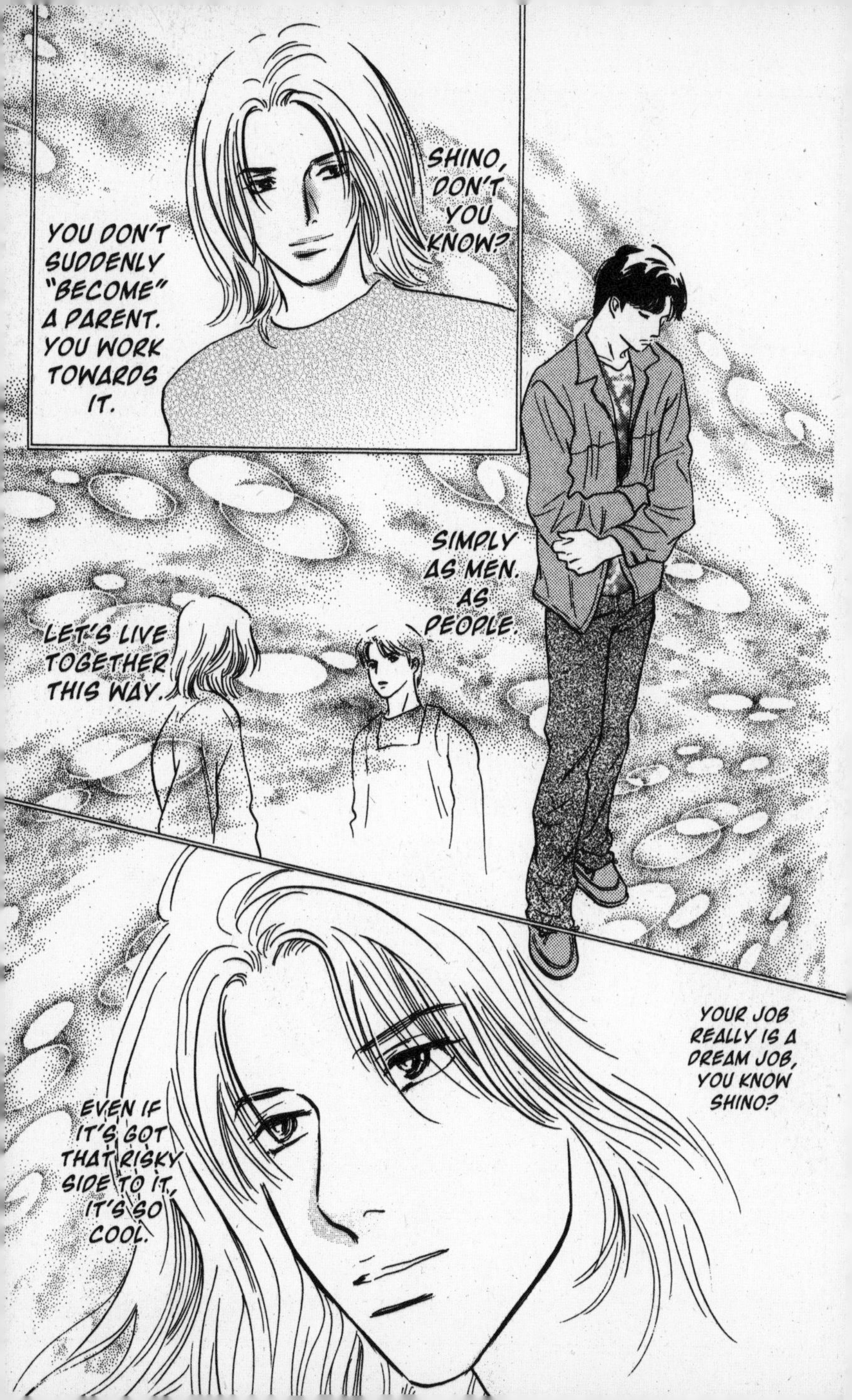
SHINO, DON'T YOU KNOW?
YOU DON'T SUDDENLY "BECOME" A PARENT. YOU WORK TOWARDS IT.
SIMPLY AS MEN. AS PEOPLE.
LET'S LIVE TOGETHER THIS WAY.
YOUR JOB REALLY IS A DREAM JOB, YOU KNOW SHINO?
EVEN IF IT'S GOT THAT RISKY SIDE TO IT, IT'S SO COOL.

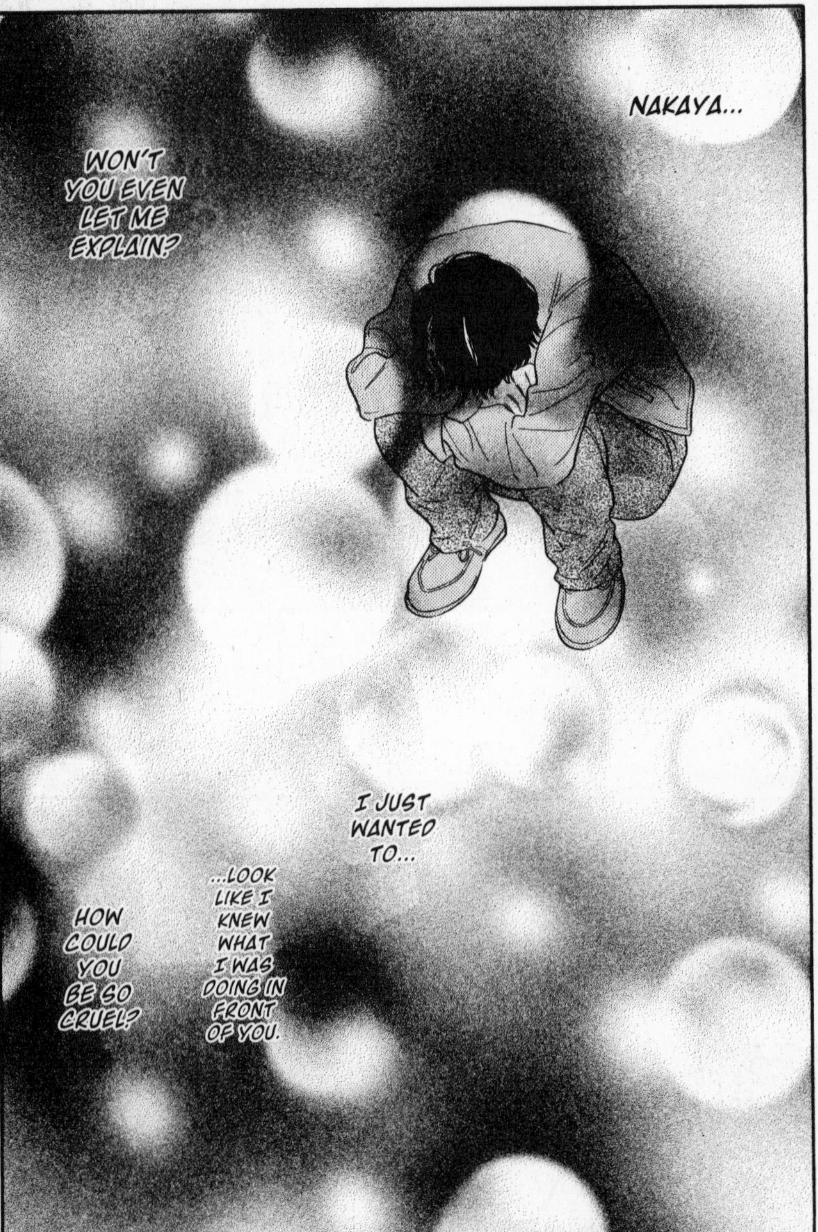
NAKAYA...
WON'T YOU EVEN LET ME EXPLAIN?
I JUST WANTED TO...
...LOOK LIKE I KNEW WHAT I WAS DOING IN FRONT OF YOU.
HOW COULD YOU BE SO CRUEL?

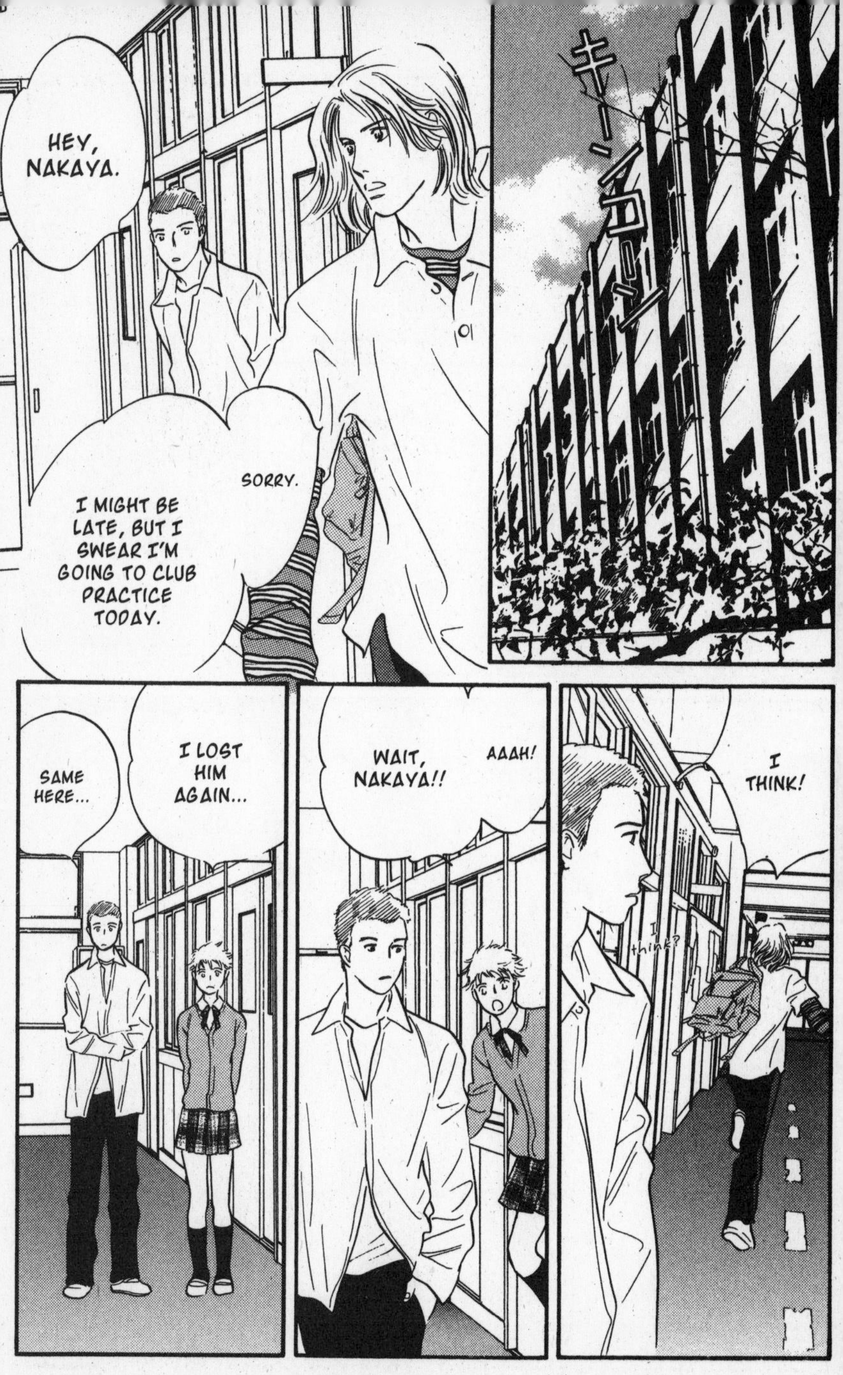
HEY, NAKAYA.
SORRY.
I MIGHT BE LATE, BUT I SWEAR I'M GOING TO CLUB PRACTICE TODAY.
I THINK!
I think?
AAAH!
WAIT, NAKAYA!!
I LOST HIM AGAIN...
SAME HERE...

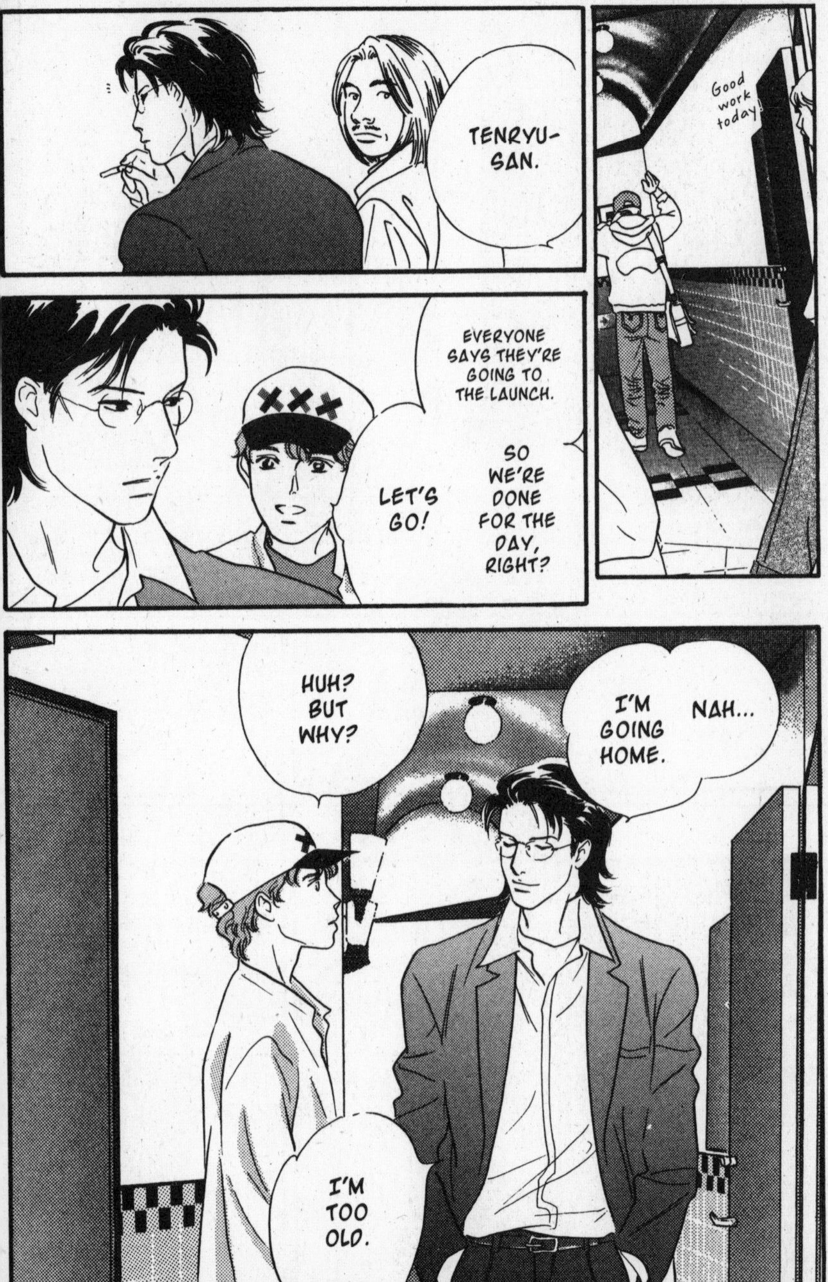
Good work today!
TENRYU-SAN.
EVERYONE SAYS THEY'RE GOING TO THE LAUNCH.
SO WE'RE DONE FOR THE DAY, RIGHT?
LET'S GO!
NAH...
I'M GOING HOME.
HUH? BUT WHY?
I'M TOO OLD.

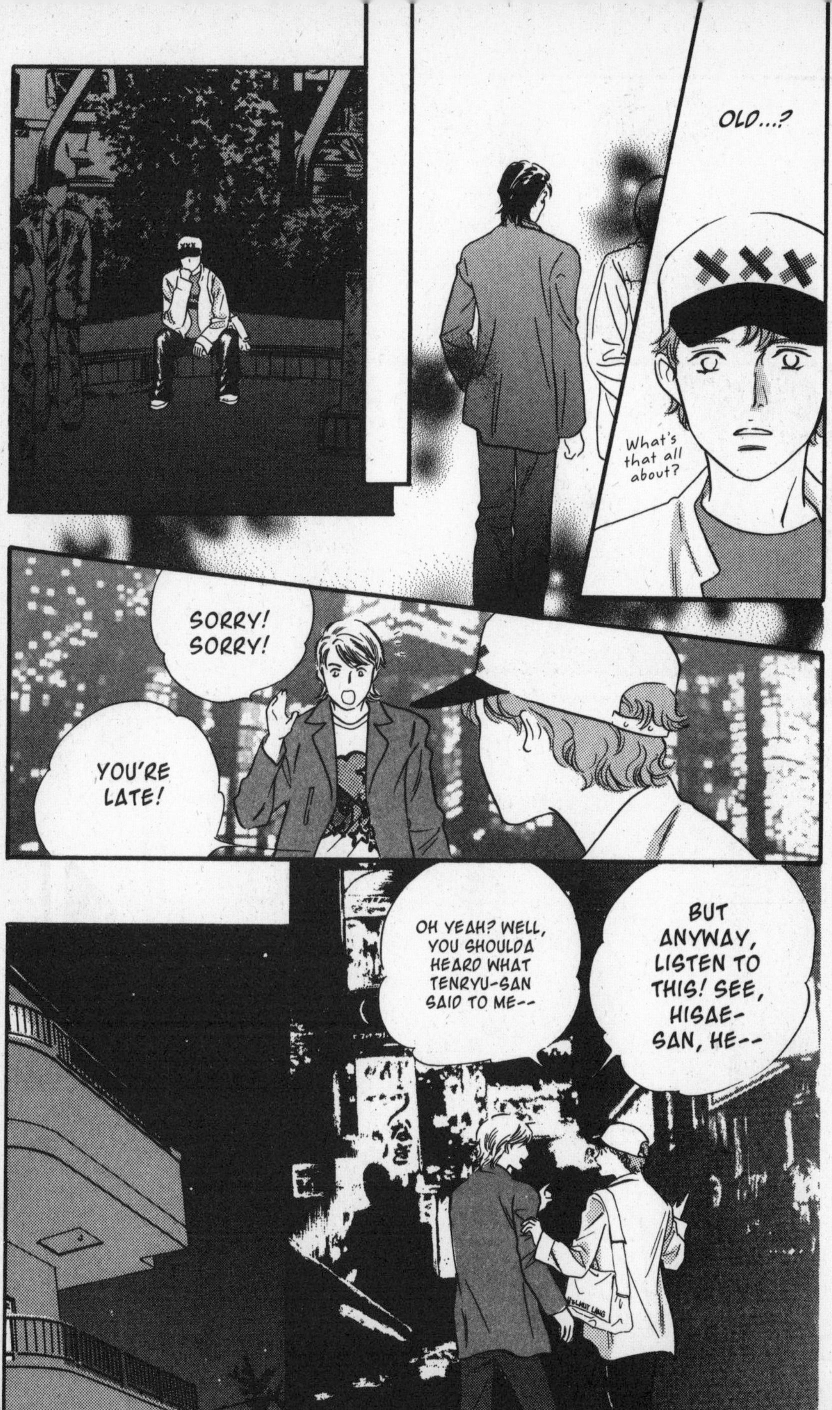
OLD...?
What's that all about?
SORRY! SORRY!
YOU'RE LATE!
BUT ANYWAY, LISTEN TO THIS! SEE, HISAE-SAN, HE--
OH YEAH? WELL, YOU SHOULDA HEARD WHAT TENRYU-SAN SAID TO ME--

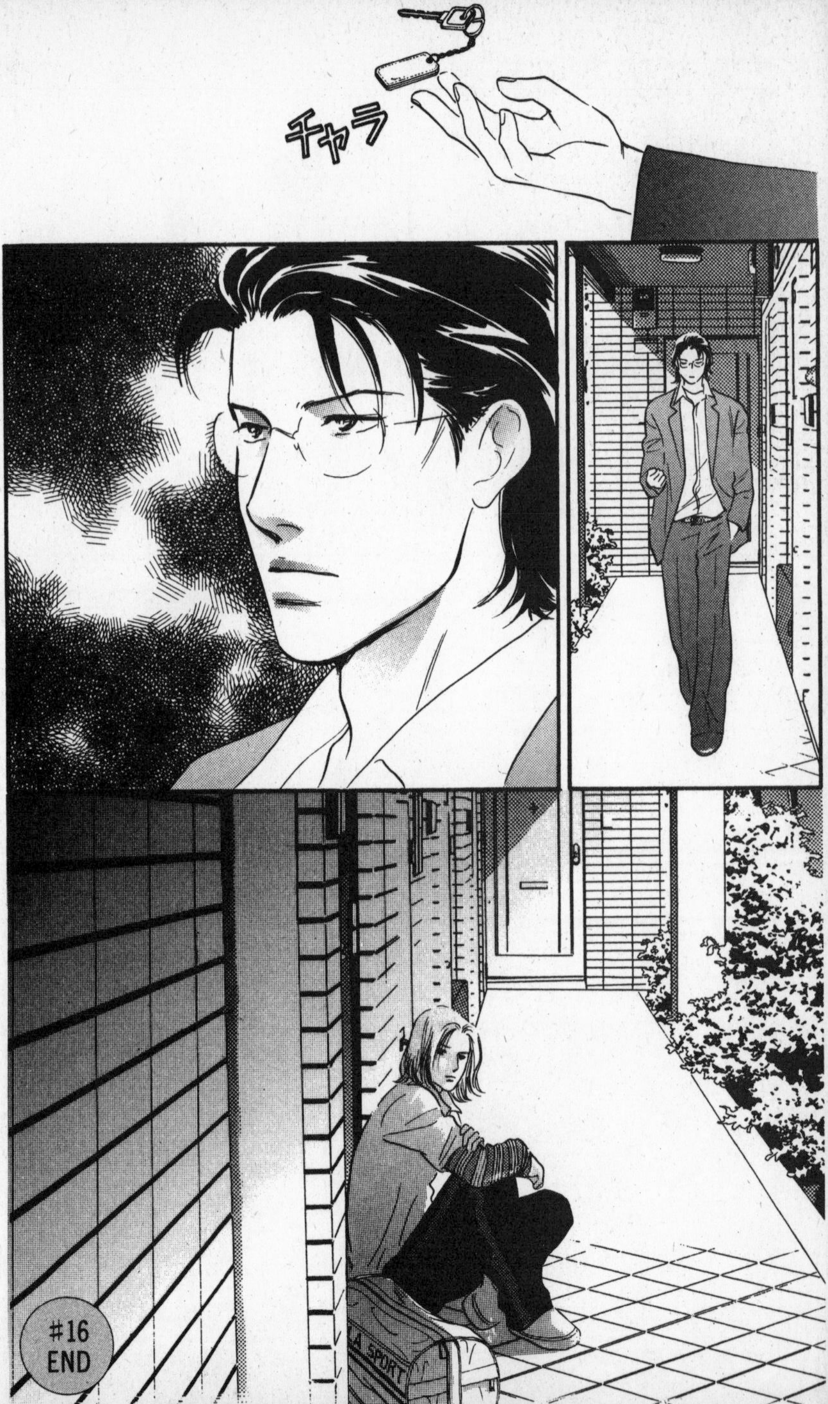
チャラ
#16 END

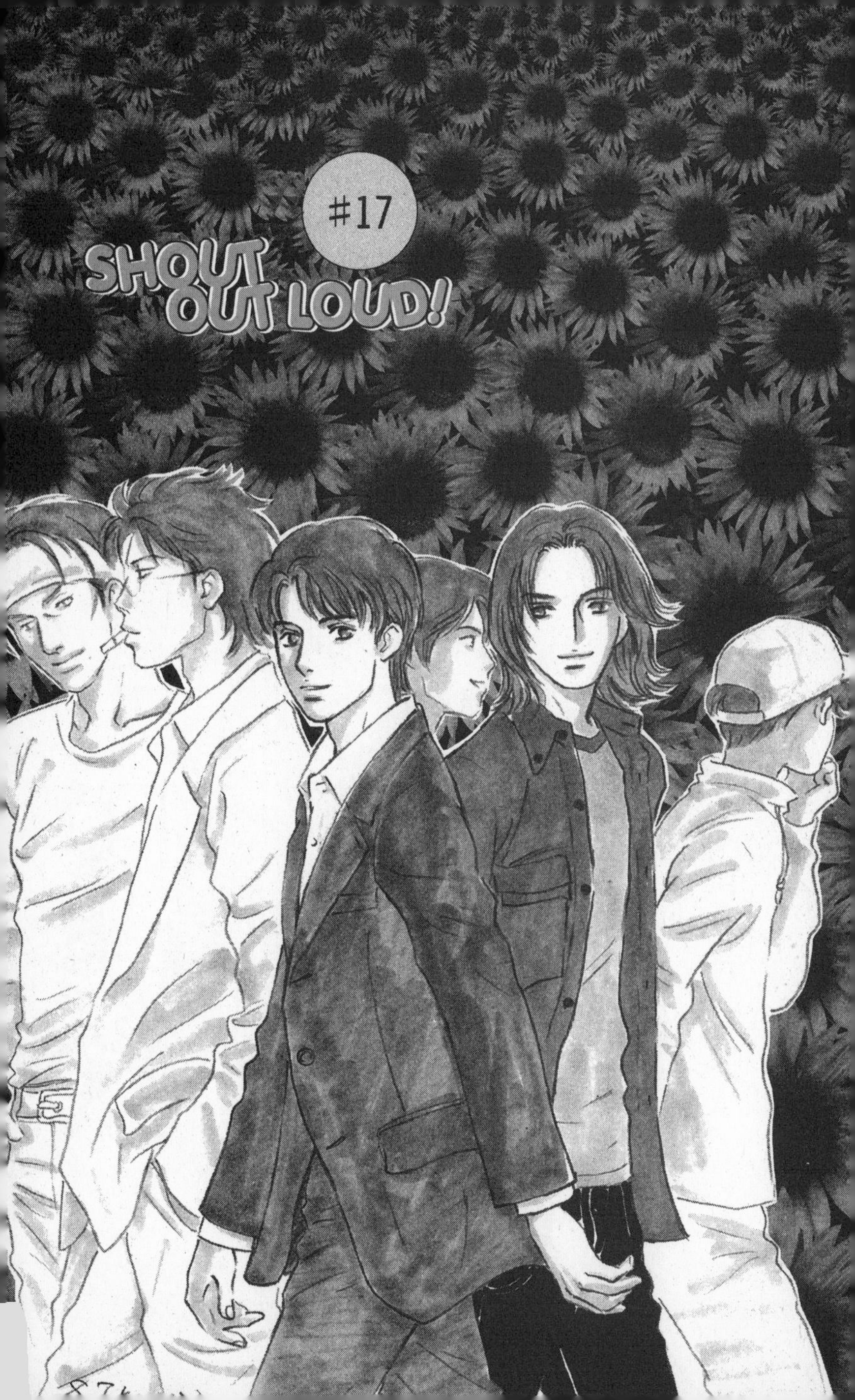
#17
SHOUT OUT LOUD!

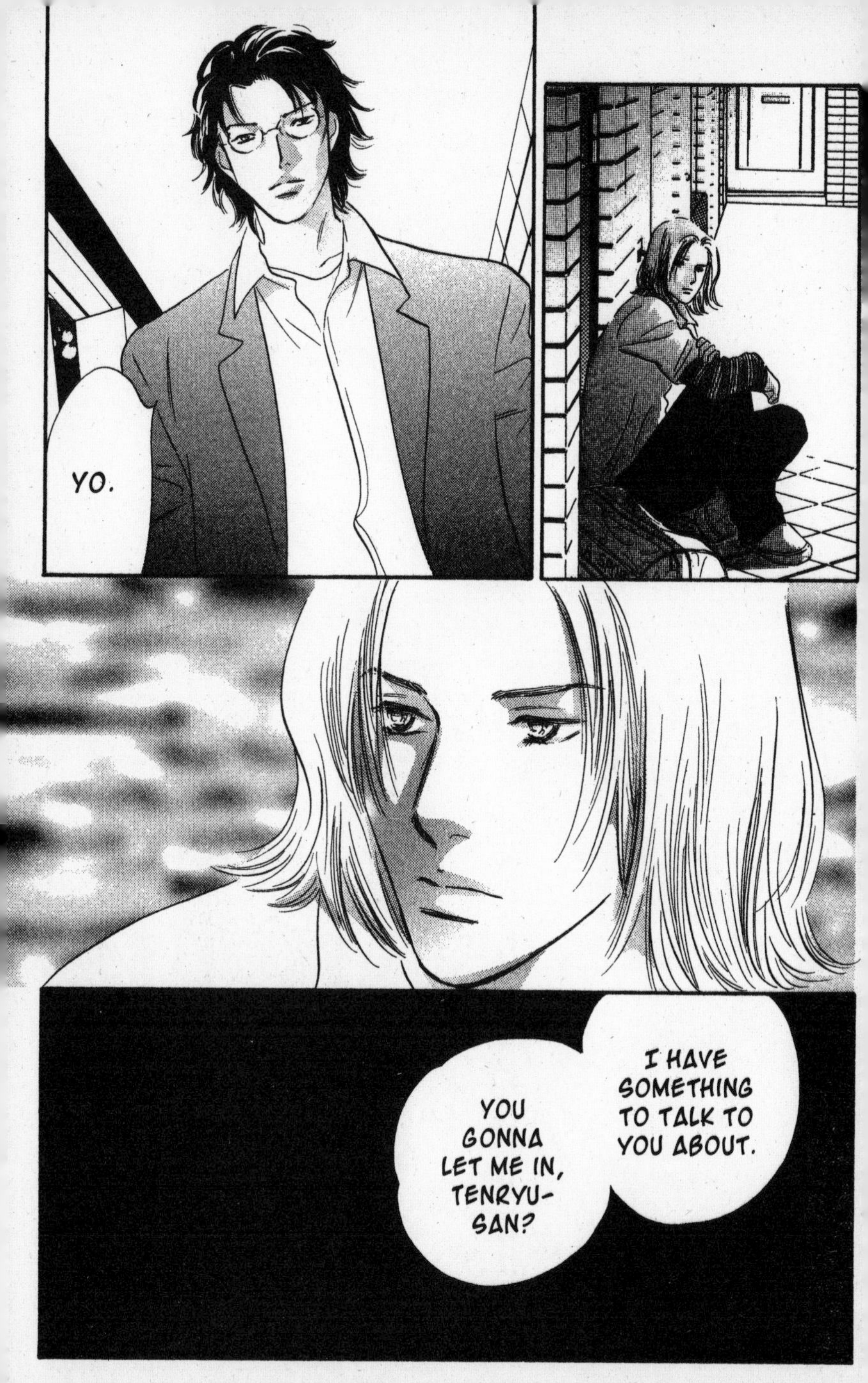
YO.
I HAVE SOMETHING TO TALK TO YOU ABOUT.
YOU GONNA LET ME IN, TENRYU-SAN?

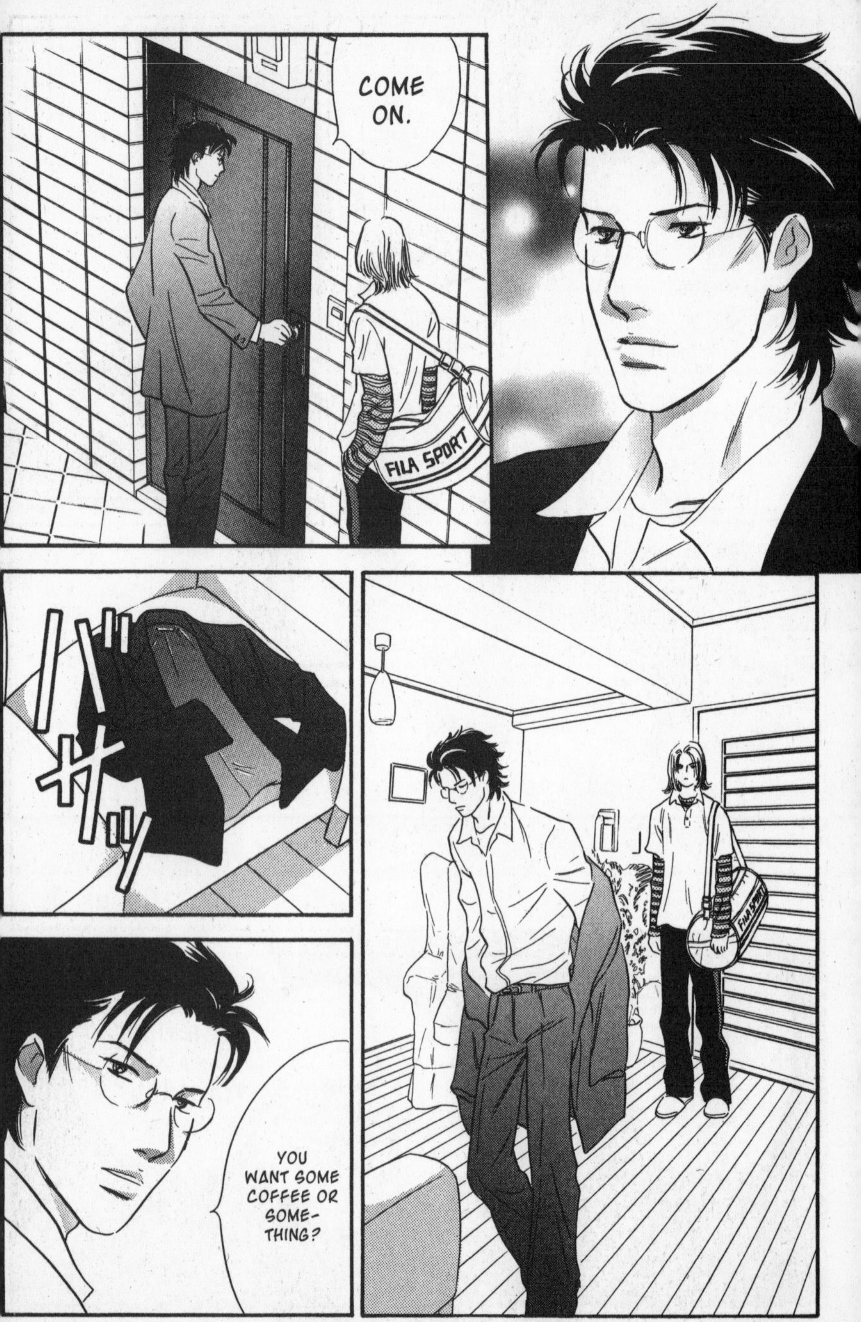
COME ON.
FILA SPORT
FILA SPORT
バサッ
YOU WANT SOME COFFEE OR SOME-THING?

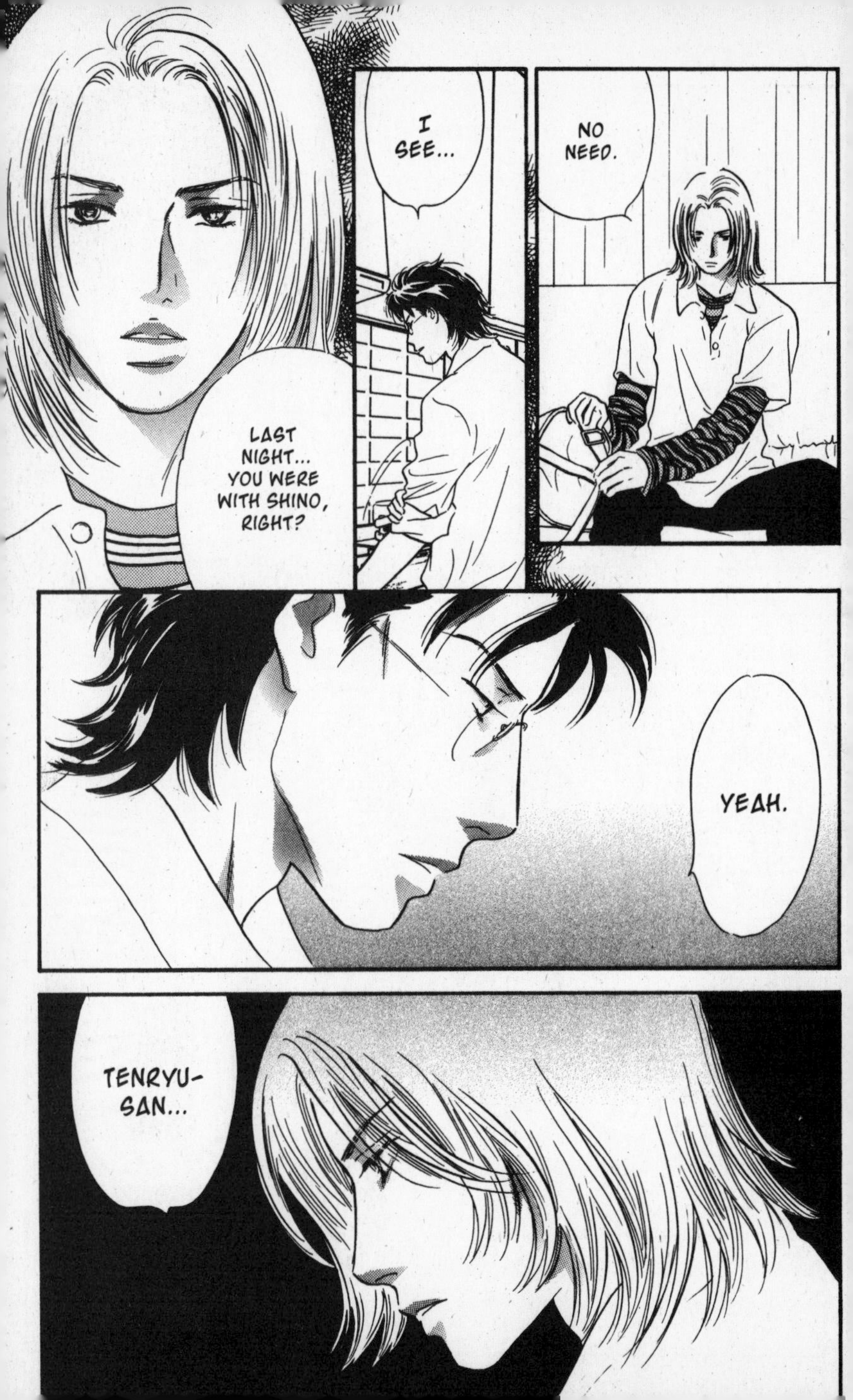
NO NEED.
I SEE...
LAST NIGHT... YOU WERE WITH SHINO, RIGHT?
YEAH.
TENRYU-SAN...

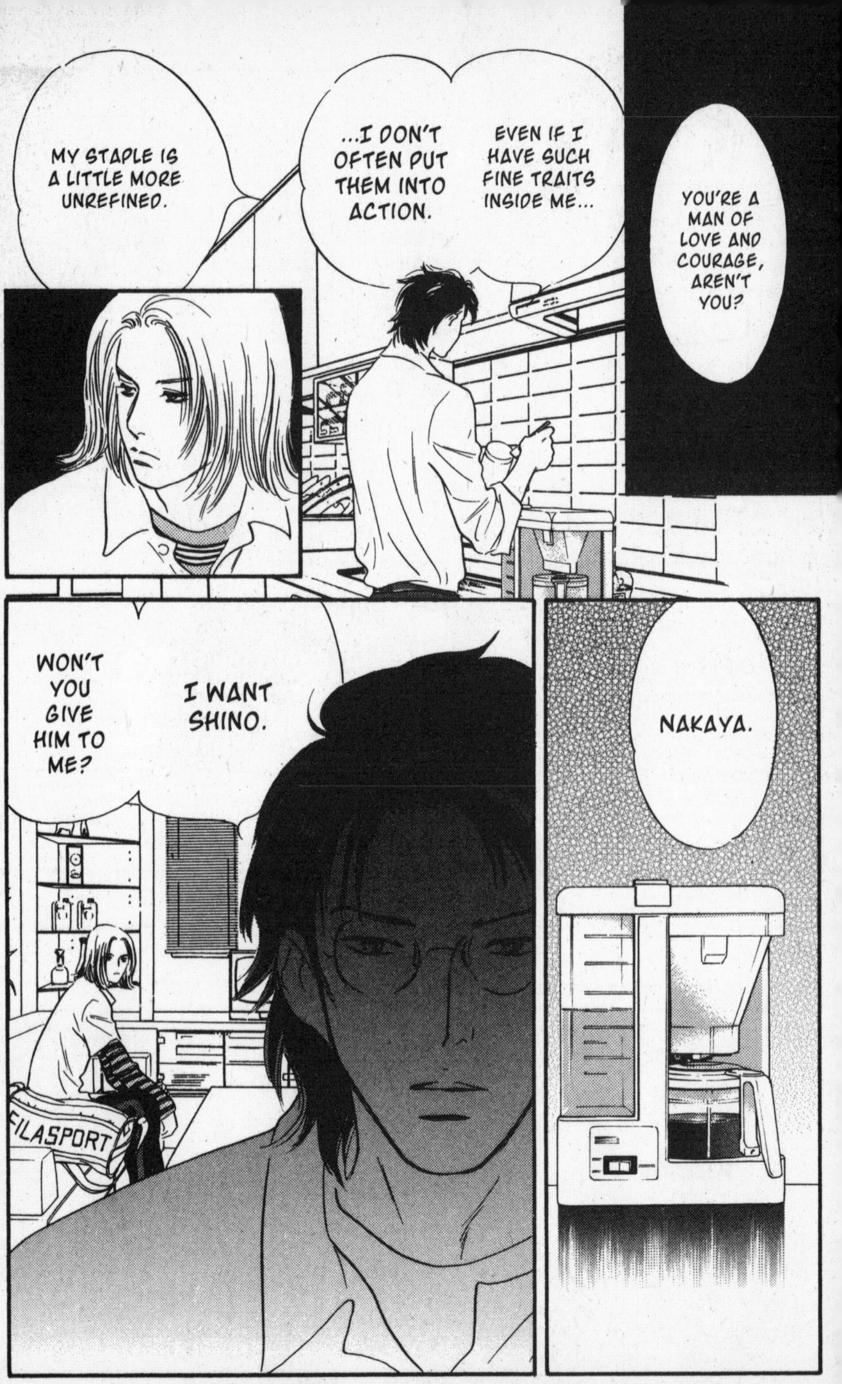
YOU'RE A MAN OF LOVE AND COURAGE, AREN'T YOU?
EVEN IF I HAVE SUCH FINE TRAITS INSIDE ME...
...I DON'T OFTEN PUT THEM INTO ACTION.
MY STAPLE IS A LITTLE MORE UNREFINED.
NAKAYA.
I WANT SHINO.
WON'T YOU GIVE HIM TO ME?
FILASPORT

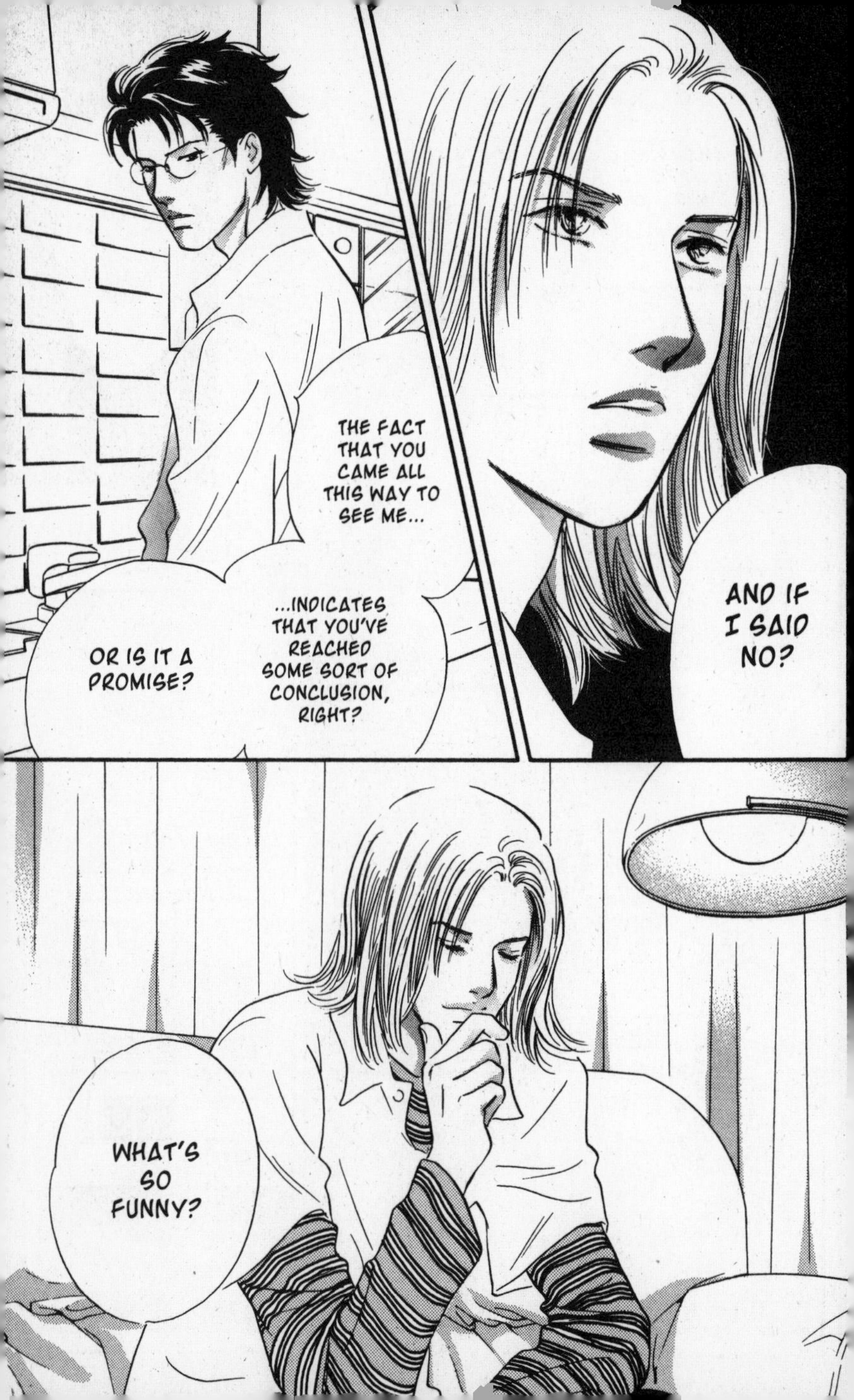
AND IF I SAID NO?
THE FACT THAT YOU CAME ALL THIS WAY TO SEE ME...
...INDICATES THAT YOU'VE REACHED SOME SORT OF CONCLUSION, RIGHT?
OR IS IT A PROMISE?
WHAT'S SO FUNNY?

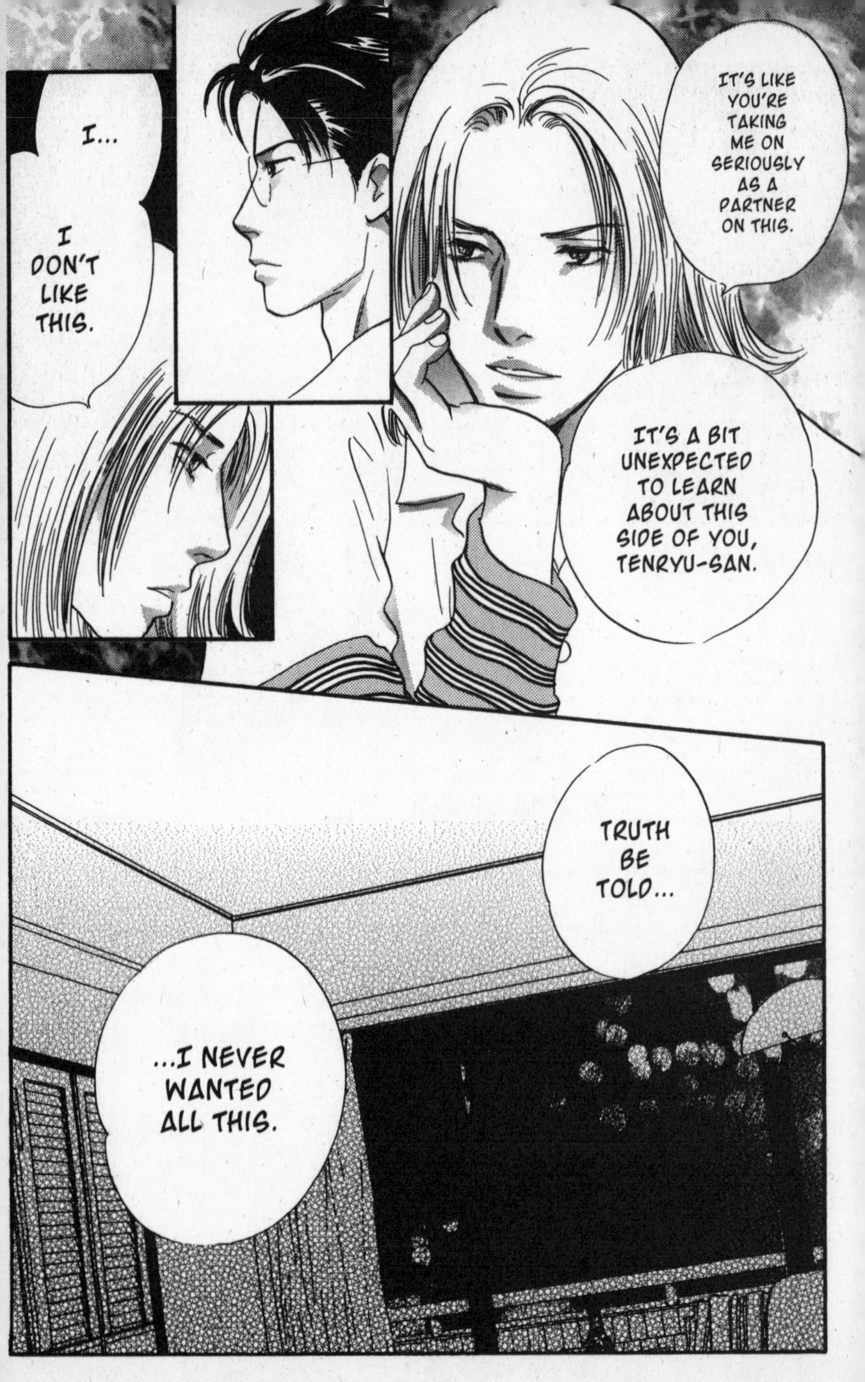
IT'S LIKE YOU'RE TAKING ME ON SERIOUSLY AS A PARTNER ON THIS.
IT'S A BIT UNEXPECTED TO LEARN ABOUT THIS SIDE OF YOU, TENRYU-SAN.
I...
I DON'T LIKE THIS.
TRUTH BE TOLD...
...I NEVER WANTED ALL THIS.

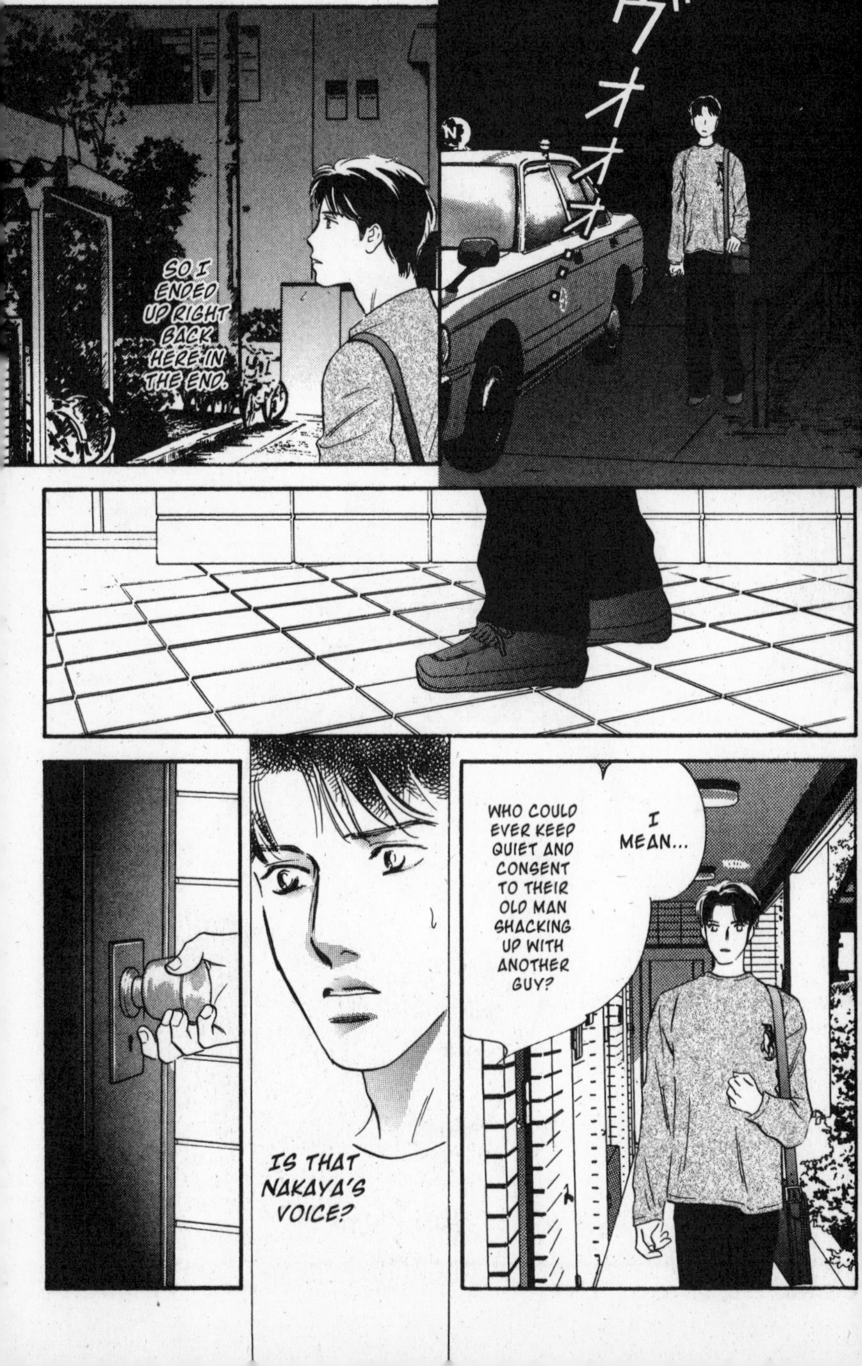
ヴオオオオ
SO I ENDED UP RIGHT BACK HERE IN THE END.
I MEAN...
WHO COULD EVER KEEP QUIET AND CONSENT TO THEIR OLD MAN SHACKING UP WITH ANOTHER GUY?
IS THAT NAKAYA'S VOICE?

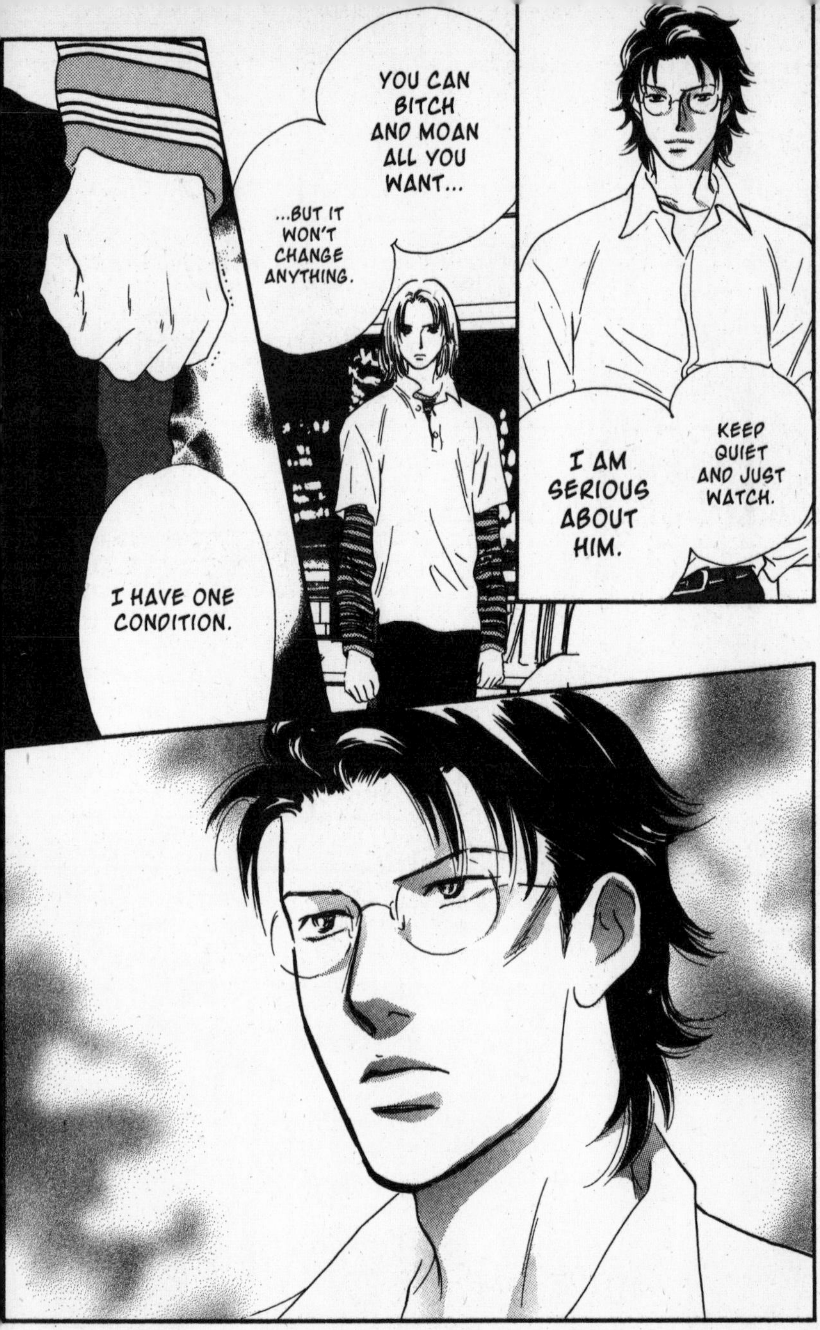
KEEP QUIET AND JUST WATCH.
I AM SERIOUS ABOUT HIM.
YOU CAN BITCH AND MOAN ALL YOU WANT...
...BUT IT WON'T CHANGE ANYTHING.
I HAVE ONE CONDITION.

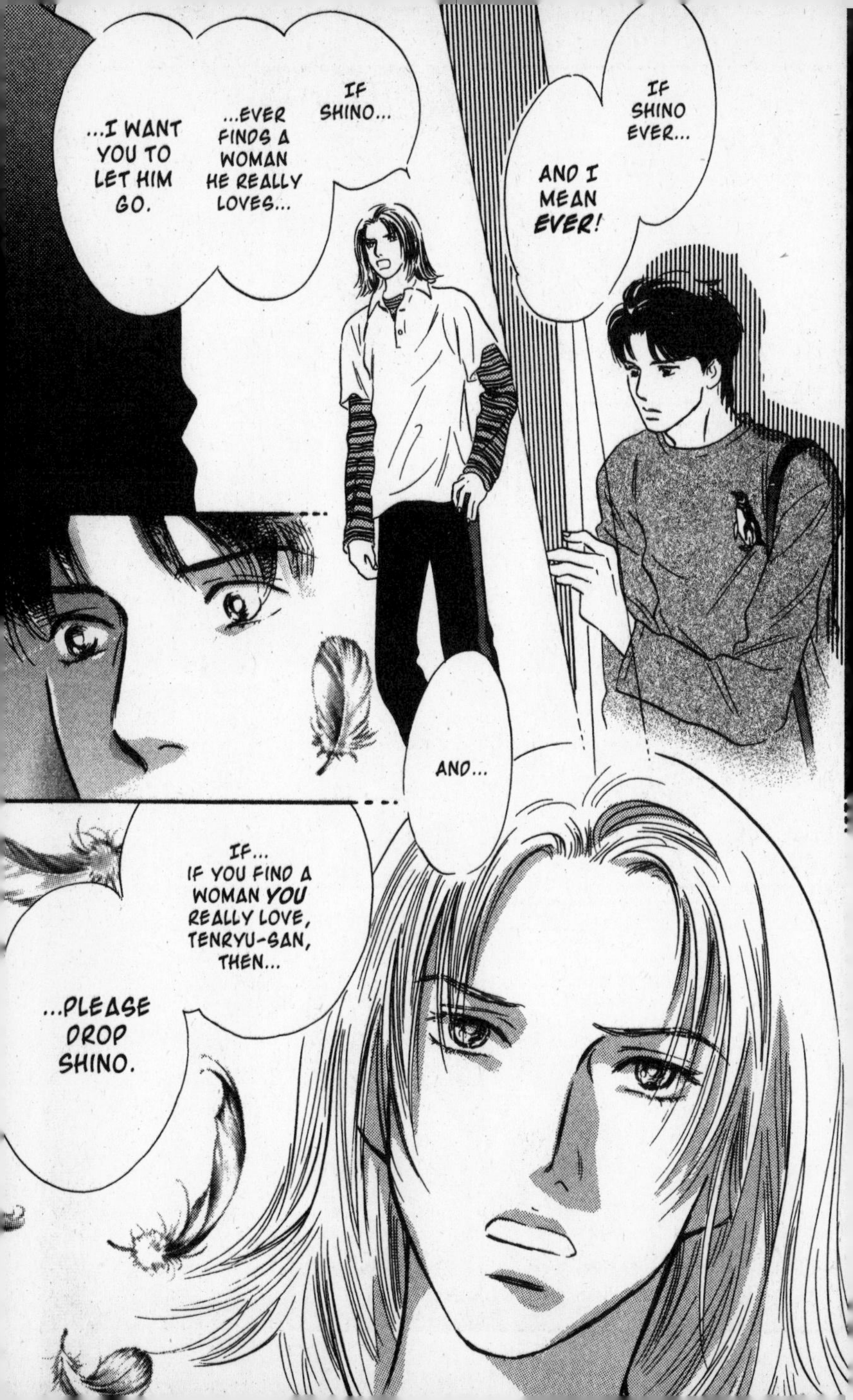
IF SHINO EVER... AND I MEAN *EVER*!
IF SHINO... ...EVER FINDS A WOMAN HE REALLY LOVES... ...I WANT YOU TO LET HIM GO.
AND...
IF... IF YOU FIND A WOMAN *YOU* REALLY LOVE, TENRYU-SAN, THEN... ...PLEASE DROP SHINO.

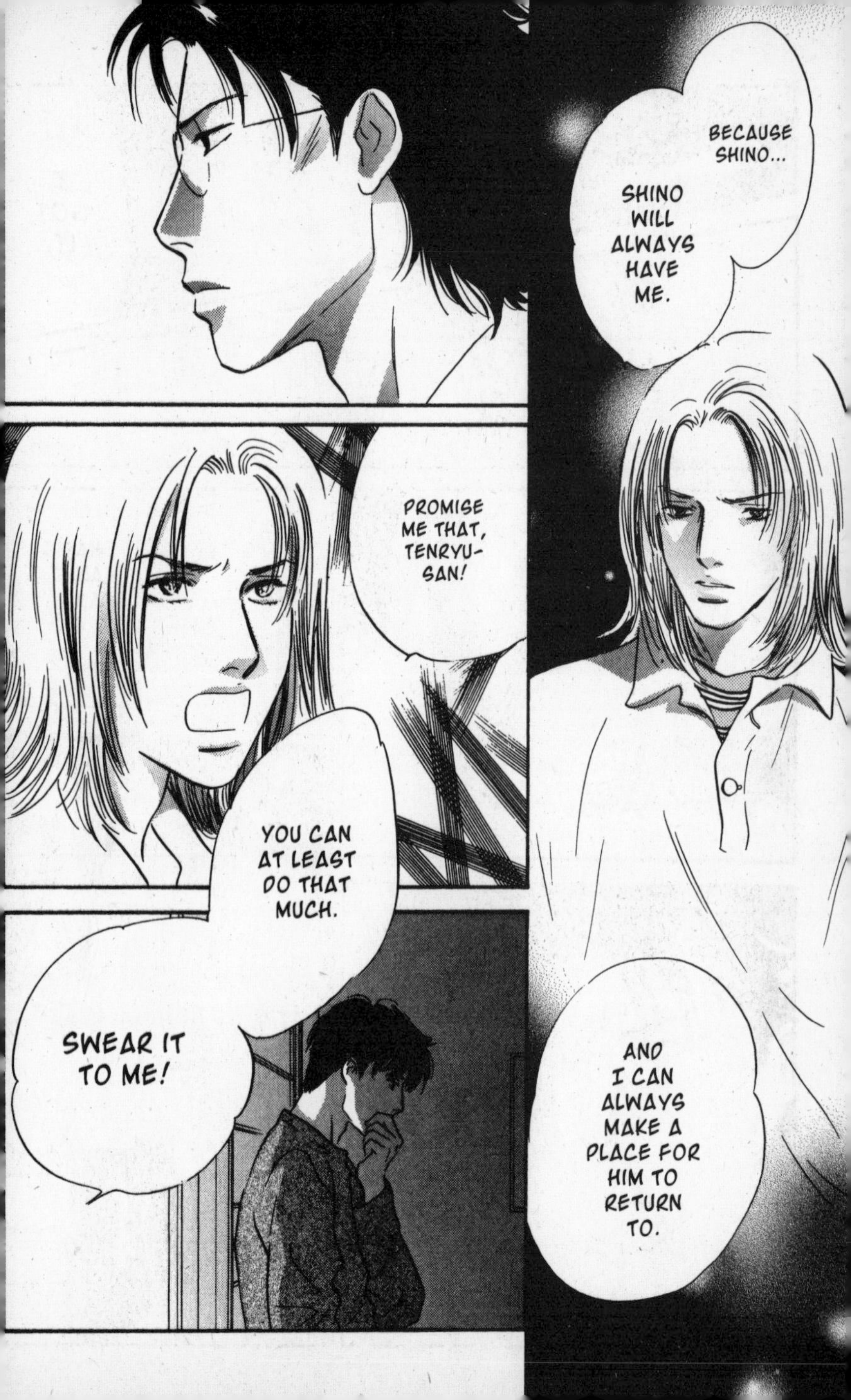
BECAUSE SHINO...
SHINO WILL ALWAYS HAVE ME.
AND I CAN ALWAYS MAKE A PLACE FOR HIM TO RETURN TO.
PROMISE ME THAT, TENRYU-SAN!
YOU CAN AT LEAST DO THAT MUCH.
SWEAR IT TO ME!

I GOT IT.

...

WHAT?

NAKAYA.

THAT'S ALL I WANTED TO SAY.

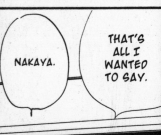

DO YOU REMEMBER WHAT I SAID BEFORE?

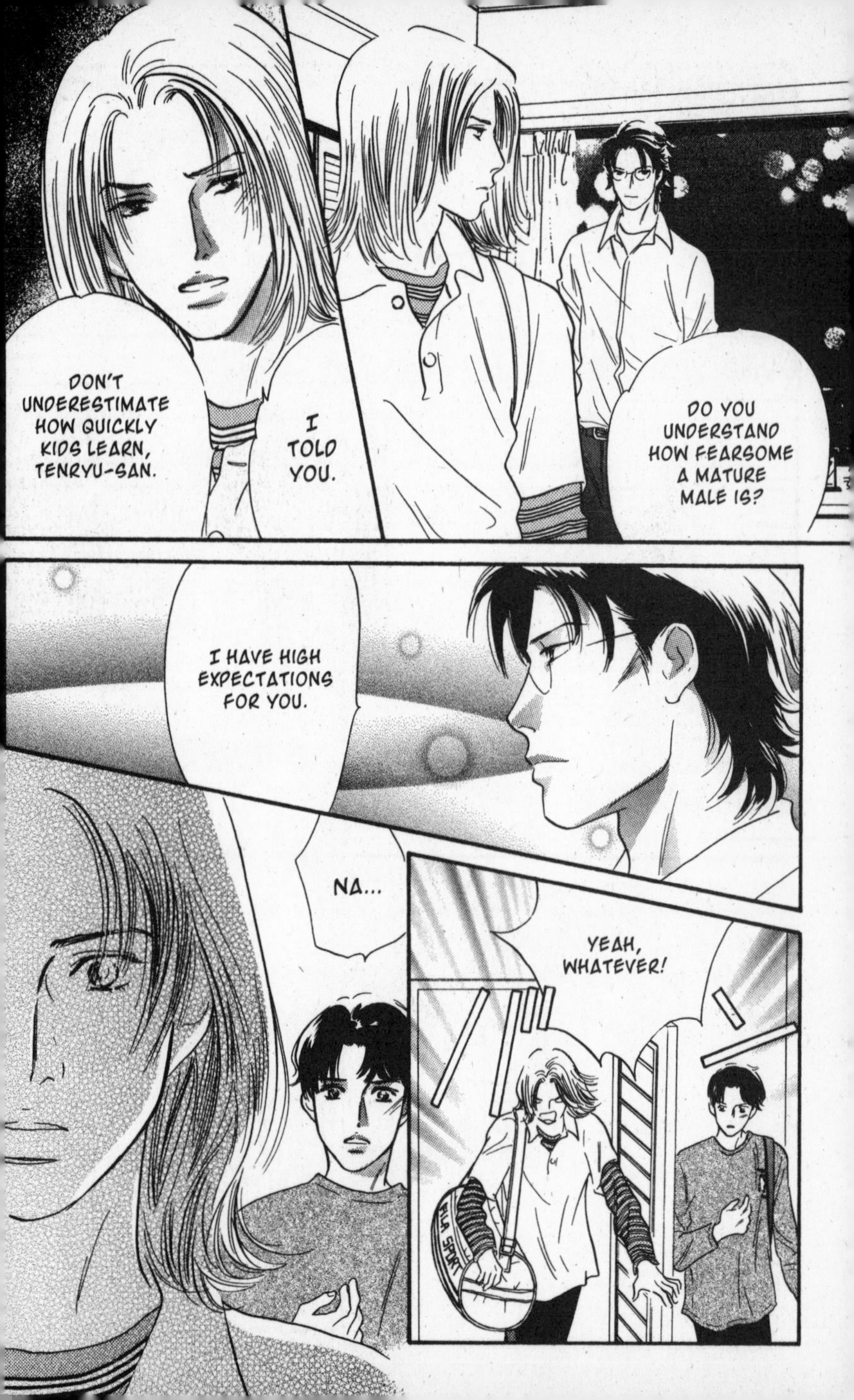
DO YOU UNDERSTAND HOW FEARSOME A MATURE MALE IS?
I TOLD YOU.
DON'T UNDERESTIMATE HOW QUICKLY KIDS LEARN, TENRYU-SAN.
I HAVE HIGH EXPECTATIONS FOR YOU.
YEAH, WHATEVER!
NA...
FILA SPORT

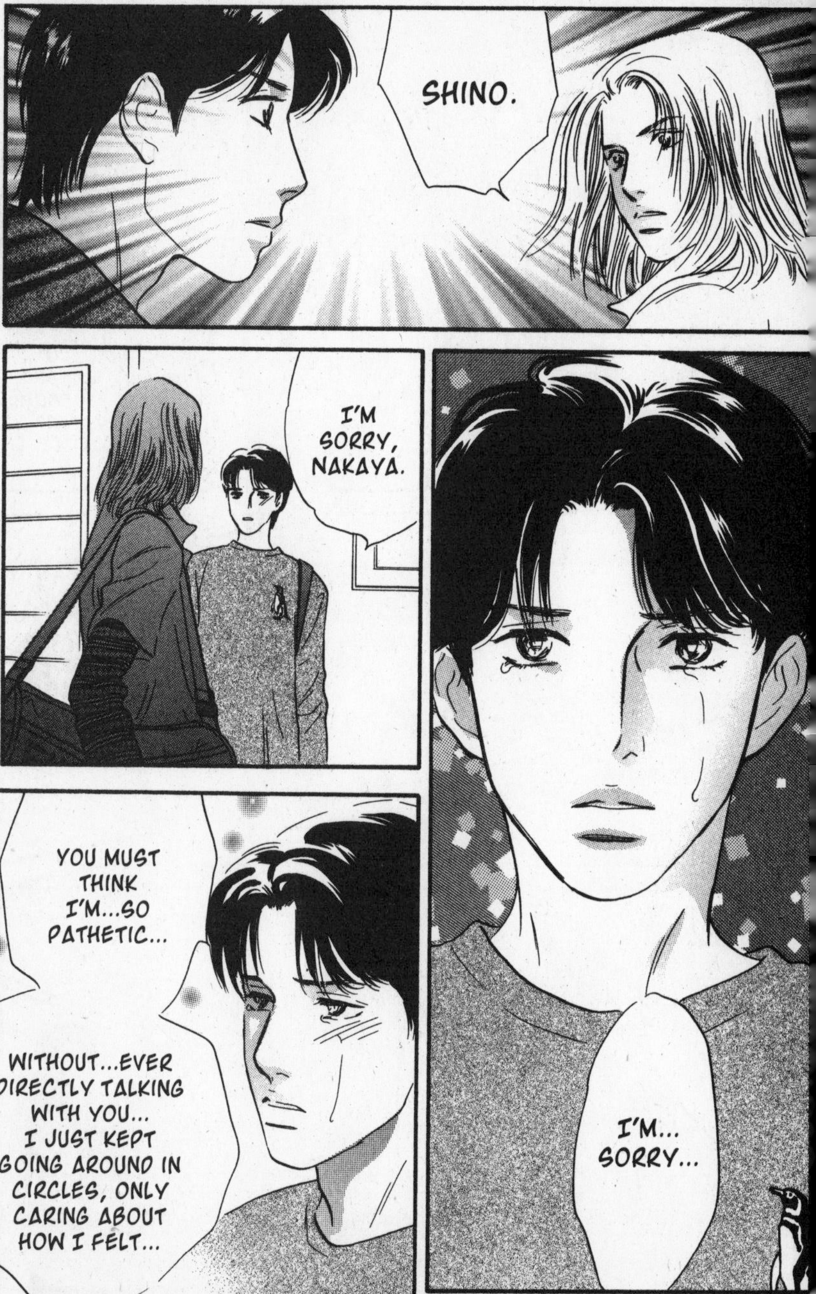
SHINO.
I'M... SORRY...
I'M SORRY, NAKAYA.
YOU MUST THINK I'M...SO PATHETIC...
WITHOUT...EVER DIRECTLY TALKING WITH YOU... I JUST KEPT GOING AROUND IN CIRCLES, ONLY CARING ABOUT HOW I FELT...

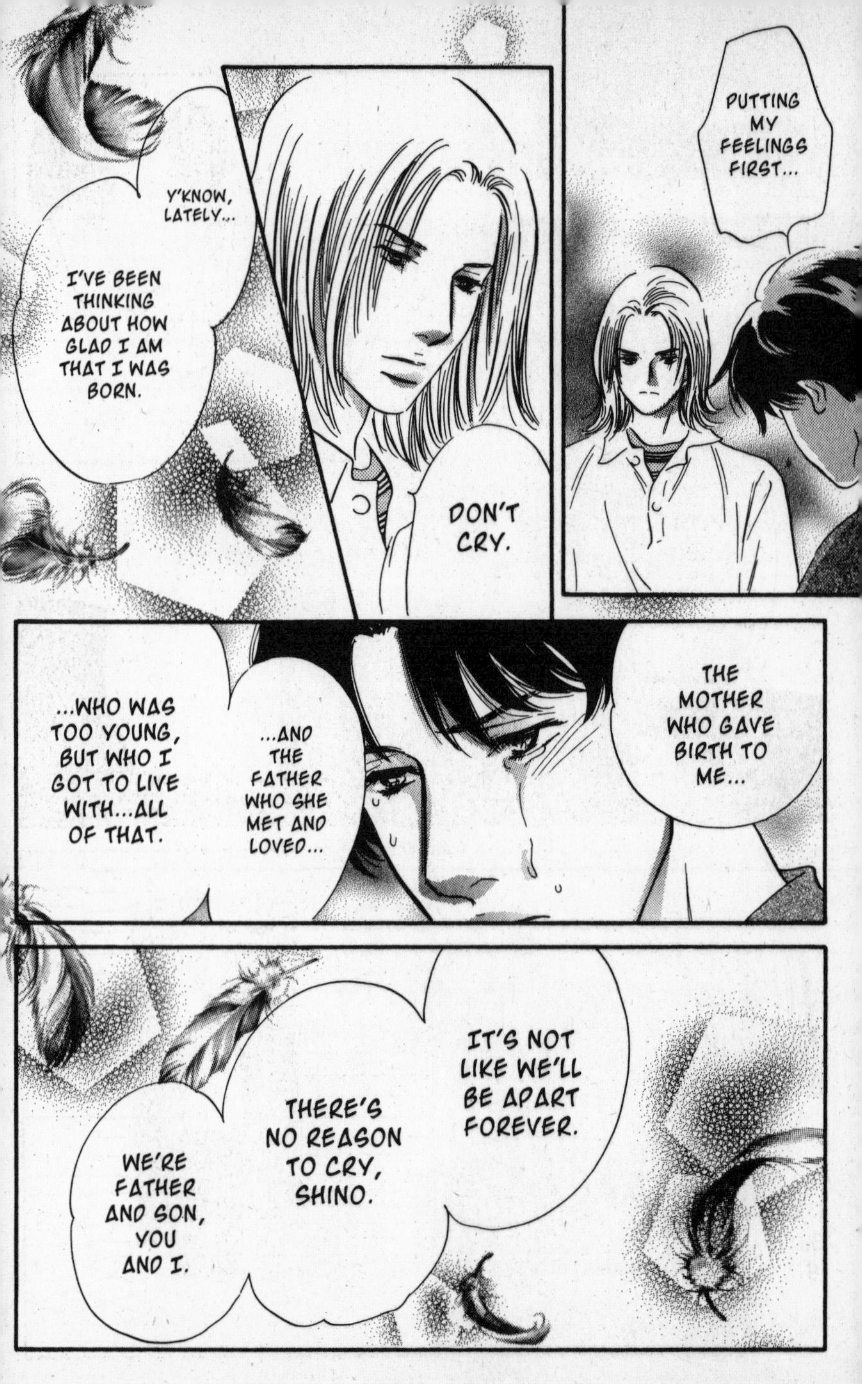
PUTTING MY FEELINGS FIRST...
DON'T CRY.
Y'KNOW, LATELY...
I'VE BEEN THINKING ABOUT HOW GLAD I AM THAT I WAS BORN.
THE MOTHER WHO GAVE BIRTH TO ME...
...AND THE FATHER WHO SHE MET AND LOVED...
...WHO WAS TOO YOUNG, BUT WHO I GOT TO LIVE WITH...ALL OF THAT.
IT'S NOT LIKE WE'LL BE APART FOREVER.
THERE'S NO REASON TO CRY, SHINO.
WE'RE FATHER AND SON, YOU AND I.

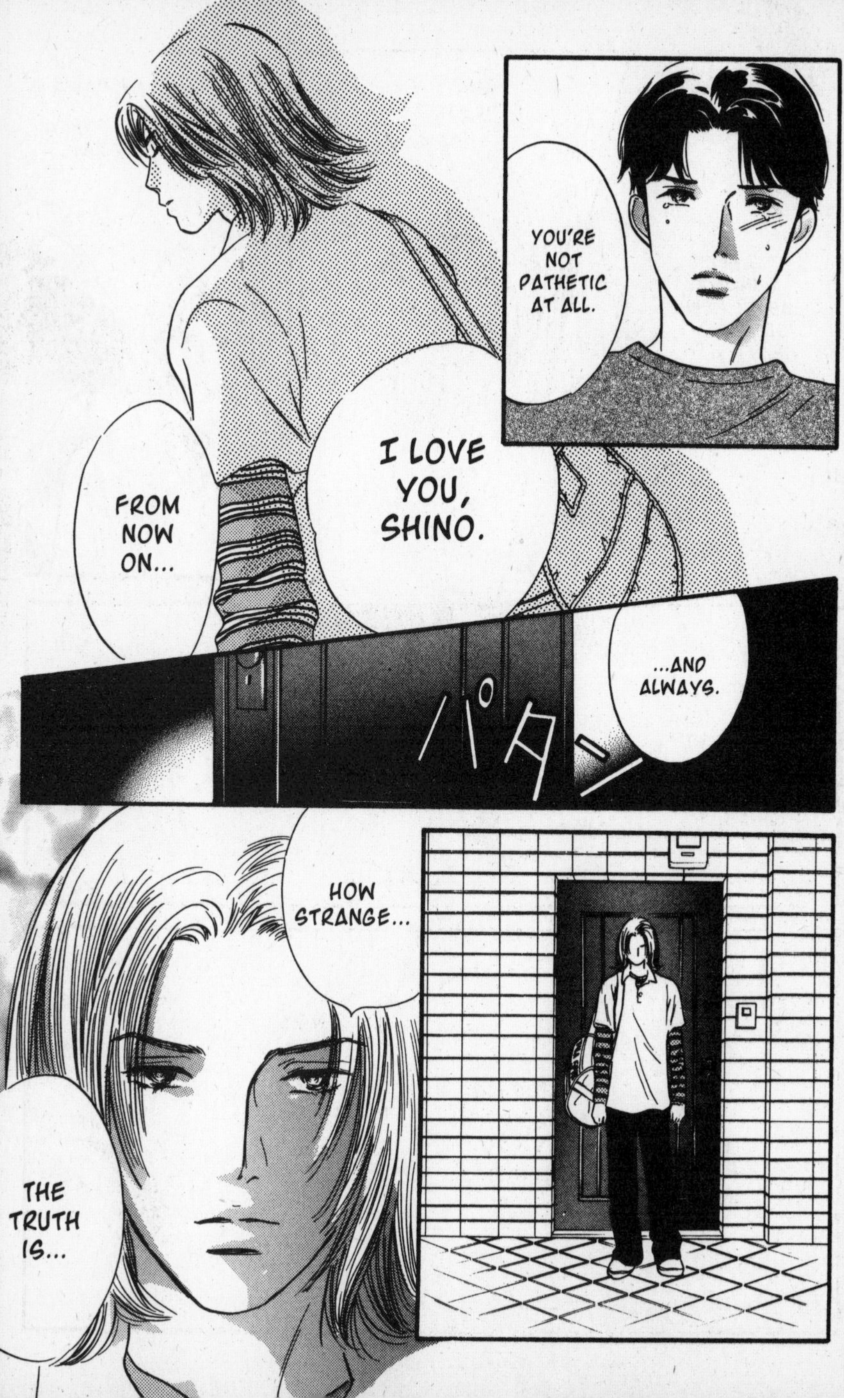
YOU'RE NOT PATHETIC AT ALL.
I LOVE YOU, SHINO.
FROM NOW ON...
...AND ALWAYS.
パターン
HOW STRANGE...
THE TRUTH IS...

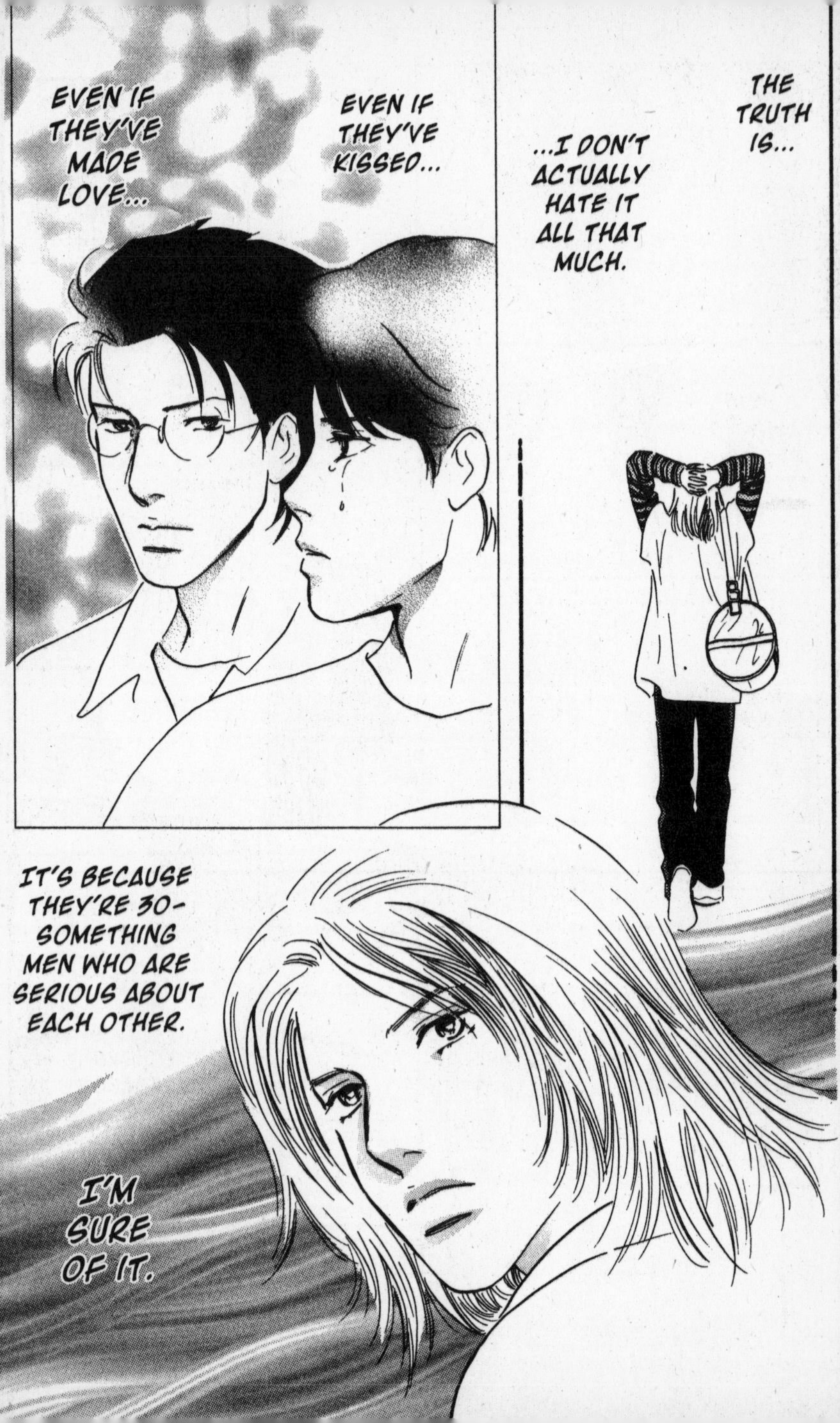
THE TRUTH IS...
...I DON'T ACTUALLY HATE IT ALL THAT MUCH.
EVEN IF THEY'VE KISSED...
EVEN IF THEY'VE MADE LOVE...
IT'S BECAUSE THEY'RE 30-SOMETHING MEN WHO ARE SERIOUS ABOUT EACH OTHER.
I'M SURE OF IT.

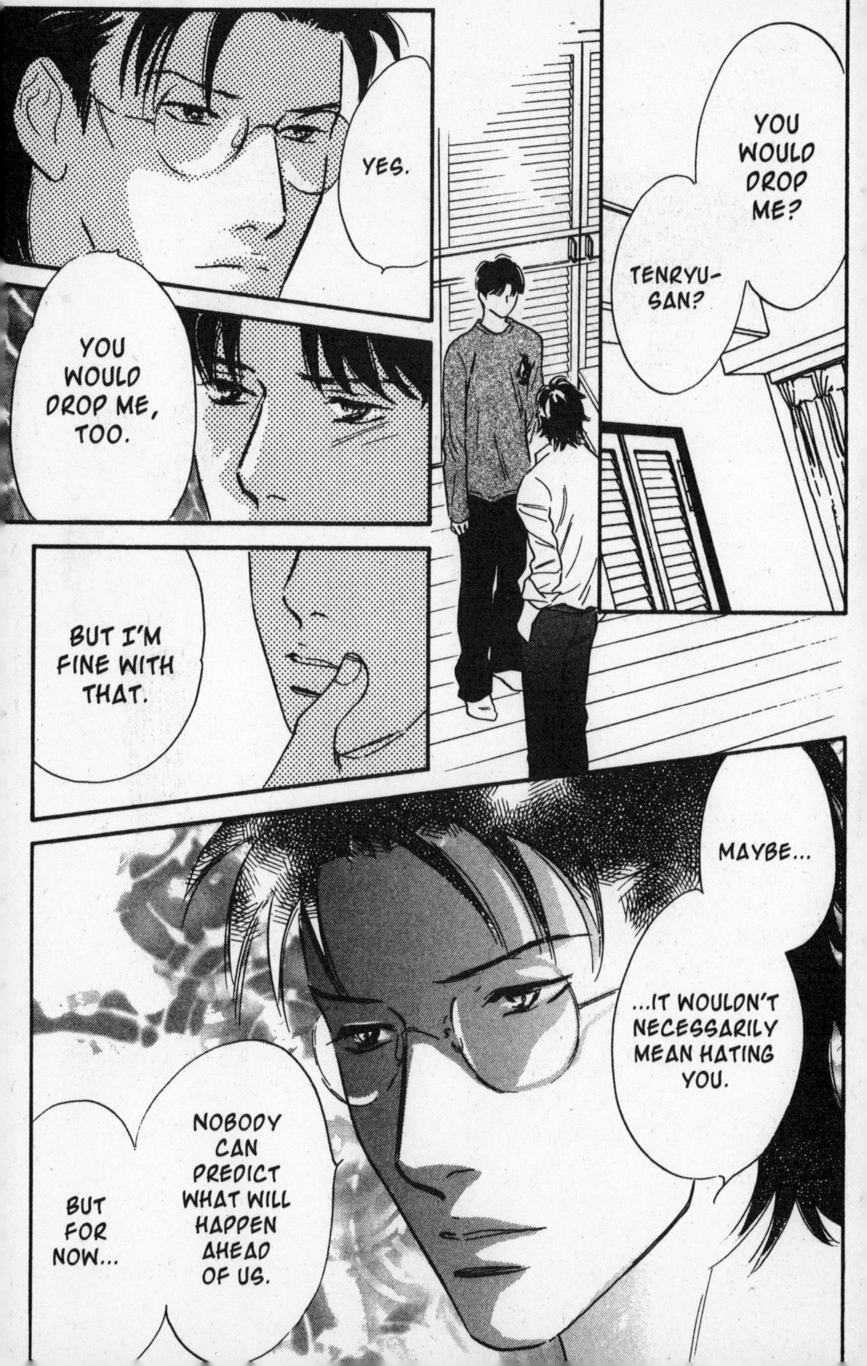
YOU WOULD DROP ME?
TENRYU-SAN?
YES.
YOU WOULD DROP ME, TOO.
BUT I'M FINE WITH THAT.
MAYBE...
...IT WOULDN'T NECESSARILY MEAN HATING YOU.
NOBODY CAN PREDICT WHAT WILL HAPPEN AHEAD OF US.
BUT FOR NOW...

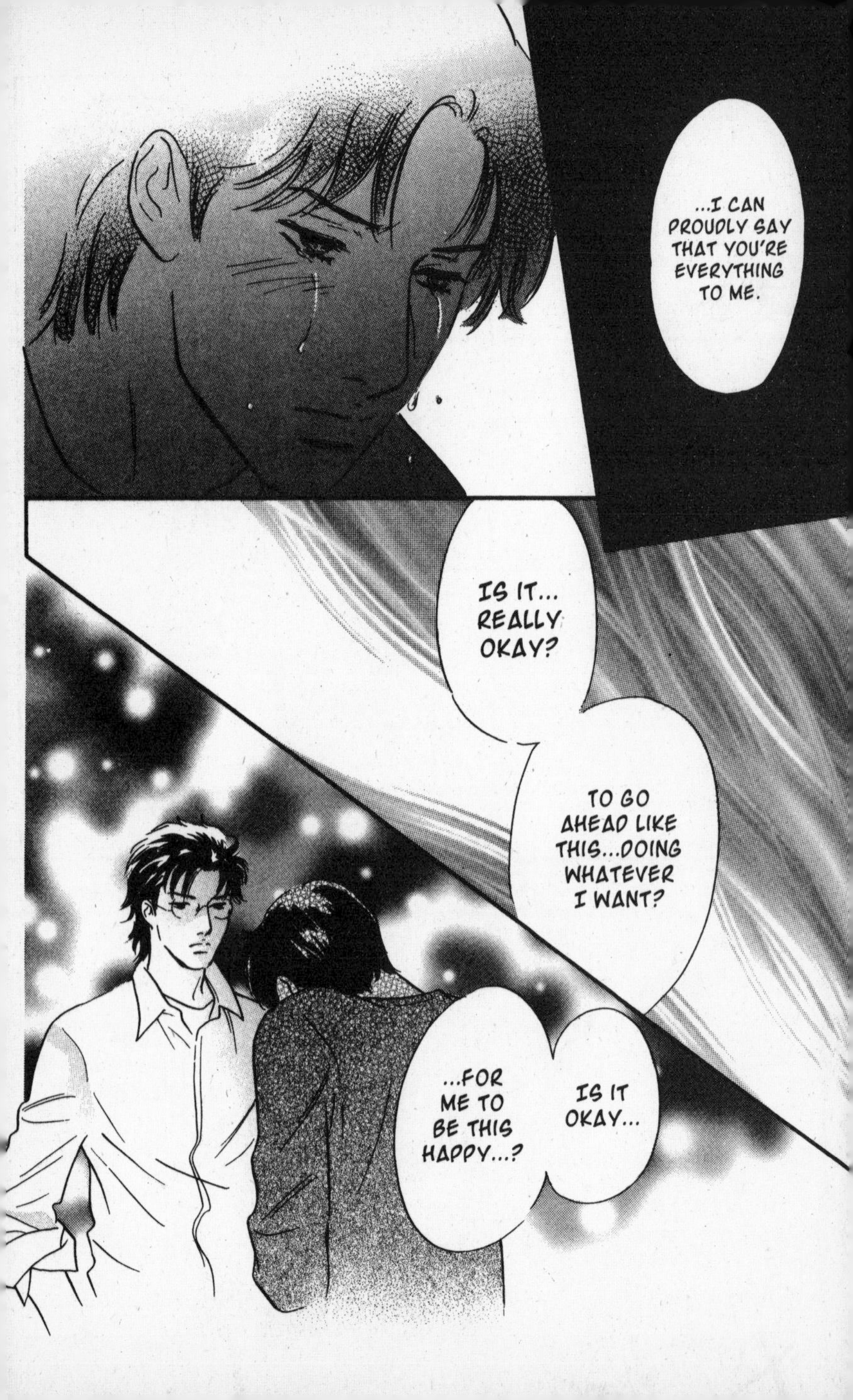
...I CAN PROUDLY SAY THAT YOU'RE EVERYTHING TO ME.
IS IT... REALLY OKAY?
TO GO AHEAD LIKE THIS...DOING WHATEVER I WANT?
IS IT OKAY...
...FOR ME TO BE THIS HAPPY...?

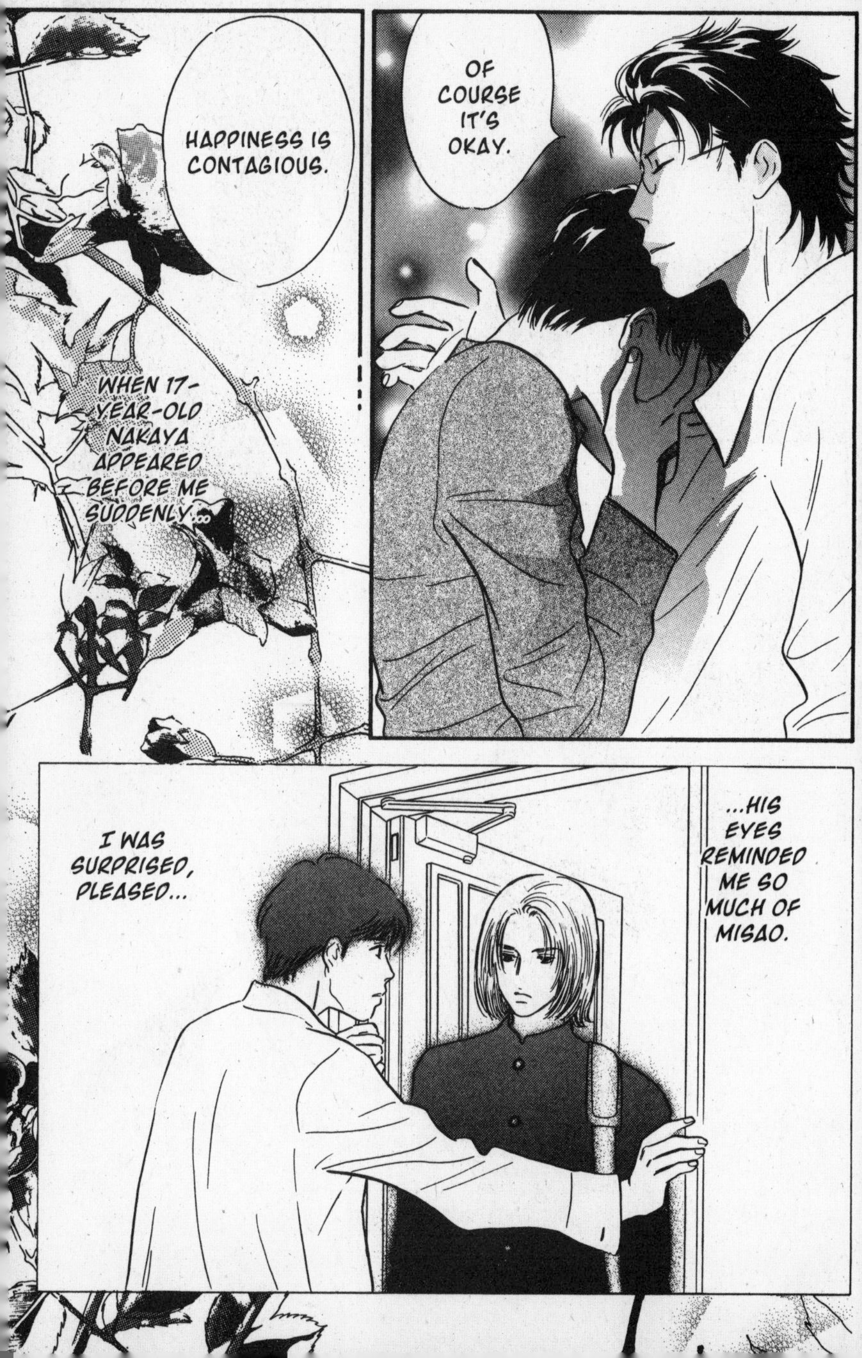
OF COURSE IT'S OKAY.
HAPPINESS IS CONTAGIOUS.
WHEN 17-YEAR-OLD NAKAYA APPEARED BEFORE ME SUDDENLY...
...HIS EYES REMINDED ME SO MUCH OF MISAO.
I WAS SURPRISED, PLEASED...

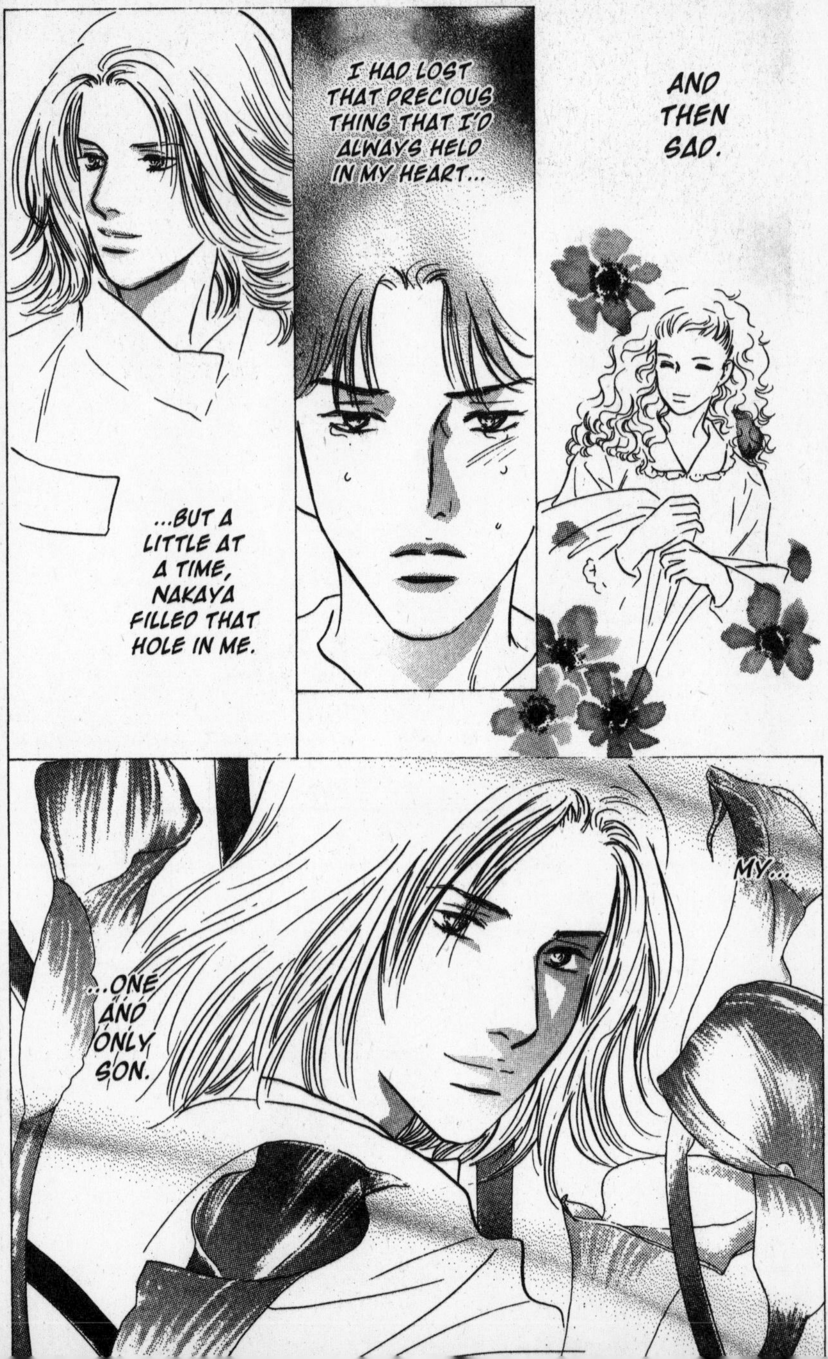
AND THEN SAO.
I HAD LOST THAT PRECIOUS THING THAT I'D ALWAYS HELD IN MY HEART...
...BUT A LITTLE AT A TIME, NAKAYA FILLED THAT HOLE IN ME.
MY...
...ONE AND ONLY SON.

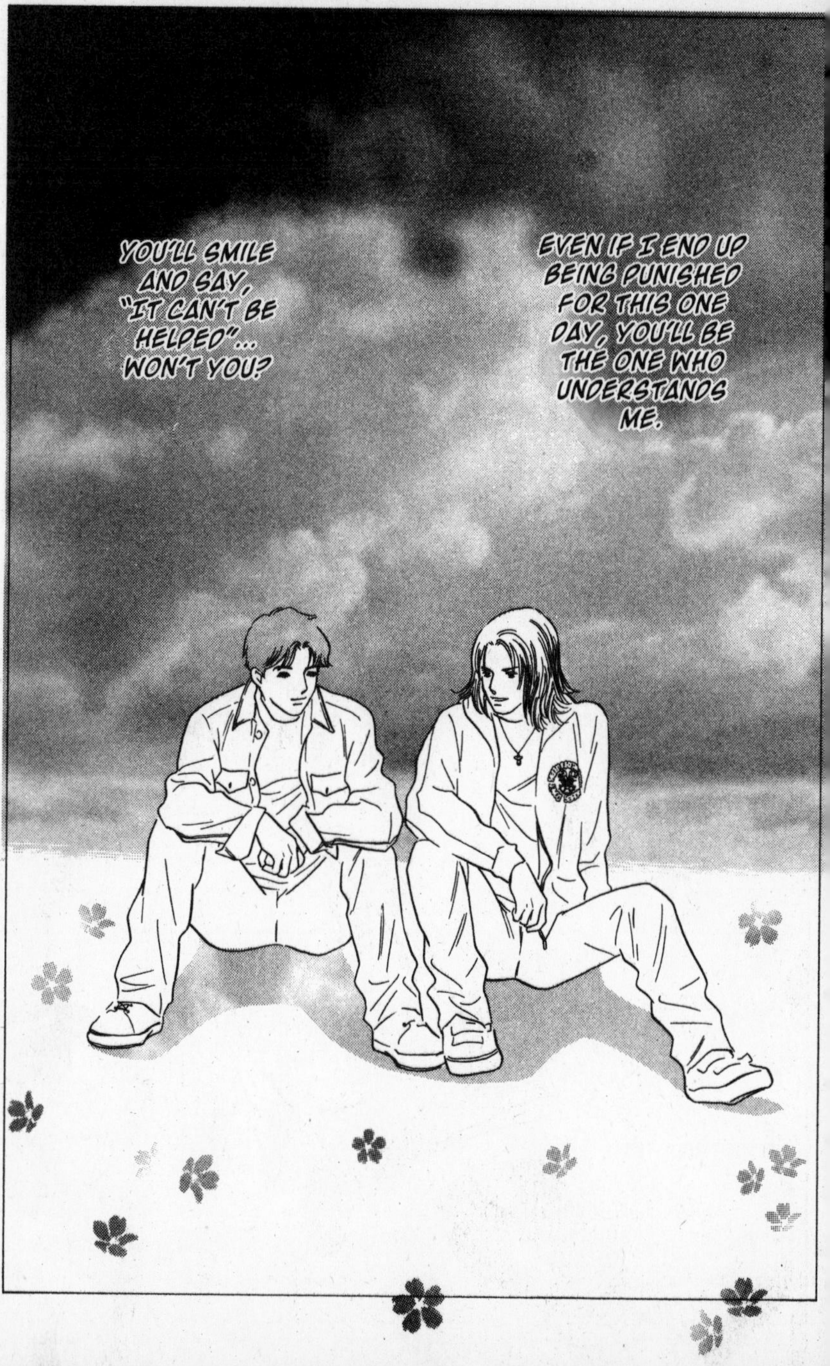
EVEN IF I END UP BEING PUNISHED FOR THIS ONE DAY, YOU'LL BE THE ONE WHO UNDERSTANDS ME.
YOU'LL SMILE AND SAY, "IT CAN'T BE HELPED"... WON'T YOU?

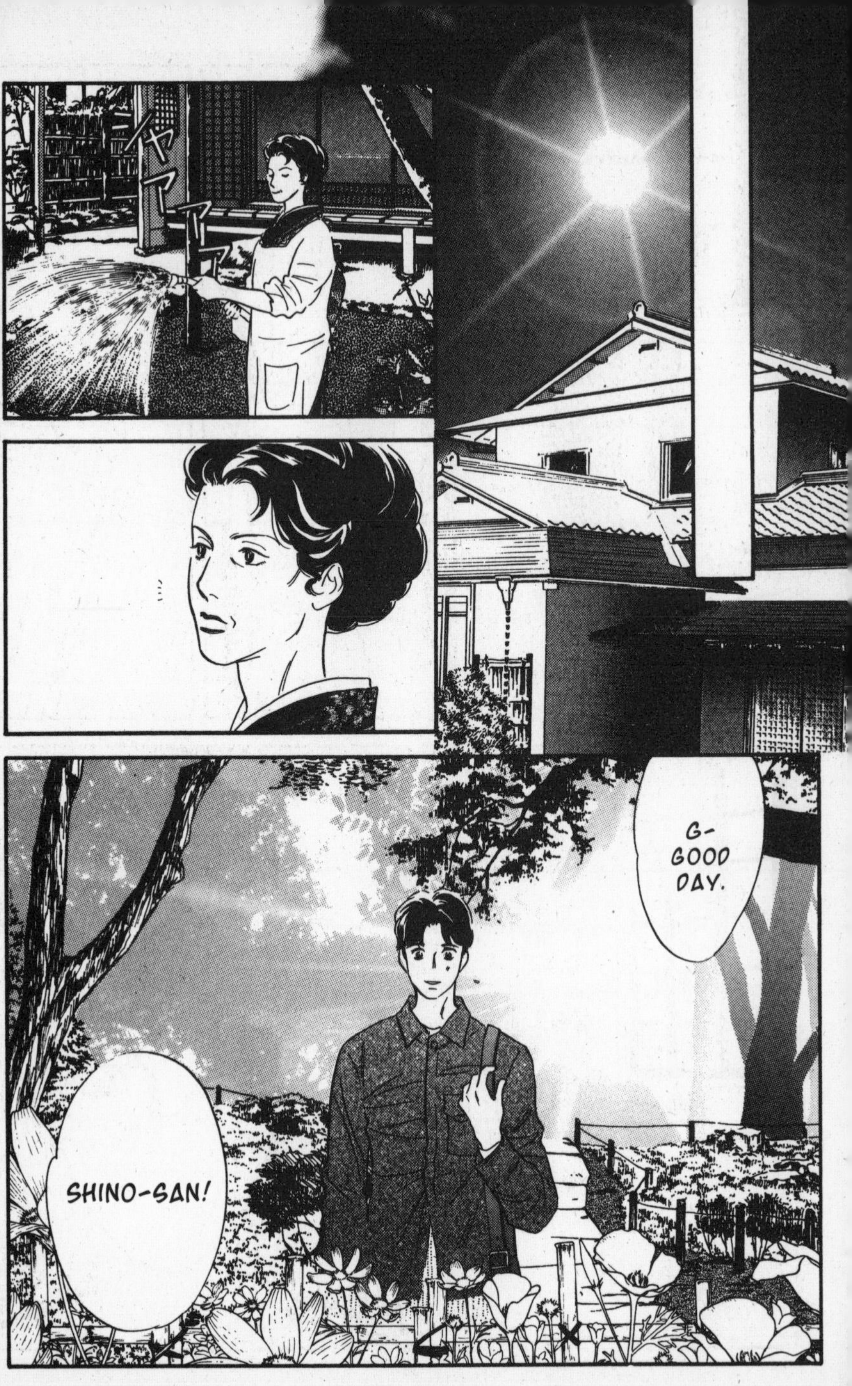
G-GOOD DAY.
SHINO-SAN!

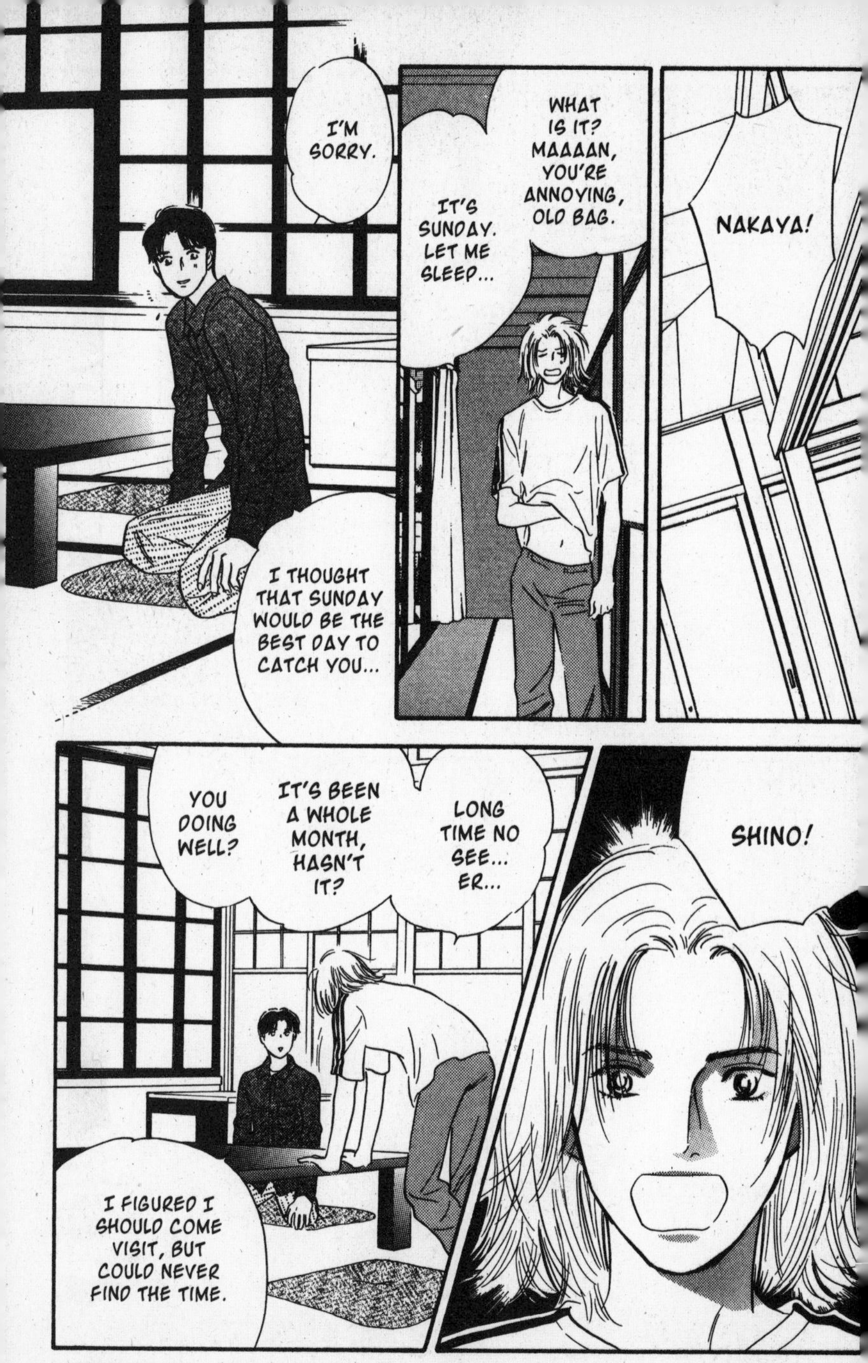
NAKAYA!
WHAT IS IT? MAAAAN, YOU'RE ANNOYING, OLD BAG.
IT'S SUNDAY. LET ME SLEEP...
I'M SORRY.
I THOUGHT THAT SUNDAY WOULD BE THE BEST DAY TO CATCH YOU...
SHINO!
LONG TIME NO SEE... ER...
IT'S BEEN A WHOLE MONTH, HASN'T IT?
YOU DOING WELL?
I FIGURED I SHOULD COME VISIT, BUT COULD NEVER FIND THE TIME.

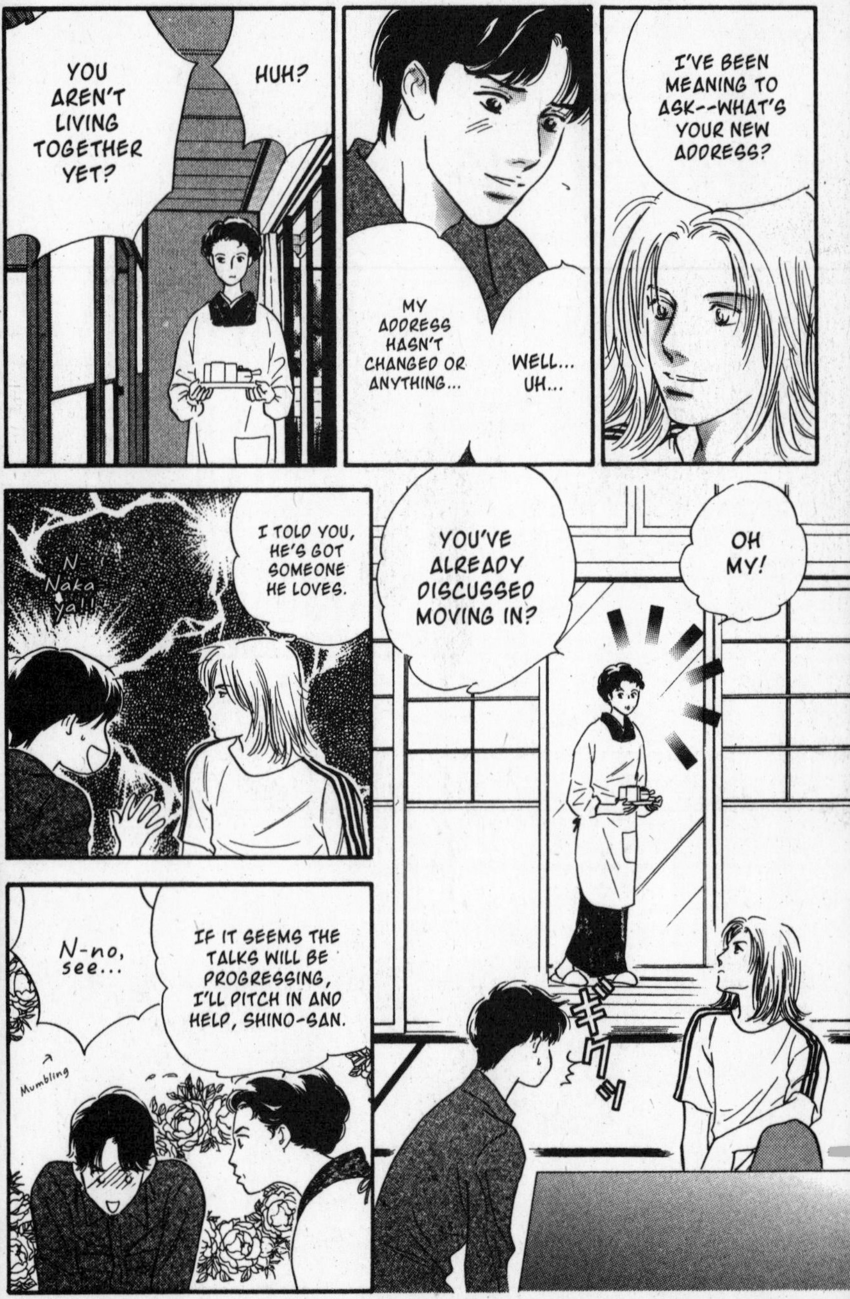
I'VE BEEN MEANING TO ASK--WHAT'S YOUR NEW ADDRESS?
WELL... UH...
MY ADDRESS HASN'T CHANGED OR ANYTHING...
HUH?
YOU AREN'T LIVING TOGETHER YET?
OH MY!
YOU'VE ALREADY DISCUSSED MOVING IN?
I TOLD YOU, HE'S GOT SOMEONE HE LOVES.
N-Naka-ya!!
IF IT SEEMS THE TALKS WILL BE PROGRESSING, I'LL PITCH IN AND HELP, SHINO-SAN.
N-no, see...
Mumbling

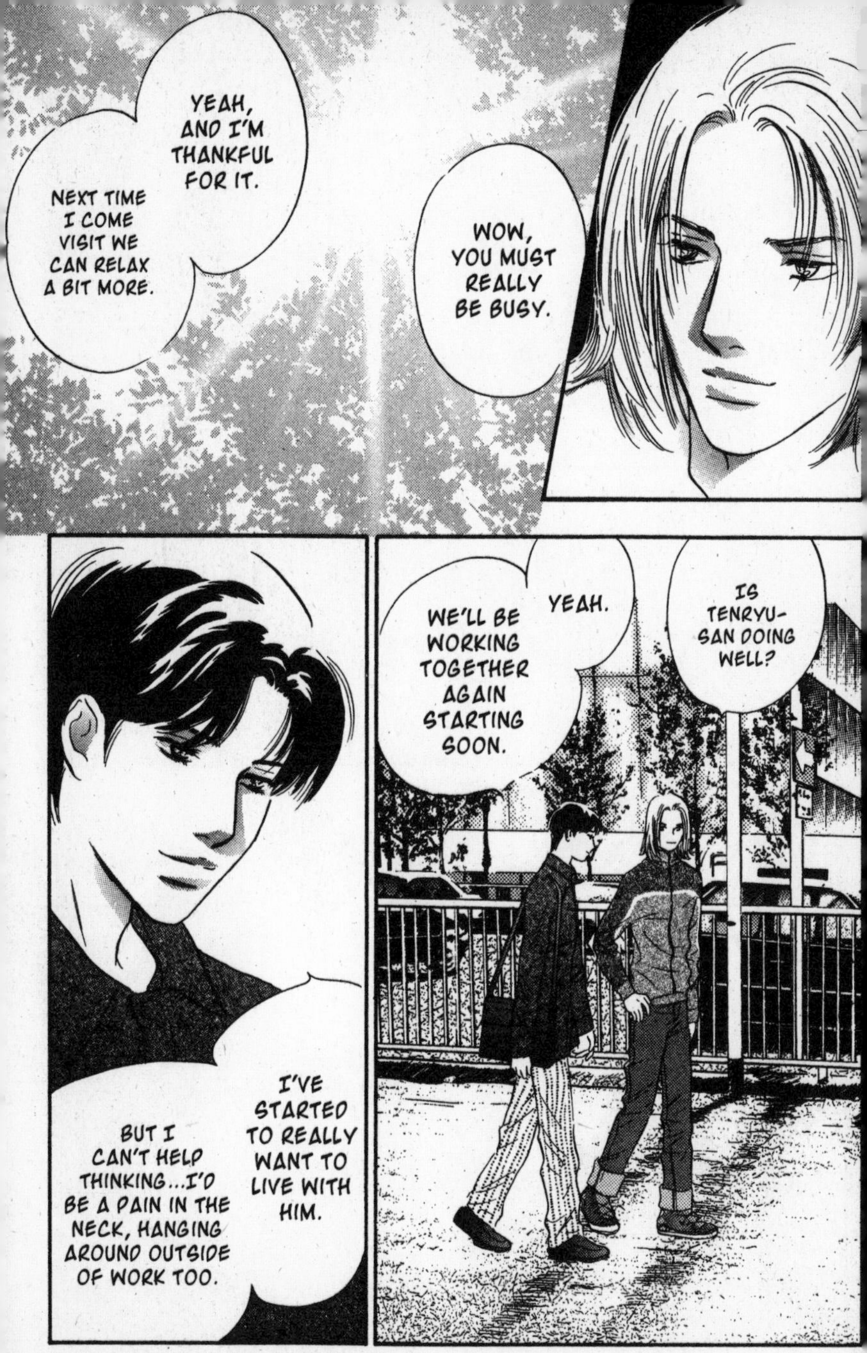
WOW, YOU MUST REALLY BE BUSY.
YEAH, AND I'M THANKFUL FOR IT.
NEXT TIME I COME VISIT WE CAN RELAX A BIT MORE.
IS TENRYU-SAN DOING WELL?
YEAH.
WE'LL BE WORKING TOGETHER AGAIN STARTING SOON.
I'VE STARTED TO REALLY WANT TO LIVE WITH HIM.
BUT I CAN'T HELP THINKING...I'D BE A PAIN IN THE NECK, HANGING AROUND OUTSIDE OF WORK TOO.

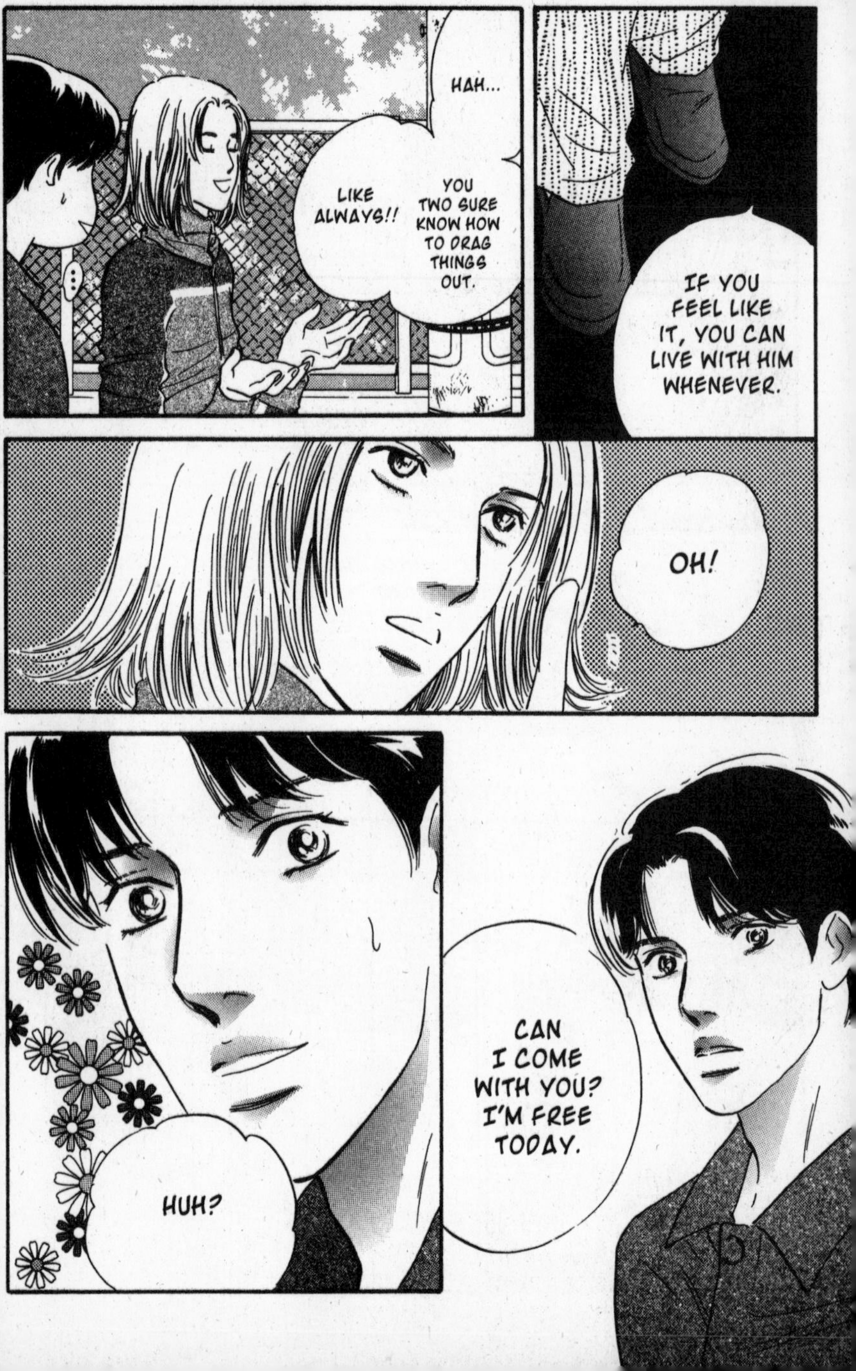
IF YOU FEEL LIKE IT, YOU CAN LIVE WITH HIM WHENEVER.
HAH...
YOU TWO SURE KNOW HOW TO DRAG THINGS OUT.
LIKE ALWAYS!!
OH!
CAN I COME WITH YOU? I'M FREE TODAY.
HUH?

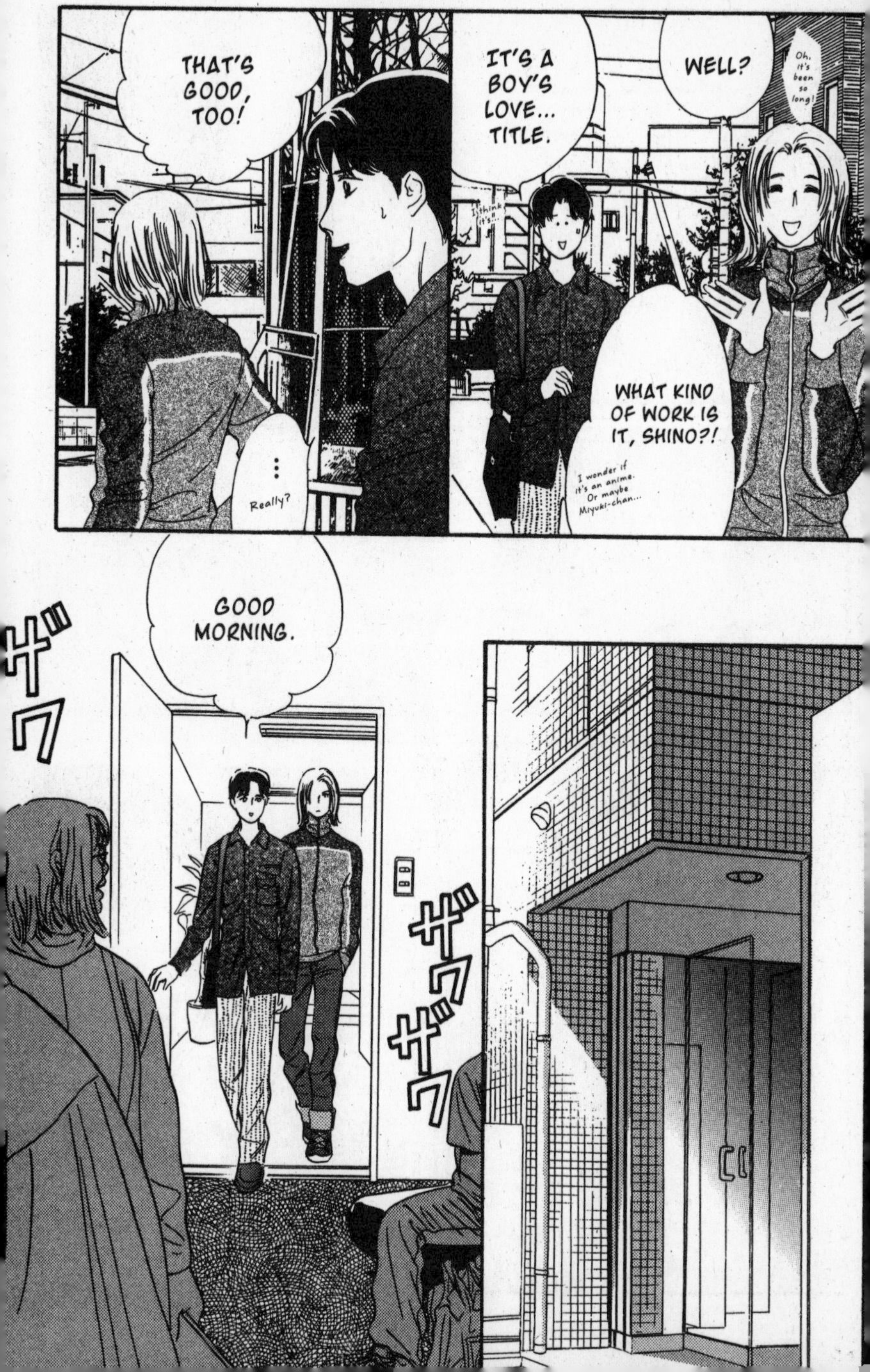
Oh, it's been so long!
WELL?
IT'S A BOY'S LOVE... TITLE.
I think it's...
WHAT KIND OF WORK IS IT, SHINO?!
I wonder if it's an anime. Or maybe Miyuki-chan...
THAT'S GOOD, TOO!
...
Really?
ザワ
GOOD MORNING.
ザワ
ザワ
ザワ

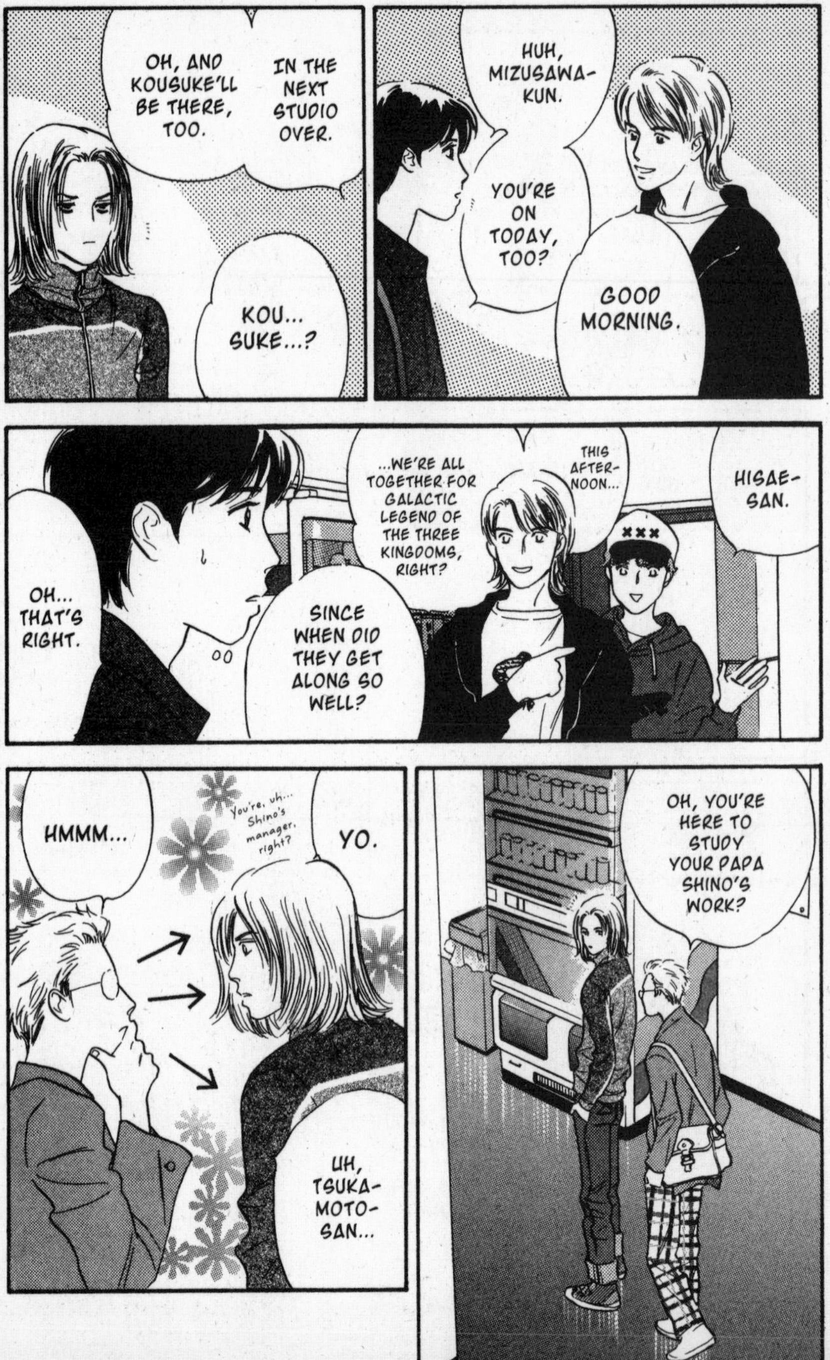
HUH, MIZUSAWA-KUN.
YOU'RE ON TODAY, TOO?
GOOD MORNING.
OH, AND KOUSUKE'LL BE THERE, TOO. IN THE NEXT STUDIO OVER.
KOU... SUKE...?
HISAE-SAN.
THIS AFTER-NOON...
...WE'RE ALL TOGETHER FOR GALACTIC LEGEND OF THE THREE KINGDOMS, RIGHT?
SINCE WHEN DID THEY GET ALONG SO WELL?
OH... THAT'S RIGHT.
OH, YOU'RE HERE TO STUDY YOUR PAPA SHINO'S WORK?
YO.
You're, uh... Shino's manager, right?
HMMM...
UH, TSUKA-MOTO-SAN...

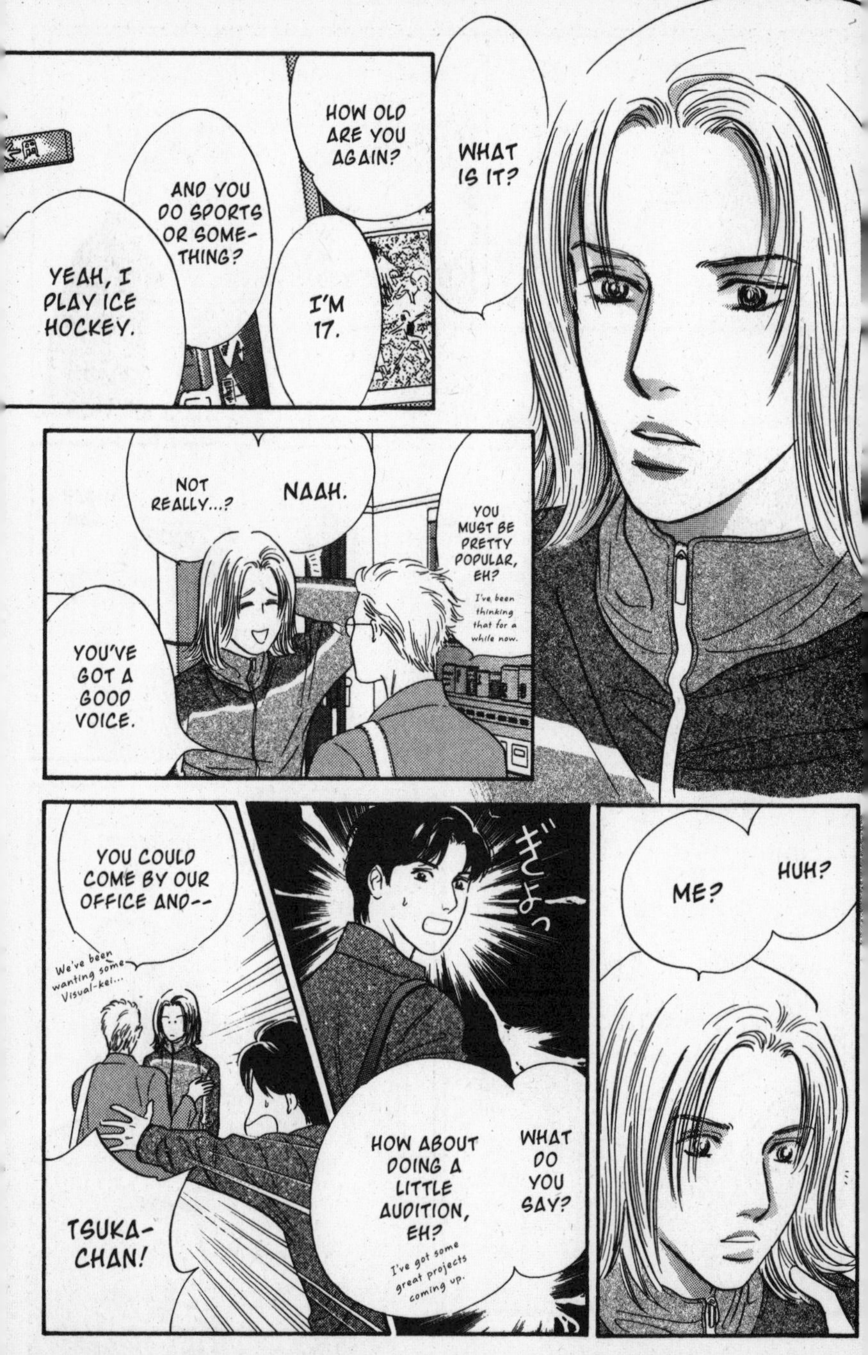
WHAT IS IT?
HOW OLD ARE YOU AGAIN?
I'M 17.
AND YOU DO SPORTS OR SOMETHING?
YEAH, I PLAY ICE HOCKEY.
YOU MUST BE PRETTY POPULAR, EH?
I've been thinking that for a while now.
NAAH.
NOT REALLY...?
YOU'VE GOT A GOOD VOICE.
HUH?
ME?
WHAT DO YOU SAY?
HOW ABOUT DOING A LITTLE AUDITION, EH?
I've got some great projects coming up.
ぎょっ
YOU COULD COME BY OUR OFFICE AND--
We've been wanting some Visual-kei...
TSUKA-CHAN!

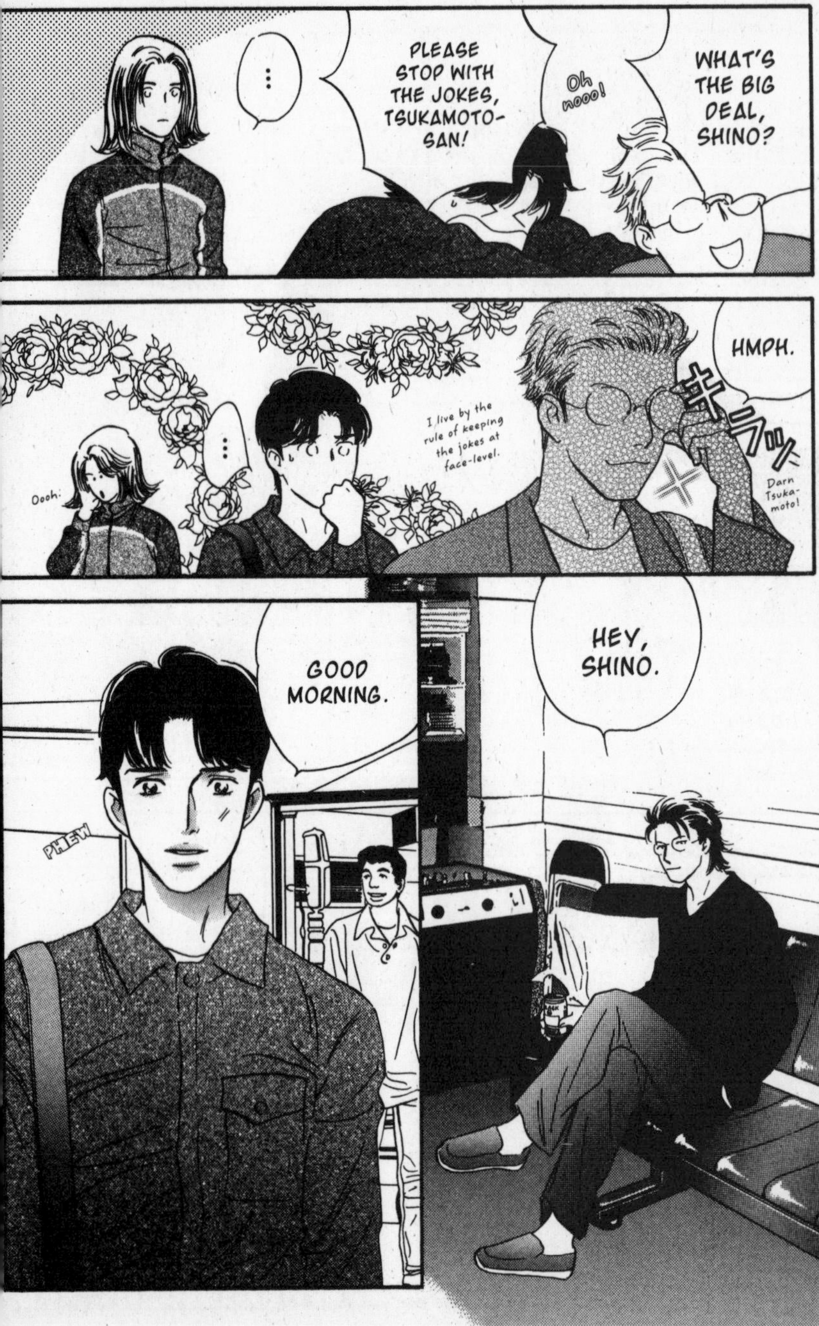
WHAT'S THE BIG DEAL, SHINO?
Oh nooo!
PLEASE STOP WITH THE JOKES, TSUKAMOTO-SAN!
...
HMPH.
キラッ
Darn Tsukamoto!
I live by the rule of keeping the jokes at face-level.
...
Oooh:
HEY, SHINO.
GOOD MORNING.
PHEW

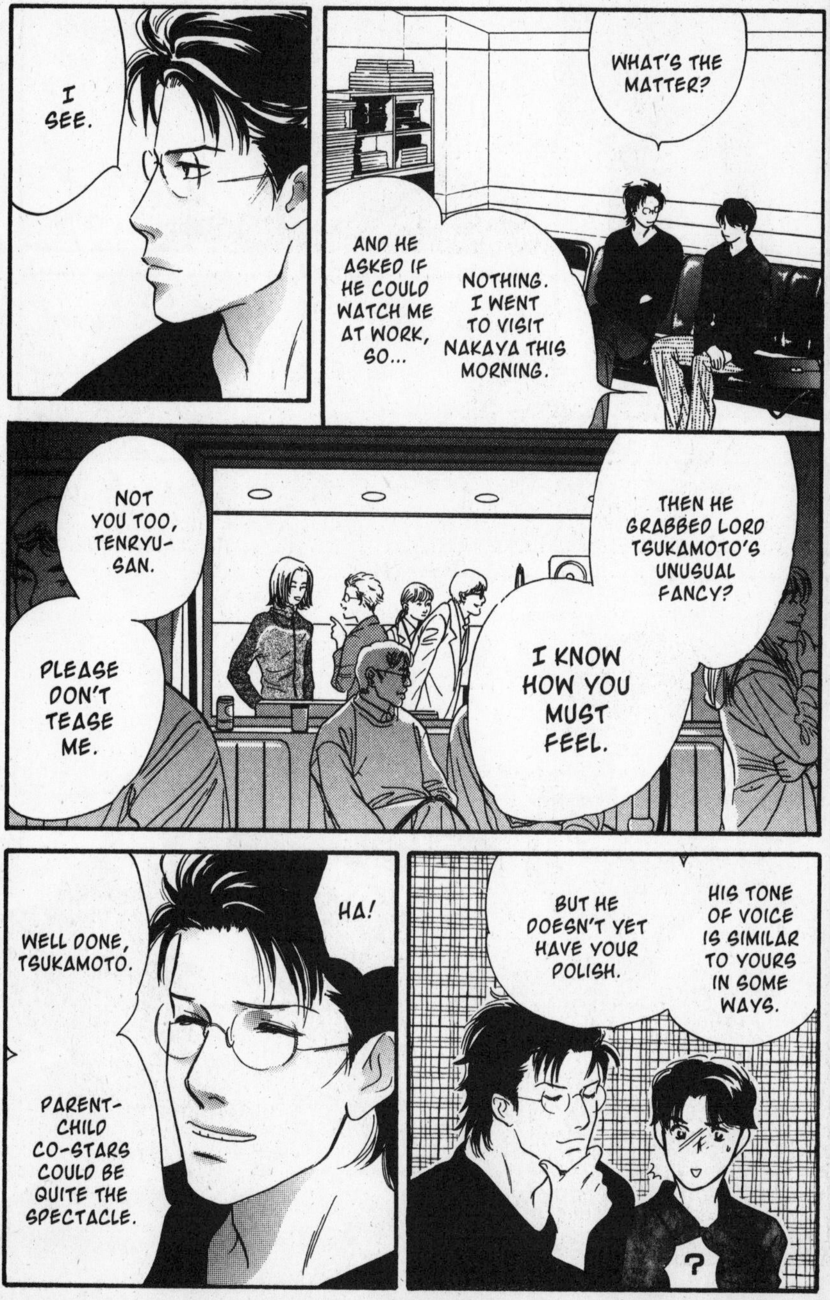
WHAT'S THE MATTER?
NOTHING. I WENT TO VISIT NAKAYA THIS MORNING.
AND HE ASKED IF HE COULD WATCH ME AT WORK, SO...
I SEE.
THEN HE GRABBED LORD TSUKAMOTO'S UNUSUAL FANCY?
I KNOW HOW YOU MUST FEEL.
NOT YOU TOO, TENRYU-SAN.
PLEASE DON'T TEASE ME.
HIS TONE OF VOICE IS SIMILAR TO YOURS IN SOME WAYS.
BUT HE DOESN'T YET HAVE YOUR POLISH.
?
HA!
WELL DONE, TSUKAMOTO.
PARENT-CHILD CO-STARS COULD BE QUITE THE SPECTACLE.

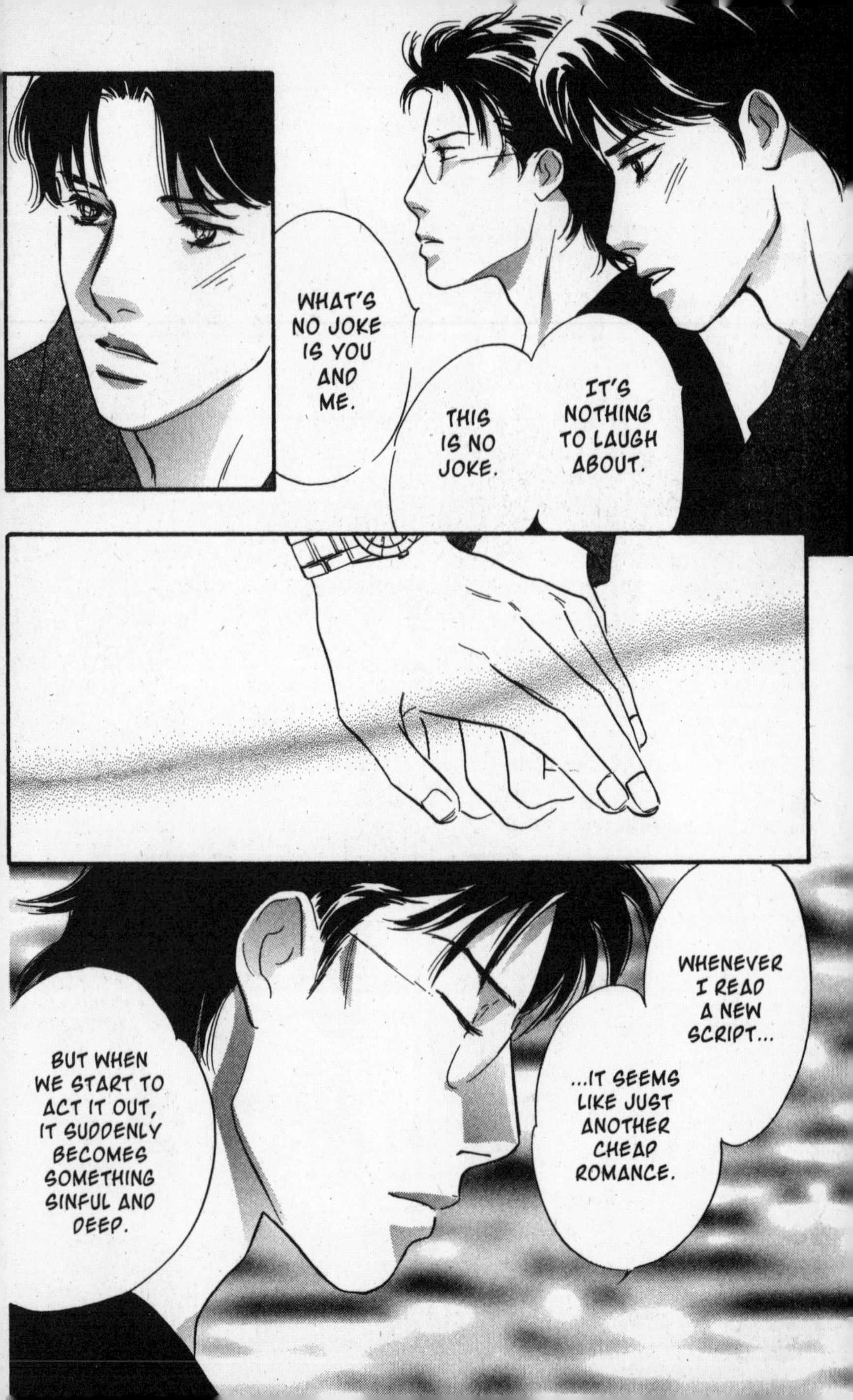
IT'S NOTHING TO LAUGH ABOUT.
THIS IS NO JOKE.
WHAT'S NO JOKE IS YOU AND ME.
WHENEVER I READ A NEW SCRIPT...
...IT SEEMS LIKE JUST ANOTHER CHEAP ROMANCE.
BUT WHEN WE START TO ACT IT OUT, IT SUDDENLY BECOMES SOMETHING SINFUL AND DEEP.

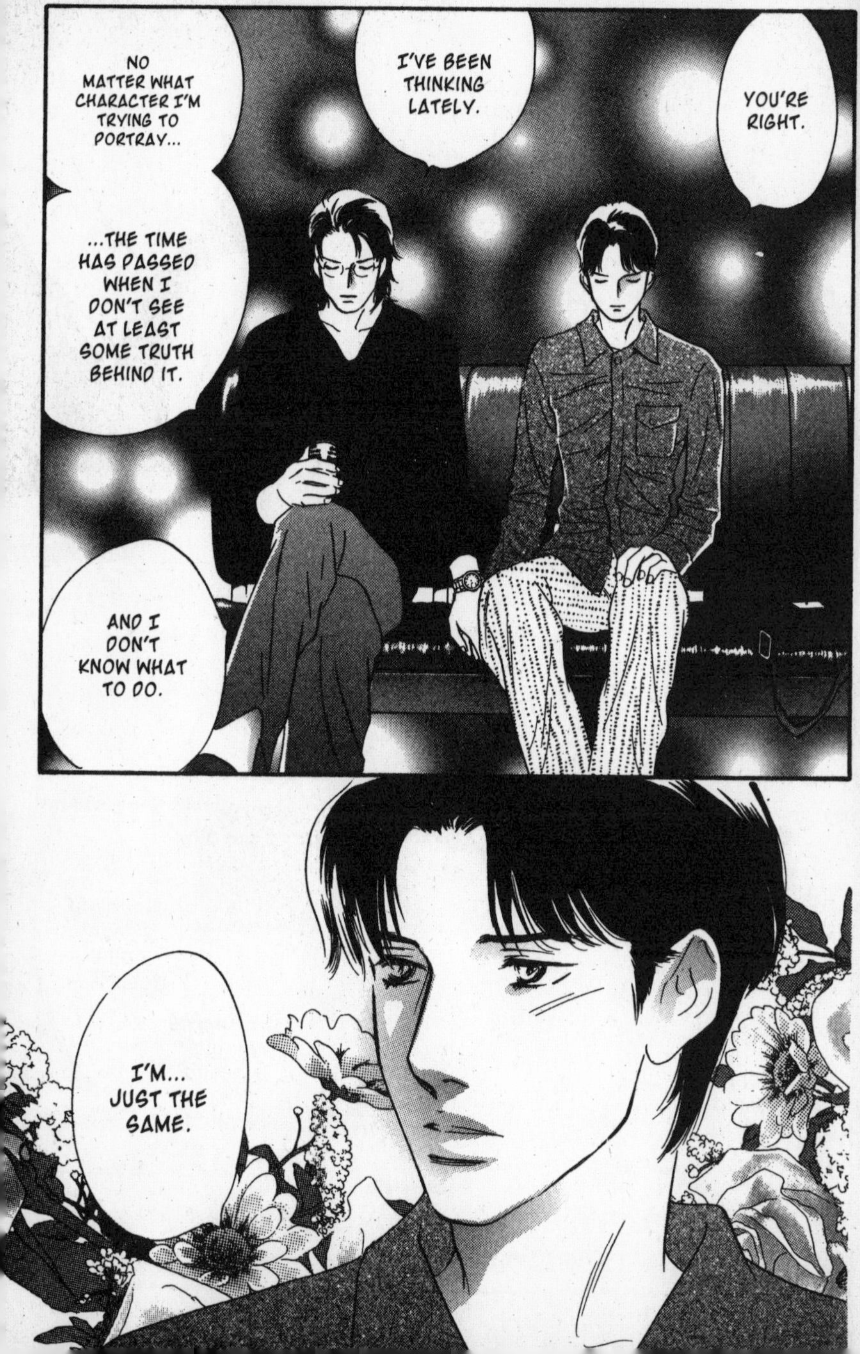
YOU'RE RIGHT.
I'VE BEEN THINKING LATELY.
NO MATTER WHAT CHARACTER I'M TRYING TO PORTRAY...
...THE TIME HAS PASSED WHEN I DON'T SEE AT LEAST SOME TRUTH BEHIND IT.
AND I DON'T KNOW WHAT TO DO.
I'M... JUST THE SAME.

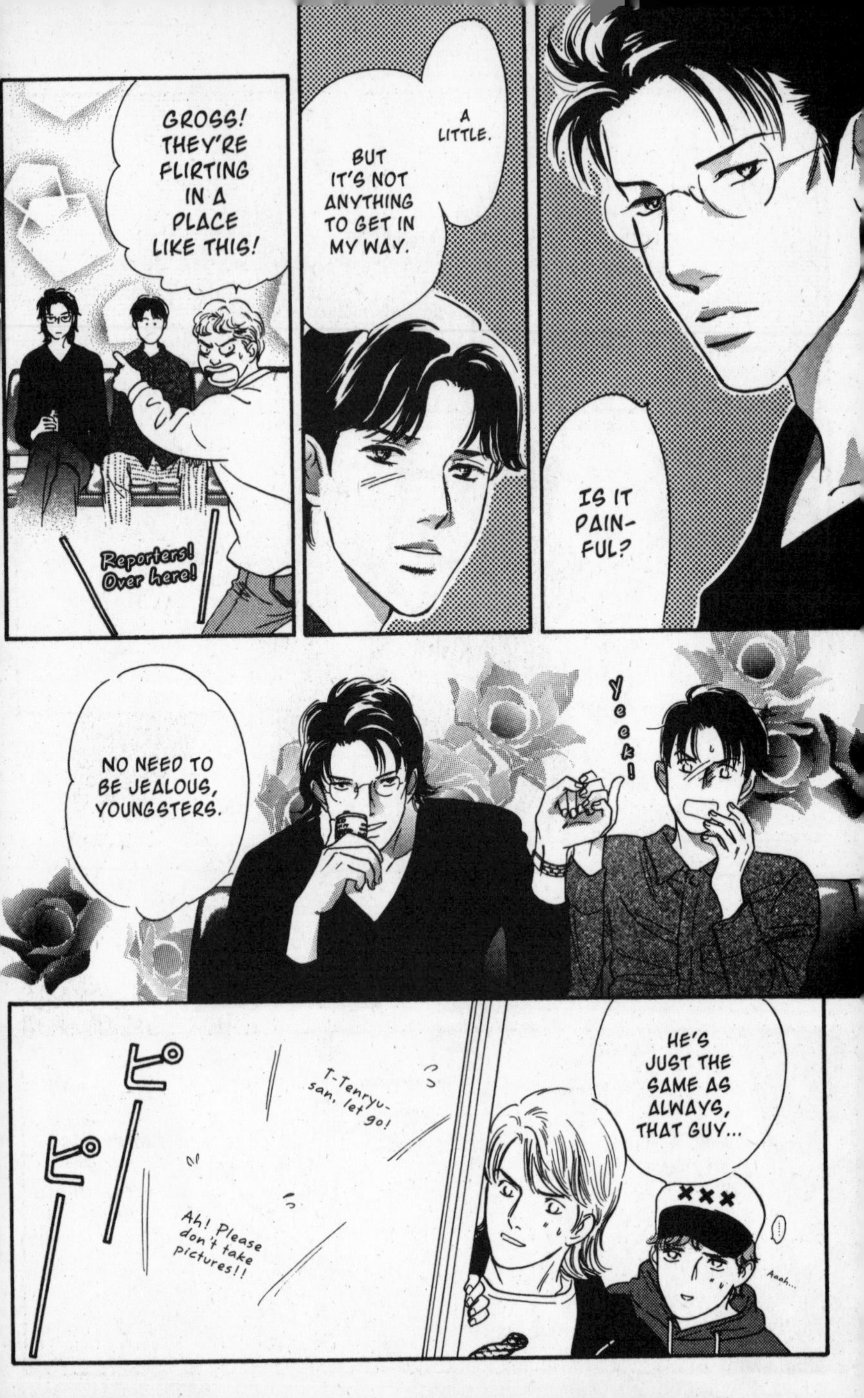
IS IT PAIN-FUL?
A LITTLE.
BUT IT'S NOT ANYTHING TO GET IN MY WAY.
GROSS! THEY'RE FLIRTING IN A PLACE LIKE THIS!
Reporters! Over here!
Yeeek!
NO NEED TO BE JEALOUS, YOUNGSTERS.
HE'S JUST THE SAME AS ALWAYS, THAT GUY...
Aaah...
T-Tenryu-san, let go!
Ah! Please don't take pictures!!
ピ
ピ

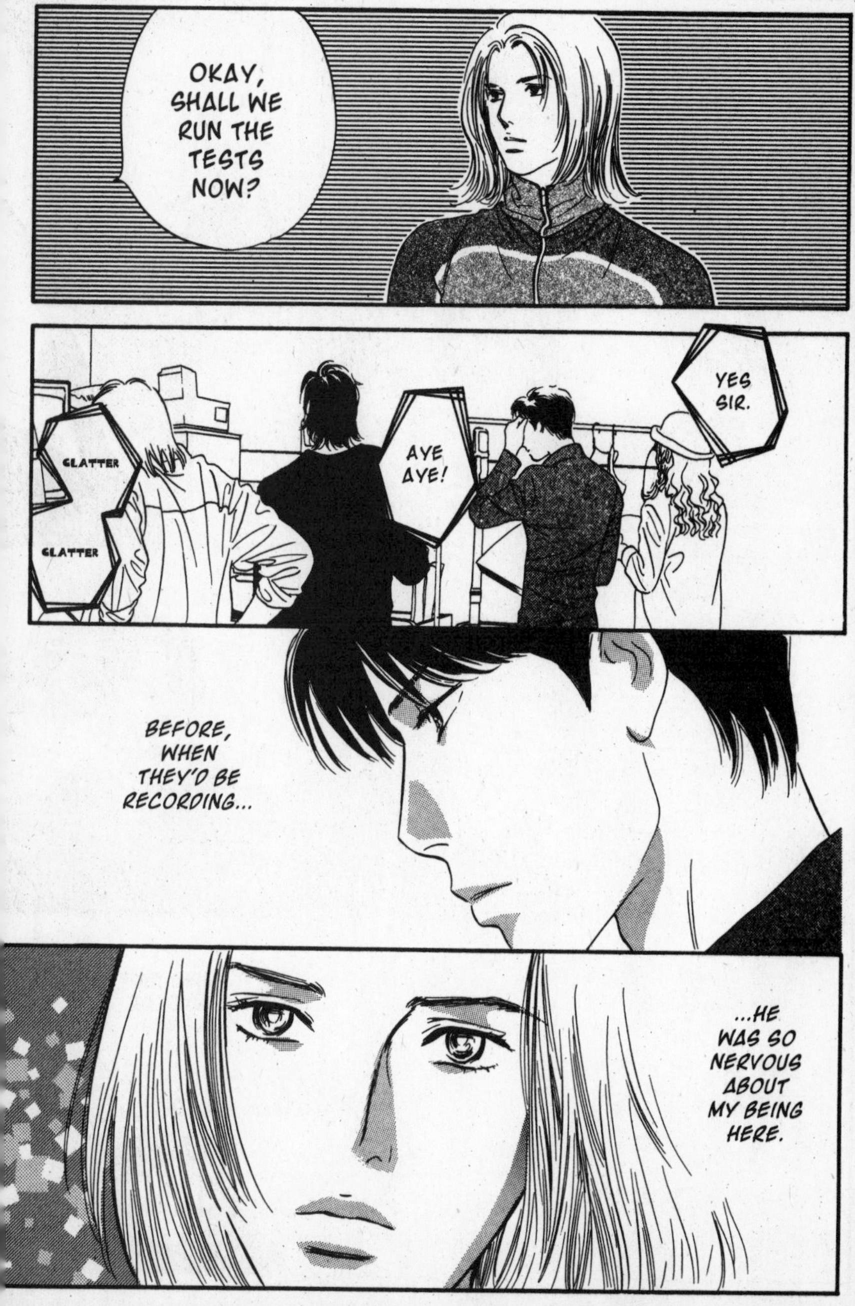
OKAY, SHALL WE RUN THE TESTS NOW?
YES SIR.
AYE AYE!
GLATTER
GLATTER
BEFORE, WHEN THEY'D BE RECORDING...
...HE WAS SO NERVOUS ABOUT MY BEING HERE.

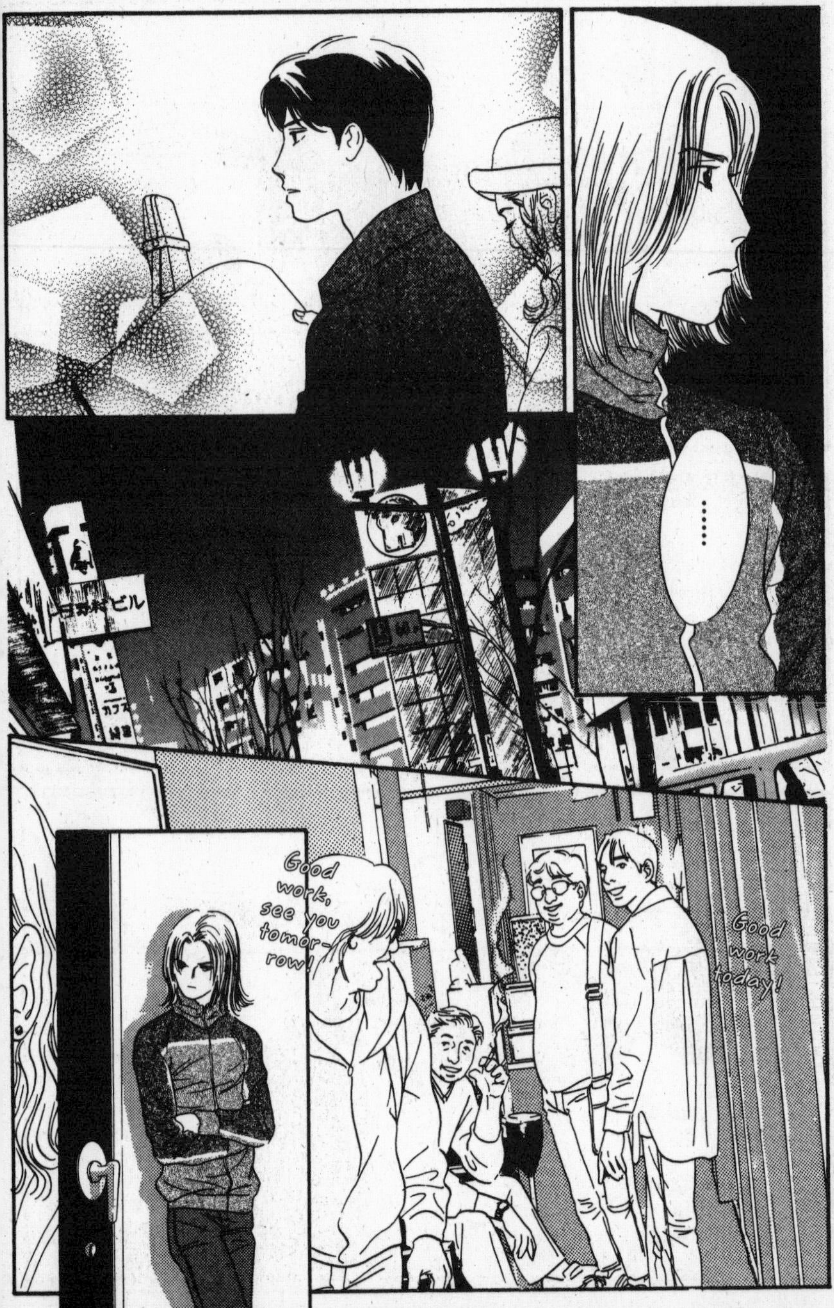
……
Good work today!
Good work, see you tomor-row!

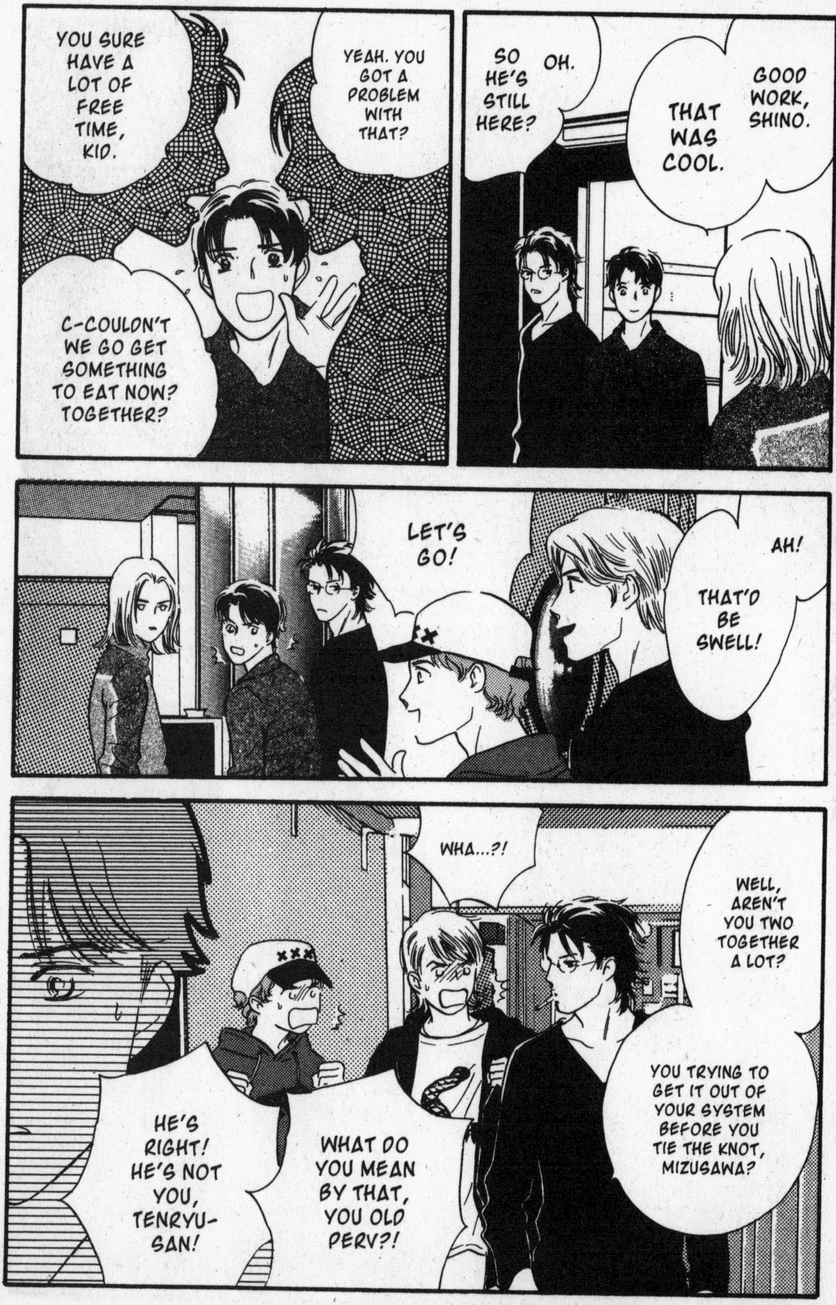
GOOD WORK, SHINO.
THAT WAS COOL.
OH.
SO HE'S STILL HERE?
YEAH. YOU GOT A PROBLEM WITH THAT?
YOU SURE HAVE A LOT OF FREE TIME, KID.
C-COULDN'T WE GO GET SOMETHING TO EAT NOW? TOGETHER?
AH!
THAT'D BE SWELL!
LET'S GO!
WELL, AREN'T YOU TWO TOGETHER A LOT?
YOU TRYING TO GET IT OUT OF YOUR SYSTEM BEFORE YOU TIE THE KNOT, MIZUSAWA?
WHA...?!
WHAT DO YOU MEAN BY THAT, YOU OLD PERV?!
HE'S RIGHT! HE'S NOT YOU, TENRYU-SAN!

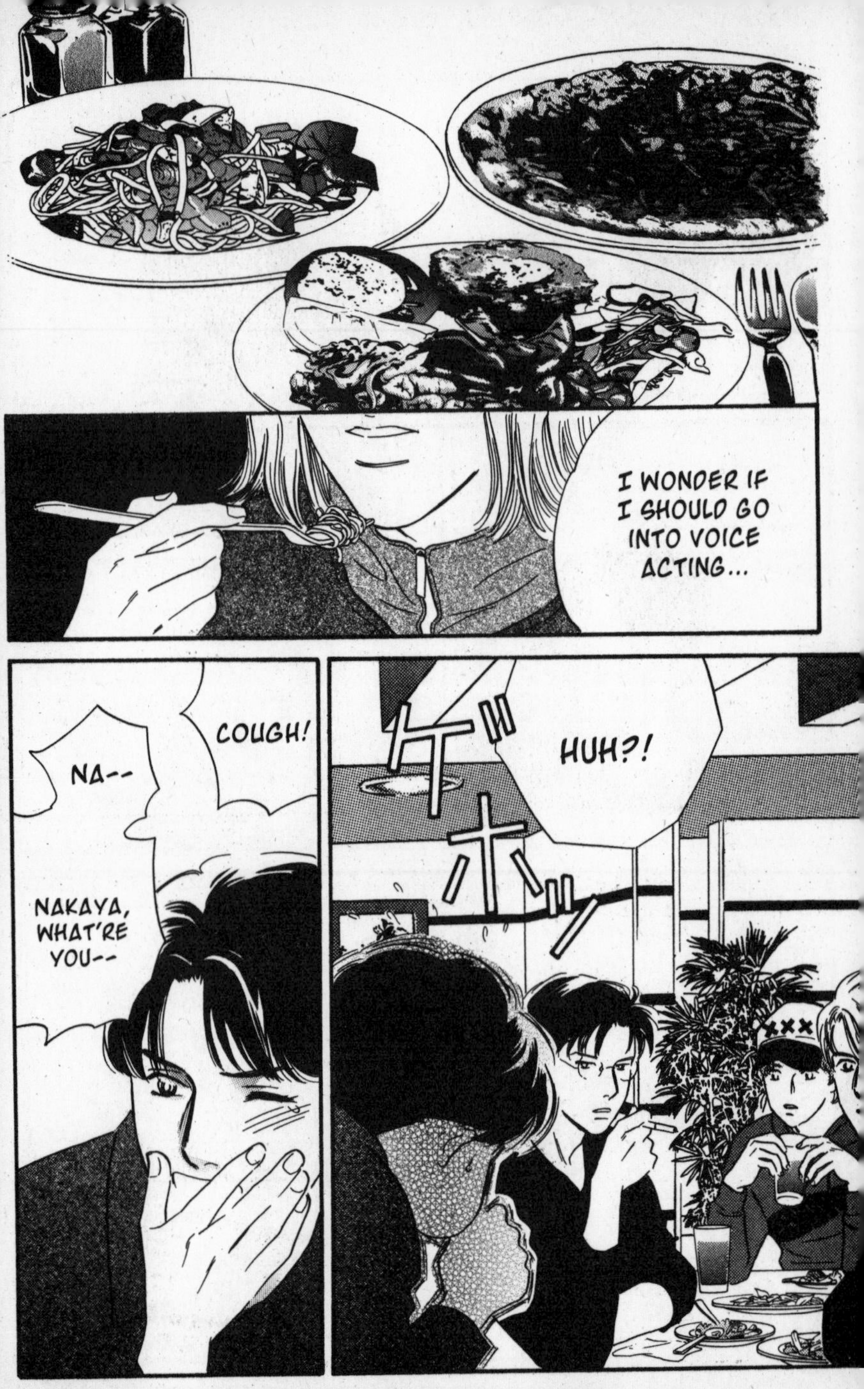
I WONDER IF I SHOULD GO INTO VOICE ACTING...
HUH?!
COUGH!
NA--
NAKAYA, WHAT'RE YOU--

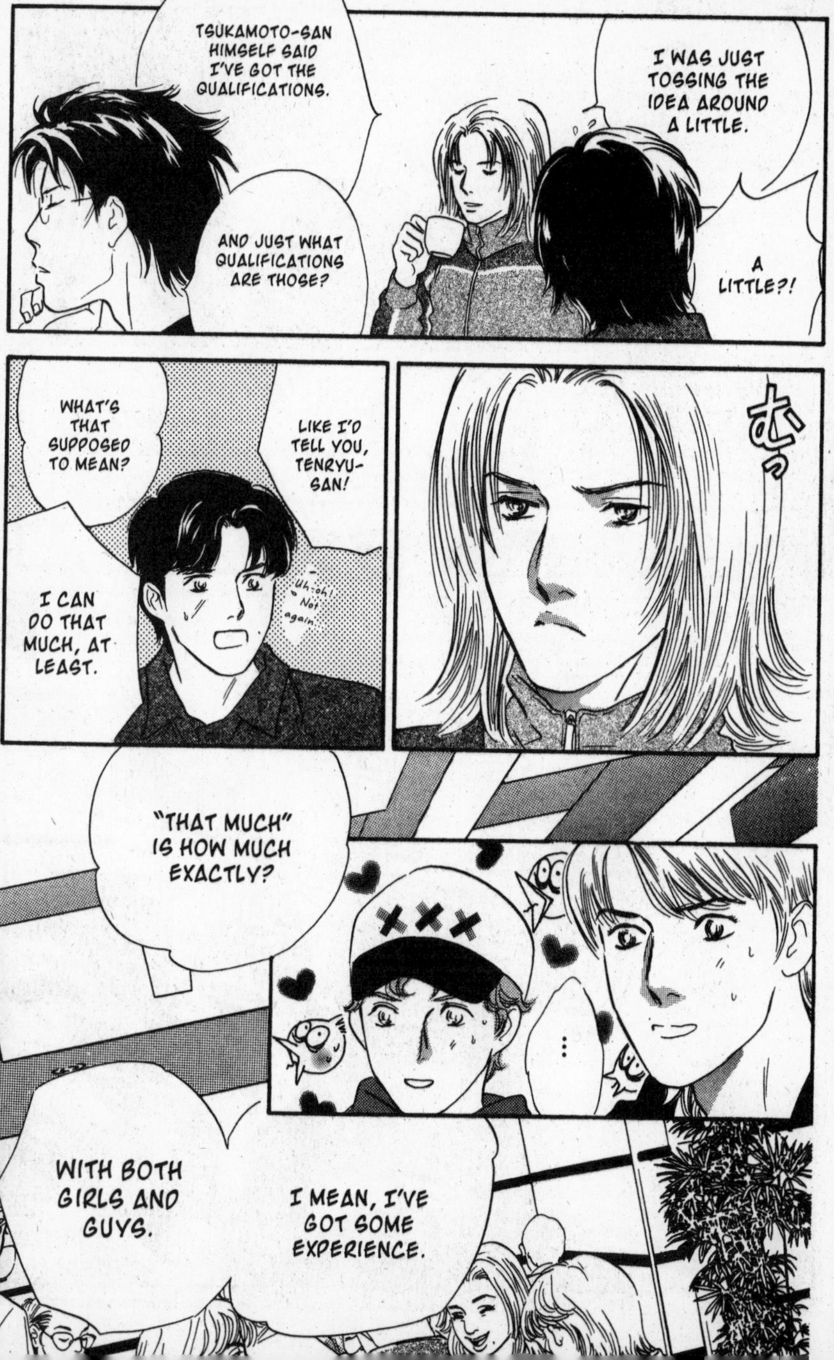
I WAS JUST TOSSING THE IDEA AROUND A LITTLE.
A LITTLE?!
TSUKAMOTO-SAN HIMSELF SAID I'VE GOT THE QUALIFICATIONS.
AND JUST WHAT QUALIFICATIONS ARE THOSE?
むっ
LIKE I'D TELL YOU, TENRYU-SAN!
WHAT'S THAT SUPPOSED TO MEAN?
Uh-oh! Not again...
I CAN DO THAT MUCH, AT LEAST.
"THAT MUCH" IS HOW MUCH EXACTLY?
...
I MEAN, I'VE GOT SOME EXPERIENCE.
WITH BOTH GIRLS AND GUYS.

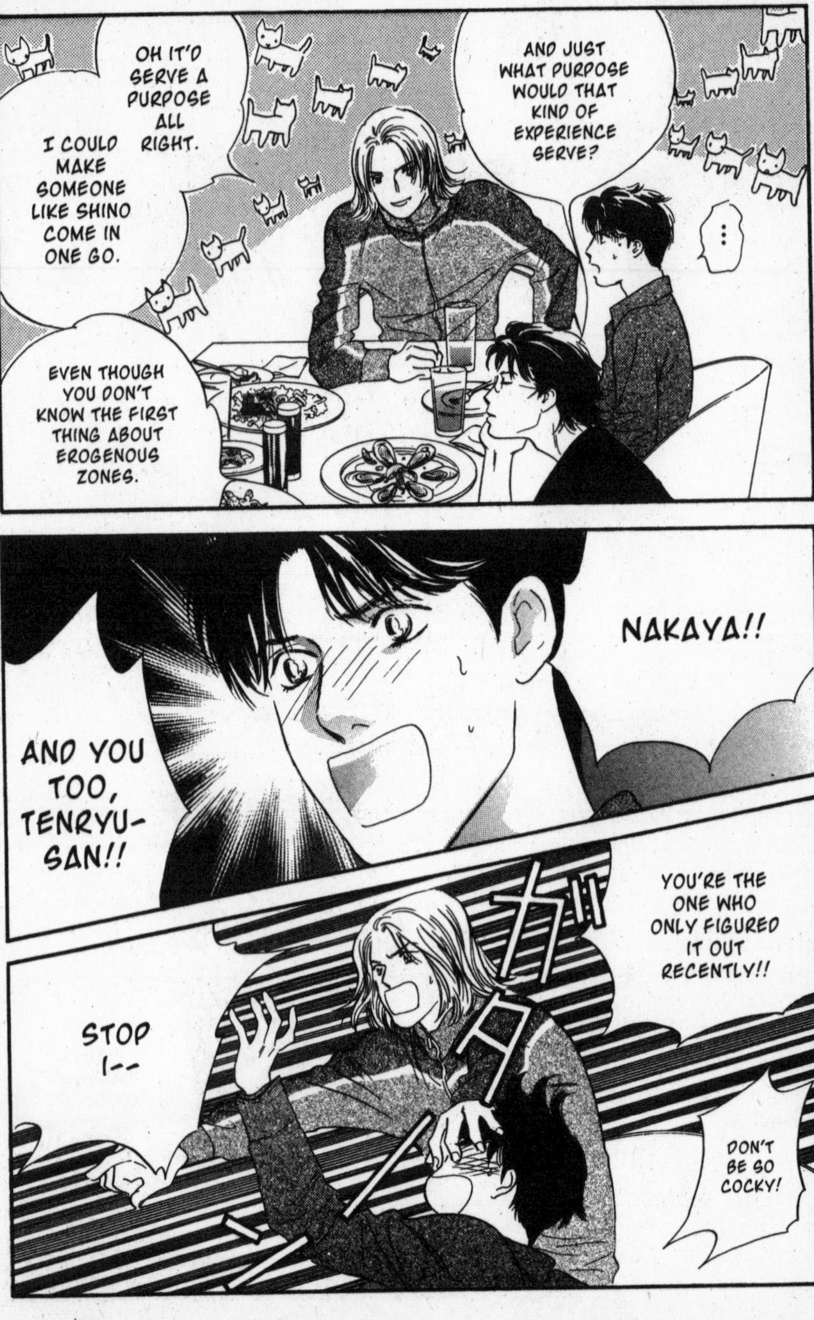
AND JUST WHAT PURPOSE WOULD THAT KIND OF EXPERIENCE SERVE?
...
OH IT'D SERVE A PURPOSE ALL RIGHT.
I COULD MAKE SOMEONE LIKE SHINO COME IN ONE GO.
EVEN THOUGH YOU DON'T KNOW THE FIRST THING ABOUT EROGENOUS ZONES.
NAKAYA!!
AND YOU TOO, TENRYU-SAN!!
YOU'RE THE ONE WHO ONLY FIGURED IT OUT RECENTLY!!
ガタ
STOP I--
DON'T BE SO COCKY!

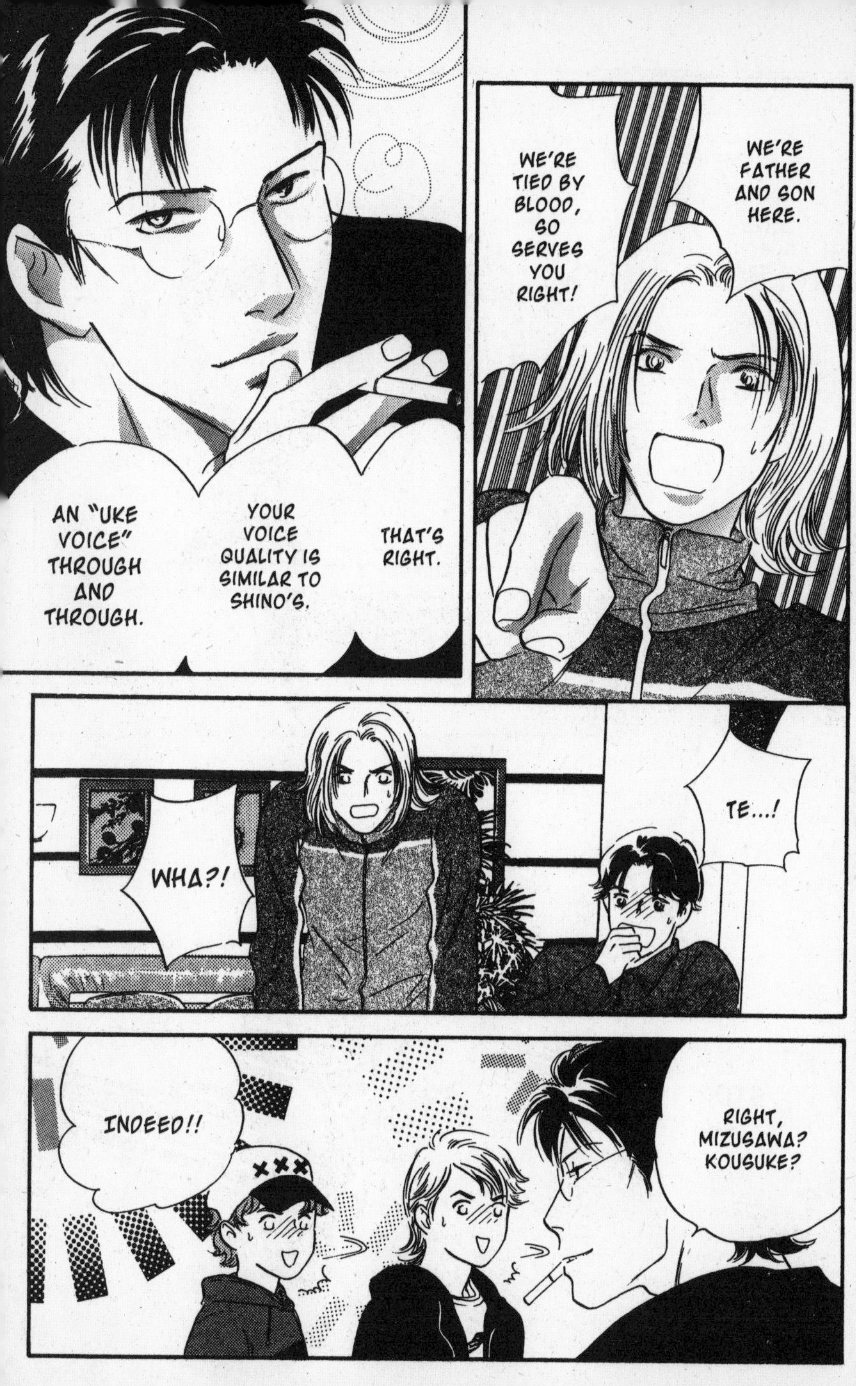
WE'RE FATHER AND SON HERE.
WE'RE TIED BY BLOOD, SO SERVES YOU RIGHT!
THAT'S RIGHT.
YOUR VOICE QUALITY IS SIMILAR TO SHINO'S.
AN "UKE VOICE" THROUGH AND THROUGH.
TE...!
WHA?!
RIGHT, MIZUSAWA? KOUSUKE?
INDEED!!

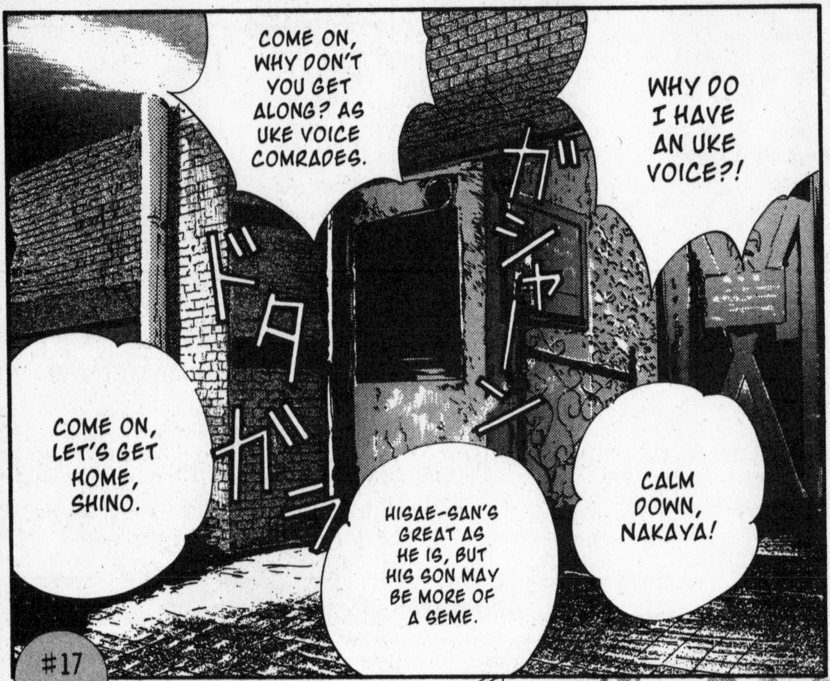
WHY DO I HAVE AN UKE VOICE?!
COME ON, WHY DON'T YOU GET ALONG? AS UKE VOICE COMRADES.
ガシャーン
CALM DOWN, NAKAYA!
HISAE-SAN'S GREAT AS HE IS, BUT HIS SON MAY BE MORE OF A SEME.
COME ON, LET'S GET HOME, SHINO.

#17 END

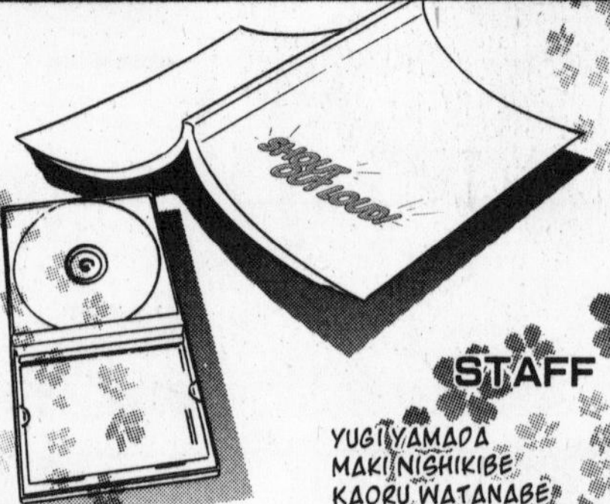

STAFF

YUGI YAMADA
MAKI NISHIKIBE
KAORU WATANABE
NOZOMI MATSUJIMA
YUMIKO SAGOTANI
CHIZUKO MARUI

YUKIKO NISHIYA
HARUMI MAKINO
TAKAKO SAITOU
KAYOKO ENDOU
AYAKO TSUIK
KYOKO SUSUI
NAOMI YOSHIDA
MIYUKI NARA

EDITOR

SAKAE SHIMAOKA
CHIHIRO NISHIGAWA

SPECIAL THANKS!

SUMAKO IKUMA
JUNKO KAWAKAMI
AMANE KAZUKI
KAZUYA FUJISAKI
HANKO KAGURAZAKA
ATSUKO SENRI
RIE IGAMI
CHIAKI OGAMO
MISSILE KAGURAI

Shout Out Loud! ⋯→ END

AFTERWORD!

"TENRYU-SAN? IS YOUR HEADACHE BETTER? THEY'LL BE STARTING THE TEST SOON, SO EVERYONE'S ALREADY INSIDE THE STUDIO..."

"..."

"TENRYU-SAN?" "..."

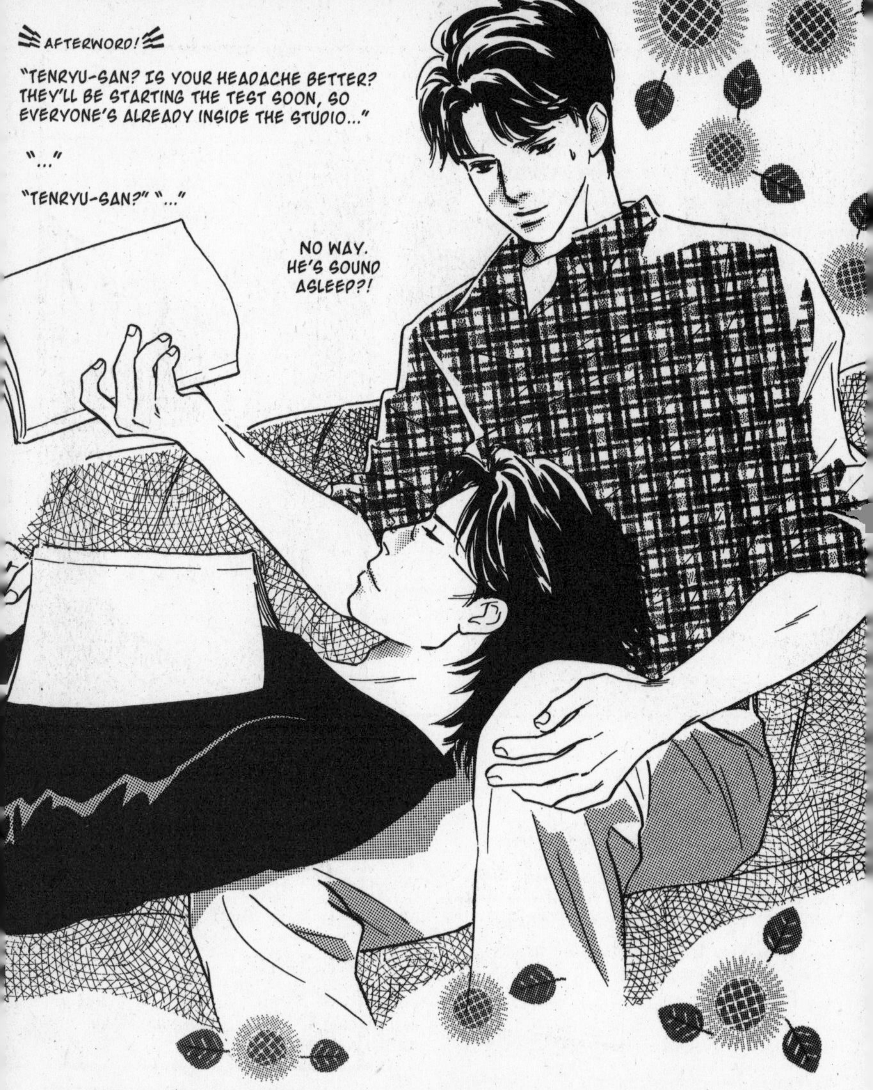
NO WAY. HE'S SOUND ASLEEP?!

A NOTE ABOUT THE "DIETER MIYUKI" THAT APPEARS THROUGHOUT THE SERIES: I WONDER IF IT'LL EVER REALLY BECOME AN ANIME. I GOT EXCITED ABOUT THE IDEA WHEN TALKING IT OVER WITH THE BOYFRIEND OF A FRIEND WHO WORKS IN A PRODUCTION STUDIO, AND A SCENARIO WRITER. WE PREPARED SOME WEAPONS, MAGICAL TRANSFORMATION ITEMS AND WHATNOT. OH, AND LISTEN TO THIS. MY DAUGHTER (IN 2ND GRADE) IS REALLY INTO MAGICAL TRANSFORMATION STORIES. HA HA HA HA.

SHE ALSO KEEPS SAYING, "PICTURES ARE WAY COOLER THAN MOMMY!" (CURSES!!) STILL, SHE'S A FEW YEARS TOO YOUNG TO BE READING ANYTHING HER DEAR OLD MOMMY MAKES. WON'T BE MUCH LONGER UNTIL THEN, EH? GYAAAH! PLEASE, DON'T READ ANYTHING THAT YOU CAN ONLY REACH WITH A FOOTSTOOL!

"Shout Out Loud!" Report on the Safe Finish to the Serialization

It sure is.
Aaaaw...
It really really is over.
It's all over.
Sheesh, they're noisy.
If I said it's over, it's over!
Sensei, Goro didn't make an appearance...
Even though he's on the cover.
Sensei?
Dammit!
Oh crap!
Oh crap!
What about Yamabe-sensei?
......
Oh! Well about that! I so completely forgot that it's actually quite refreshing!
You call that a punch-line?
I wonder why that could be.

Notice about "Shout Out Loud!" fansite

Hello, everyone. This is Takaguchi.
Thank you for all your support.
Amongst you hardcore fans, one particularly zealous one named "Jun-jun-san" has made a fansite for "Shout Out Loud!" for all of you.
I also hang out there and add oil to the flame, making it fun for all of you.
It's fun! Please come and check it out!

Kisekae Land

Inside "Shout Out Loud!" Memorial Hall

Plans for a Takaguchi homepage are also underway.

Please come check it out, too!
How should I put this... This is a work that I really went all out on while drawing...

When you say "Boys" it was more like a sappy tale of a couple of middle-aged men and their whispered sweet nothings... (Ugh, I don't like putting it that way at all.)

The keywords are "baby-faced middle-aged man" and "voice actors."

And I think Takaguchi and her voice-fetish have been outed. Even to this day, I'm a huge fan of the voice actor Akio Ootsuka. ♡♡♡

By the way, production for the third "Shout Out Loud!" drama CD has been decided!!! (I hope they schedule it for spring...)

I think it might be a mail order-only thing so please keep an eye on CIEL and the fansite for more info! We'll keep you posted! Thanks! ♡

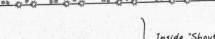

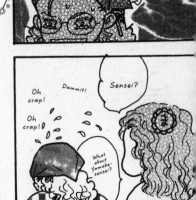

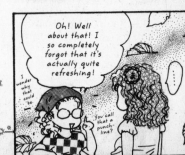

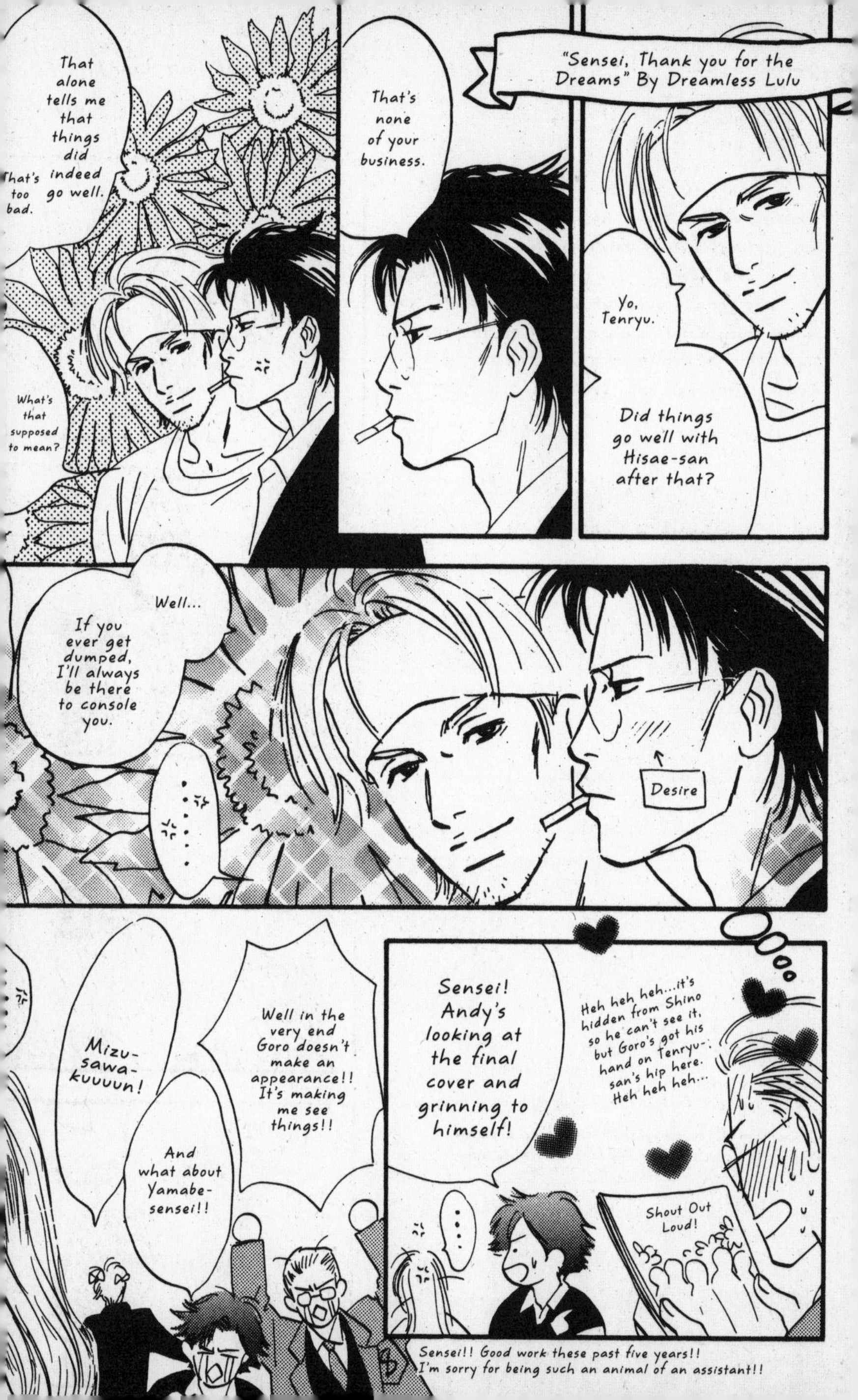
"Sensei, Thank you for the Dreams" By Dreamless Lulu
Yo, Tenryu.
Did things go well with Hisae-san after that?
That's none of your business.
That alone tells me that things did indeed go well.
That's too bad.
What's that supposed to mean?
Well...
If you ever get dumped, I'll always be there to console you.
Desire
......
Heh heh heh...it's hidden from Shino so he can't see it, but Goro's got his hand on Tenryu-san's hip here. Heh heh heh...
Sensei! Andy's looking at the final cover and grinning to himself!
Shout Out Loud!
....
Well in the very end Goro doesn't make an appearance!! It's making me see things!!
Mizu-sawa-kuuuun!
And what about Yamabe-sensei!!
Sensei!! Good work these past five years!!
I'm sorry for being such an animal of an assistant!!

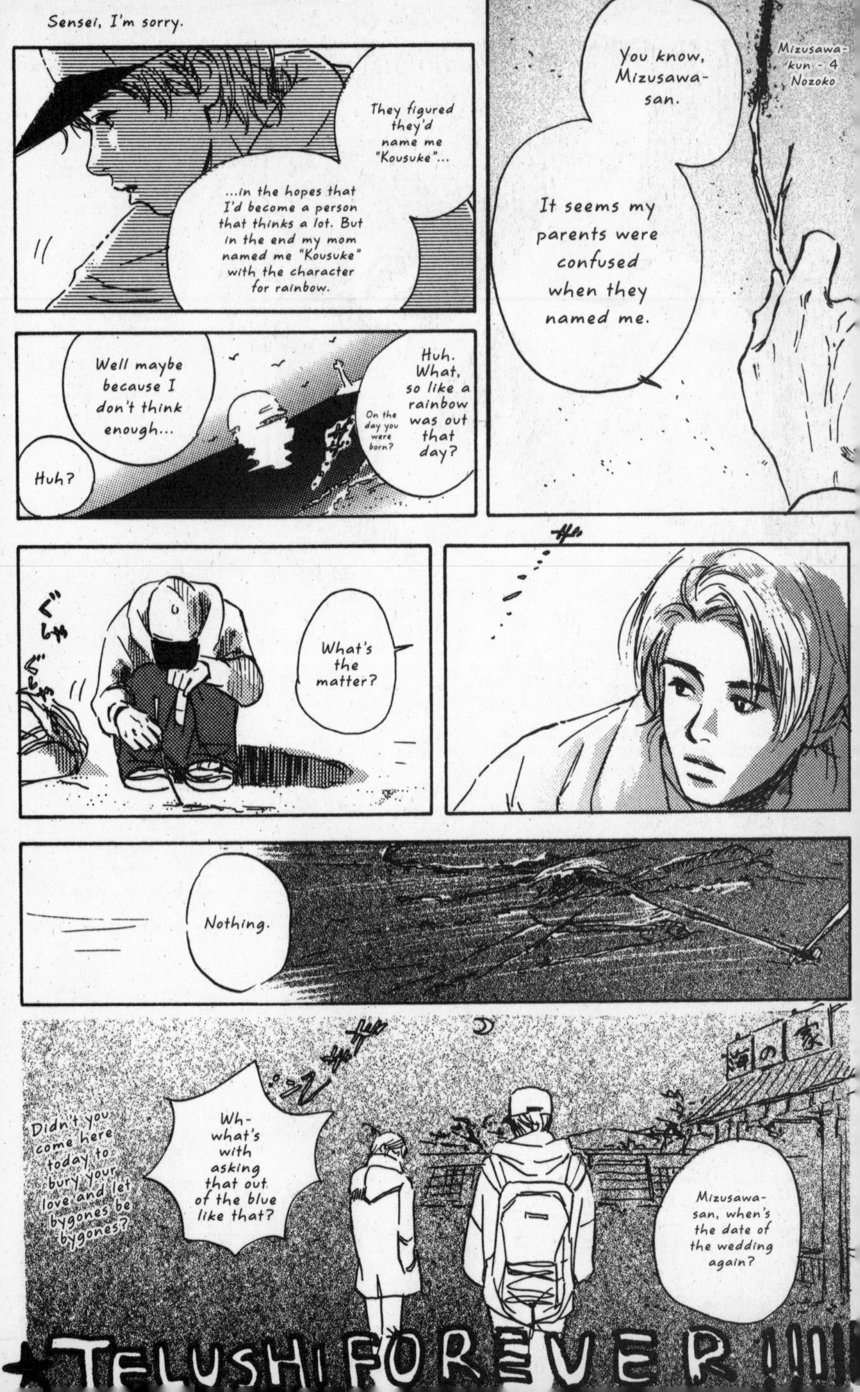
Mizusawa-kun - 4 Nozoko
You know, Mizusawa-san.
It seems my parents were confused when they named me.
Sensei, I'm sorry.
They figured they'd name me "Kousuke"...
...in the hopes that I'd become a person that thinks a lot. But in the end my mom named me "Kousuke" with the character for rainbow.
Huh. What, so like a rainbow was out that day?
On the day you were born?
Well maybe because I don't think enough...
Huh?
What's the matter?
Nothing.
海の家
Mizusawa-san, when's the date of the wedding again?
Wh-what's with asking that out of the blue like that?
Didn't you come here today to bury your love and let bygones be bygones?
TELUSHI FOREVER !!!!

A LETTER FROM CANADA?

BY NABEZOU

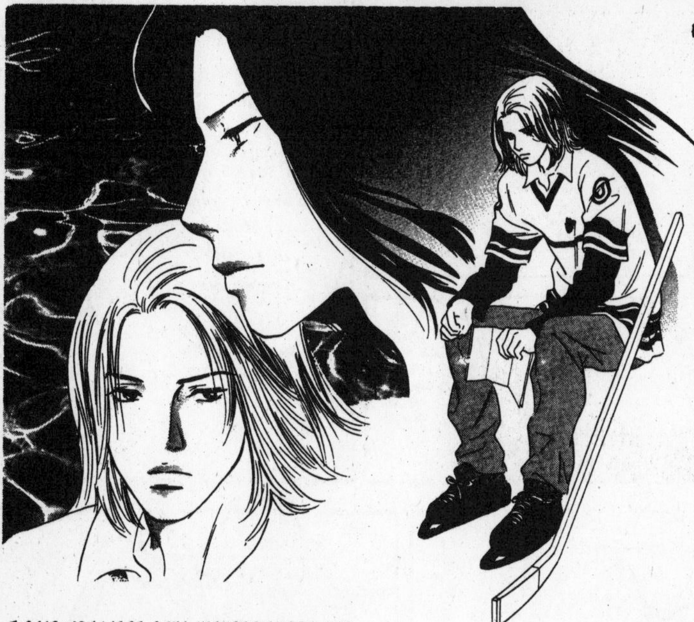

I'M SORRY LEAVING LIKE THAT WITHOUT SAYING ANYTHING.

I'M THE EDITOR FOR THE JUNIOR ARTISTS HERE NOW. I GUESS YOU COULD SAY I'M NOT DOING ANYTHING THAT DIFFERENT FROM MY TIME IN JAPAN.

I SAID YOU WERE STILL INEXPERIENCED AND ASKED IF YOU COULD PULL OFF AN ADVENTURE, BUT THAT'S NOT ACTUALLY WHAT I FELT INSIDE.

IF I WANTED TO BRAINWASH YOU, I COULD DO IT ANYTIME. BUT THAT'S NO FAIR AT ALL, SO I GUESS THAT'S WHY I RAN AWAY.

FROM HERE ON OUT, IT'S OKAY FOR YOU TO GET SOME SENSE AND CHANGE. AND YOU DON'T HAVE TO CHANGE, BUT JUST TAKE THE NEXT STEP, PLEASE.

IT WAS SELFISH OF ME TO BE PICKY ABOUT THE COUPLINGS.

I WANT YOU TO LET ME BE SELFISH.

GOODBYE.

AND FOR NOT BEING ABLE TO CALL YOU A FRIEND, PLEASE FORGIVE ME.

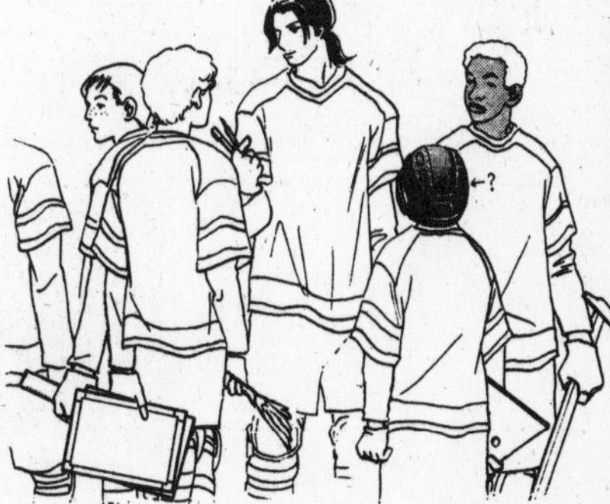
←?

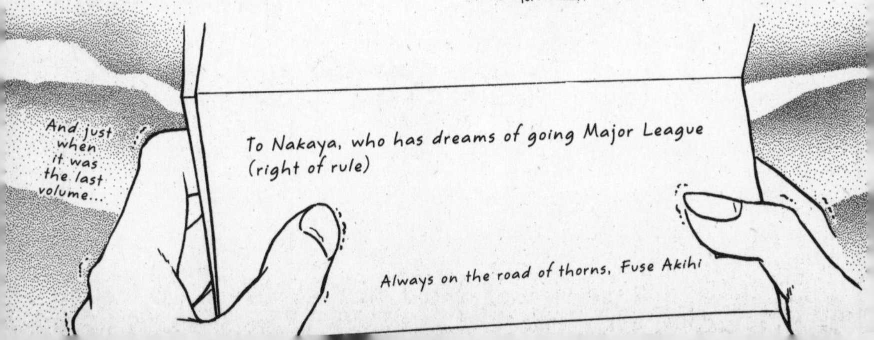
To Nakaya, who has dreams of going Major League (right of rule)
Always on the road of thorns, Fuse Akihi
And just when it was the last volume...

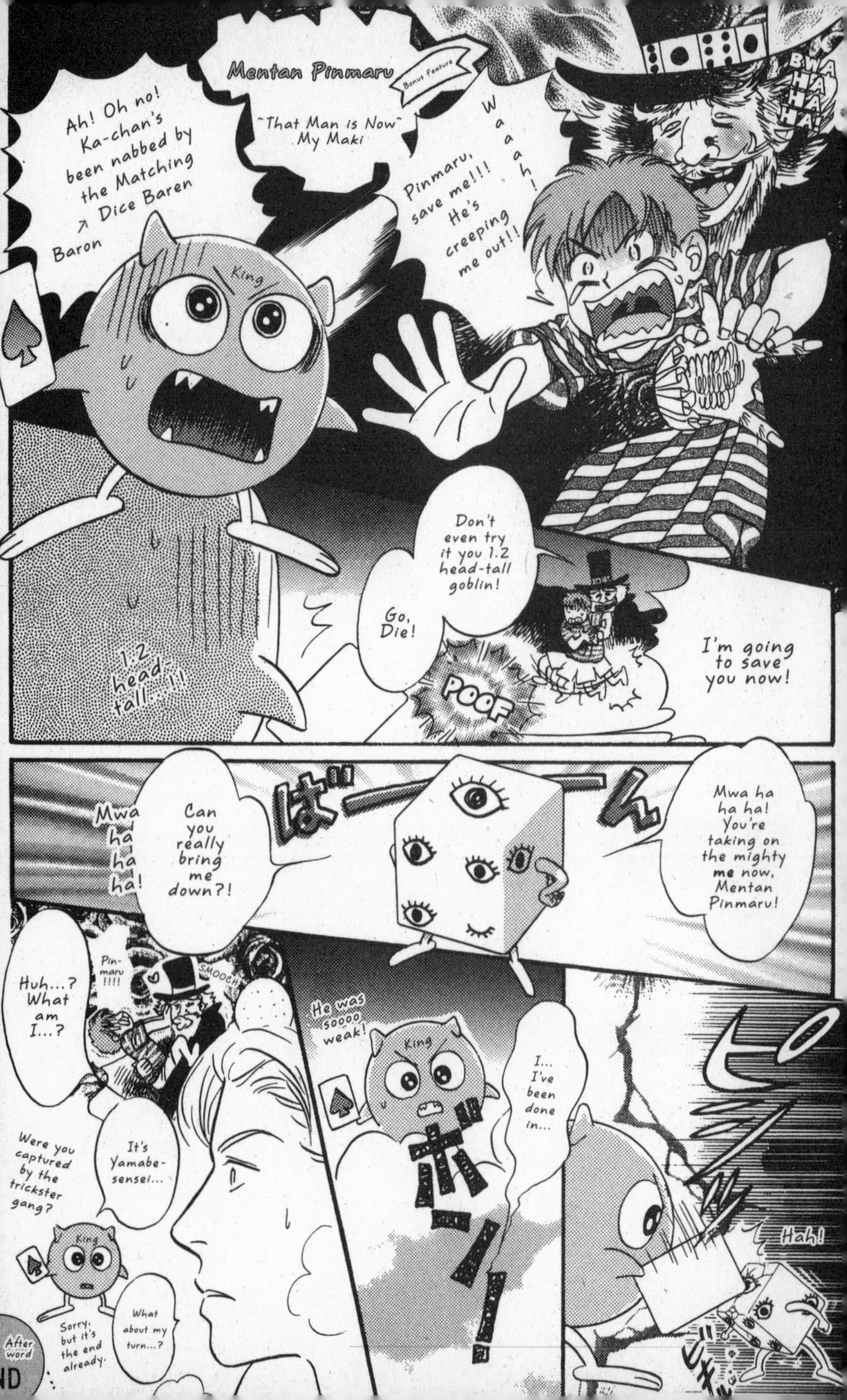

BWA HA HA HA HA!
Waaah!
Pinmaru, save me!!! He's creeping me out!!
Mentan Pinmaru
Bonus Feature
~That Man is Now~ My Maki
Ah! Oh no! Ka-chan's been nabbed by the Matching Dice Baren
Baron
King
I'm going to save you now!
Don't even try it you 1.2 head-tall goblin!
Go, Die!
POOF
1.2 head-tall...!!
Mwa ha ha ha! You're taking on the mighty me now, Mentan Pinmaru!
ば——ん
Can you really bring me down?!
Mwa ha ha ha!
Hah!
I... I've been done in...
He was soooo weak!
King
Pin-maru!!!!
SMOOCH
Huh...? What am I...?
It's Yamabe-sensei...
Were you captured by the trickster gang?
King
What about my turn...?
Sorry, but it's the end already.
After word

SHOUT OUT LOUD! VOL. 5
Created by Satosumi Takaguchi

ISBN: 978-1-59816-320-9

First Printing: August 2007
10 9 8 7 6 5 4 3 2 1
Printed in the USA

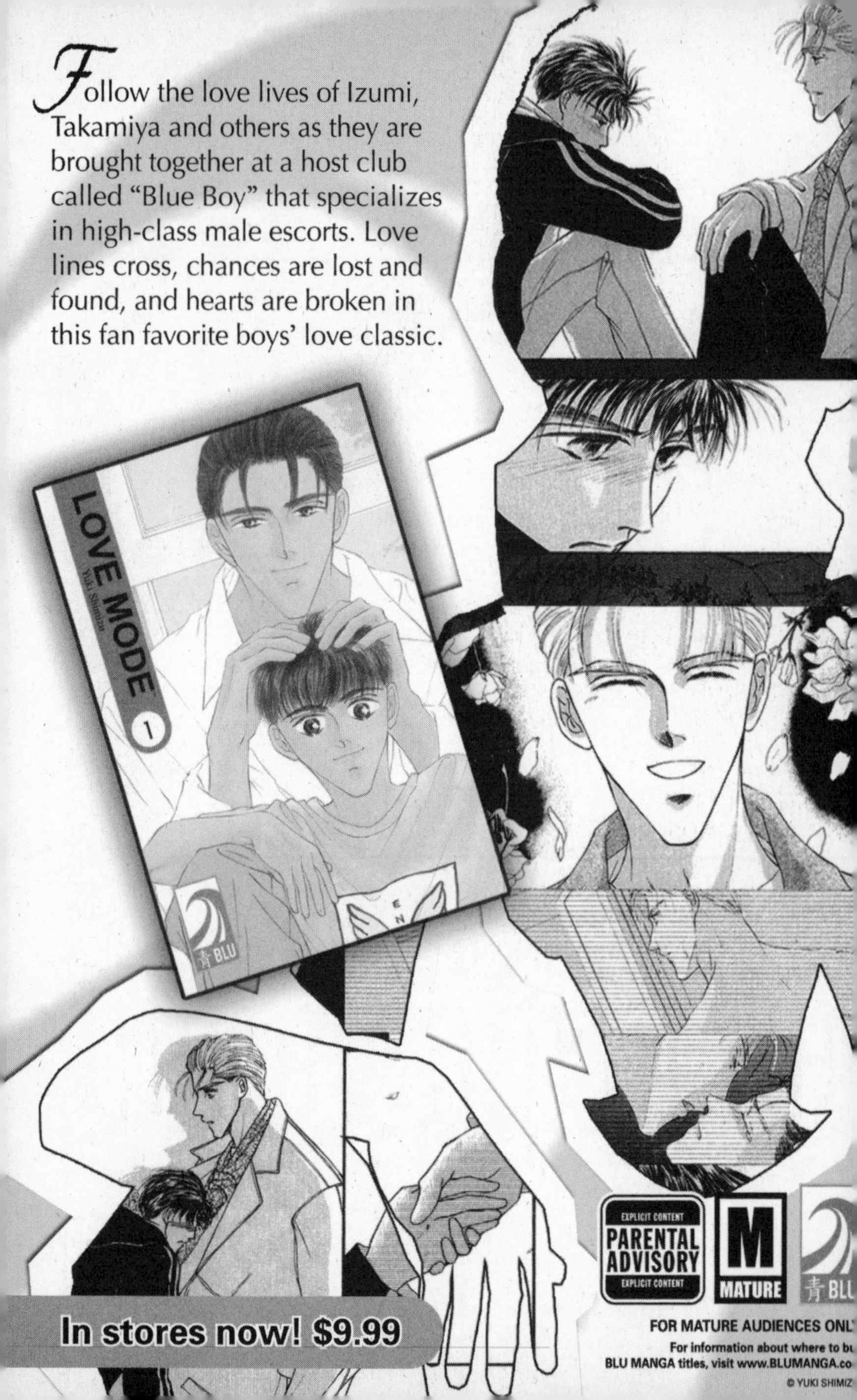
Follow the love lives of Izumi, Takamiya and others as they are brought together at a host club called "Blue Boy" that specializes in high-class male escorts. Love lines cross, chances are lost and found, and hearts are broken in this fan favorite boys' love classic.
LOVE MODE
Yuki Shimizu
1
青 BLU
In stores now! $9.99
EXPLICIT CONTENT
PARENTAL ADVISORY
EXPLICIT CONTENT
M
MATURE
青 BLU
FOR MATURE AUDIENCES ONL
For information about where to bu
BLU MANGA titles, visit www.BLUMANGA.co
© YUKI SHIMIZ

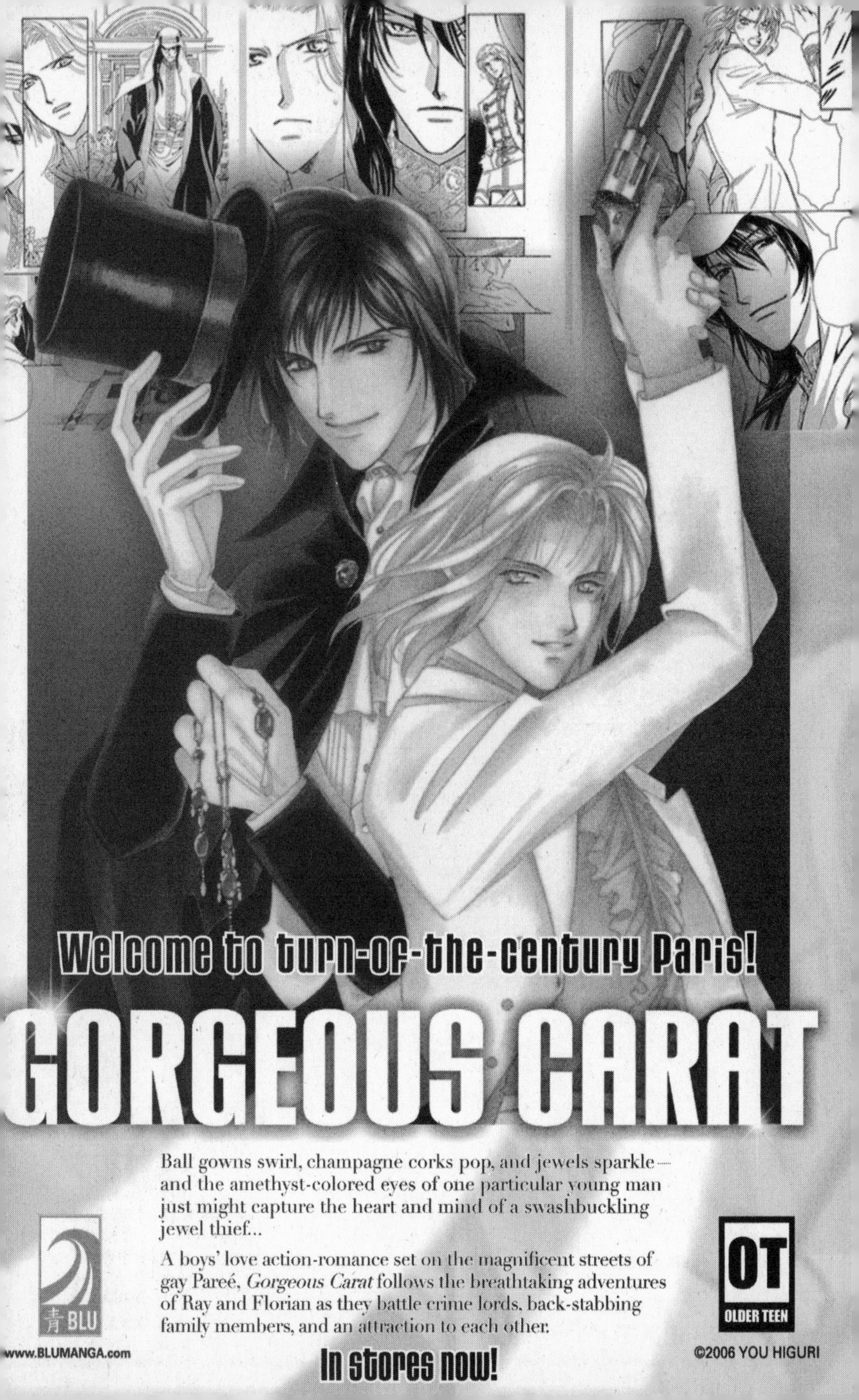

THE REVOLUTION OF LOVE
STARTS IN THE NIGHT.

In *Lovers in the Night*, Fumi Yoshinaga weaves the story of a bratty French nobleman named Antoine whose unspoken passion for his uptight and proper butler, Claude, erupts on the eve of the French Revolution. *Truly Kindly*, the companion work, presents several new tales, including the tragic story of Claude's uncle and his own noble lover.

Famed creator of *Gerard and Jacques* and *Antique Bakery* Fumi Yoshinaga conjures up an enchanting tale of forbidden love.

Where schoolwork is the last thing you need to worry about...

When Keita is admitted to the prestigous all-boys school Bell Liberty Academy, his life gets turned upside down!

Filled with the hottest cast of male students ever put together, this highly anticipated boys' love series drawn by You Higuri (*Gorgeous Carat*) is finally here!

Liberté! Egalité! Fraternité!...and Love!

Become enraptured by a thrilling and erotic tale of an unlikely pair of lovers during the tumultuous times of the French Revolution. Freed from a high-class brothel, noble-born Jacques becomes a servant in Gerard's house. First seduced by his new master's library, Jacques begins to find himself falling for the man as well...but can their love last in the face of the chaos around them?

stop

blu manga are published in the original japanese format

go to the other side and begin reading